T3-AKC-124

Debt, Crisis and Reform in Bolivia

International Finance and Development Series

Published in association with the Institute of Social Studies

General Editor: **E. V. K. FitzGerald**, Professor of Economics, Institute of Social Studies, The Hague, and Director, Finance and Trade Policy Research Centre, University of Oxford

The International Finance and Development Series reflects the research carried out at The Hague and associated centres in Europe, Asia, Africa and Latin America on the relationship between international capital flows and the process of structural adjustment in less-developed economies. The studies in this series share a common analytical approach based on the use of advanced social accounting techniques and the explicit modelling of the economic behaviour of institutional sectors, which in turn permit a new approach to macroeconomic policy design.

Titles include:

Karel Jansen
EXTERNAL FINANCE IN THAILAND'S DEVELOPMENT

Karel Jansen and Rob Vos (*editors*)
EXTERNAL FINANCE AND ADJUSTMENT

Luis Carlos Jemio
DEBT, CRISIS AND REFORM IN BOLIVIA
Biting the Bullet

Joke Luttik
ACCOUNTING FOR THE GLOBAL ECONOMY

Rob Vos
DEBT AND ADJUSTMENT IN THE WORLD ECONOMY

Rob Vos and Josef T. Yap
THE PHILIPPINE ECONOMY
East Asia's Stray Cat?

Howard White (*editor*)
AID AND MACROECONOMIC PERFORMANCE

Debt, Crisis and Reform in Bolivia

Biting the Bullet

Luis Carlos Jemio
Senior Economist
Corporación Andina de Fomento
Bolivia

in association with
Institute of Social Studies

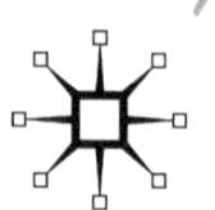

First published 2001 by
PALGRAVE
Houndmills, Basingstoke, Hampshire RG21 6XS and
175 Fifth Avenue, New York, N. Y. 10010
Companies and representatives throughout the world

PALGRAVE is the new global academic imprint of St. Martin's Press LLC Scholarly and Reference Division and Palgrave Publishers Ltd (formerly Macmillan Press Ltd).

ISBN 0–333–96103–X

This book is printed on paper suitable for recycling and made from fully managed and sustained forest sources.

A catalogue record for this book is available from the British Library.

Library of Congress Cataloging-in-Publication Data
Jemio M., Luis Carlos.
Debt, crisis and reform in Bolivia : biting the bullet / by Luis Carlos Jemio.
p. cm. — (International finance and development series)
Includes bibliographical references.
ISBN 0–333–96103–X
1. Debts, Public—Bolivia. 2. Structural adjustment (Economic policy)—Bolivia. 3. Bolivia—Economic conditions—1982– 4. Bolivia—Economic conditions—1952–1982. I. Title. II. Series.
HJ8574 .J46 2001
339.5'0984—dc21

2001032119

10 9 8 7 6 5 4 3 2 1
10 09 08 07 06 05 04 03 02 01

Printed and bound in Great Britain by
Antony Rowe Ltd, Chippenham, Wiltshire

Contents

List of Tables

List of Figures

Glossary of Acronyms and Abbreviations

ANMM	Asociación de Mineros Medianos
ASOBAN	Asociación de Bancos
BAB	Banco Agrícola de Bolivia
BAMIN	Banco Minero
BANEST	Banco del Estado
BCB	Banco Central de Bolivia
b/d	barrels/day
CBF	Corporación Boliviana de Fomento
CBO	Central Obrera Boliviana
CD	Central Bank Certificate of Deposit
CDD	Certificado de Devolución de Depósitos
CEDLA	Centro de Estudios pare el Desarrollo Laboral y Agrario
CEPB	Confederación de Empresarios Privados de Bolivia
CET	Centro de Estudios del Trabajo
CGE	Computatable General Equilibrium
CIPCA	Centro de Investigacion y Promocion del Campesinado
COMIBOL	Corporación Minera de Bolivia
CPI	Consumer price index
CRA	Certificado de Reintegro Arancelario
EMV	Empresa Metalúrgica de Vinto
ENDE	Empresa Nacional de Electricidad
ENAF	Empresa Nacional de Fundiciones

ENFE	Empresa Nacional de Ferrocarriles
ENTEL	Empresa Nacional de Telecomunicaciones
ESAF	Extended Structural Adjustment Facility
FABOCE	Fábrica Boliviana de Cemento
FANCESA	Fabrica Nacional de Cemento
FINEX	Gerencia de Financiamiento Externo del Banco Central de Bolivia
FIS	Fondo de Inversión Social
FLACSO	Facultad Latinoamericana de Ciencias Sociales
FONDESIF	Fondo de Desarrollo del Sistema Financiero
fob	free on board
FSE	Fondo Social de Emergencia
HCL	Hydrochloride
HIID	Harvard Institute for International Development
IDB	Inter-American Development Bank
ILDIS	Instituto Latinoamericano de Investigaciones Sociales
ILO	International Labor Organization
INE	Instituto Nacional de Estadística
INVOFIN	Indice de Volumen Físico de la Industria
ISIC	International Standard Industrial Classification of All Economic Activities
LAB	Lloyd Aéreo Boliviano (Bolivian national airlines)
LASP	Latin American Studies Program, Cornell University
LDC	Less Developed Country
LIBOR	London Inter-Bank Offer Rate
MACA	Ministerio de Asuntos Campesinos y Agropecuarios
NAFIBO	Nacional Financiera Boliviana
NAU	Northern Arizona University
NBER	National Bureau of Economic Research
NEP	New Economic Policy
NFPS	Non Financial Public Sector
NFS	Non Financial Sector
PIL	Planta Industrializadora de Leche
PREALC	Programa Regional del Empleo para América Latina y elCaribe
RF-CGE	Real Financial Computational General Equilibrium
ROW	Rest of the World

RW	Rest of the World
SAFCO	Sistema de Administración Financiera y Control
SAM	Social Accounting Matrix
SIRESE	Sistema de Regulación Sectorial
SNA	System of National Accounts
UIS	Urban informal sector
UNICEF	United Nations Children's Fund
UNITAR	United Nations Institute for Training and Research
USAID	United State Agency for International Development
YPFB	Yacimientos Petrolíferos Fiscales Bolivianos

Glossary of Terms and Organizations

Asociación de Bancos	Private banking association
Asociación de Mineros Medianos	Private Miners' Association
Banco Agrícola de Bolivia	Agricultural Bank of Bolivia
Banco Central de Bolivia	Bolivian Central Bank
Banco del Estado	Bolivian State Bank
Banco Minero	Mining Bank
Bolsin	system of public auctioning of foreign exchange
Bonosol	'solidarity bonds'; dividends for Bolivians over 65 from proceeds of privatization
Central Obrera Boliviana	Bolivian Labour Union
Centro de Estudios del Trabajo	Labour Studies Centre
Certificado de Devolución de Depósitos	Commercial Bank Deposit Rebate Certificates

Certificado de Reintegro Arancelario	Rebate Certificate; 10 per cent rebate on duties, paid to agricultural exporters
Confederación de Empresarios Privados de Bolivia	Bolivian Private Entrepreneurs' Association
Corporación Boliviana de Fomento	Bolivian Development Corporation
Corporación Minera de Bolivia	Bolivian Mining Corporation
Empresa Metalúrgica de Vinto	Bolivian Smelting Company
Empresa Nacional de Electricidad	National Electricity Company
Empresa Nacional de Ferrocarriles	National Railway Company
Empresa Nacional de Fundiciones	National Smelting Company
Empresa Nacional de Telecomunicaciones	National Telecommunications Company
Fábrica Boliviana de Cemento	Bolivian Cement Factory
Gerencia de Financiamento Externo del Banco Central de Bolivia	External Finance Division, Central Bank of Bolivia
Fondo de Inversión Social	Social Investment Fund
Fondo de Desarrollo del Sistema Financiero	Fund for the Development of the Financial System and Productive Sector
Indice de Volumen Físico de la Industria	Manufacturing Physical Volume Index
Instituto Nacional de Estadística	National Statistics Institute

Lloyd Aéreo Boliviano	Bolivian National Airlines
Ministerio de Asuntos Campesinos y Agropecuarios	Ministry of Agriculture and Peasants' Affairs
Nacional Financiera Boliviana	Bolivian Financial Institution
Planta Industrializadora de Leche	National Milk Factory
Plan de Todos	Plan for Everyone
Programa Regional del Empleo para América Latina y el Caribe	Regional Employment Programme for Latin America and the Caribbean
Sistema de Administración Financiera y Control	Financial Administration and Control System
Yacimientos Petrolíferos Fiscales Bolivianos	Bolivian Petroleum Company

Series Editor's Preface

In the early 1990s there were apparently strong indications that stable and sustainable economic growth could be – and was being – achieved in Latin America. This 'new stage' was held to be the virtuous reward for a combination of conservative economic and fiscal policies on the one hand, and a strategy of domestic deregulation and integration to the world economy on the other. Much of this optimism was based on good short-term macroeconomic results and foreign capital inflows, and the wave of financial crises that struck the region in the second half of the decade indicated that markets were much more difficult to manage than had been anticipated. It has now become clear that sound economic policy would have to take into account the heterogeneous nature of Latin American economies and the asymmetric way in which they are linked to the world economy.

Poverty had increased in Latin America during the 'lost decade' of the 1980s: wages fell, unemployment rose and welfare provision deteriorated as a result of repeated stabilization attempts. However, the opening up of the economies of the region was supposed to reverse this trend in the 1990s. An increased dispersion of incomes was anticipated as the logical (and indeed desirable) consequence of liberalization. Nonetheless, national governments and international agencies believed that higher economic growth rates would counterbalance the increased inequality so that absolute and relative poverty could decrease. This did not occur, and in consequence the economic policy agenda at the outset of the twenty-first century still has much in common with that at the beginning of the twentieth: educational deficits and social exclusion, fiscal and financial instability and vulnerability to global economic shocks.[1]

The roots of these recurrent problems in achieving sustainable economic growth lie in the heterogeneous behaviour of the Latin American economies. This is why the 'Finance and Development' research group at The Hague took as a central proposition that the response of the economy to external shocks depends upon the distinct investment and savings decisions of the main economic agents and the relationship between them.[2] Our research programme attracted a number of exceptional doctoral students, among whom Luis Carlos Jemio stood out for his meticulous attention to statistical detail and determination to come to grips with the complexity of the Bolivian economy. He set out to produce an alternative framework for the analysis of the numerous external shocks, stabilization policies, adjustment programmes and structural reforms that Bolivia has gone through during the past quarter-century. The alternative framework is lucidly set out in this book, and Luis Carlos has been able to implement his approach in his home country both as head of the government's statistical agency and as a leader of Bolivia's major policy research centre (UDAPE).

The author makes the strong claim that both existing neo-orthodox and structuralist approaches are unable to explain the impact of external shocks on short-term macroeconomic equilibrium and long-term growth in developing countries. This is for a number of reasons: first that both are too aggregated to capture the heterogeneous nature of even a small economy such as that of Bolivia, rarely going beyond a broad distinction between the public and private sectors. Capital markets are fragmented, meaning that the neo-classical assumptions about the response to interest rate changes are invalid. Again, the structuralist assumption as to foreign exchange constraints is plainly not valid for some sectors, particularly the 'informal' (i.e. narcotics) sector in Bolivia, even though the government and 'formal' sectors may be constrained by the central bank in this way.

Second, the behaviour of institutions changes over time. This is due both to the learning process itself, which means that the reactions to external impulses change, and to the fact that in each period stocks of assets and liabilities are 'inherited' from the previous period. In this sense the approach of our research team is 'path dependent' and the power of that approach is clearly illustrated in this book, where Luis Carlos carefully traces the adjustment of the real and financial sectors through well defined sub-periods in Bolivia's recent past. In particular, he has achieved a significant disaggregation of the accumulation balance which shows how changing macroeconomic rules oblige agents to adjust their ex ante plans. Further, he has the central bank and private commercial banks as active agents in his model, rather than as passive channels for the investment and saving of other sectors, which is a valuable innovation.

The computable general equilibrium (CGE) model which forms the heart of this book goes well beyond the basic framework developed by our team[3] and set out in the case studies of Thailand and Philippines in this *Series*.[4] By careful econometric estimation he establishes individual supply-demand microeconomic adjustment models for *each* productive sector separately. By including full accounting matrices at the beginning and end of each period, he can trace the changes in the asset-liability positions of individual agents (or rather, institutional groups) during the adjustment process. Thus the effect of external shocks on the wealth position of each group can be tracked, and the way in which agents shift their portfolios, including external assets, can be explained. The identification of urban upper-income households is an innovation in itself but also allows their wealth portfolio allocation to reflect capital flight very clearly.

The treatment of the 'informal' cocaine economy in the model is noteworthy. The rigorous estimation of narcotics transactions within a social accounting framework is a real innovation, showing their effect on exports, financial balances, foreign exchange availability and so on. Luis Carlos' modelling of the drugs economy and capital flight allow him to track the increasing 'dollarization' of the Bolivian economy in an interesting way. This in turn reduces the capacity of the monetary authorities to reach macroeconomic balance and holds important lessons for the rest of Latin America, where currency substitution is increasingly widespread. In response to repeated external shocks and inept economic policies, the private sector in Latin American has embarked upon dollarization as its own 'adjustment policy'. The US dollar has come to perform most of the functions of money: as a unit of account, store of value and means of exchange. The emergence of parallel economies – whether based on narcotics, tax evasion or just pure 'informality' – is closely related to this process.

The simulation of the responses to external shocks in the form of changes in the terms of trade, international interest rates and capital inflows in this book is also significant. This simulation allows the author to run a neutral (i.e. 'do nothing') macroeconomic policy as the base case, and then rigorously compare the orthodox (i.e. 'Washington consensus') and heterodox responses to external shock. Each policy is then evaluated in terms of the out-turn for growth, poverty and investment. What becomes clear is that repeated attempts at conventional stabilization, while partially successful in terms of reducing inflation and over-valued exchange rates, do little or nothing to stimulate exports or investment, let alone to reduce poverty.

The average income of Latin Americans in 1999 was some five times higher than in 1900.[5] Nonetheless, the ratio between per capita incomes in Latin America and the United States stayed precisely the same – 13 per cent. In fact, so little 'catching up' has been achieved that average income in the region is still only two-thirds of the US level at the outset of the new century. Why that should be so in the case of Bolivia – and what might be done to construct sustainable growth in the future – are the lessons of this book.

Valpy FitzGerald
Oxford and The Hague
December 1999

Notes

1. Rosemary T. Thorp *Latin America in the Twentieth Century: Poverty, Progress and Exclusion* Washington DC: Inter-American Development Bank (1999)

2. For a more extensive explanation, see Karel Jansen and Rob Vos (eds) *External Finance and Adjustment: Failure and Success in the Developing World* Basingstoke: Macmillan (1997).

3. Rob Vos in particular.

4. Rob Vos and J. Yap, *The Philippines Economy – East Asia's Stray Cat?* Basingstoke: Macmillan (1996), and Karel Jansen *External Finance in Thailand's Development* Basingstoke: Macmillan (1997).

5. That is, about US$ 1000 as opposed to US$ 200, both at 1970 purchasing power parity – see my statistical appendix to Thorp *op cit.*

Introduction

1 An Approach to the Study of External Shocks, Macroeconomic Adjustment and Stabilization Policies in Bolivia

This book puts forward an appropriate framework for the analysis of external shocks, macroeconomic adjustment and stabilization policies in less developed countries (LDCs), based on the Bolivian experience between 1970 and 1995. This book argues that existing neo-orthodox and structuralist macroeconomic approaches are limited in their ability to explain the impact of external shocks on short-term macroeconomic equilibrium and long-term economic growth in LDCs.

First, orthodox models, such as the Monetary Approach to the Balance of Payments (MABP) (IMF 1977; Frenkel and Johnson 1976) or the structuralist Two-gap and Three-gap models (Chenery and Strout 1966; Bacha 1984, 1990), are far too aggregated to capture the heterogeneous nature of a developing economy such as Bolivia. In their analytical frameworks, disaggregation does not go beyond a distinction between private and public sectors. At that aggregated level, saving-investment behaviours (especially within the private sector) are assumed to be homogeneous, whereas in reality the private sector comprises socioeconomic groups whose saving-investment behaviours tend to be essentially different. Therefore key microeconomic aspects crucial for the interpretation of macroeconomic adjustment are lost or simply ignored. For instance, the orthodox hypothesis of a stable private accumulation balance, which sees interest rates as determining savings and savings availability as determining investment (IMF 1987a), cannot explain the saving-investment behaviour of all the heterogeneous economic actors commonly found in developing economies. Interest rates alone cannot bring fragmented capital markets into equilibrium (even allowing for financial liberalization) and thus bring all government, formal and informal sector accounts into balance simultaneously. On the other hand, the structuralist hypothesis that economic growth is constrained by the overall import capacity of the economy appears not to be valid for all sectors in the Bolivian case. During the 1980s, for instance, the informal sector had access to large amounts of foreign exchange, but investment did not react significantly, since informal profit-earners preferred to invest their surpluses outside the country. The structuralist hypothesis explains the government and formal sector's situation during this period quite well, where the reduced import capacity imposed a binding constraint on output and investment.

Second, existing theoretical approaches tend to be atemporal in the sense that the underlying assumptions explaining sectoral saving-investment behaviours are regarded as being unchanged over time; their interpretations of macroeconomic adjustment therefore tend to disregard the effects of different external and internal environments on the way in which sectoral and macroeconomic adjustments take place. A changing external environment can substantially change the conditions under which adjustment takes place and, consequently, the adjusting mechanisms change from one period to another.

From the analysis of the main macroeconomic events that occurred in Bolivia over the last two and a half decades, it is evident that the various economic groups (public sector, corporate sector, and informal sector) have tended to follow different financial behaviours. Even more, each individual sector's accumulation behaviour has tended to change over the period in response to heavy external shocks. The key patterns observed were as follows.

(i) The 1970s

Increased capital inflows and export revenues expanded the public sector's availability of funds. In response, public sector consumption and investment expanded, boosting activity and employment in the formal sector. A large part of these resources was transferred to the private sector in order to promote its role in economic activity. The private sector, however, did not respond to the resulting favourable conditions by increasing investment, but preferred to take these surpluses outside the country, initiating capital flight.

(ii) The first half of the 1980s

Heavy external shocks in the form of reduced capital inflows, higher interest payments and lower export revenues greatly reduced the public sector's availability of funds. The government did not adjust its outlays to the much lower level of resources available in order to avoid recession, and began increasingly to finance its deficit through money creation. The outcome was hyperinflation. The informal (including the illegal coca trade) sector started generating large surpluses from the coca business. These resources circulated within the informal channels of the economy and were maintained largely beyond any kind of government control. Employment in the informal sector increased sharply.

(iii) After the 1985 stabilization programme

After the 1985 stabilization programme, the government's investment and consumption were brought into line with its available funds. As a result, the fiscal deficit, money creation and inflation were brought under control. In addition, the public sector's relations with international creditors were normalized and external finance to the country was restored. Despite the reduction of the fiscal deficit, it was not completely eliminated, and the remaining gap was financed through open-market operations that pushed the domestic interest rate upwards.

Financial liberalization and a higher domestic interest rate boosted bank deposits in the domestic financial system, as funds were repatriated from abroad, with some switching from informal to formal financial intermediaries. The higher interest rates also prevented private investment taking off as expected within the new economic model.

(iv) After the 1990s structural reforms

The structural reforms initiated in 1993, known as the second-generation reforms, are expected to substantially change the behaviour of the economic agents in the future. The state enterprises have been transferred to the private sector, through the capitalization process. This is expected to increase substantially the levels of foreign direct investment to the country, especially in the telecommunications, electricity, hydrocarbons, transport sectors, and water services. The government's role has been redefined, limiting it to investment activities in human and physical capital and to the provision of a sectoral regulatory framework. The reforms introduced to the financial system give greater autonomy to the Central Bank and limit the government's prospects to finance its deficits through Central Bank credit. The government, therefore, has to reduce its deficits to levels compatible with the concessional external finance it can secure.

Finally, the third major shortcoming of existing theoretical approaches is that they are partial in their analysis. To capture adequately the characteristics of a developing economy open to trade, four key relationships (balances) must be specified (Taylor 1987):

(i) supply-demand balances for the productive sector,
(ii) accumulation balances for socioeconomic agents and institutions,
(iii) financial balances, and
(iv) external balances.

These four key relationships have to be included in any model to ensure the complete consistency of the whole system. Leading theoretical approaches give only a partial explanation of macroeconomic adjustment, however, since they tend to focus their analyses on only some of these balances For example, the MABP focuses on monetary balances while the 'Three-gap' model focuses on external, fiscal and internal balances.

To deal with these problems, this book puts forward a more disaggregated approach to the understanding of external shocks, macroeconomic adjustment and stabilization policies in Bolivia. The rationale behind this approach is that only through an understanding of the individual sectoral financial behaviours of the various social groups and institutions can a proper understanding of the functioning of the economy as a whole be obtained. In this way, a more realistic and subtle picture is obtained of the processes underlying macroeconomic adjustment. This is obviously essential for a more subtle and plausible interpretation of macroeconomic adjustment in a developing economy such as Bolivia and for a more insightful macroeconomic policy design.

This is achieved by:

(a) carrying-out macroeconomic analysis at a disaggregated level, and studying the behaviour of individual accumulation balances for all economic agents (companies, households, government and financial institutions) during the 1970s, 1980s and first half of the 1990s. This will explain how the institutional settings that govern each agent's financial behaviour (for example, the objectives, constraints in the different markets they face, bargaining power, and so on), have determined adjustment to external shocks and policy interventions, in each of these individual balances;
(b) observing closure changes by periods of time for each of the balances, depending on prevailing external and internal conditions;
(c) incorporating both the non-financial and financial sectors in the analysis. Macroeconomic equilibrium is therefore understood as the result of the simultaneous interaction of all balances;
(d) including a considerable disaggregation to the analysis of the productive sector behaviour and incorporating the informal sector, which does not appear in other macroeconomic analytical models.

The stylized facts derived from the discussion of each of the economic agents' adjustment behaviours are used to formulate sectoral behavioural models, which are the building blocks of a macroeconomic model for Bolivia. This model links macroeconomic adjustment to sectoral adjustment behaviours. This approach regards macroeconomic adjustment in Bolivia as being the result of the interaction of the different socioeconomic groups, each of them having different adjustment behaviours, through the different markets of the economy.

In order to capture the linkages between groups and sectors, a detailed social accounting matrix (SAM) with a considerable disaggregation of the productive sector and of socioeconomic groups was constructed. This SAM is the core of a Computatable General Equilibrium (CGE) model, which focuses in particular on the financial behaviour of sectors. This model is used in simulation exercises that show in detail how the various sectors and groups in the Bolivian economy react to external shocks and domestic policy responses. The model is referred to as the RF (real financial) CGE model, and has the following characteristics:

First, the model places special emphasis on changes in class relationships and income distribution as the main determinants in bringing macroeconomic adjustment. The various economic agents interact through different markets mostly regulated by institutional factors that in most cases are not purely price signals. There are many adjusting mechanisms through which excess demand in the different markets is cleared: changes in the levels of output or imports or relative price movements may bring adjustment to the goods and services market, whereas the income distribution among economic actors, investment levels, or interest rates may vary to equilibrate the financial market.

Second, the emphasis of the RF-CGE model is placed on the financial behaviour of the different institutions and socioeconomic groups (FitzGerald and Vos 1989). Although the model singles out economically relevant sets of individuals and institutions in groups related to functional categories of income distribution (wages, corporate profits, receipts of non-corporate enterprises, government), this breakdown is still useful for differentiating financial behaviours since propensities to save, consumption and investment behaviour, access to credit, portfolio choice, and power over price formation are assumed to differ across these various economic categories of agents.

The impacts of shocks and policy interventions on the economy as a whole and on each of the individual sectors are tested numerically through this CGE model. The effects of unfavourable external shocks to an economy are normally judged in terms of the behaviour of key macroeconomic variables, measuring the degree of success in achieving the different objectives (such as GDP growth, price stability, income distribution, employment, and external equilibrium). In the same way, the soundness of a determined economic policy is judged in terms of its effectiveness in achieving these macroeconomic goals.

The RF-CGE model is utilized to assess the macroeconomic impact of external shocks and to evaluate the effectiveness of various stabilization policy packages applied to cope with them. The model is also used to test the impact of structural reforms implemented in Bolivia during the 1990s. The detailed picture provided by the RF-CGE model is crucial for a proper understanding of macroeconomic adjustment and therefore for a more subtle design of policy responses.

2 Macroeconomic Policy Objectives, External Shocks and Policy Responses

2.1 Policy Objectives

Broadly speaking, the main objectives of macroeconomic policies are:

(a) *Long-term economic growth leading to economic development.* The degree of achievement of this variable is normally measured in terms of GDP growth or in terms of the share of investment in total GDP. The RF-CGE model provides a detailed picture of sectoral output growth over time. Therefore, the output of those sectors most affected by an external shock can readily be identified. Moreover, since the RF-CGE model includes separate accumulation balances for the different groups and institutions, detailed assessments can be made of the impact of an external shock on sectoral saving-investment behaviours in the short and long runs. In all cases, a more subtle policy response can be designed to cope with the negative effects of such a shock.

(b) *Equitable income distribution leading to the eradication of poverty and the satisfaction of basic needs.* Bolivia is one of the poorest countries in the Western Hemisphere and it is extremely important to understand how poverty is aggravated or ameliorated when a shock occurs or a policy package is implemented. The RF-CGE model provides a detailed picture of the resultant income distribution structure after an external shock has worked its way through the system. The soundness of alternative policies in ameliorating the impact of an external shock on the poorest groups of society can be evaluated in a very detailed way through the model.

(c) *Sustainable internal and external equilibria.* Price stability and balance of payments equilibrium are among the most important objectives in IMF- or World Bank-sponsored stabilization programmes. Although the control of inflation cannot be considered as an objective in itself, and although external equilibrium acts more as a constraint than an objective, experience has shown that both conditions are necessary (but not sufficient) for long-term macroeconomic development.

The RF-CGE model provides detailed information about different sectors' price behaviour in response to shocks so that those sectoral prices contributing most to inflation can readily be identified. In addition, a detailed picture of the effects of shocks on the balance of payments is obtained through the model. The significant detail obtained of each sub-balance in the balance of payments is very important for improved policy design.

(d) *Employment and capacity utilization.* Underutilization of existing productive resources is something that a resource-scarce country like Bolivia cannot afford. Since some sectors within the RF-CGE model are characterized by excess capacities, the short-run macro-adjustment takes place in terms of changes in output (capacity utilization). Therefore, an indiscriminately restrictive policy implemented to cope with balance of payments and inflation problems can cause unnecessary losses in terms of output and employment. By providing detailed sectoral output behaviour, the RF-CGE model helps not only to evaluate the effectiveness of different policies to cope with the negative effects of external shocks on employment and capacity utilization, but it also helps to identify the most subtle and accurate policy response so that unnecessary costs can be avoided.

2.2 External Shocks and Policies

As discussed above, external shocks have had a negative effect on Bolivia's pursuit of its main macroeconomic objectives. Although the RF-CGE model gives the possibility for a wide range of simulation exercises aimed at measuring these impacts and the effects of alternative policies, the focus of this book is on the shocks that have affected the country's macroeconomic development the most.

The external shocks that occurred at the beginning of the 1980s were the most damaging in terms of all macroeconomic objectives. These shocks were identified as (a) higher interest payments, (b) lower export revenues, and (c) negative capital inflows.

In general, shocks such as these tend to impose serious budget constraints on the public sector and a very heavy foreign exchange constraint on the economy as a whole. In the first instance the country could, if possible, choose to make no adjustment and to compensate foreign exchange losses by resorting to external finance or by reducing foreign exchange reserves. Since crises of confidence usually occur when a country has experienced adverse external shocks, such additional external finance might not be available in the quantities required; besides, foreign exchange reserves are limited, and might very soon dry up. In that case adjustment is unavoidable.

The external balance will first tend to adjust through lower imports, since exports and external finance cannot be expanded. Lower imports will also have a negative effect on domestic output. As a result, supply is greatly reduced, creating an excess demand in the market for goods and services.

Three alternative policy responses are open to the country at this stage. The first is that the economic authorities take no action and leave the economy to adjust by itself (as was the Bolivian case in the early 1980s). In this case, aggregate demand is not brought into line with the lower levels of supply, and adjustments occur through changes in the nominal value of total supply. This leads to higher prices (inflation) and large foreign exchange rate depreciations.

The second alternative is that the country adopts an orthodox stabilization programme in line with IMF and World Bank prescriptions (as in Bolivia in the late 1980s). The orthodox stabilization programme focuses, in the short term, on controlling aggregate demand and bringing it into line with the lower levels of supply resulting from the shock.

The third proposed alternative, usually termed the heterodox option, resists adjustments to the demand side alone, and thus calls for measures to increase supply in real terms by removing some of the structural constraints that limit output expansion.

The RF-CGE model helps us to evaluate numerically the effectiveness of each of the alternative policy responses in restoring the external and internal imbalances created by the shocks.

2.3 Structural Reforms

Since 1993, Bolivia, like the vast majority of developing countries, has undertaken a broad programme of structural reforms. This reform programme includes a programme of capitalization of state enterprises (that is, privatization based on increased share capital), a reform of the pension system, an education sector reform and an administrative reform of decentralization of public expenditure programmes through the 'popular participation' and 'decentralization' laws.

The RF-CGE model is utilized to assess the macroeconomic and sectoral impacts of the reforms. The capitalization process is expected to increase foreign direct investment in the telecommunication, electricity, transport, hydrocarbons and mining sectors. The pension reform will have impacts on government and private savings. The education reform and the Strategy for the Productive Transformation of the agricultural sector (Ministry of Finance, 1996) are expected to increase labour productivity in the medium to long term. The RF-CGE model simulations furnish a detailed picture about the impacts of the reform programme, both at the macro and sectoral levels.

3 Outline of this Book

This study follows a bottom-up approach to the study of external shocks, macroeconomic adjustment and stabilization policies.

Chapter 1 analyses the main macroeconomic events in Bolivia over the last two and a half decades. The analysis highlights the impact of external shocks and policies on sectoral and macroeconomic adjustments. This chapter evaluates the competing explanations available about macroeconomic performance in Bolivia. To interpret Bolivia's most important macroeconomic events, this chapter then discusses the main structural characteristics of the Bolivian economy which should be incorporated into the analysis in order to attain a proper understanding of how the Bolivian economy works. The chapter concludes that this understanding, which is crucial for a more subtle policy design in response to external shocks, requires an analysis of macroeconomic adjustment within a more disaggregated framework.

Chapter 2 discusses, in detail, the external shocks experienced by the Bolivian economy over the last two and a half decades, to give a clear picture of their dimensions. This is important to understand the sectoral adjustments discussed in subsequent chapters. Furthermore, this chapter discusses the trends followed by the main macroeconomic variables linked to the external sector, namely exchange rates, reserves and trade balances.

Chapter 3 discusses accumulation balance behaviours over the last two and a half decades for the most relevant socioeconomic groups and non-financial institutions of the Bolivian economy: households, companies, public enterprises and the government. The key stylized facts about the saving-investment and financial behaviours of each agent are identified.

Chapter 4 concentrates on the accumulation behaviour of the financial institutions, namely the Central Bank and the commercial banks. A detailed analysis of how financial institutions adjusted to the external shocks over the last two and a half decades is carried out in the first part of the chapter. The stylized facts identified are used to define adjustment rules and closures in the balance for each financial institution. Likewise, this chapter discusses the expected changes in the adjustment behaviour of financial institutions that will result from the reforms implemented during the 1990s.

In Chapter 5 the discussion moves to an analysis of the relations between the external shocks and the supply-demand adjustments made by productive activities. The balances for the main sectors and the alternative closures are discussed in light of the observed output and price behaviours over the last two and a half decades. From this analysis, key stylized facts are obtained that are later used in the construction of individual supply-demand microeconomic adjustment models for each sector. The main findings of Chapter 5 confirm the hypothesis that the various productive sectors have tended to adjust following quite different patterns of response to external shocks, and that these adjustment rules have tended to change over the period.

In Chapter 6 an attempt is made to develop a more disaggregated analysis. A reduced SAM-based model is set up with limited disaggregations of the productive sector and of socioeconomic groups. The reduced model is used to trace the shocks and adjustments in Bolivia in three periods: the 1970s, 1980–85 and 1985–95. The alternative adjustment mechanisms for each period are clearly specified in a consistent manner. This chapter places emphasis on (a) clarifying the differences in the adjustment behaviours of each agent; (b) identifying the changing nature of the rules that condition sectoral adjustment over time; and (c) confirming the value of adopting a disaggregated approach to the study of macroeconomic adjustment in an LDC.

Chapter 7 discusses the results obtained from a number of counterfactual exercises on the macroeconomic effects of different external shocks and policy packages. The effects of the shocks discussed above (in section 3.2), such as the terms of trade, international interest rates and capital inflows, are simulated numerically through the RF-CGE model. Three policy alternatives are introduced in order to cope with the negative effects of the shocks: no policy response, an orthodox policy and a heterodox policy. The policy measures included within each of these alternative policy packages are clearly specified. The effectiveness of the various policies is judged in terms of the macroeconomic objectives outlined in section 3.1 (growth, income distribution, inflation, employment and balance of payments), and the most relevant policy conclusions derived from the simulations are set out. Finally, in Chapter 7 numerical simulations of the foreseen impacts of the structural reforms are undertaken. Their effects on growth, income distribution, domestic savings and investment rates are tested through the RF-CGE model. The main findings of this simulation are discussed. Chapter 8 summarizes the most important findings of this book and puts forward the main conclusions. Finally, this book has two appendices. Appendix A develops and presents the fully-fledged SAM for Bolivia, which links the non-financial and financial sectors of the economy. It includes considerable disaggregation of the productive sector (including the informal sector), of socioeconomic groups and institutions, and of financial assets in the accumulation balance for each agent. The financial part of the SAM is set up in terms of stocks, so that portfolio decisions can be incorporated within the CGE model. Appendix B presents the equations of the RF-CGE model. All the sectoral models constructed in previous chapters are linked within the RF-CGE model. Closures at the macroeconomic level are also clearly defined.

1 The Approach of this Book to the Study of External Shocks and Policy Analysis

1.1 Introduction

As explained in the introduction, this book argues that adjustment to external shocks, in a less developed country like Bolivia, crucially depends on the institutional features that determine the macroeconomic functioning of the country, as well as on the socioeconomic structure that determines the direction of adjustment. This chapter analyses how these institutional settings, that are particular to the functioning of the Bolivian economy, have determined macroeconomic adjustment to external shocks in the country over the last two and a half decades.

Section 1.2 briefly discusses the trends followed by the main macroeconomic variables during the 1970s, 1980s and 1990s. Those trends have strongly been determined by the external shocks that the country faced over these two and a half decades. Section 1.3 analyses the interpretations given by different observers of the Bolivian economy regarding the main causes that determined the country weak macreoeconomic performance. These observers' interpretations differ with respect to the origin of the high rates of indebtedness and inflation, the low rates of growth and the high levels of poverty the country has exhibited over the long-term. Section 1.4 discusses the general features of the Bolivian economic structure that are crucial to explain macroecoconomic events in the country. Section 1.5 puts forward a disaggregated approach to the study of external shock and macroeconomic adjustment. The ways this approach mitigates the shortcomings of the more traditional neo-classical and structuralist approaches are explained in this section. Finally, section 1.6 puts forward some concluding remarks to this chapter.

1.2 The Bolivian Economy in the 1970s, 1980s and 1990s

There are two characteristics that have distinguished the Bolivian economic performance over the last two and a half decades: the high dependency on foreign capital inflows and the large participation of the government in economic activity. Figures 1.1 and 1.2 show that while the country benefited from positive transfers of foreign resources during the 1970s, the economy grew fast, fuelled by public investment, and inflation was kept low. When transfers of foreign resources became negative during the first half of the 1980s, growth was negative and the country suffered hyperinflation. When Bolivia regained access to foreign finance after the 1985 stabilization program, positive growth was regained and inflation was brought under control.

The large and rapid changes that occurred in the international financial markets during the 1970s, 1980s and 1990s brought about strong external shocks to the Bolivian economy. The country very quickly moved from a period of relatively abundant foreign exchange and external finance availability (during the 1970s) to a period of extremely acute foreign exchange shortage (in the 1980s) and once again started to

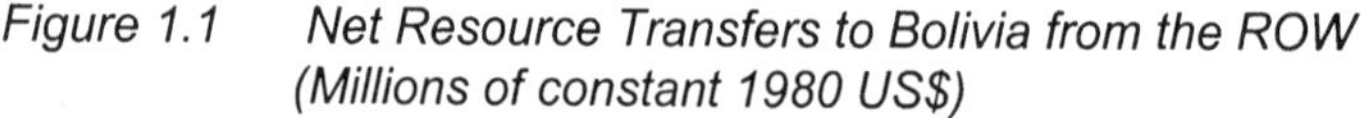

Figure 1.1 Net Resource Transfers to Bolivia from the ROW (Millions of constant 1980 US$)

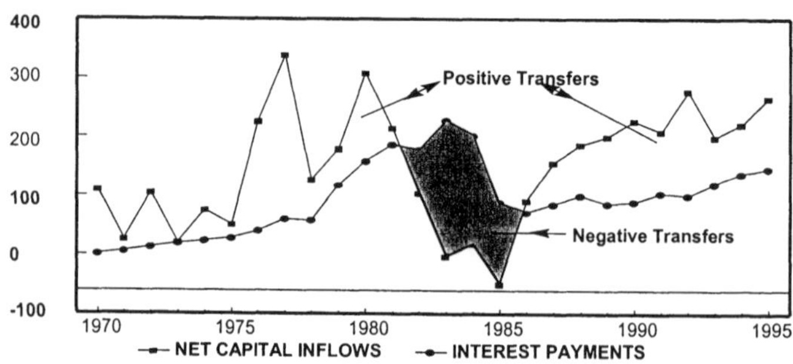

Figure 1.2 *GDP Growth and Inflation*

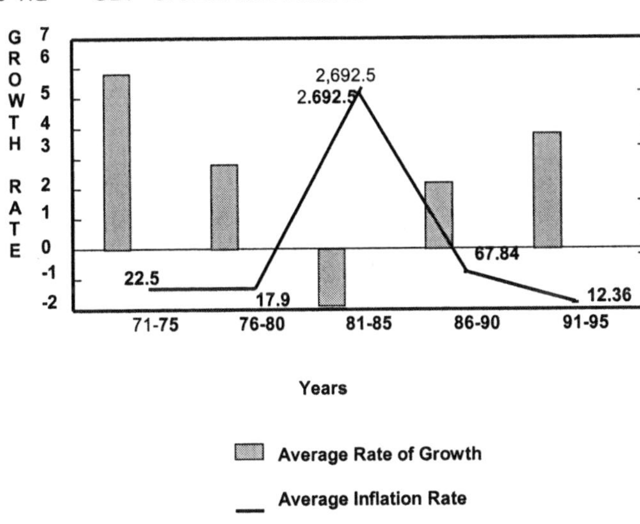

Source: Jemio and Antelo (1996)

receive foreign capital inflows once the country stabilized its economy and normalized its relations with international credit institutions after the 1995 stabilization programme.

These external shocks have dramatically modified the financial positions of the various economic agents in Bolivia over the last two decades, giving rise to an uneven pattern in the country's macroeconomic adjustment. The government and private sector have responded to the external shocks in quite different fashions, and the way the shocks worked their way through the system seems also to have experienced fundamental changes over the period.

In the 1970s, the country experienced a series of favourable external shocks:

(a) An oil, gas and commodity price boom associated with the discovery of hydrocarbon fields greatly increased the country's export potential.
(b) This export boom made the country attractive to foreign financial entities. A large public debt was accumulated in the 1970s. Capital

inflows grew to US$300 million per year at the peak in 1978–79, of which more than 90 per cent went to the public sector.

Adjustment to the relatively abundant foreign exchange during the 1970s exacerbated the weaknesses of Bolivia's development pattern in two ways.

First, it further increased the role of the state in the economy. The accumulation of capital needed for Bolivia's long-term development became a government responsibility. The 1970s saw the creation of relatively large, complex and inefficient state-owned metallurgical and agro-industrial factories, and of several public sector industrial plants.

Second, it accelerated the acquisition of foreign assets (capital flight). The government pursued a development strategy aimed at favouring a larger participation of the private sector in economic activity. In that process, large amounts of resources were transferred from the public to the private sector through credit. Private investment was also promoted through price incentives and wage controls, but the private sector did not react as expected, preferring to invest their surpluses outside the country. According to various estimates (World Bank 1985b; Ramos 1980), accumulated capital outflows amounted to over 60 per cent of the value of the debt accumulated during the years 1971–81.

During the 1980s the country experienced a series of negative external shocks that drastically changed the accumulation behaviours of both the public and private sectors.

(a) External capital inflows to the public sector were interrupted in 1978–79 by a change in the commercial banks' perception of Bolivia's export potential and debt-servicing capacity. This led the banks to reduce their exposure, leaving the Bolivian government without the substantial foreign inflows needed to help service its large external debt.
(b) In 1982 Bolivia was hit by the recession in the industrialized world, which led to a sharp decline in its official exports. At the same time the outbreak of the debt crisis resulted in a further retrenchment of foreign finance.
(c) The country's debt-service burden increased sharply because of higher interest rates.

Adjustment to these adverse external conditions proved to be extremely difficult and painful. During the first half of the 1980s, falling exports and constrained industrial production due to the lack of imported inputs and capital goods led to a continuous fall of GDP. Besides, the external payments problem was directly linked to a rising fiscal deficit; the unfavourable trend in exports reduced tax incomes, while high interest payments on foreign debt pushed up expenditures. The government cut investment, but current expenditures proved to be more difficult to reduce due to social and political pressures. Since external finance was practically non-existent, the growing deficits were continuously financed through money creation. This process eventually brought about a deep economic crisis characterized by falling output, external imbalances and hyperinflation.

During the 1980s, however, the country's access to external resources did not completely disappear. Some US$400 million per year (UDAPE 1990b) entered the economy from the illegal cocaine business, which, during this decade, became the paramount source of foreign exchange to the economy. High international prices due to increased demand in the developed countries and the underemployment and falling real wages created by the economic crisis resulted in a widespread pursuit of multi-occupational livelihood strategies in the informal sector, many within the coca-cocaine economy. During the 1980s, the level of output, employment and investment in the formal sector contracted, while employment in the informal sector boomed. Given their illegal origins, the government was unable to tax or have any kind of control over these surpluses in order to finance its activity.

The stabilization programme implemented in 1985, known as the New Economic Policy (NEP), completely redefined the roles of the public and private sectors in the economy. The NEP centred on a sharp reduction of the non-financial public sector deficit and the strengthening of market forces. The policies included a massive devaluation and a unification of the exchange rate, increases in public sector prices (in particular of domestic petroleum products), and reductions in government expenditures to levels that could be financed by available funds.

The NEP was also part of a broader structural adjustment programme aimed at changing the whole functioning of the economy by reducing the influence of the state on production, increasing reliance on the price system in the different markets (goods, labour and capital), and promoting private sector initiatives. The framework of incentives adopted under the NEP (including free convertibility of foreign exchange, elimination of price controls, reduced government intervention in labour contracts, financial liberalisation, and commitment to price stability) was designed to encourage greater private sector participation in the economy. These reforms have been largely maintained under the Paz Zamora government (1989–93) and widened in scope under the government of president Sánchez de Lozada that took office in August 1993. The recent reforms include a programme of capitalization of state enterprises (that is, privatization based on increased share capital), a reform of the pension system, an education sector reform and an administrative reform of decentralization of public expenditure programmes through the 'popular participation' and 'decentralization' laws.

The reforms were highly successful in stabilizing the economy and in reducing internal and external imbalances:

(a) Macroeconomic indicators continue to show stability as inflation has been kept down below 20 per cent per annum since 1989 and has been below the 10 per cent mark since 1993.
(b) GDP growth has been steady since the introduction of the economic reforms (2–4 per cent per year).
(c) The country also largely succeeded in renegotiating part of its external debt and in restoring relations with international creditors. This restored the flow of external finance to the country, mostly to the public sector.
(d) As a result of financial liberalization, bank deposits increased substantially due to repatriation of funds from abroad to take advantage of higher interest rates and some switching from informal to formal financial intermediaries. This has increased the amount of loanable funds within the economy.
(e) Net foreign exchange reserves increased to almost US$1 billion by 1996, having been negative in 1985.

The programme has been less successful in achieving other macroeconomic objectives, however.

(a) The fiscal deficit was greatly reduced but not completely eliminated. The remaining deficit was financed through foreign loans and debt instruments such as certificates of deposit (CDs) issued by the Central Bank and Treasury bonds, paying high interest rates. Domestic saving remains at very low levels and investment finance has relied mostly on foreign borrowing.

(b) The aggregate private investment response to the change in the business environment since 1985 has been limited due to the high interest rate resulting from the Central Bank's open-market operations, inadequate infrastructure and uncertainty about the long-term application of the programme.

(c) GDP growth has been positive and stable since 1987. However, on average, it has remained just above population growth. As a result, per capita income and consumption have increased very little. The unemployment rate increased from 15 per cent in 1984 to 20 per cent on average during the second half of the 1980s and real wages have deteriorated since 1985.

1.3 The Bolivian Debate on Macroeconomic Performance

Over the last two decades, the Bolivian macroeconomic behaviour has been anything but stable. As is evidenced by Table 1.1, the country has moved from a period of relatively rapid growth and price stability (1972–75), to a period of economic decline (1976–79), to a period of economic crisis characterized by hyperinflation and large decreases in real GDP (1980–85), and eventually to a period of price stability but low economic growth under the New Economic Policy (1985–95). Analysts of the Bolivian economic reality have offered a number of interpretations of the macroeconomic events that have occurred over the last two and a half decades.

Advocates of the neoclassical paradigm argue that the weaknesses of the Bolivian economic development pattern before 1985 were deeply rooted in the government intervention in economic activity. According to the World Bank (1985b, p.ii), increased government intervention in economic activity,

> ...has been steady and relatively independent of the political orientation of successive Governments. Conservative Governments have not attempted to reverse the trend; if anything, they have strengthened the

> management and efficiency of the public sector bureaucracy as, for example, during the 1970s, without questioning or redirecting the role of the state in the economy. More radical Governments have increased Government involvement by expanding the scope of state activities. For example, Gulf Oil in Bolivia was nationalized in 1969, as was a large mine belonging to United States Steel (Mina Matilde) in 1971. In 1983, a public enterprise was established in a sector – passenger and freight surface transportation – that had previously been free from Government intervention.

The World Bank (ibid, p.4) further argues the this process has built up, over time, a mutual mistrust between the private sector and important segments of the population with two consequences:

> First, the private sector has come to feel that participation in Bolivia's development process entails an unacceptable degree of risk and has therefore continued, whenever possible, to accumulate assets abroad. Second, the Government has chosen to compete with the private sector in activities that are more suited to the latter (such as consumer goods,

Table 1.1 Bolivia: Selected Economic Indicators

	1972–75	1976–79	1980–85	1986–90	1991–96
		(average percentage changes)			
GDP at constant 1980 prices	5.6	1.4	–1.9	1.7	4.0
Consumer price index	17.8	20.4	983.6	13.9	12.2
Net domestic credit	15.4	35.2	264.8	24.54	18.9
– To the public sector	-27.2	51.3	245.1	14.7	3.8
– To the private sector	42.1	29.4	289.2	59.2	31.3
		(average millions of U.S. dollars)[a]			
Exports f.o.b.	368.9	741.3	768.6	639.8	1018.2
Imports c.i.f.	351.2	736.8	664.9	770.3	1261.0
Current account balance	–17.2	–189.8	–172.2	–281.7	-330.1
		(average percentage of GDP)[b]			
Surplus/deficit of the non-financial public sector	0.9	–8.9	–13.2	–4.7	-3.9

Notes: [a] Annual averages.
[b] Estimate based on the 'errors and omissions' item of the balance of payments.

agro-industry and metallurgy), while giving inadequate attention to the production of public goods in which it has a natural role to play.

The pitfalls of this style of economic management, according to the World Bank (ibid, p.4),

> ...did not become fully evident until 1980s ... In the 1970s, an export boom associated with the discovery of hydrocarbon fields which indicated the possibility of sizeable petroleum and gas deposits, made the country attractive to foreign financial entities and exacerbated the weaknesses of Bolivia's development pattern. It further increased the role of the state in the economy, and accelerated private capital flight.

In the same vein, the IMF (1987b) argues that during the second half of the 1970s, 'Bolivia's economy was beset by declining economic growth, sluggish domestic savings, and a widening external current account deficit, owing mainly to a lax fiscal policy – with public sector deficits averaging more than 9 per cent of GDP during the period – and an inappropriate exchange rate policy'.

During that period, the IMF argues, '...ample availability of foreign finance made it possible to defer the implementation of corrective measures.

A more structuralist version has been put forward by Devlin (1986) and by Devlin and Mortimore (1983, p.220); they argue that the easy availability of financial resources deposited in international financial markets initiated large financial flows towards developing countries, bringing about a process of 'supply-led' indebtedness. In response to the enlarged capacity to obtain external resources, the Bolivian authorities tried to achieve rapid development by siphoning almost all the domestic credit to the private capitalist sector and leaving the public sector to secure finance abroad at higher costs. This option was chosen for three reasons. First, transnational banks were not inclined to lend directly to the private sector and preferred to finance investment by the public sector, especially in the profitable exporting sectors. Second, the Bolivian economic authorities believed that large transfers of resources to the private sector would bring about increased private investment and therefore faster development. Third, the costs of finance from international banks were relatively low in real terms in that period.

Other authors (Ramos 1980, p.222; 1989, p.268; Dunkerley 1984, p.228; Hinojosa and Espinoza 1983) confirm the previous observation;

they argue that the development strategy applied during the late 1970s benefited the higher socioeconomic strata of society. Thus, large resources were transferred to the capitalist sector mainly through the expansion of domestic credit.

Moreover, the wage policy applied during that period was also designed to generate additional investable surpluses to the private capitalist sector through a more unequal income distribution. During the 1970s wages were strictly controlled while prices increased at an average rate of 30 per cent per annum. As a result, wage-earners' share of national income dropped from 47 to 31 per cent (Ramos 1980, p.179). Despite this large availability of resources, however, the groups that benefited from the development strategy implemented during the 1970s failed to translate these resources into productive investment, choosing instead to use them for luxury consumption (Rivas 1989) and to finance capital flight (Ramos 1980).[1]

The acute economic crisis of the early 1980s, which is closely related to the external debt accumulated during the 1970s, also finds different interpretations under different perspectives.

The World Bank and IMF, although they acknowledge that the external shocks that occurred in the late 1970s and early 1980s had large negative impacts in the Bolivian economy, maintain that the economic crisis arose mainly because successive governments failed to implement coherent macroeconomic programmes to cope with the external shocks. Each of the eight packages applied between 1979 and February 1985, '...failed in one or another crucial area of the economy. Some provided insufficient devaluation (e.g. the November 1983 package); others were unclear regarding wages and interest rate policies (e.g. the April 1984 programme)...' (World Bank 1985b, p.10). The rigid foreign exchange regime, according to the World Bank (ibid, p.11) '...has been one of the main causes of increases in the money supply, and thus in inflation...' because '... public sector revenues depend significantly on the level of the official exchange rate and domestic prices are influenced by the exchange rate in the parallel market.'

Sachs (1987, p.280) identifies three factors as being fundamental to the rise of hyperinflation: first, the cutoff of international lending and the increase in international interest rates in the early 1980s were the main factors that led to hyperinflation; second, the recourse to seigniorage (i.e. the inflation tax) jumped as the net international resource transfer turned negative; and third, the increasing inflation caused the tax system to collapse.

The IMF (1987b, p.20) argues that at times,

> the authorities adjusted the official exchange rate and publicly controlled prices or approved measures to increase tax revenues. These attempts to contain the public sector deficit, however, were undermined by strong political pressures aimed at increasing real wages. In particular, widespread strikes brought the economy to a standstill. In response to these pressures, the authorities imposed interest rate ceilings, tightened price controls, and indexed minimum wages in all sectors of the economy to inflation.

According to the IMF, the sharp increase in the demand for dollars, which resulted in a severe dis-intermediation in the financial system, has to be attributed to the accelerating inflation, administered interest rate, and the growing overvaluation of the peso.[2] Output contraction, on the other hand, (ibid, p.19) 'can be largely attributed to the absence of any coherent economic policies manifested in a continuously expanding deficit of the non-financial public sector, which crowded the private sector out of the organized financial markets'.

Critics of the IMF and World Bank position identify the external shocks as being the main factors for initiating the economic crisis. Morales and Sachs (1989, p.21) argue that, 'The hyperinflation under [President] Siles was not so much a result of new spending as the inability to restrain spending in the face of falling foreign loans, falling tax revenues, and higher debt service payments abroad'. The external shock of the early 1980s therefore brought about an increased fiscal deficit (which was mainly financed through Central Bank credit due to the narrowness of the Bolivian financial market) and lower levels of investment and output; these two factors are regarded as being the main causes for the beginning of hyperinflation.

In the same vein, R. Morales (1987a, p.9) argues that the hyperinflationary process in Bolivia mainly originated in the effects of external shocks on the fiscal balance; these shocks being 'the drop in the value of mining and hydrocarbon exports, the heavy burden of the external debt service, and the unwillingness of international financial institutions to grant new loans to Bolivia'.

Morales (1987b) also argues that two other factors greatly contributed to hyperinflation: the distorted structure of the markets for consumer goods, and the 'dollarization' of the economy. The first factor, according to Morales, is associated with both the unequal income distribution, which translates into non-homogeneous demand, and with the existence of oligopolies and other concentration mechanisms among suppliers.

The same distributional argument is utilized by Pastor (1991), who explains the Bolivian hyperinflation as being partly the result of unresolved social conflicts, where workers and capitalists were unable to arrive at some explicit agreement about the distribution of income and instead struggled for an increased income share by continually raising nominal claims:

> ...widening government deficits and their monetisation can also be understood in distributional terms: generally, workers clamour for more social spending while capitalists resist surrendering the social surplus (in the form of tax revenues) that will fund these expenditures. If external finance is available, the inflationary impact of such social conflict can be dampened; if such financing is not available, monetarisation is required and inflation can result (ibid, p.217).

Against this background, Pastor argues that the pressures faced by the government to maintain and even increase real wages 'must be seen in the light of stagnant wages in the 1970s and a dramatic decline in labour's share of income during 1980–82. The labour movement had supported Siles Zuazo and viewed his presidency as an opportunity to make up for those past losses'.

Ramos (1989, p.272) explains hyperinflation in terms of the inability of the government to control speculative factors and corruption, losing progressively its capacity to conduct economic policy. According to Ramos, certain social actors (including private banks and import traders) '...utilized their power to obtain high profits through speculative operations with the dollar and essential goods. Central Bank credit to the private sector was diverted, to a large extent, towards speculative operations which very quickly resulted in price increases'.

The main objective of the 1985 New Economic Policy (NEP) in the short term was to stabilize the economy by reducing hyperinflation and restoring the external balance; in the long term, however, it was conceptualized as a far more ambitious political plan aimed at completely changing the accumulation model based on state capitalism that had been applied since 1952. In that context, the NEP's emphasis on reducing the size of the public sector was seen not only as a means of reducing hyperinflation by cutting the fiscal deficit and, therefore, of money creation, but also as a way of reducing government intervention in economic activity. The NEP, according to the World Bank (1989, p.15), 'constituted a consistent and comprehensive programme designed to increase the reliance of productive activities on the price system and on private sector initiative, reduce the influence of the state on production, and increase the efficiency of the public sector administration'.

The NEP has been quite successful in bringing price stability; long-term growth and structural reforms, however, have proved to be more difficult to achieve after seven years of application of the programme. The success of the NEP in bringing price stability is explained differently by various authors.

According to the IMF (1987b), price stability has been mainly achieved '...through the improvement of public sector finances and the elimination of price distortions'.

Sachs (1987) identifies the exchange rate as being the main determinant of Bolivian inflationary expectations; he therefore places more emphasis on the exchange rate stabilization as having '...played the pre-eminent role in the immediate disinflation, while fundamental fiscal policy changes were necessary to maintain the stable exchange rate over time'.

Pastor (1989, p.233), on the other hand, maintains that the fundamental problems that caused hyperinflation were:

> the pressure of debt payments which eroded public finance while distributional conflict produced both a wage-price spiral and an inability to resolve exactly which social sector would bear the brunt of the budget adjustment necessary to close the public sector deficit. . . the NEP attacked these fundamental problems by adopting an orthodoxy that attracted new funds and pushed the burden of the adjustment on the lower-income groups'.

Public sector balance disequilibrium and exchange rate instability were proximate causes of inflation. The deficit was reduced by 'raising gasoline prices and then installing a new regressive tax system'; the exchange rate, on the other hand, was supported by '...dumping scarce reserves, borrowing abroad, and raising the interest rate to attract capital flight home'.

Other observers highlight the financial support provided by the foreign exchange in the form of revenues from the cocaine trade as being essential for the success of the stabilization programme. According to Dunkerley (1992, p.228), '...on the basis of "errors and omissions" in the National Accounts, the formally registered infusion of *narcodollares* was at least US$64 million in 1986 (much higher thereafter)'.

The lack of long-term growth, on the other hand, is also rationalized in different ways; some analysts (World Bank 1989; Candia 1991) see the Bolivian economic model as being in a 'situation of incomplete [structural] adjustment' (Candia 1991, p.51) because crucial reforms needed to achieve long-term growth (such as privatization of public enterprises, rationalization of government expenditures) were not fully implemented. Therefore, large distortions still remain in many sectors of the economy, bringing uncertainty to the economic agents and preventing them from getting the right price in order to undertake investment. Particular attention is paid to the persistent fiscal deficit which has resulted in a crowding out of the the private sector through higher interest rates (Fisher 1991; Mierau-Klein and Page 1991; Calvo 1991; Trigo 1991; Boada 1991).

Other authors focus on the much deeper structural constraints that characterize the Bolivian economy, as being crucial in preventing private-initiative-led long-term growth. Among these factors are the lack of investment in physical infrastructure (Mierau-Klein and Page 1991) and in human capital (Behrman 1991).

Schuh (1991) emphasizes the inadequate attention paid to the agricultural sector in Bolivia, given its importance in terms of employment and of food supply. An adequate supply of food, according to Schuh, is the only way to protect the real incomes of the poorest sectors of society.

Machicado (1991) and UDAPE (1991) highlight the segmented and monopolistic nature of the financial sector as having obstructed an efficient allocation of resources. Machicado (ibid, p.37) argues that in the Bolivian financial system '...there is a group of banks that serves certain enterprises'.

Toranzo (1991) stresses that the NEP has been designed to promote the private initiative of the formal capitalist sector of society, and has completely excluded the new entrepreneurial groups within the 'informal sector'.

The impact that the second-generation reforms will have on economic growth and poverty alleviation is also the subject of profound controversies. Government authorities (Ministry of Finance, 1997) argue that the reforms will substantially increase growth, by removing the structural constraints, which have so far limited the country's prospects to attain long-term growth and development. These constraints are: low rates of domestic saving and investment, lack of infrastructure, low investment levels in human capital, and little access to advanced technology. The capitalization of public enterprises is expected to boost investment and technology transfers to key sectors of the economy: hydrocarbons, telecommunications, electricity, transport and mining; the pension reform will help to develop a long-term capital market in Bolivia and thus promote higher rates of domestic savings; and the education reform and popular participation are expected to bring about an increase in labour productivity and a more equitable income distribution. The setting up of a transparent and stable regulatory system will also promote private investment. Critics of the structural reforms carried out by the government since 1993 are more sceptical about the capacity of the reforms to deliver growth and development. They argue that the investment boost resulting from the capitalization process, will take place in capital-intensive sectors, with little impact on employment and thus on poverty reduction.

Other authors (Vos, Lee and Mejía, 1998) argue that

> Bolivia's initial conditions do not seem to provide the best prospects for a smooth transition towards the creation of a 'virtuous cycle' of growth, employment creation, and poverty reduction. Firstly, its export orientation shows heavy reliance on primary commodities (agriculture and mining), most of which is produced with low labour intensity. The collapse of world markets of minerals (tin in particular) led to a decline in one part of export sector, while expansion of agricultural export production in Santa Cruz area (soya, in particular) also mainly applies large scale technologies. Secondly, its small and underdeveloped industrial base makes a shift towards labour-intensive, export-oriented manufacturing more difficult. Thirdly, low educational levels of the major part of the population would indicate the need for sustained high investment in education for many years to provide better trained works

force. Fourth, compensatory programs such as the Emergency Social Fund (FSE) and the Social Investment Fund (FIS) cannot be expected to fully make up the social cost of the economic recession and restructuring by their sheer nature (they were designed to be temporary, small scale in nature, targeted to specific groups, and, in principle, not meant to override universal provisioning of basic social services).

In summary, analysts have provided a wide variety of interpretations to Bolivian macroeconomic behaviour over the last two and a half decades; some have tended to identify with the orthodox position that excessive government intervention has prevented the efficient working of the market mechanism in order to guarantee long-term growth. Indiscriminate government intervention is therefore seen as the main explanation for the external debt that built up in the 1970s and the intense economic crisis of the early 1980s. Although this tendency has been reversed since 1985, the structural changes have not gone far enough to guarantee an adequate functioning of market forces, and this has obviously delayed the renewal of growth.

Other analysts have explained these events in terms of the external shocks to the Bolivian economy over the last two decades. It has been argued that the negative impacts of these shocks have been amplified by the structural and institutional factors that characterize the Bolivian economy. These factors include: the high levels of dependence of production, investment and public sector revenues on the external sector; oligopolistic structures in the financial and goods-and-services markets; distributional conflicts that have created political tensions and instability; and the lack of physical and human infrastructures. These structural features, which are discussed in more detail in next section, must be included in any analytical framework in order to obtain an accurate understanding of macroeconomic adjustment in Bolivia.

1.4 General Features of the Bolivian Economic Structure

According to various authors (Cariaga 1982; J.A. Morales 1982), the most representative institutional features of the Bolivian economy are: the coexistence of modern and traditional modes of production, the existence of a large and growing informal sector (including the illegal production of coca and unrefined cocaine), a significant dependence on the external sector, the high level of public sector intervention in economic activity, and the existence of an underdeveloped and highly segmented financial market.

This section discusses each of these structural features.

1.4.1 Dual productive structure

The Bolivian productive sector is characterized by the coexistence of traditional modes of production, activities of non-corporate units, such as family-run, subsistence-oriented productive units, and modern modes of production, incorporated capitalistic units that employ mainly hired labour.

This occurs not only across productive sectors but also within the same sector. In the agricultural sector for instance, 93 per cent of the productive units are smallholders working plots averaging only 7 hectares. Although they grow 70 per cent of the country's food, they own only 11 per cent of the agricultural land. In contrast, 40,000 large estates occupy 89 per cent of the land and produce most of the commercial commodities for overseas markets.

This segmented structures, by which distinct technology modes co-exist simultaneously in the delivery of similar commodities or services, can be found in most productive activities in Bolivia (such as agriculture, mining, manufacturing, construction and services).

1.4.2 Growth of the informal sector

During the economic crisis of the first half of the 1980s the importance of informal sector activities increased rapidly. Although reliable data are difficult to obtain, it is clear that the informal sector now makes up a large portion of the Bolivian economy (Blanes Jimenez 1989).

Informal economic activity is also high in urban areas. According to the 1976 national census, excluding domestic services, about 47 per cent of the working urban population in Bolivia is involved in the informal economy (Casanovas and Escobar 1988). In 1983, 152,215 economic units were identified in the larger urban centres, but only 8,340 (5.5 per cent) employed five or more workers. The remaining 143,875 establishments (94 per cent of the total) employed 48.4 per cent of the population (INE 1983).

1.4.3 Dependence on the external sector

The dependence of the Bolivian economic performance on external factors (both foreign trade and capital flows) is significant. Despite efforts by various governments to achieve even small-scale industrialization in order to limit the country's dependence on foreign trade, the Bolivian economy is still very open, or very dependent upon foreign trade. By 1996, exports and imports averaged 20 and 25 per cent of GDP, respectively. By these measures Bolivia is one of the most open of Latin American economies.[3]

While imports have mostly comprised staple foods (wheat) and manufactured goods, historically the composition of Bolivian official exports has been dominated by a small number of commodities. During the 1970s minerals and hydrocarbons accounted for 67 and 20 per cent of official Bolivian exports, respectively; tin exports alone comprised 42 per cent of total official exports. During the 1980s hydrocarbons increased its share to 41 per cent and minerals fell to 47 per cent. Natural gas alone represented 39 per cent of total exports. During the 1990s, non-traditional exports picked up and reduced the importance of mining and hydrocarbon exports. Bolivia is therefore largely a primary quasi-mono-product commodity exporter. This factor makes the economy extremely vulnerable to international market fluctuations.

The importance of the external sector was augmented during the 1980s by the increased significance of illegal coca export revenues, estimated at US$115 million and US$600 million in 1978 and 1986, respectively (INE 1990). UDAPE estimated coca and unrefined cocaine export revenues at US$1.5 billion[4] and US$700 million in 1987 and 1989, respectively (UDAPE 1990c).

Capital flows have also played a key role in shaping the behaviour of the Bolivian economy. The large external debt accumulated during the 1970s that went to finance current account deficits and capital flight largely explains the economic crisis witnessed in the first half of the 1980s. It lowered the country's import capacity, reduced access to new credit, and reduced control over domestic macroeconomic management. After the 1985 stabilization program, access to foreign resources was recovered and the country was able to stabilize its economy and reassume growth.

1.4.4 Public sector participation in economic activity

The public sector has played an important role in the Bolivian economy, not only in terms of government policy design, but also through its direct participation in production. In 1978 all government units, including decentralized agencies and mixed enterprises, provided for 25 per cent of GDP, 70 per cent of investment and 48 per cent of gross savings (INE 1989d). By 1986, although government participation in GDP had reduced to 19 per cent, in investment to 50 per cent, and in gross savings to 36 per cent, the level of public sector involvement in economic activity is still one of the highest in Latin America. Some of the reforms implemented during the 1990s, (such as the capitalization and privatization of the public enterprises) have considerably reduced the public sector's involvement in activities that produce goods and services; the public sector, however, accounted for 50 per cent of total investment in 1995.

1.4.5 Underdeveloped financial system

Financial intermediation in Bolivia is carried out by commercial banks, private sector development banks (of which only one plays a significant role in the market) and non-bank financial intermediaries (including savings and loans associations and credit unions).

The degree of competition within the system fell during the economic crisis, when most international banks left Bolivia. In addition, nine domestic banks have been liquidated after the stabilization programme of 1985. The public banks consisting of three banks with specific development objectives – the State Bank (BANEST), the Agricultural Bank (BAB) and the Mining Bank (BAMIN) – were closed in 1992, as a governmental policy aimed at withdrawing the state from commercial banking activities. In 1994, two commercial banks were closed due to financial insolvency.

As of December 1996, Bolivia had 17 private commercial banks, of which 13 are classified as domestic and four as foreign. The financial market in Bolivia has an oligopolistic structure, with four banks holding 54 per cent of total deposits and 53 per cent of total capital.[5]

1.5 The Disaggregated Approach to Macroeconomic Adjustment

An important conclusion that can be drawn from this discussion is that the conventional theoretical approaches (MABP, Mundell-Fleming models, Two-gap and Three-gap models) are far too aggregated to include all the structural factors that are crucial in explaining the Bolivian economy's adjustment to external shocks over the last two decades.

For instance, a key assumption of the neoclassical models that is in clear contradiction with what has been observed in the Bolivian reality is the homogeneity of the private sector's accumulation balance behaviour; this assumption suggests that non-financial private sector agents (households, corporate enterprises, non-corporate firms, and small peasants) have the same saving-investment behaviours. In other words, the savings decisions of all these agents are explained by the hypothesis that rational consumers attempt to maximize their utility by allocating a lifetime stream of earnings to an optimum lifetime pattern of consumption, while their investment decisions are based on a portfolio analysis that considers rates of return differentials among different assets.

Very clearly, neoclassical models fail to integrate in their analyses the institutional characteristics of the economy at hand, which underline market forces (Fitzgerald and Vos 1989) and therefore cannot explain the saving-investment behaviour of all the heterogeneous economic actors found in developing economies in general and the Bolivian economy in particular. Crucial institutional characteristics have to be taken into account. For instance, rural households and small producers tend to save their own surpluses for investment; faced with credit rationing and high loan costs, they tend to be self-financing and therefore their investments are determined by their capacity to save. Their investments are concentrated in housing, farm improvements, or transport equipment as part of the expansion of their own income opportunities (Jansen 1987). The capacity of households and small producers to generate surpluses depends on their own productivity as well as on their internal terms of trade.

Rich households, on the other hand, have demonstrated their preferences for investment in luxurious housing and in financial deposits in offshore banks.

For large enterprises, depreciation funds, retained profits and preferential access to bank loans provide the main sources of finance. Enterprises have easier access to bank credit than do small producers, since large businesses are usually organized in oligopolistic groups associated with banks that can guarantee the required liquidity on the basis of the profits of the group as a whole (Leff 1976; Drake 1980). Generally speaking, large enterprises do not face financial constraints in investment; a profitable investment has no problem in finding finance.

Wage-earners show low saving rates in developing countries once household incomes are disaggregated. The wage rate will determine the capacity of the wage-earner to generate savings. In the enterprise sector, wages tend to be negotiated collectively, while in the small-scale sector there is a market-clearing wage.

Finally, the government has resorted to several measures in order to generate investable surpluses: to increase tax rates so that revenues exceed current expenditures, inflationary finance as a tax on money that redistributes resources for investment to the government, and obtaining external finance. State investment, which accounts for more than half of non-housing fixed capital formation in Bolivia, has been a function of a perceived development strategy rather than of considerations of profitability.

Structuralist models, on the other hand, are also too aggregated to capture most of the structural features of a developing economy such as Bolivia. The hypothesis embodied in the Three-gap model that economic growth is constrained by the overall import capacity of the economy explains quite well the government and formal sector's situation, where the reduced import capacity imposed a binding constraint on growth. However, the Three-gap hypothesis appears not to be valid in all cases; for instance, during the 1980s the Bolivian informal sector had access to large amounts of foreign exchange. Nevertheless, investment did not react significantly since informal profit-earners preferred to invest these surpluses outside the country (capital flight). This has brought about a situation in which we find two coexisting sectors within the economy, facing quite different constraints. On the one hand, the formal sector and the government were foreign exchange constrained, because the level of state output was likely to be increased through new investment and utilization of excess capacity, but the lack of foreign finance offset this possibility. The informal private sector, on the other hand, demonstrated a very low absorption capacity. It has access to foreign exchange through illegal export earnings, but its capacity to use them productively has proved to be very limited. Therefore, investment by the sector has not reacted significantly and these resources have been used mainly to finance imports and capital outflows.

1.5.1 The need for a disaggregated framework

A more realistic approach to the study of external shocks and adjustment in Bolivia should start by singling out economically relevant sets of individuals and institutions into groups related to a functional category of income distribution. For the specific purpose of this research, we need to distinguish at least the following economic agents:

(i) wage-earners,
(ii) non-corporate enterprises in the informal sector,
(iii) corporate private enterprises in the formal sector,
(iv) public enterprises,
(v) the government.

The justification for this breakdown is based on the hypothesis that each of these institutional sectors has a particular accumulation balance behaviour, including the acquisition of financial liabilities and assets. All the institutional sectors accumulate (that is, invest, save, lend, and borrow) in fundamentally different ways with different objectives and under different conditions. Therefore, their reactions to external shocks (such as an increase in capital inflows received by one particular sector) and their interactions with the other sectors follow specific behavioural rules with consequent repercussions on macroeconomic equilibrium. We now analyse some of the distinguishing characteristics of these various socioeconomic groups.

(i) Wage labour households

The main source of income for this category is wages. The propensity of wage-earners to save is very low, especially when consumer durables and housing are counted as deferred consumption. Wage labour can be divided into two groups:

(a) The poor and unskilled, whose wage incomes are spent entirely on wage goods and who face a fairly competitive labour market. With little or no access to means of production, they must sell their labour for whatever they can get.
(b) Skilled and administrative workers, who have greater control over their wage levels (through trades union action) and the capacity to acquire consumer durables. The savings (and investment) of this group are mostly confined to the purchase (or direct construction) of housing.

(ii) Non-corporate enterprises

This category comprises two groups in the case of Bolivia:

(a) A wide range of activities by peasants, artisans, petty traders, and so on, which take place in competitive markets. Their main sources of income are the profits earned in small enterprises, including the imputed incomes of self-employed workers and the family labour they employ. Consumption, production, savings and investment decisions take place within the same unit on the basis of total household income. Their investment largely takes the form of purchasing equipment or expanding labour employment in order to enhance production and income. This investment is limited by available resources, which typically consist of their own surplus income (savings) plus credit from informal money lenders and some rationed amount of government credit channelled through state-owned development banks. Their main relation to the formal banking system, if any, is as depositors.
(b) The so-called 'parallel economy'. This level is used to suggest the parallel and illicit nature of an economic system that avoids regulation by, and contributions to, the state and its formal economy. It includes those small-scale informal-sector activities pursued by households that may contravene state laws and regulations (for example, by money-changing, contraband imports, gold panning), as well as large-scale criminal activities involving fractions of 'rogue' capital in search of large profits, such as those associated with the drug business. Although threatened by coercive action, the subterranean economy can be self-sustaining and capable of generating high rates of accumulation (that is normally used to finance capital

flight) and can exist as a parallel, if not autonomous, economic system.

(iii) Corporate enterprises

Privately-owned firms which have a registered legal status. In practice this category mostly refers to companies applying modern, large-scale production techniques. To a large extent they may have the market power to influence prices, but may encounter market size limitations on output (unless exporting). They finance their investment mainly out of depreciation and retained profits of the group. Bank credit can easily be obtained, although it may be largely used for working capital needs. Their easy access to bank credit may be even larger; in many LDCs non-financial corporate enterprises also tend to have close ties with domestic banking groups (Leff 1976). Thus, their investment is not usually limited by savings but rather by expected profitability in the medium term based on projected sales volumes.

(iv) Public enterprises

State-owned enterprises that face controlled prices on their output. They mostly operate in exporting activities. Their investment expenditures are largely financed from low-cost state bank credits and from foreign borrowing.

(v) The government

Comprises the government administration. Fiscal deficits can be financed by tax revenues or foreign borrowing, although both may be limited due to political resistance by taxpayers and credit rationing on the side of international banks and aid donors. Domestic resources need not be constrained to the extent that money creation can be used. Therefore public investment is not limited in the first place by savings and means of payments as such, but rather by the consequences of fiscal deficits for macroeconomic instability.

1.5.2 The need for a multi-sectoral model

To capture adequately the characteristics of a developing economy open to trade, one needs to specify four key relationships (balances):

(i) supply-demand balances for each productive sector,
(ii) accumulation balances for each socioeconomic agent and institution,
(iii) financial balances,
(iv) external balances.

These four relationships must be included in any macroeconomic model, although the degree of disaggregation of each of them might change from model to model. The leading theoretical approaches give only partial explanations of macroeconomic adjustment since they tend to focus their analyses on only some of these balances. For example, the MABP focuses only on the financial and external balances so that it has to make unrealistic a priori assumptions about the natural tendency of an economy towards full-employment output or about the homogeneity of the behaviour of the private sector.

The inclusion of all these balances ensures that each sector of the economy is accounted for in the analysis and that all the relevant variables are determined simultaneously within the model.

Normally, output and price formation are determined within the supply-demand balances; saving-investment decisions within the sectoral accumulation balances; the transfer of savings from sectors with excess to sectors with deficits of savings are modeled within the financial balances; and, finally, external balances assure overall consistency of domestic equilibria with external constraints.

1.5.3 The need to differentiate closures

Finally, existing theoretical models tend to be a-temporal in the sense that their underlying assumptions are constant over the period. Their visions of which mechanisms bring about ex-post equilibrium tend to be constant, regardless of the effects that changing external and internal environments could have in determining the adjustment.

As emerged from the discussion in the previous section, however, the mechanisms that brought about adjustment to the Bolivian economy changed substantially over the different periods considered. During the 1970s, for instance, the large availability of external resources allowed the country to run up large current account deficits, and adjustment came through a lower level of reserves. During the early 1980s, external finance was discontinued and the external sector became more of a constraint that imposed adjustment on the economy through other mechanisms such as output contraction and large income shifts. After the implementation of the NEP in 1985, the external sector constraint was eased by restoring external financial relations and by allowing illegal flows to enter the legal financial system.

1.6 Conclusions

The main objective of this research is to try to overcome the shortcomings of the leading theoretical approaches through the construction of an alternative explanatory model. For that purpose, a computatable general equilibrium (CGE) model is constructed and utilized in numerical simulations (Dervis et al. 1982).

The RF-CGE model is inspired by the structuralist tradition in formulating and applying CGE models in economies in the developing world (Taylor 1990). These models emphasize class relationships and income distribution changes; as Taylor points out, they rely more explicitly on the analytical heritage of Keynes, Kalecki and Kaldor.

The various economic agents interact through different markets mostly regulated by institutional factors, which in most cases are not purely price signals. In the RF-CGE model constructed in this research, emphasis is placed on the financial behaviours of the various institutions and socioeconomic groups (FitzGerald and Vos 1989).

A clear advantage in utilizing a CGE model is the fact that it is built around the accounting framework provided by a social accounting matrix (SAM) (Alarcón et al. 1991; Round and Pyatt 1985). The SAM provides the model with an integrated and consistent system of accounts for the analysis of income formation, distribution and spending of disaggregated production units and socioeconomic groups. Financial relations logically complement such a system of accounts, matching sectoral and institutional savings surpluses and deficits.

The SAM brings together data that can also be found in the more traditional types of National Accounts (including input-output data for the various branches of the economic activity), as well as disaggregated data concerning the interrelations between income distribution, saving-consumption, investment and financial transactions for the various social groups included in the model. In this respect, the SAM also provides a quite suitable framework for the construction of structuralist models.

Notes

1. This is a widely shared observation; see also Hinojosa and Espinoza (1983); Devlin and Mortimore (1983).

2. The peso was substituted by the boliviano as Bolivia's currency unit in September 1985 as part of the New Economic Policy (NEP).

3. In countries such as Colombia, Peru, Chile and Paraguay, these percentages never exceed 15 per cent over the same period.

4. Throughout this book, the term billion is used in the American sense; that is, one billion = 1,000,000,000.

5. According to the World Bank (1989), the major banks fix both deposits and interest rates, and competition is carried out largely through advertising in order to increase market share.

2 External Shocks and External Sector Trends

2.1 Introduction

This chapter discusses in detail the external shocks that affected Bolivia's economic performance over the last two and a half decades. During the 1970s, Bolivia enjoyed large capital inflows from international commercial banks and increased 'official' export revenues. The country had access to levels of foreign exchange that exceeded the economy's absorption capacity. Hence, capital flight became a feature of Bolivia's external adjustment. During the 1980s, illegal sources of revenue also became important. This access to foreign exchange resulted in the tendency for the real exchange rate to appreciate in the long run, reducing export competitiveness and encouraging imports.

The segmented nature of the foreign exchange market during the first half of the 1980s is identified as the main reason for the emergence of greatly differentiated official and parallel exchange rates. The market segmentation conditioned sectoral adjustment, depending on each sector's access to one or other source of foreign exchange. The public sector, which could only resort to the shrinking official sources of foreign exchange, had to adjust by reducing its import capacity, while the private sector, which had access to both markets, benefited from exchange rate differentials and generated large surpluses that went to finance asset accumulation abroad (capital flight).

Section 2.2 discusses the external shocks that have conditioned Bolivia's economic performance over the last two and a half decades.

The patterns followed by capital inflows, debt servicing and external terms of trade are analysed for the three periods under study: the 1970s, 1980–85 and 1986–95. Section 2.3 analyses how external shocks, brought about by the varying external conditions, have affected Bolivia's external sector trends. Bolivia's current account balances, foreign exchange reserves position and exchange rate policies have been conditioned by the substantial shifts observed in the pattern followed by foreign capital inflows and by the terms of trade. Finally, Section 2.4 offers some concluding remarks.

2.2 External Shocks

2.2.1 Capital Inflows

Capital inflows to Bolivia have fluctuated sharply over time, as shown in Tables 2.1, 2.2 (a), 2.2 (b) and 2.3.

(a) During the 1970s

Between 1970 and 1973, Bolivia's access to external credit adhered to the patterns of the 1960s: a high level of dependence on official sources of credit from the United States and from the Inter-American Development Bank, and, to a lesser extent, on credits from the German government and from the IMF.

Table 2.1 *Net resource transfers to Bolivia from the rest of the world (yearly average in millions of constant 1990 US$)*

	1971–74	1975–79	1980–85	1986–89	1990–95
Net Capital Inflows		418.1	160.5	196.4	216.3
Public Debt		405.9	160.0	202.7	211.1
– Public Enterprise	97.1	196.4	9.3	25.9	53.9
– Central Bank	15.9	9.6	8.8	76.7	63.9
Private Banks	13.2	12.2	0.5	-6.2	5.2
Interest (paid)	52.7	129.4	262.5	107.8	105.1
Net Transfer		288.7	–102.0	88.6	111.2

Sources: Author's estimates based on BCB (a; various issues) and the World Bank's *World Debt Tables* (various issues)

Table 2.2a *Bolivian external public debt structure, 1970–95, according to borrower institution (debt outstanding as of 31 December in millions of US$)*

	1970	1975	1980	1985	1990	1995
Non-financial public sector	497.7	837.7	2121.1	3030.6	3261.0	3725.5
a. General govt.	325.9	500.3	1259.6	2511.9	2818.5	3056.7
b. Public entrp.	171.8	337.4	861.5	518.7	442.5	668.8
Financial public sec.	19.5	47.7	154.3	263.8	517.9	798.1
Central bank	11.6	14.0	65.9	166.9	456.3	593.8
Others	7.9	33.7	88.4	96.9	61.6	204.3
Private sector	7.2	11.2	36.9	0.0	0.0	0.0
TOTAL	524.4	896.6	2312.3	3294.4	3778.9	4523.6

Sources: Author's estimates based on BCB (b; various issues) and the World Bank's World Debt Tables (various issues)

Beginning in 1974, Bolivia gained access to commercial sources of credit. Thanks to the higher export prices in international markets, the country rapidly increased its exports and accumulated foreign exchange, both of which were very important indicators of creditworthiness for the transnational banks. Besides, an oil, gas and commodity boom associated with the discovery of hydrocarbon fields, indicating the possibility of sizeable petroleum and gas deposits, made the country attractive to foreign financial investors. Average annual capital inflows grew to more than US$300 million at their peak in 1975–78.

According to the Bolivian Central Bank's balance of payments statistics and the World Bank's world debt tables, the country received around US$1.3 billion in net terms between 1971 and 1978 (80 per cent of which was received after 1975). Of this total, 43 per cent went to the central government, 39 per cent to public enterprises, 12 per cent to the Central Bank and 6 per cent to other financial institutions (commercial banks). During this period, interest payments were relatively low, so that the country benefited from a net resource transfer of close to US$1 billion.

Table 2.2b Bolivian external public debt structure, 1970–95, according to borrower institution (percentage of debt outstanding as of 31 December)

	1970	1975	1980	1985	1990	1995
Non-Financial Public Sector	94.9	93.4	91.7	92.0	86.3	82.4
a. General govt.	62.1	55.8	54.5	76.2	74.6	67.6
b. Public entrp.	32.8	37.6	37.3	15.7	11.7	14.8
Financial public sec.	3.7	5.3	6.7	8.0	13.7	17.6
Central Bank	2.2	1.6	2.8	5.1	12.1	13.1
Others	1.5	3.8	3.8	2.9	1.6	4.5
Private Sector	1.4	1.2	1.6	0.0	0.0	0.0
TOTAL	100.0	100.0	100.0	100.0	100.0	100.0

Sources: Author's estimates based on BCB (a; various issues) and the World Bank's *World Debt Tables* (various issues)

(b) First half of the 1980s

The accumulation of debt to finance publicly sponsored investment was interrupted after 1980 by a change in the foreign commercial banks' perception of Bolivia's export potential and debt-servicing capacity. Net capital inflows effectively received by the public sector went down from more than US$300 million in 1978 to US$100 million in 1982. Interest payments became a burden. Between 1979 and 1982 the country paid US$640 million in interest. As a result, during these four years, the country only received US$263 million as a net resource transfer. As the debt-service burden increased sharply in 1982 because of higher interest rates and lower exports, Bolivia ceased to service its foreign debt. In early 1983, however, Bolivia agreed with commercial banks on a schedule to eliminate the arrears and complied with this schedule until April 1984, when it again stopped servicing its foreign debt.

In 1979–82, 58 per cent of the resources received went to the government, 23 per cent to public enterprises, 17 per cent to the Central Bank and 2 per cent to other financial institutions.

Between 1983 and 1985 external financing had virtually disappeared and net capital inflows became negative; i.e. capital payments exceeded capital receipts on average by about US$180 million a year.

Table 2.3 *Bolivian external public debt structure, 1970–95, according to sources of credit (percentage of debt outstanding as of 31 December)*

	1970	1975	1980	1985	1990	1995
Suppliers	37.6	13.3	4.5	0.5	0.5	0.0
Private Foreign Banks	0.0	17.9	35.6	21.2	5.6	0.0
Multilateral Organizations	11.4	19.9	26.2	26.5	45.1	59.6
Bilaterals	37.6	42.4	31.0	50.7	47.8	40.4
State's Bonds	13.3	6.5	2.7	1.1	0.9	0.0
TOTAL	100.0	100.0	100.0	100.0	100.0	100.0

Sources: BCB (b; various issues)

Moreover, the country effectively paid around US$519 million in interest. As a result, Bolivia transferred US$555 million abroad during these three years.

(c) Following the 1985 stabilization programme

Within a few years of the introduction of the stabilization programme in 1985, net capital transfers to the country became again positive, since the country normalized its relations with international credit institutions. The external debt strategy under the NEP concentrated on the reduction of the country's private foreign debt in order to restore its international creditworthiness. Whereas in 1980 private creditors owned almost half the total of public disbursed debt, during 1986–89 that fraction fell to less than 1 per cent, whereas credit from official sources, the only sources prepared to lend to the Bolivian government, tripled. Since then Bolivia has been able to substantially reduce its private foreign debt. In 1987, the country repaid two-thirds (US$473 million) of the principal due to international banks (with overdue interest being waived), through cash buy-backs at 11 cents per dollar face value of debt, using money deposits in an IMF rescue account set up by friendly nations. In 1993, an additional reduction of US$170 million was obtained, practically eliminating Bolivia's debt to international private creditors. Although private commercial debt is no longer a problem for Bolivia, the public sector has not obtained any other credit from private banks since 1985.

The bilateral debt was also addressed through several negotiations at meetings of the Paris Club, which allowed Bolivia to take advantage of the different debt-reduction initiatives adopted by creditor countries, first under the Toronto terms in 1990 and the London terms in 1992. Following Bolivia's qualification for the Naples terms in 1995, it achieved a reduction of 67 per cent in its debt stock. With regards to bilateral debt, reductions additional to those agreed by Paris Club were obtained through direct negotiations with creditor countries.

During the period 1986–95 the country received, in net terms, US$2.055 billion (US$205 million a year on average). Interest payments were renegotiated so that Bolivia paid US$1.037 billion in interest (US$104 million a year on average). Thus the net resource transfers to the country reached US$1.018 billion over this period, most of which went to the government (45 per cent) and to the Central Bank (33 per cent). Public enterprises received only 21 per cent of net capital inflows. Most of the finance to the country after 1985 has come from multilateral financial institutions, especially from the Inter-American Development Bank (IDB). The outstanding Bolivian debt to the IDB has increased from US$470 million in 1985, to US$1,430 in 1995.

It is worth highlighting that after 1990, foreign direct investment inflows started picking up, reaching US$372 million in 1995. This is the result both of investment commitments due to the capitalization of public enterprises, and other foreign investment flowing to different sectors in the economy.

2.2.2 External terms of trade

Bolivia's economic performance has been heavily affected by wide fluctuations in its external terms of trade, illustrated in Figure 2.1.

(a) During the 1970s

During the 1970s, Bolivia benefited from very positive external market conditions for most of its export commodities. Between 1972 and 1980, the price of tin increased by more than 300 per cent, the price of natural gas more than ten fold as a result of much higher oil prices in international markets, and the prices of non-traditional exports went up by

Figure 2.1 *Bolivia's terms of trade, 1971–89 (1980 = 100)*

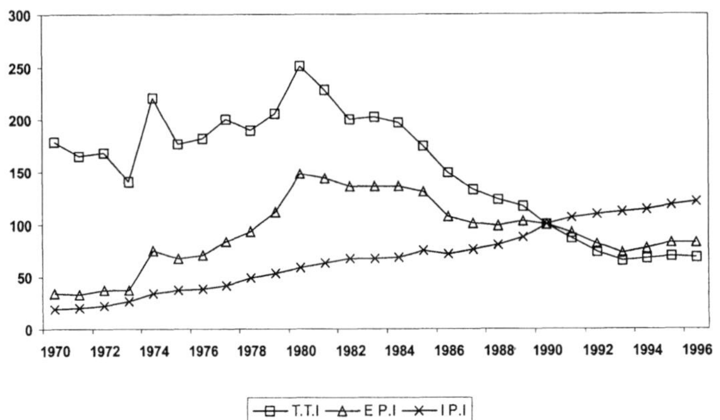

Sources: World Bank *World Debt Tables* (various issues); BCB (a; various issues).

more than 270 per cent. Since import prices increased by more than 180 per cent, the country's terms of trade improved by 50 per cent over the decade.

(b) During the first half of the 1980s

During the first half of the 1980s, the overall export price index deteriorated by 10 per cent. The price of tin fell by almost 30 per cent, but this was compensated by an increase in the price of natural gas of more than 50 per cent. Between 1980 and 1985, import prices increased by 22 per cent. The net outcome was a 30 per cent reduction in the country's terms of trade.

(c) Following the NEP

During the period 1985–1995, Bolivia's external terms of trade deteriorated sharply (by 60 per cent). The overall export price index went down by 40 per cent as a result of a 66 per cent reduction in the price of tin, due to the collapse of the international tin market in 1986. The export price of natural gas fell by 70 per cent, once Argentina (Bolivia's main importer of gas) discovered sizeable gas deposits in its own territory. However, the price index for non-traditional exports increased by 76 per cent. On the other hand, import prices went up by 57 per cent between 1985 and 1995.

2.3 External Sector Trends

It has been argued in this book that, besides the legal foreign trade and current transactions recorded in official balance of payments statistics, in the Bolivian economy a large trade of goods and services also takes place through unofficial channels. Table 2.14 presents the official figures for the current account transactions and capital movements recorded by the Central Bank. Before a more detailed analysis of the current account's behaviour is undertaken, it is important to point out that, during the two and a half decades under analysis, Bolivia's unofficial transactions with the rest of the world have tended to increase, while official transactions have tended to shrink.

2.3.1 Exchange Rate Policy

Bolivia followed a fixed and unified foreign exchange system from 1957 to 1982. During these years, the exchange rate remained remarkably stable, and only one devaluation was undertaken (in October 1972). After 1982, when external capital inflows fell sharply, the government was reluctant to devalue the Bolivian peso.

In March 1982, the fixed foreign exchange system collapsed, and a dual system was implemented, with an overvalued, highly rationed official rate system, and a totally divergent parallel rate. During the 1970–85 period, the official exchange rate (as measured by the parity exchange rate; see Figure 2.2) tended to appreciate, causing a loss of export competitiveness and encouraging imports. The tendency for the real exchange rate to appreciate was reinforced by the fixed exchange rate policy adopted during the 1970s, and the large lags between inflation and nominal devaluations during the first half of the 1980s.

In August 1985, as part of the stabilization programme, a system of public auctioning of foreign exchange (Bolsin) was introduced. Under this system, the exchange rate was devalued and permanently adjusted to inflation. The exchange rate tended to depreciate in real terms and thus to maintain the competitiveness of the tradable sector. As can be seen in figure 2.2, the real multilateral exchange rate depreciated by about 97 per cent between 1986 and 1996, mostly due to the stabilization policies followed by Bolivia's main trading parties, particularly Latin America.

2.3.2 Balance of Payments

The external shocks described above have affected the country's external-sector performance.

(a) During the 1970s

Between 1970 and 1972, Bolivia presented an equilibrated current account balance with surpluses averaging an amount equivalent to US$3.6 million (0.3 per cent of GDP) per year. Exports stood at US$228 million in 1970 (20 per cent of GDP) of which 90 per cent comprised mining exports. That year imports reached US$158 million (15 per cent of GDP), of which 80 per cent were imports of capital goods and intermediate inputs. Then there was a substantial increase in the level of exports, which rose to US$338 million (26 per cent of GDP) in 1973 and to US$650 million (31 per cent) in 1974. This was the result of the increase in hydrocarbon exports, which share in total exports increased from 6 per cent in 1970 to 30 per cent in 1974. As a consequence, in 1974 the current account balance registered a surplus equivalent to 7.5 per cent of GDP. Bolivia also gained access to external credit when international

Figure 2.2 *The official and parallel parity exchange rates (base year 1989)*

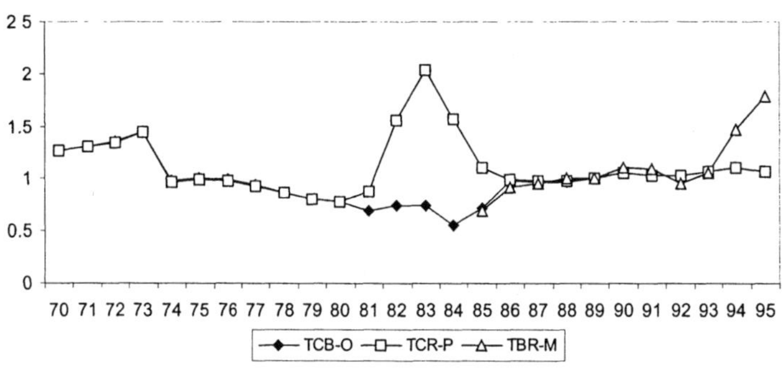

Sources: World Bank (1985b); UDAPE (1997a)

commercial banks re-evaluated the country's creditworthiness as a result of a more favourable perception of its export potential. Foreign finance increased from 1.7 per cent of GDP in 1973 to 3.5 per cent in 1974.

Between 1975 and 1979, however, large current account deficits became a feature of the Bolivian economy, averaging US$172.5 million (5 per cent of GDP) per year. The share of exports[1] (such as minerals, hydrocarbons and agro-industry) in total GDP fell from 31 per cent in 1974 to 22.1 per cent in 1975, and remained at that level until the end of the decade (on average at 21.9 per cent of GDP per year). Export prices, which had increased by 71 per cent in 1974, fell again in 1975 by 25 per cent. Between 1976 and 1980, export prices steadily increased (tin and natural gas prices more than doubled between 1976 and 1979), and the quantities exported fell by 21 per cent and 46 per cent for minerals and hydrocarbons, respectively.

The exchange rate policy adopted during the 1970s damaged the export sector competitiveness by inducing an exchange rate overvaluation (see Figure 6.3). The official nominal exchange rate was fixed between 1972 and 1979, while inflation, measured by the GDP implicit deflator, stood at around 20 per cent per year over the whole decade.

The current account deficit swelled due to increased levels of imports and interest payments. The share of imports in GDP went up from 17.3 per cent in 1974 to 23.8 per cent in 1975, and stood at 21 per cent for the rest of the decade. On the other hand, interest payments increased from 1.2 per cent of GDP to 3.6 per cent in the same period.

The current account deficits observed during the second half of the 1970s were financed by sizeable capital inflows, which averaged an equivalent of 6.8 per cent of GDP per year between 1975 and 1979. This amount not only covered the deficit, but also went to finance capital flight. Using the methodology presented in Appendix 2.1, it is estimated that more than US$1 billion left Bolivia to acquire external assets during the 1970s.

(b) During the first half of the 1980s

During the first half of the 1980s, the share of exports in total GDP fell even further (to 15 per cent of total GDP), even though international prices and export quantities for natural gas rose by 57 and 8 per cent, respectively. Between 1980 and 1984, the prices for minerals fell in international markets, (for example, the price of tin fell by 27 per cent), and the quantities of agro-industrial and mineral products exported declined by 70 and 26 per cent, respectively. Moreover, during the period of high inflation, the official exchange rate deteriorated significantly in real terms, resulting in an even greater overvaluation of the exchange rate and further decline in export competitiveness.

Interest payments on the external debt became an increasingly heavy burden; during the early 1980s they accounted for 5.2 per cent of GDP compared with only 1.5 per cent per year during the 1970s. Capital inflows fell to an amount equivalent to 3.2 per cent of GDP in 1981 and thereafter became negative (–1.5 per cent of GDP per year between 1982 and 1985).

During the first half of the 1980s, the maintenance of a fixed exchange rate came to be regarded as sign of successful economic policy, while devaluation came to signify failure. The government tried to keep the nominal exchange fixed after the Central Bank stopped sales of foreign exchange at the official rate in June 1981, while capital inflows were falling and the public sector deficit was still at its high 1970s level. In spite of accelerating inflation during 1980–85, the nominal exchange rate was readjusted only seven times (in each of the six economic packages plus one isolated adjustment in August 1984), and always insufficiently. When the Central Bank stopped the unrestricted sale of foreign exchange, the excess demand for foreign exchange was redirected towards the increasingly important parallel market. Maintaining the exchange rate at an artificially low level forced the government to ration foreign exchange through administrative schemes that hindered production. As the World Bank (1985b, p.14) pointed out,

> Allocations of foreign exchange have been erratic. No clear guidelines have been stated and applications for foreign exchange have had uncertain and irregular outcomes. Some applications for a particular type of good have been accepted quickly while others for the same type of goods have taken months, or have been inconsistent over time. In 1973, the Central Bank gave priority to servicing debt to commercial banks, while in 1984 it serviced multilateral and bilateral debt first. The probability that foreign exchange would be used in a productive way has thus become low.

The reduced access to foreign exchange had a devastating effect on the country's capacity to import (at least through official channels). Officially recorded imports as a share of GDP fell from 21 per cent in the late 1970s to only 10.6 per cent in the early 1980s. This was particularly damaging for the overall functioning of the economy since official imports comprise the bulk of the country's imports of capital goods and intermediate inputs. This situation imposed a very tight foreign exchange constraint on the economy.

As official exports fell, estimated unofficial exports (mainly of coca and unrefined cocaine) expanded from 4 per cent of GDP during the second half of the 1970s to 18 per cent in the first half of the 1980s. The increase in prices brought about an expansion in production of coca leaves. The shift from official to unofficial (illegal) sources of foreign exchange brought about several changes within the Bolivian economy.

First, it brought about a change in the composition of imports. During the second half of the 1970s, the share of official imports in GDP was 21 per cent, while estimated contraband imports accounted for 5.7 per cent. During the first half of the 1980s, the share of officially recorded imports in GDP fell to 10.6 per cent, resulting from repeated devaluations and a contraction in demand. The share of contraband in GDP, on the other hand, increased to almost 9 per cent. The fact that importers had to resort to buying foreign exchange on the parallel market caused the marginal cost of acquiring foreign exchange (and thus the price of imported goods) to be determined by the parallel rate. Variations in the parallel market rate during that period were closely correlated with the consumer price index; by August 1985, immediately prior to the introduction of the NEP, the parallel rate was 15 times the official rate.

Second, the shift from official to unofficial sources of foreign exchange brought about a substantial increase in the level of capital outflows, which increased as a share of GDP from 3.6 per cent during the second half of the 1970s to 8.8 per cent in 1980. Obviously, the foreign exchange for capital flight was no longer obtained from official sources, but from unofficial ones.

(c) After the 1985 NEP

The NEP introduced substantial changes in the functioning of the Bolivian external sector. The exchange rate was unified, foreign exchange controls and prohibitions against denominating domestic transactions in foreign currency were lifted, the system of quantitative restrictions was dismantled, and a low uniform tariff rate was imposed. An auction system was instituted to determine the exchange rate, with free access. This system allowed the Central Bank to buy and sell foreign exchange obtained from official and un-official sources. Residents were permitted to hold foreign exchange and enter into contracts for domestic transactions denominated in foreign currency. The immediate result was a 93 per cent depreciation of the exchange rate, followed by a substantial repatriation of capital ('errors and omissions' amounted to 3.1 per cent of GDP positive in 1985).

These policies achieved a much more realistic official exchange rate, which improved incentives for the production of tradable goods. However, the share of official exports as a proportion of total GDP fell even further to only 12 per cent. Although the official exchange rate depreciated significantly in real terms after the 1985 stabilization programme, the resulting gain in competitiveness by the export sector was offset by significant reductions in international prices for most Bolivian export commodities. International tin prices plummeted by 40 per cent after the collapse of the tin market in 1985. Also, the prices of natural gas paid by Argentina to Bolivia suffered continuous reductions between 1985 and 1989, although the international price of the commodity did not. In 1989 the price paid by Argentina was 43 per cent lower than in 1985. Moreover, export quantities of minerals declined by 16 per cent between 1986 and 1989.

Exports of timber, agricultural products and other manufacturing benefited from the exchange rate devaluation, tax incentives and better international prices. Non-traditional export quantities showed a threefold increase between 1985 and 1989, and the value exported of non-traditional products rose from 0.5 per cent of GDP in 1985 to 5.9 per cent in 1990. As a result, total export earnings went up from 11 per cent of GDP in 1985 to 18.9 in 1990. Total export revenues fell to 12 per cent of GDP in 1992 and 1993, due to new reductions in the price and volumes of natural gas sold to Argentina. However, non-traditional exports kept their positive trend, increasing to 7 per cent of GDP by 1995 and bringing total export value to about 16 per cent of GDP.

Table 2.4 Official balance of payments (percentage of GDP)

	1972	1973	1974	1975	1976	1977
Balance of Goods and NFS	1.1	1.4	8.7	−5.7	−1.3	−0.5
Trade Balance	5.7	8.7	13.6	−1.8	1.7	3.3
Exports (fob)	20.0	26.8	31.0	22.1	23.4	22.3
Minerals	14.5	17.9	18.4	13.1	14.4	15.2
Hydrocarbons	3.5	5.3	9.2	6.4	5.8	4.2
Agro-Industry	2.1	3.6	3.3	2.6	3.2	2.9
Imports (cif)	14.3	18.1	17.3	23.8	21.7	19.0
Consumer	3.5	3.6	3.6	4.4	3.8	3.8
Intermediate	5.0	6.2	6.4	8.3	6.8	5.8
Capital	5.8	8.3	7.3	11.2	11.1	9.4
Balance of NFS	−4.6	−7.3	−4.9	−3.9	−3.0	−3.8
Interests	−1.3	−1.3	−1.2	−1.1	−1.1	−1.9
Other Factors	−0.5	−0.6	−0.8	−0.4	−0.4	−0.4
Transfers	1.1	1.2	0.7	0.4	0.5	0.6
Balance on Current Account	0.4	0.8	7.5	−6.8	−2.2	−2.2
Direct Investment	−0.9	0.4	1.2	1.5	0.7	0.7
Net Official M<	8.8	1.7	3.5	4.5	8.2	10.5
Exceptional Financing	0.0	0.0	0.0	0.0	0.0	0.0
Other Long Term Capital	0.0	0.0	0.0	0.0	0.0	0.0
Net Short Term Capital	0.0	−0.2	−0.1	−0.1	0.0	1.2
Net Use of IMF Resources	0.1	1.0	−0.2	0.0	−0.9	0.0
Unpaid Gas Receipts from Argentina	0.0	0.0	0.0	0.0	0.0	0.0
Errors and Omissions	−3.1	−8.7	−6.7	−4.0	−6.9	−1.1
Changes in Reserves	0.3	−0.8	1.7	−0.2	5.0	−2.1

Source: Author's own estimates, based on INE (1997) and BCB (b; various issues)

Table 2.4 Official balance of payments (percentage of GDP), continued

	1978	1979	1980	1981	1982	1983
Balance of Goods and NFS	–4.8	–3.7	4.0	–2.2	3.2	2.0
Trade Balance	–1.1	–0.7	7.5	1.2	5.9	4.2
Exports (fob)	19.3	19.7	20.7	15.6	15.0	13.8
Minerals	13.7	13.6	12.9	8.8	7.0	5.9
Hydrocarbons	3.3	3.4	4.4	5.3	6.6	7.0
Agro-Industry	2.3	2.7	3.4	1.5	1.4	0.9
Imports (cif)	20.3	20.4	13.2	14.4	9.1	9.6
Consumer	4.2	4.3	3.4	3.7	1.6	1.1
Intermediate	5.7	6.6	5.0	5.4	4.1	4.8
Capital	10.4	9.6	4.8	5.3	3.3	3.7
Balance of NFS	–3.7	–3.0	–3.5	–3.4	–2.7	–2.2
Interests	–2.7	–3.6	–5.0	–5.3	–6.5	–5.1
Other Factors	–0.4	–0.9	–0.3	–0.5	–0.4	–1.0
Transfers	1.0	1.2	1.2	0.6	0.8	1.8
Balance on Current Account	–6.9	–7.0	–0.1	–7.4	–2.9	–2.3
Direct Investment	0.6	0.9	0.9	1.2	0.5	0.1
Net Official M<	6.7	4.1	5.6	3.3	–3.0	–6.0
Exceptional Financing	0.0	0.0	3.7	4.7	5.9	13.3
Other Long Term Capital	0.1	1.2	–0.6	–0.1	–0.5	–0.1
Net Short Term Capital	0.9	–0.8	–3.5	–1.2	0.0	–0.5
Net use of IMF resources	0.4	0.0	0.2	0.1	0.0	0.0
Unpaid Gas Receipts from Argentina	0.0	0.0	0.0	0.0	0.0	0.0
Errors and Omissions	–4.4	–9.1	–4.7	–1.8	–8.1	–3.1
Changes in Reserves	1.4	1.0	–2.8	–3.4	–1.9	–2.6

Source: Author's own estimates, based on INE (1997) and BCB (b; various issues)

Table 2.4 Official balance of payments (percentage of GDP), continued

	1984	1985	1986	1987	1988	1989
Balance of Goods and NFS	1.7	–1.5	–2.3	–5.4	–3.8	–3.5
Trade Balance	3.5	0.1	–0.2	–3.8	0.2	4.3
Exports (fob)	9.2	11.6	13.6	11.5	13.0	17.3
Minerals	4.3	4.6	4.2	4.2	6.0	8.5
Hydrocarbons	4.6	6.5	7.1	5.2	4.8	4.5
Agro-Industry	0.3	0.6	2.4	2.1	2.3	4.3
Imports (cif)	5.7	11.5	13.9	15.3	12.8	13.0
Consumer	1.1	2.3	2.8	3.8	2.8	2.9
Intermediate	2.4	4.8	5.0	6.2	5.0	5.5
Capital	2.2	4.4	6.0	5.3	5.0	4.7
Balance of NFS	–1.8	–1.6	–2.0	–1.6	–4.0	–7.8
Interests	–3.9	–5.5	–5.4	–5.0	–5.3	–4.7
Other Factors	–0.4	–0.9	–0.9	–0.3	–0.4	–0.7
Transfers	1.0	1.4	2.1	2.4	4.0	3.3
Balance on Current Account	–1.6	–6.5	–6.5	–8.2	–5.5	–5.6
Direct Investment	0.1	0.2	0.3	0.7	0.7	0.7
Net Official M<	–2.0	–4.1	–2.1	–0.8	3.2	3.1
Exceptional Financing	3.1	6.2	6.6	7.8	3.1	1.8
Other Long Term Capital	–0.1	–0.2	–0.5	–0.1	–0.4	–2.8
Net Short Term Capital	0.2	–0.5	–0.1	–0.2	–2.0	–1.2
Net Use of IMF Resources	0.0	0.1	0.0	–0.2	0.0	0.0
Unpaid Gas Receipts from Argentina	–2.4	–1.7	–0.1	–1.9	–0.2	–0.1
Errors and Omissions	1.4	2.0	4.7	1.3	1.0	0.9
Changes in Reserves	–1.0	4.8	2.4	–1.6	–0.2	–3.0

Source: Author's own estimates, based on INE (1997) and BCB (b; various issues)

Table 2.4 *Official balance of payments (percentage of GDP), continued*

	1990	1991	1992	1993	1994	1995
Balance of Goods and NFS	–2.3	–3.7	–8.2	–8.8	–4.9	–5.1
Trade Balance	4.7	–2.1	–6.9	–7.1	–2.4	–4.3
Exports (fob)	18.9	15.9	12.6	13.1	17.5	17.4
Minerals	8.4	6.7	6.5	6.3	6.9	7.8
Hydrocarbons	4.7	4.5	2.4	1.8	1.8	2.3
Agro-Industry	5.9	4.7	3.7	5.0	8.8	7.2
Imports (cif)	14.2	18.1	19.5	20.2	19.8	21.7
Consumer	3.1	3.9	3.6	3.9	4.7	4.3
Intermediate	5.5	7.0	7.5	7.7	7.9	8.6
Capital	5.6	7.2	8.3	8.6	7.2	8.8
Balance of NFS	–7.1	–1.6	–1.3	–1.7	–2.6	–0.8
Interests	–4.2	–3.4	–2.9	–3.1	–2.8	–2.7
Other Factors	–0.8	–0.6	–0.5	–0.5	–0.4	–0.4
Transfers	3.6	3.6	4.4	4.2	4.8	3.6
Balance on Current Account	–3.8	–4.1	–7.3	–8.2	–3.3	–4.6
Direct Investment	0.7	1.8	2.1	2.1	2.1	5.7
Net Official M<	2.1	1.5	2.7	1.6	2.2	2.0
Exceptional Financing	3.0	3.6	3.1	2.6	1.9	2.9
Other Long Term Capital	0.0	–0.2	1.7	0.5	–0.5	–0.7
Net Short Term Capital	–0.1	0.3	0.7	2.4	1.6	1.2
Net Use of IMF Resources	0.0	0.0	0.0	0.0	0.0	0.0
Unpaid Gas Receipts from Argentina	–0.4	–0.1	0.1	2.1	0.4	0.0
Errors and Omissions	0.7	–1.0	–2.6	–0.6	–2.0	–4.2
Changes in Reserves	2.3	1.7	0.5	2.4	2.3	2.3

Source: Author's own estimates, based on INE (1997) and BCB (b; various issues)

The NEP also undertook a radical revision of trade policy to eliminate quantitative restrictions and establish a uniform tariff rate. All import prohibitions and trade licensing requirements were abolished, with the exception of controls on sugar and wheat. As a result of the liberalization of the trade regime, there was a shift from unofficial to official import channels. Official imports recovered to 20 per cent of GDP in 1995. Intermediate imports comprised 40 per cent of total imports, capital goods 40 per cent, while consumer goods dropped to 20 per cent.

By 1989, interest payments abroad were reduced to 4.9 per cent of GDP and by 1995 to 2.5 per cent, as part of the external debt was renegotiated. This further contributed to the amelioration of the country's foreign exchange constraint.

2.4 Conclusions

In summary, the external sector's balance of the Bolivian economy went through substantial changes during the whole period under analysis. During the 1970s, an export boom and increased capital inflows brought high levels of (public) investment and economic growth. However, the levels of foreign exchange available were beyond the country's capacity to use them productively. Part of these resources was used to finance increased import levels (consumption, inputs and capital goods) and to increase reserves in the financial system. Excess foreign exchange was taken out of the country (capital flight). Interest payments were not significant.

During the first half of the 1980s, there was a clear segmentation in the country's external balances, which created a very large gap between the official and parallel exchange rates. While foreign exchange supply to the official exchange market fell dramatically, due to lower export revenues and capital inflows, demand increased sharply, mostly due to external debt servicing. This situation reduced the country's capacity to import capital goods and intermediate inputs, with a consequent negative effect on investment and production. At the same time, foreign exchange supply to the parallel exchange market increased as coca proceeds rose rapidly, and importers (mostly of consumer goods) increasingly turned to this market to obtain foreign exchange. Excess foreign exchange in the parallel market went to finance capital flight.

Under the NEP, the two foreign exchange markets were unified. This measure helped the Central Bank to obtain 'unofficially' generated foreign exchange, and the country's access to external credit was normalized. Besides, higher interest rates, resulting from the stabilization programme, encouraged short-term capital inflows. This situation helped the productive sector ameliorate the foreign exchange constraint it faced during the hyper-inflation years, and hence the Central Bank was able to accumulate foreign reserves.

Finally, from 1995 onwards, foreign direct investment became more significant as a source of foreign savings, as a result of the capitalization of public enterprises.

Appendix 2.1
Estimated Capital Flight

Capital flight comprises all those financial assets that are not accounted for by official statistics. That is, all foreign exchange reserves demanded by domestic private agents, as well as unrecorded capital outflows.

There are no reliable figures for the amounts of resources channelled through informal financial markets, but some methodologies have been developed to give estimates (FitzGerald and Sarmad 1990; see Vos 1990).[2] According to Vos (1990), the World Bank provides one of the widest alternative measures of private capital outflows, in which a residual measure of private capital outflows in effect equals the sum of net (short-term) foreign assets acquired by the banking sector and the private non-banking sector, plus errors and omissions.

Other approaches exclude foreign assets held by the banking sector (Morgan Guarantee 1986; Vos 1990). According to this 'exclusive' definition, private capital outflows would be equal to:

$$\Delta A = \Delta F + \Delta IF - \Delta R - CAD - \Delta A_b = \Delta A_p + EO$$

where:

ΔA = Private capital outflows
ΔF = Net long-term capital inflows
ΔIF = Net direct foreign investment (inflow)
ΔR = Net changes in official reserves
CAD_o = Official current account deficit

$\Delta A_b =$ Net increase in the (short-term) external assets of deposit money banks

$\Delta A_p =$ Net increase in the (short-term) external assets of the private non-banking sector

$EO =$ Errors and omissions

In this thesis the 'exclusive' definition of capital outflows is partly adopted, but in the Bolivian case, it is also necessary to consider the external flows from the illegal cocaine trade and contraband imports. Therefore, the figures obtained by means of the 'exclusive' Morgan Guarantee definition of private capital movements have to be corrected by the estimated unofficial current account balance (CABuo), namely the balance between unrecorded exports (mostly unrefined cocaine) and contraband imports.

The final definition of private capital outflows would therefore be:

$$\Delta A_t = \Delta A + CAB_{uo}$$

The figures obtained appear in Table 2.A.1.

The World Bank (1991) estimates that the accumulated private capital outflows (excluding narcotics proceeds and unrecorded imports) by 1990 were over US$1 billion. This estimate is consistent with figures obtained using the 'exclusive' Morgan Guarantee definition (see Table 2.A.1).

Table 2.A.1 Measures of private foreign asset accumulation, 1970–89 (US$ million)

Year	Errors and Omissions	Unofficial Trade Balance	Capital Flight
1970	–32	–23	9
1971	–127	–68	59
1972	–208	–116	92
1973	–258	–142	117
1974	–402	–147	256
1975	–430	–160	269
1976	–551	–186	366
1977	–845	–262	583
1978	–1 022	–366	657
1979	–1 099	–345	754
1980	–1 503	–270	1 233
1981	–1 700	37	1 737
1982	–1 617	203	1 820
1983	–1 501	491	1 991
1984	–1 501	837	2 338
1985	–1 218	1 416	2 634
1986	–999	1 936	2 935
1987	–934	2 340	3 275
1988	–890	2 196	3 086
1989	–850	2 330	3 180
1990	–814	2 388	3 202
1991	–870	2 292	3 162
1992	–1 017	2 247	3 264
1993	–1 052	2 219	3 271
1994	–1 173	2 177	3 350
1995	–1 445	2 145	3 590

Sources: BCB (b; various issues); INE (1997)

Notes

1. The official figures on Bolivia's external economic relations are kept by the Central Bank of Bolivia. The National Accounts, however, complement the Central Bank's figures by providing estimates on external transactions such as contraband imports and coca exports which, due to their illegal nature, are not conducted through official channels.

2. See Vos (1990) for a detailed discussion on the different methodologies.

3 Sectoral Accumulation Balances in the Bolivian Economy

3.1 Introduction

The discussion in chapter 2 demonstrated that Bolivia faced strong external shocks over the last two and a half decades. Large fluctuation in the quantities of foreign capital inflows to the country has affected its overall macroeconomic performance. During the 1970s, the large supply of financial resources available in international financial markets allowed the Bolivian government to acquire large amounts of foreign debt. During that period growth and investment rose rapidly. During the 1980s, when the debt crises developed, Bolivia transferred a large quantity of resources abroad through debt service payments. During that period, growth plummeted and inflation increased to world record levels. After 1985, when the stabilization programme was introduced, positive capital inflows restarted again, stability was attained and positive growth rates were recovered. During this process, Bolivia also faced extremely sharp changes in its terms of trade. During the 1970s and first half of the 1980s there was a positive trend in prices for most of the country's export products. However, from 1985 onwards prices of minerals and gas deteriorated sharply. The country literally had to develop its export base from scratch. The results, of course, were a complete restructuring of the economy's productive base, large changes in the employment structure, and, therefore, significant shifts in income distribution among sectors.

The ways in which the different socioeconomic sectors (households, private companies, the government, public enterprises and the financial sector) responded to the external shocks followed different patterns. The direction of adjustment for each of these sectors has been determined by their particular institutional settings, namely the structure of the markets they operate in, broad and specific objectives that guide their economic actions, access to credit or other sources to finance investment, and so on.

This chapter discusses the individual adjustment patterns followed by different groups in response to external shocks and policy over the last two and a half decades. Six socioeconomic groups are identified: government, state enterprises, companies and three household categories (upper-urban, lower-urban and rural). Every economic agent's accumulation balance adjusted to shocks following its own specific rules through which ex-post equilibrium was achieved.

This chapter also argues that these adjustment mechanisms have not been stable, but have tended to change over time in response to external as well as internal shocks and policy interventions. The aim of this chapter is to discuss, in depth, which of these mechanisms were paramount in bringing adjustment to each of the Bolivian agents' accumulation balances over the last two and a half decades. The stylized facts to be found throughout this discussion will eventually help us to develop behavioural models for each of the economic agents. Econometric tests will be carried out in order to verify that the data available support the accumulation balance models developed throughout the chapter.

Section 3.2 discusses, at a general level, adjustments for the public and private sectors. This section tries to highlight that public and private sector adjustments were closely related during the 1970s; in fact, the large public external debt accumulated during that decade had, as a counterpart, an almost equivalent accumulation of private external assets. The relation between private and public sector adjustments during the 1980s adopted a different pattern, as public sector access to external funds was reduced and the private sector began to receive large surpluses from the coca trade. This section also discusses how public and private sector interactions have developed after the 1985 stabilization and the subsequent structural adjustment programmes were put into practice. The changes that the structural reforms implemented since 1993 are expected to have on private-public interactions are also pointed out in this section.

Sections 3.3 and 3.4 deal with the more specific aspects of the public sector's accumulation balance behaviour. These sections discuss, respectively, accumulation balance behaviours of the government and public enterprises in response to the external shocks of the 1970s, 1980s and first half of the 1990s. Based on these discussions, these sections identify the stylized facts that are most characteristic of the behavioural adjustment rules for both sectors' accumulation balances.

Section 3.5 discusses the sectoral behaviour of the corporate sector. The most significant adjustment mechanisms that brought equilibrium to company accumulation balances over the last two and a half decades are identified here; these stylized facts are later used in the construction of a behavioural model for the Bolivian corporate sector.

Section 3.6 concentrates on household accumulation balance adjustments; the microeconomic behaviours of upper-urban, lower-urban and rural households during the 1970s, 1980s and 1990s are discussed in detail, and behavioural models are developed for each household category.

Finally, section 3.7 presents some concluding remarks.

3.2 Accumulation Balance Adjustments for the Public and Private Sectors

3.2.1 The public sector

One of the most distinctive characteristics of the Latin American development pattern after the Great Depression and the Second World War, has been the increasing involvement of the state in economic activity. According to Veliz (1980, pp.238; 258–9), the strategic position of the state in controlling export activities in Latin America allowed successive governments to control foreign exchange earnings and to play a central role in the process of industrialization through the allocation of these resources. Thus the state was able to consolidate its position in at least three key aspects of economic policy: it became the main financial entity able to give credit to private industrial enterprises; it assumed the role of referee in the process of income redistribution through the implementation of social policies; and it assigned to the public sector a dynamic role, channelling the required financial resources for the development of an adequate industrial infrastructure, and for the creation of the productive sectors that would form the basis of the new industrial economy. This centralist tradition, which has characterized Latin American development strategies, has made the Latin American experience distinct from those of most of the more advanced capitalist countries.

The development strategy applied in Bolivia after the 1952 revolution gave the state a central role. This strategy was followed by successive governments until 1985 regardless of their political orientation. As a result, the public sector played an increasingly important role in the Bolivian economy, not only in terms of government policy, but also through its direct participation in production, employment and investment. The process of capital accumulation became heavily influenced by the state, which has been responsible for over two-thirds of all such accumulation since 1952 (World Bank 1985b, p.4).

The continuous and growing involvement of the state in economic activity has demanded an equal increase in the amount of finance. Over the periods considered here, the government resorted to various sources in order to finance its activities.

After the 1952 revolution, government saw nationalization as a way of controlling foreign exchange in order to finance investment in other sectors of the economy. Governments continuously extracted resources from the mining sector through exchange rate overvaluation, increased export taxes, and reduced funds for investment in mining. This process eventually resulted in a chronic undercapitalization of the state mining company COMIBOL.

During the 1950s and 1960s most major public investment projects were sponsored by official multilateral and bilateral agencies. For example, the government plan to develop the lowlands was financed almost entirely by bilateral agencies.

(a) During the 1970s

In the 1970s, after the military government headed by Colonel Banzer took power, the confluence of three dynamic elements hinted at the possibility of a much faster economic growth and development of the Bolivian economy in which the public sector would play a key role: (i) a clear economic strategy imposed through a hard stabilization programme, (ii) an export boom in which the state was the main beneficiary, and (iii) a large inflow of external credit mostly directed to the public sector (more than 90 per cent of Bolivian external debt accumulated between 1973 and 1979 was acquired by the public sector). In that context, during the 1970s the role of the state increased and oriented toward providing support to the private sector in three forms: to provide basic economic and social infrastructures; to mobilize financial resources; and to undertake direct productive investment aimed at increasing the limited fiscal base of the state (Irving 1979).

In this context, the 1970s saw the creation of relatively large, complex and inefficient state-owned industrial plants. Between 1970 and 1975, the public sector accounted for 75 per cent of total investment compared with 52 per cent in the period from 1964 to 1969. Much of this increase corresponded to the growth in decentralized agencies and state enterprises. In 1977, all government units, including decentralized agencies and mixed enterprises, provided for 33 per cent of GDP, 13 per cent of employment, 59 per cent of exports, 70 per cent of investment, and 23 per cent of national savings. Table 3.1 shows that, because of the large increase in capital inflows (equivalent to 8.9 per cent of GDP on average during the period 1976–1980), investment by the public sector increased to 12.2 per cent of GDP.

The relatively easy access to foreign exchange during the 1970s exacerbated the weaknesses of Bolivia's development pattern; besides increasing the role of the state in the economy, it accelerated the accumulation of external assets by the private sector (capital flight). The easy availability of foreign exchange during the 1970s helped the government to transfer a large part of these resources to the private sector in order to promote its participation in economic activity. Ramos (1980)

Table 3.1 Public Sector Balance (percentage of GDP)

	1972–75	1976–80	1981–85	1986–90	1991–95
Gross Savings	3.8	3.0	–8.1	1.1	2.9
Investment	5.0	12.2	4.5	6.9	9.0
Other Capital (Net)	–0.3	0.2	–0.7	1.0	2.3
Deficit/Surplus	0.9	–8.9	–13.2	–4.7	-3.9
Total Financing	–0.9	8.9	13.2	4.7	3.9
External Finance	0.0	6.3	1.8	3.3	3.9
Domestic Finance	–0.9	2.6	11.4	1.3	0.0

Sources: INE (1997); BCB (c; various issues); UDAPE (1997a)

maintains that government transferred to the private sector not only the resources obtained through public foreign borrowing, but also part of the surpluses generated by public enterprises. He further argues that public enterprises were obliged to pay heavy taxes to the Treasury and to sell foreign exchange to the Central Bank at an extremely undervalued official exchange rate. These resources were later transferred to the private sector in the form of credits and overvalued contracts for the execution of public works. In the same vein, other authors (Ramos 1980, p.102; Devlin and Mortimore 1983 p.116; Rivas 1989, p.73; Ugarteche 1986), concur that the development strategy implemented during the 1970s identified the state with privileged capitalist groups in the private sector and to a large extent subordinated the state to them.

In spite of the unprecedented degree of political stability during the 1970s, private entrepreneurs did not find investing in Bolivia an attractive proposition. Although the government issued policy statements encouraging foreign and domestic private sector entrepreneurs to invest in Bolivia, new private investment flows failed to materialize. The capital inflows were partially offset by capital outflows: capital flight (and unrecorded imports) amounted to over 60 per cent of the value of the debt accumulated during the years 1971–81 (World Bank 1985b, p.6). The government's foreign borrowing for public investment therefore effectively financed the accumulation of privately owned assets abroad.

The accumulation of debt to finance publicly sponsored investment was interrupted in 1978–79 by a change in the foreign commercial banks' perception of Bolivia's export potential and debt-servicing capacity. This led the banks to reduce their exposure, leaving Bolivia without the substantial foreign inflows needed to help service its large public external debts – debts which had in turn financed a capital stock that could not contribute to repaying them.

(b) Between 1980 and 1985

By the end of 1980, Bolivian access to the private international capital markets had dried up. An emergency rescheduling with the commercial banks was completed in 1981, but this soon fell apart. The World Bank and the IMF also ceased lending. However, although the accumulation of public debt was limited by the slow-down of new commitments, this debt continued to grow through the build-up of arrears and interest payments and their *de facto* capitalization, and through continued use of short-term credit facilities.

Under this extreme shortage of foreign finance, the authorities pursued a fiscal policy that was even more lax than in previous years, in order to avoid further output contractions. As the debt-service burden increased sharply in 1982 because of higher interest rates and lower export revenues, Bolivia ceased to service its foreign debt. At the same time, the Siles government was called upon to satisfy pent-up social and economic demand. The demands on the government were heightened by the fact that it represented a coalition of forces on the political left that pressed for increases in social spending, public sector employment, and public sector pay, but that lacked the political base to raise tax revenues to fund such spending. External finance had virtually disappeared and the rising deficit was financed entirely by Central Bank credit, which resulted in an acceleration of inflation and eventually hyperinflation.

The Siles government actually proposed several stabilization programmes during 1982–85, but in each case they were overturned by public protest, by key constituencies of the government, or by political opposition in the Congress.

Sachs (1987, p. 280) identifies three fundamental aspects of the rise of hyperinflation. First, the cutoff in international lending and the increase in international interest rates were the main initiating factors in the outbreak of hyperinflation in the early 1980s, since government met the drop in net international financing and higher debt-servicing costs through an increase in the inflation tax. In the first half of the 1980s, the Siles administration ceased virtually all debt-service payments to private creditors.

The second important characteristic of the inflation dynamic, as identified by Sachs, is that the seigniorage (i.e. the inflation tax) jumped as the net international resources transfer turned negative, with seigniorage fluctuating around a new high plateau during the period of the Siles government.

The takeoff in inflation after 1981 followed closely the jump in seigniorage, as should be expected from almost any monetary theory of hyperinflation. However, during 1982–85 the inflation rate continued to accelerate even though seigniorage collection did not rise steadily after its one-time jump. According to Sachs, this pattern is familiar from Cagan's original model of hyperinflation. Assuming that expectations of inflation adjust slowly to actual inflation, and that the demand for real money balances is a function of expected inflation, a permanent increase in the seigniorage needs of the government (as occurred after 1981) will produce an inflation rate that rises over time while the stock of real money balances declines. If the new seigniorage level is sufficiently high, then inflation will rise without bounds in the Cagan model.

The third important aspect of the inflation dynamics, according to Sachs, was that the increasing inflation caused the tax system to collapse, with total government revenues falling (via the Olivera-Tanzi effect) from around 10.4 per cent of GDP in 1981 to about 1.3 per cent in the first half of the 1985. Therefore, the constancy of the seigniorage tax did not reflect a constant underlying path of real revenues and real expenditures, but rather a path of falling real tax revenues matched by a lagged but steady drop in real spending. The most important cuts in spending were in public investment and then in international debt-servicing (as the country went into virtually complete default to private creditors by the end of 1984).

(c) The 1985 stabilization programme

The main aims of the 1985 stabilization programme introduced by the newly elected centre-right government of President Victor Paz Estenssoro were to reduce inflation, to restore the external balance, and to lay the foundation for sustained growth (IMF 1987b). In order to achieve the programme objectives, the key policy actions centred on controlling the public sector deficit (World Bank 1989, p.17):

- A devaluation and subsequent managed float of the exchange rate. This measure helped to reduce the fiscal deficit by increasing public enterprise export revenues.
- An immediate reduction in the fiscal deficit through a sharp increase in public sector prices (especially the price of domestic oil), combined with a public sector wage freeze;
- Spending by the public enterprises was limited to revenue collection, Central Bank credit was strictly controlled and public enterprises were required to deposit their revenues in custody accounts with the Central Bank – with the use of these funds dependent on the approval of the Ministry of Finance.
- A comprehensive tax reform was introduced in order to make the entire tax system more buoyant while simplifying the tax collection process.

The policy package had the desired effect of closing the budget deficit, although the falling world prices of tin and natural gas significantly reduced export revenues and public sector incomes.

The measures included in the stabilization programme curtailed the financing requirements of the non-financial public sector, and their overall deficit fell from 20 per cent of GDP in 1984, to 8 per cent in 1985, and to 5.5 per cent in 1989. On average, between 1985 and 1989 the whole public sector deficit was 4.7 per cent of GDP. During the first half of the 1990s, the overall fiscal deficit fell further (by on average 3.9 per cent of GDP). A general improvement in the tax collection administrative system and the successive successful renegotiations of the bilateral public debt within the Paris Club framework resulted in higher fiscal revenues and lower debt-service expenditures. However, the lower gas export price set under the agreement renegotiated with Argentina in 1992 translated into lower fiscal incomes.

As the deficit declined, the government relied increasingly on external financing and was able to significantly reduce its recourse to the domestic financial system, thereby reducing the 'crowding-out' effects on private activity. Between 1991 and 1993, the public sector resorted to domestic finance (Central Bank credit). Open market operation policies were introduced to offset the monetary effects of the fiscal deficit finance (issuing of Central Bank Certificates of Deposits (CDs)). This policy generated internal pressures on interest rates, which maintained their high – albeit slowly reducing – levels.

However, from 1994 onwards fiscal deficits further declined to around 2 per cent of GDP below the levels of foreign finance available. Consequently, domestic credit to the non-financial public sector contracted. According to the IMF (IMF 1996), the Bolivian authorities are aiming at limiting the fiscal deficit to a level that can be fully financed from concessional external resources. During the 1990s, the Bolivian government and the IMF signed three ESAF arrangements, establishing specific targets for the fiscal deficit and domestic credit expansion. During this period, fiscal policy was largely aimed at complying with the financial programmes agreed upon with the IMF.

(c) The structural reforms

Starting in 1993, the government of Gonzalo Sanchez de Lozada launched the capitalization and popular participation programmes.

These two reforms, in conjunction with a major education reform, comprise the Sanchez de Lozada government's Plan de Todos (plan for all) (Ministry of Finance, 1997; Graham, 1997).

The capitalization programme differs from traditional approaches to privatization of state-owned enterprises, in that it invests the proceeds of sales of state-owned enterprises in a new private social security scheme, and distributes the dividends from those investments in the form of 'solidarity bonds' to all Bolivians 65 and older. The capitalization thus combines two objectives: privatization and social security reform.

Under capitalization, the government allows a strategic investor – selected through a competitive bidding process – to purchase 50 per cent of the shares in the privatized company. Instead of paying the government for the enterprises, the strategic investor agrees to invest the agreed amount in the enterprise within a fixed period of time. The other 50 per cent of the shares are turned over to the Bolivian population, in the form of shares in a new private pension scheme. The dividends from the shares, which are invested by two pension funds, are distributed annually to all Bolivians over the age of 65, in payments of approximately US$250. All Bolivians, regardless of whether they contribute to the new pension fund scheme, receive the dividend payments, which are called Bonosol or solidarity bonds. All workers who are currently contributing to the public pension scheme receive compensation, paid by the National Treasury, for their past contributions, and their retirement accounts are transferred to a new private pension system, which is managed by the new pension fund and regulated by the state. For workers who retired under the old system, the law requires that all their benefits and the payment of pensions be met by the National Treasury.

The popular participation reform (followed by the administrative decentralization) is a major re-allocation of fiscal revenues from the central government to the departmental and municipal levels, in conjunction with the devolution of responsibility for the management and delivery of social services to the municipalities. Popular participation increases the level of general tax revenues going from central to local government from 10 to 20 per cent. The law stipulates that 85 per cent of co-participation resources must go to investment rather than to operating expenditures. In addition, the expenditures are now allocated on a per capita basis. The law also gives municipal governments increased facilities for generating local revenues. The structural reforms substantially redefine the functioning of the public sector in several ways. First, the capitalization and privatization of public enterprises transfer to the private sector the responsibility for all investment previously in the hands of state owned firms; thus, the remaining public investment can focus on the social and infrastructure sectors. Second, some of the structural reforms entail larger fiscal costs in the short term (as in the case of the pension reform); therefore higher fiscal deficits are expected during the transition period. Third, as will be explained in more detail in Chapter 4, the reforms introduced to the financial system enhance the Central Bank's autonomy, thus greatly diminishing the public sector's capacity to resort to Central Bank credit in order to finance its deficits

In summary, the public sector's accumulation balance behaviour has changed constantly over the periods under analysis.

During the 1970s, the easy availability of foreign exchange both encouraged and financed greater public sector involvement in economic activity; foreign capital inflows to the state also encouraged large transfers of resources to the private sector.

During the first half of the 1980s, the increasing debt burden and the world economic recession triggered a large fiscal imbalance that was entirely financed through Central Bank credit. The macroeconomic impact of this policy was reflected in a process of severe hyperinflation.

By 1995, the public sector deficit was greatly reduced, although not eliminated. The remaining deficit was financed by borrowing from both external and domestic sources. At a macroeconomic level, the government's domestic borrowing resulted in higher interest rates, which tended to crowd out private investment. However, from 1994 onwards external finance stood above the fiscal deficit levels, resulting in the contraction of domestic credit to the NFPS.

Finally, the structural reforms begun in 1993 redefine government accumulation behaviour in four fundamental ways: a) they transfer to the private sector the investment and financial operations of the public enterprises; b) they decentralize government expenditures to the departmental and municipal levels; c) they increase fiscal costs during the transition period of the structural reforms; and d) limit access of government to Central Bank credit.

3.2.2 The private sector

The adjustment of the accumulation balance for the private sector also tended to change over time. During the 1970s this adjustment was closely linked to public sector behaviour, but in the 1980s it followed a pattern that became increasingly independent of public sector performance.

According to National Accounts and other estimates,[1] between 1972 and 1975, the private non-financial sector as a whole (all households and companies) displayed a saving-investment surplus averaging 1.9 per cent of GDP: savings stood on average at 11.8 per cent and investment at 9.9 per cent of GDP during that period (see Table 3.2).

Because private external borrowing in Bolivia was acquired largely by private banks rather than by households or non-financial companies, the only other source of funds available to the private non-financial sector was bank credit, which, during 1972 and 1975, increased on average by 3.5 per cent of GDP a year. This was matched by an equivalent expansion in the demand for domestic assets (currency, demand deposits and quasi-money). Given that there were no other sources and uses of funds available to the non-financial private sector, companies and

Table 3.2 Non-financial private sector accumulation balance (percentage of GDP)

	1972–75	1976–79	1980–85	1986–89	1990–96
Gross Savings	11.8	9.7	13.7	5.2	3.3
Investment	9.9	7.3	3.9	4.9	5.8
Saving Surplus	1.9	2.4	9.8	0.3	–2.5
Net Domestic Asset Accumulation	0.1	0.0	–1.7	0.3	–0.8
– Domestic Asset Accumulation	3.4	3.8	10.7	5.0	8.0
– Domestic Liability Accumulation	3.5	3.8	9.0	5.6	8.8
Net Foreign Asset Accumulation	1.8	2.4	11.5	0.9	–1.7

Sources: INE (1989b); R. Morales (1985); UDAPE (1997a)

households had to have invested (on average) an amount of resources equivalent to 1.8 per cent of GDP per year in external assets (capital flight).

During the second half of the 1970s, savings and investment by the private sector fell when the economy started showing lower prospects for sustainable growth. Capital outflows were on average equal to 2.4 per cent of GDP per year.

When the country went through the severe external financial constraints during the first half of the 1980s, the private sector still benefited from high profits, preferential access to non-indexed domestic credit and access to foreign currency at the official undervalued exchange rate. According to National Accounts figures, between 1980 and 1985, the non-financial private sector presented an average saving-investment surplus equal to 19.8 per cent of GDP. This large savings surplus resulted from four factors:

(a) During the hyperinflationary period, there were large transfers of income from the public to the private sector as a result of the much lower levels of taxation and the provision of foreign exchange at the official exchange rate. According to the World Bank

> ... the large fiscal deficit partly reflects the subsidy implicit in providing foreign exchange at the official exchange rate when the prices charged by users of this foreign exchange reflected the value of the parallel market rate. Reckoning the subsidy as the difference between the exchange rate in the parallel market and the exchange rate in the official market times the Central Bank's foreign exchange sales (some US$800 million in 1983/84) provides a figure slightly over 20 per cent of GDP in 1983 and 1984. The public sector deficit is thus indirectly financing a large income redistribution in favour of who obtain foreign exchange at the official rate. (World Bank 1985b, pp.11–12)

(b) A significant reduction in private consumption and investment; during the hyperinflationary period there were large income shifts from sectors whose incomes depended upon non-indexed remuneration (wage-earners) to sectors that were able to protect their incomes against inflation (profit-earners). These income shifts, coupled with the propensity to consume differentials among households, brought about a sharp reduction in consumption.

(c) Between 1980 and 1985 the production of coca, and the illegal income it generated, expanded very rapidly, by more than 150 per cent. The bulk of the surpluses went to finance capital flight, thus contributing significantly to the non-financial private sector's savings surplus (11 per cent of GDP on average).

(d) Private investment fell significantly from an amount equivalent to 7.3 per cent of GDP in 1975–79 to only 3.9 per cent in 1980–85. The main reason for this sharp contraction has to be found in the highly uncertain economic and political climate in Bolivia at that time.

In relation to the other sources of funds available, bank credit to the private sector increased by 9 per cent of GDP per year. The bank loans obtained by companies and households during the hyperinflation routinely became almost insignificant within one or two months, but capitalists were able to opportunely transform their non-indexed liabilities into indexed assets through the acquisition of foreign exchange and real estate. Access to information was also crucial for opportunistic portfolio reshuffles, which brought considerable capital gains.

The acquisition of domestic financial assets by the non-financial private sector also expanded significantly in 1980–85. In nominal terms, the stock of domestic financial assets increased by 10.7 per cent. Most of that expansion can be attributed to the large expansion of currency issued by the Central Bank in order to finance the public sector deficit and was, in one way or another, demanded by the private sector. The stock of currency expanded in nominal terms by 6 per cent of GDP on average, reaching 12.6 per cent of GDP at its peak in 1984. However, hyperinflation quickly eroded domestic asset stocks to such an extent that the value of the stocks outstanding at the end of the high-inflation period were practically equal to the changes in the asset stock (flows) during that period.

To equilibrate its accumulation balance, the non-financial private sector therefore acquired external assets amounting, on average, to 18 per cent of GDP per year (capital flight). As explained above, most of the resources that went to finance capital flight during that period came from the surpluses generated in the production of coca and unrefined cocaine.

Between 1986 and 1989, according to National Accounts estimates, on average the private sector's saving-investment surplus fell to an amount equivalent to 0.3 per cent of GDP. This reduction can be entirely attributed to the contraction of savings, to an amount equivalent to 5.2 per cent of GDP. Investment remained depressed during the period, averaging only 4.9 per cent of GDP. The private sector's savings surplus was complemented by bank credit, which increased by almost 5.6 per cent of GDP per year. The acquisition of domestic financial assets averaged 5.0 per cent of GDP, which was a substantial reduction compared to the level observed during 1980–85. This reduction can be explained by the sharp reduction in the amount of currency created to finance the public sector deficit. As a result, the amount left for the acquisition of external assets fell sharply, to 0.9 per cent of GDP.

In the period 1990–1996, on average the private saving deficit increased to 2.5 per cent of GDP because of lower savings and increased investment. The higher levels of investment recorded can partly be explained by the increased levels of direct foreign investment recorded in the last three years. A higher saving deficit vis-á-vis investment demand did not cause a reduction in the net asset acquisition by the private sector, as lending to the private sector increased and the acquisition of foreign assets became negative. The last of these movements could mean that the private agents repatriated financial resources that were deposited in offshore banks, to take advantage of the higher domestic interest rates resulting from the financial liberalization.

In summary, the pattern of private sector adjustment changed over time. During the 1970s, it was closely linked to the public sector behaviour, and it benefited from the highly favourable domestic conditions created by the public sector aimed at encouraging private sector activities. The government also made large resource transfers to the private sector through credit, high prices for public works contracts, and low prices for public goods and services. However, the private sector did not react to these favourable conditions with more investment, since transfers only encouraged capital flight. The large public external debt accumulated during the 1970s was, therefore, accompanied by an equally large accumulation of external assets by the private sector, mostly deposited in offshore banks (see Figure 3.1).

Figure 3.1 *External asset positions of the public and private sectors (US$ million)*

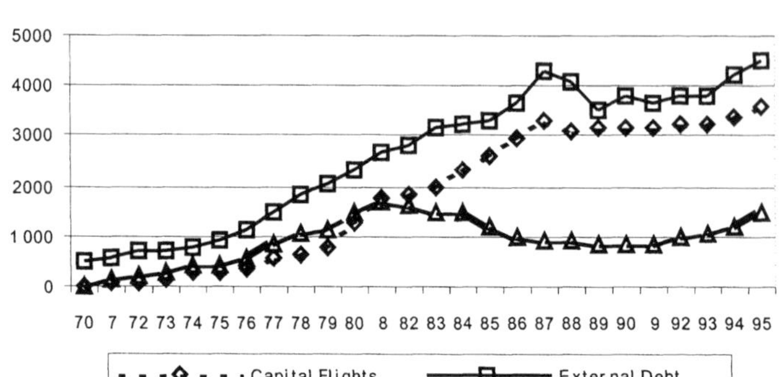

Source: World Bank, *World Debt Tables*

During the first half of the 1980s, private sector adjustment became more independent of the behaviour of the public sector for two reasons. First, during the 1980s the state was almost bankrupt and stopped transferring resources to the private sector (at least directly), since its resources were inadequate even to finance its own activities. Large income transfers took place through a much lower level of taxation and through the sale of state-generated foreign exchange at the highly undervalued official exchange rate. Second, the private sector benefited from windfall gains from the illegal production of coca and its by-products. Most of the surpluses thus generated went to finance luxury imports and capital flight. (The low level of private investment within Bolivia may be explained by the uncertain macroeconomic and political conditions which prevailed in that country.) Thus, while the outstanding public external debt kept growing, due to arrears and de-facto capitalization of interest, the private sector found an alternative source of finance to increase its accumulation of external assets (coca).

After the introduction of the NEP in 1985, the public sector adjusted to a much lower level of activity, in accordance with its much lower availability of resources. The public sector deficit was significantly reduced but not eliminated; therefore some public sector domestic borrowing was still required, which in turn pushed up the interest rate and crowded out private investment. The public sector also tried to capture part of the foreign exchange from coca by authorizing the Central Bank to buy foreign exchange without asking its origin. The private sector reduced capital flight and increased the acquisition of domestic financial assets that became more attractive due to their higher interest rates.

The rest of this chapter discusses adjustments for the accumulation balances of the individual economic agents, in both the public and private sectors. Within the public sector, the balance adjustments for the government and for public enterprises are discussed separately. Within the private sector, there are four agents: companies, higher-income households in urban areas, lower-income households in urban areas, and lower-income households in rural areas.

3.3 Accumulation Balance Adjustment for the Government

(a) During the 1970s

During the 1970s, government revenues increased from an amount equivalent to 8 per cent of GDP in 1970 to 12 per cent in 1976. This increase was primarily the result of higher transfers from public enterprises. Public enterprise contributions to the Treasury went up from an amount equivalent to 0.6 per cent of GDP in 1971 to an average of 4.5 per cent in 1973–78. This obviously represented a great drain on the resources of COMIBOL and YPFB. Conversely, tax receipts from the private sector stood at a very low level throughout the decade (around 2.5 per cent of GDP). The increased resources received by the government through public enterprise transfers and foreign borrowing made it unnecessary to increase the levels of private taxation (Table 3.3).

Government expenditures, on the other hand (see Table 3.4), increased consistently throughout the 1970s. The availability of foreign resources and much higher income revenues pushed government consumption from an amount equivalent to 10.2 per cent of GDP in 1972 to 14.4 per cent in 1978. Interest payments (especially on the accumulated external debt), jumped from an amount equivalent to 0.6 per cent of GDP in 1972 to 1.5 per cent in 1977. The share of public sector wage payments was initially reduced from 6.5 per cent of GDP in 1972 to 6

Table 3.3 Government income (percentage of GDP)

	Private Sector			Public Sector				Other Taxes	Total
	Custom	Internal taxation	Sub-total	Mining	Oil	Export taxes	Sub-total		
1970–75	2.7	3.6	6.3	1.0	0.9	1.0	2.9	0.6	9.8
1976–80	2.4	4.0	6.5	1.7	1.3	0.7	3.7	0.7	10.9
1981–85	0.9	1.7	2.6	0.3	1.5	0.0	1.8	0.7	5.2
1986–90	1.4	4.2	5.6	0.0	5.8	0.0	5.8	1.0	12.4
1991–96	1.3	10.0	11.3	0.0	6.3	0.0	6.3	0.5	18.1

Sources: BCB (c; various issues)

per cent in 1975, as part of the 1972 stabilization programme. In 1976, however, wage earnings by public employees began to recover, reaching 7.1 per cent of GDP in 1979, once the labour movement recovered some of its bargaining power after the years of political hardship experienced during the first half of the decade.

Public investment, on the other hand, grew rapidly during the 1970s in response to capital inflows. General government fixed capital formation went up from 2.3 per cent of GDP in 1972 to 7.8 per cent in 1977. As mentioned above, despite the relative political stability that characterized that period, private entrepreneurs did not find investing in Bolivia an attractive proposition, so that the accumulation of capital needed for Bolivia's long-term development became the government's responsibility. The availability of foreign finance played an important role in explaining the expansion in government investment; according to Ramos (1989, p.266), this was because public investment was conditioned to the negotiations with the international financial institutions which eventually defined investment priorities: 'The most common way in which Bolivia obtained credit was based upon project presentation; credits were not provided globally so that government could decide on their utilization according to its own priorities, but were provided on the basis of specific projects presented, which first had to be approved by the financial institutions themselves.'

Except for 1974, the government consistently showed a saving-investment deficit throughout the 1970s. Between 1973 and 1977, these deficits were mostly financed by foreign borrowing. External credits allowed the government not only to finance its deficit but also to increase its deposits in the Central Bank and therefore to contract the amount of domestic credit to the public sector. At the end of the decade, as the amount of external finance fell significantly, the government increasingly resorted to domestic sources as a means of financing its deficits. There is a common perception among several authors that during the 1970s Bolivia borrowed resources beyond its needs (Hinojosa and Espinoza 1983, p.14; R. Morales 1985, p.14; Devlin 1986, p.9). Morales (ibid.) further argues that '...Bolivia has taken its external indebtedness far beyond its external financial needs. The excess has been absorbed by capital flight and unrecorded imports.' Morales calculates that between 1973 and 1981, the required external credit for an efficient functioning of the economy was around US$880 million, yet Bolivia received more than US$1.9 billion, an excess of more than $US 1 billion . The government obtained enough external loans not only to cover its saving-investment gap but also to increase its deposits in the Central Bank and, therefore, to contract the level of domestic credit to the public sector. Central Bank credit to the government contracted every year between 1973 and 1977.

(b) During the first half of the 1980s

During the first half of the 1980s, government income went down sharply as inflation increased. During 1979–85 tax revenues fell mostly because tax collection was inefficient, and delays meant that inflation eroded the value of the tax revenues. Taxes on public enterprises also fell as a consequence of deteriorating export revenues due to a seriously undervalued official exchange rate. Government revenues fell as low as 2.1 per cent of GDP in 1984.

During the first half of the 1980s, government expenditures grew almost without control until they reached an amount equivalent to 20 per cent of GDP in 1984. This sharp increase was the result of higher wage payments to public servants (public sector wage payments reached 8.2 per cent of GDP in 1984) and a threefold increase in the amount of interest payments on the external debt.

Government investment, on the other hand, fell sharply once the country stopped receiving external credits. By 1980 investment was down to an amount equivalent to 2.4 per cent of GDP, and remained at a

Table 3.4 *The accumulation balance for the government (percentage of GDP)*

	1972	1973	1974	1975	1976	1977	1978	1979	1980	1981	1982	1983
Tax Income	8.0	9.8	12.1	11.8	15.4	15.2	14.7	13.0	11.2	10.4	5.6	3.7
Other Current Incomes (Net)							0.0	0.0	0.0	0.0	0.0	0.0
Total Incomes	8.0	9.8	12.1	11.8	15.4	15.2	14.7	13.0	11.2	10.4	5.6	3.7
Wages and salaries	6.5	5.7	6.0	6.0	6.7	6.4	6.8	7.1	8.5	8.0	6.5	5.8
Goods and services	2.5	2.9	2.5	2.9	2.8	2.7	3.0	2.7	3.8	3.8	2.7	2.0
Interests	0.6	0.8	0.7	1.2	1.1	1.5	1.2	1.1	1.6	1.9	3.0	2.7
Transfers	0.5	0.4	0.2	0.4	1.6	1.6	1.4	1.6	2.6	2.5	1.2	1.8
Others	0.0	0.0	0.0	0.0	0.8	1.7	2.0	2.2	1.7	2.6	7.0	7.0
Total Expenditures	10.2	9.9	9.4	10.6	13.0	13.9	14.4	14.7	18.2	18.7	20.4	19.3
Transfers	0.0	0.0	0.0	0.0	0.0	0.0	0.0	0.0	2.8	4.4	3.7	2.4
Gross Savings	−2.2	−0.1	2.7	1.2	2.3	1.3	0.3	−1.7	−4.2	−3.8	−11.1	−13.2
Fixed Capital Formation	2.3	1.5	2.4	1.8	5.9	7.8	5.6	5.6	2.4	2.4	1.3	1.3
Other Capital (Net)							−0.2	0.0	0.1	0.2	0.1	0.1
Overall Deficit/Surplus	−4.5	−1.6	0.2	−0.6	−3.7	−6.6	−5.1	−7.3	−6.7	−6.5	−12.6	−14.6
Total Financing												
External Finance	0.7	3.2	2.2	1.7	5.2	5.5	2.6	1.5	4.8	3.1	2.1	0.5
Domestic Finance	3.7	−1.6	−2.4	−1.1	−1.5	1.1	2.5	5.8	1.9	3.4	10.5	14.1

Sources: Author's own estimates based on: 1972–75 BCB (a; various issues), 1976–79 World Bank (1985b), 1980–95 UDAPE (1997)

Table 3.4 *The accumulation balance for the government (percentage of GDP), continued*

	1984	1985	1986	1987	1988	1989	1990	1991	1992	1993	1994	1995
Tax Income	2.1	3.0	6.0	7.9	9.5	14.7	16.3	17.3	17.4	17.6	18.6	19.6
Other Current Incomes (Net)	0.0	0.0	0.0	0.0	0.0	0.0	0.0	0.0	0.0	0.0	0.0	0.0
Total Incomes	2.1	3.0	6.0	7.9	9.5	14.7	16.3	17.3	17.4	17.6	18.6	19.6
Wages and salaries	8.2	5.5	5.0	6.0	7.7	7.6	7.6	7.5	8.4	8.9	9.2	9.3
Goods and services	2.1	2.4	2.6	2.9	3.2	3.0	2.6	2.8	2.6	2.4	2.0	2.4
Interests	2.2	4.5	4.3	3.4	3.7	3.6	3.2	3.4	2.7	2.3	1.8	2.2
Transfers	2.0	1.2	1.3	1.6	1.1	1.9	2.4	2.1	2.1	2.2	3.1	3.0
Others	5.7	2.0	0.5	0.5	2.2	–0.2	2.0	1.9	2.1	2.8	2.0	2.2
Total Expenditures	20.2	15.6	13.7	14.3	17.8	15.9	18.0	17.6	18.0	18.6	18.0	19.2
Transfers	2.8	6.8	9.3	5.7	7.3	0.9	1.0	1.1	1.2	1.1	0.9	2.7
Gross Savings	–15.8	–5.8	1.6	–0.7	–1.0	–0.4	–0.6	0.8	0.6	0.1	1.4	3.0
Fixed Capital Formation	1.7	1.9	3.1	2.3	4.9	5.5	4.6	5.2	6.0	5.8	6.3	6.2
Other Capital (Net)	0.1	0.1	–1.0	–0.7	–0.7	–1.3	–1.6	–1.6	–2.5	–1.2	–2.4	–1.8
Overall Deficit/Surplus	–17.1	–7.9	–0.5	–2.2	–5.2	–4.5	–3.6	–2.8	–2.8	–4.5	–2.4	–1.4
Total Financing												
External Finance	0.5	3.4	5.3	3.8	4.0	2.2	2.0	0.6	0.5	0.7	–0.1	–1.9
Domestic Finance	16.6	4.4	–4.8	–1.6	1.2	2.4	1.6	2.2	2.3	3.8	2.5	3.3

Sources: Author's own estimates based on: 1972–75 BCB (a; various issues), 1976–79 World Bank (1985b), 1980–95 UDAPE (1997)

very low level; government fixed capital formation stood on average at 1.7 per cent of GDP between 1980 and 1985.

Due to the weak revenue performance and sustained increase in current expenditure, the government deficit grew from 6.5 per cent of GDP in 1981 to 17 per cent in 1984. These deficits were entirely covered through credit from the Central Bank. The reluctance to adjust the official exchange rate has thus entailed a passive monetary policy whereby the Central Bank was instructed by the Ministry of Finance to finance the fiscal deficit. This deficit partly reflected the subsidy implicit in providing foreign exchange at the official exchange rate when the price charged by importers that had access to official sources of foreign exchange reflected the value of the parallel market rate.

(c) After the 1985 stabilization programme

Once the NEP was implemented in 1985, government revenues recovered significantly. The price policy for public goods and services under the NEP substantially increased tax revenues for the government (especially from the sale of gasoline), and tax reforms implemented in 1977 improved tax collection from the private sector. As a result, government revenues increased to 10.5 per cent in 1989.

Government expenditures were drastically reduced to only 13 per cent of GDP in 1986. Wage payments were cut to only 5 per cent in 1986, but later recovered to almost 7.7 per cent of GDP. Interest payments, however, increased to 4.5 per cent of GDP in 1985 once the official exchange rate was devalued. This represented an extremely heavy burden for the government budget. The government continued the complete moratorium on repayments of principal and interest to commercial creditors, despite the strong urging of the IMF to resume debt servicing (Sachs 1987, p.281). In 1990 interest payments fell sharply when Bolivia successfully renegotiated part of its external debt.

Government investment expenditures rose very rapidly between 1986 and 1989, as public finance in general improved and external funds for public investment started flowing in response to Bolivia's adjustment effort. The cumulative increase in government fixed investment over this period was 83 per cent in real terms, leading to a recovery of government investment from 1.9 per cent of GDP in 1985 to 5.5 per cent in 1989.

But despite the success of the stabilization programme in reducing government imbalances, the deficit was not completely eliminated. It stood at 0.5 per cent of GDP in 1986, the year after the stabilization programme was implemented, it rose to 2.2 per cent in 1987, to 5.2 per cent in 1988 and to 4.5 per cent in 1989. Although part of the deficit was covered by external finance, starting from 1988 the government began to resort to Central Bank credit. As discussed before, the monetary effect of this policy was neutralized by means of a contractionary monetary policy.

During the 1990s, although YPFB's transfers to the government decreased because of lower gas export prices, revenues increased sharply (to 19.6 per cent of GDP in 1995). This was the result of the stability attained, better tax administration and the 1994 tax reform. Between 1990 and 1995, government expenditures also increased, by almost 1.2 per cent of GDP. This was the result of higher wage increases to public employees. Wage payments went up from 7.6 per cent of GDP in 1990 to 9.3 per cent in 1995. New negotiations of the bilateral external debt further reduced the interest payments burden to 2.2 per cent of GDP in 1995.

Government investment, on the other hand, went up from 4.6 per cent of GDP in 1990 to 6.2 per cent in 1995. Due to the decentralization and popular participation reforms, there has been a radical institutional change in the composition of public investment. Municipalities and prefectures have increased their share in total public investment.

(d) Changes introduced by the structural reforms

The structural reforms implemented during the 1990s, redefine government's balance adjustment in several ways. First, access to credit coming from the Central Bank has been radically restricted under the new Central Bank Law. Thus, government deficits were reduced to levels that could be financed by concessional external resources. Second, the pension reform has transferred to the National Treasury all the liabilities of the 'pay as you go' system. This entails increased fiscal costs that will be covered by a combination of fiscal adjustment and the issue of public bonds that will be bought by the pension funds. Third, under the popular participation and decentralization laws, the National Treasury transfers directly to the municipalities and prefectures 20 per cent of the national tax revenues. This introduces a certain degree of inflexibility to the management of government's budget.

In summary, government balance has followed particular adjustment patterns in response to external shocks over the last two and a half decades. Government current incomes obtained from domestic taxation, both direct and indirect, varied depending on tax rates and on the levels of corporate profits and household incomes. The rapid increase in tax revenues observed during the 1970s is explained by the increase in corporate profits (mostly public enterprises). The slump in tax revenues during the first half of the 1980s is explained by the reduction in corporate profits and lower activity levels in the formal sector (due to the increased informalization of economic activity). The tax reforms implemented in 1986 and 1994 were aimed at increasing tax revenues through an expansion of the tax base and an improvement in tax administration.

The government's current expenditures, on the other hand, mostly comprise wage payments and the acquisition of goods and services necessary for government operations. Econometric tests (see Appendix 3.1) show that government expenditures are significantly correlated with:

(a) A lagged value of the same variable which indicates the rather rigid level and structure of government expenditures, given that the government is responsible for providing basic services such as education, health and defence (Requena 1990).
(b) External finance received by the government.
(c) Inflation, which is negatively correlated with government consumption, and indicates the negative impact of hyperinflation on government real expenditures once private economic agents started behaving according to rational inflationary expectations.

Interest payments depended on the level of the government's outstanding debt, the current international interest rate and the official exchange rate. These payments swelled when government indebtedness increased, and decreased when debt payments were reprogrammed. Part of the debt stock was eliminated in successive renegotiations between the Bolivian government and its bilateral creditors.

Government investment proved to be quite responsive to external finance. During the 1970s it increased in response to higher capital inflows. Between 1980 and 1985, external flows to Bolivia stopped, and government investment dropped to 2 per cent of GDP. After 1985, when relations with financial institutions and the flow of new foreign loans were re-established, government investment recovered to 3.5 per cent of

GDP. Annual data show that government investment has been sensitive to foreign financial flows.

There were two ways in which the government covered its saving-investment gap: (a) by obtaining external loans (when available); and (b) by resorting to Central Bank credit (public sector borrowing from private domestic sources was non-existent in Bolivia until 1988).

During the 1970s there was a rapid expansion in the amount of funds loanable to developing countries, once the large surpluses obtained by OPEC countries were deposited in international capital markets; in addition, Bolivia's international creditworthiness increased substantially due to higher export prices and improved political stability. As a result, Bolivia had unusually easy access to external finance and the country borrowed far beyond its needs. In terms of the government's accumulation balance closure, that implies that Central Bank credit to the government acted as the ultimate closure of the balance, by absorbing the excess funds available to the government through a negative change in the level of domestic credit.

Government borrowing from the Central Bank also acted as the main closure for the government's balance during the 1980s. During the early 1980s, government access to external sources of finance virtually disappeared when the international banks began to doubt the country's debt-servicing capacity. The government resorted to Central Bank credit as its only source of finance. Domestic credit to the government expanded, on average, by almost 9 per cent of GDP per year during that period.

After the stabilization programme, foreign credit was restored, and the government could use this to finance part of its deficit. Central Bank finance to the government, on the other hand, was restricted when the government was forced to adjust expenditures and revenues in order to control its deficit. However, domestic credit was still needed to cover part of the deficit and expanded by 3.3 per cent of GDP between 1985 and 1989.

Finally, the structural reforms entail a reduction in government access to Central Bank credit, an increase in deficit due to the pension reform, and a decentralization of government expenditures to regional government due to popular participation and decentralization laws.

3.4 Accumulation Balance Adjustment for Public Enterprises

Public firms' adjustment behaviour experienced substantial changes over the two and a half decades under analysis.

(a) During the 1970s

During the 1970s, there was a sharp increase in the gross incomes of public enterprises, as favourable external market conditions brought about record high international prices for the country's major export commodities (oil, natural gas, tin and silver). The quantities exported also increased, so that total incomes and gross profits of public enterprises rose significantly. However, the development strategy adopted during that period was aimed at promoting private sector activities. Consequently, the surpluses generated by state firms should not have been reinvested within the sector, but transferred to the private sector, so that this sector would make more efficient use of these resources.

The government appropriated public enterprises' surpluses through at least three types of mechanisms: first, a heavy tax on the output of state enterprises was created, and especially on YPFB and COMIBOL, without regard for their cost structures (Devlin and Mortimore 1983, p.174). Between 1974 and 1979, public firms paid an amount equivalent to 5.3 per cent of GDP (20 per cent of their gross incomes) to the Treasury. Second, public enterprises' export earnings were reduced substantially because export proceeds had to be converted at an exchange rate that was fixed between 1972 and 1979, during which time prices increased by 282 per cent. Third, domestic prices for goods and services produced by public firms were kept low, increasing domestic consumption and restricting export capacity (in 1976 for instance, YPFB exported 8 million barrels of crude for US$112.6 million and sold 6.6 million barrels to the domestic market for US$64.3 million). As a result of these substantial drains, public enterprise savings stood at only 2.8 per cent of GDP,which was insufficient to finance investment (see Table 3.5).

Public enterprise investment, however, increased sharply during the 1970s; it stood at 7.3 per cent of GDP over the period, but the viability of many of the investment projects was poor. YPFB started a vast investment programme to increase its oil refining capacity, but little was invested in prospecting for and exploration of new oil fields. According to Devlin and Mortimore (1983, p.166), the economic groups in power at that time were 'interested in large projects for which they could ask external finance from international banks'. In the mining sector again, there were large investments in mineral processing (volatilization, flotation and pre-concentration), and far too little in exploration to expand proven reserves. As a result, production declined as existing reserves were exhausted.

Because the government appropriated public enterprises' surpluses in taxes , these public enterprises had to obtain investment finance through external borrowing. The public enterprises acquired a sizeable external debt. Between 1974 and 1978, 26.4 per cent of the total external finance received by the country was directed to public enterprises. Additional finance was also required from the Central Bank.

(b) During the first half of the 1980s

Starting from 1981, public enterprises' gross incomes fell sharply from 28.9 per cent of GDP in 1981 to only 15.5 per cent in 1984. That sharp reduction was caused by a number of factors: the outbreak of the world recession reduced most export prices; the quantity produced also deteriorated as foreign exchange shortages constrained productive capacity, due to the impossibility of importing essential inputs; and export proceeds had to be converted at the extremely undervalued official exchange rate.

In spite of the lower levels of gross income, during the first half of the 1980s, public enterprises still had to make considerable transfers to the government; these amounted to an average of 3.6 per cent of GDP (15.2 per cent of their total annual sales). They also had to pay much higher interest on the external debt accumulated during the 1970s (equivalent to 1.3 per cent of GDP per year), so that savings deteriorated sharply from an amount equivalent to 5.3 per cent of GDP in 1980 to an average of only 1.8 per cent of GDP during the period 1981–85.

At the same time, the lower levels of external capital inflows were reflected in a decrease in public enterprise investment to just 2.7 per cent of GDP per year during the period 1981–85, a level that was insufficient even to replace capital consumption.

The overall public enterprise deficit was on average equivalent to 1.5 per cent of GDP per year during 1981–85 (reaching a maximum of 3.6 per cent in 1984), but this average hides differences in the performance of individual enterprises. Despite the official exchange rate undervaluation and low domestic prices for hydrocarbon by-products, YPFB was able to generate surpluses, whereas other public enterprises such as COMIBOL and ENFE showed consistent deficits. Indeed, COMIBOL's deficit constituted one of the main components of the overall non-financial fiscal deficit during that period.

In the first half of the 1980s, external credit to public enterprises was non-existent. The only source available to finance their global deficit was through domestic credit from the Central Bank.

(c) *After the stabilization programme*

After the 1985 stabilization programme, one of the main priorities of the NEP was the control of public firms' deficits, by means of the following measures: (a) state enterprises, especially COMIBOL, were restructured to reduce the drain on public finances and to increase the efficiency of the mining sector (COMIBOL's labour force was cut from 30,000 to 7,000 employees); (b) curtailed access of state enterprises to Central Bank credit; (c) state enterprises were studied with a view to future privatization; (d) all price controls and marketing boards were eliminated; (e) the domestic prices of gasoline products were increased to international levels; and (f) railroad tariffs, electricity rates and telephone charges were increased.

Despite these reforms, however, after 1985 the gross incomes of public enterprises fell even further (to only 13.6 per cent of GDP in 1989). Although the large devaluation and public domestic price adjustments implemented under the stabilization programme increased these gross incomes, other factors helped to reduce them: the collapse of the tin market in 1985 slashed international tin prices and therefore COMIBOL's income; besides, COMIBOL's incomes were further squeezed by much lower levels of production once the government ordered the shutdown of the most unprofitable mines (COMIBOL's gross income went down from 2.2 per cent of GDP in 1986 to 0.1 per cent in 1987).

In contrast, YPFB's gross income benefited from domestic price and exchange rate adjustments, and increased from an equivalent of 7.8 per cent of GDP in 1984 to 11.3 per cent in 1987. These income gains, however, were utilized by the government to finance deficits in other public sector institutions. As a result, public firms' transfers to the gov-

Table 3.5 *The accumulation balance for public enterprises (percentage of GDP)*

	1973	1974	1975	1976	1977	1978	1979	1980	1981	1982	1983	1984
Current Income	26.2	31.4	24.4	25.8	27.5	26.9	28.5	28.9	24.2	26.2	18.4	15.5
Intermediate Consumption						11.5	13.1	14.0	11.2	11.9	10.5	7.1
Wages and Salaries						4.7	5.3	4.2	3.4	2.7	2.1	3.9
Indirect Taxes	3.1	7.5	5.2	4.7	5.4	4.6	4.7	2.8	4.4	3.7	2.4	2.8
Operating Surplus						6.2	5.4	7.9	5.2	7.8	3.5	1.8
Net Other Current						0.1	0.1	0.6	1.7	2.6	1.0	0.7
Interests	0.4	0.5	0.5	0.6	0.6	1.4	2.1	2.0	1.7	1.2	1.2	0.5
Gross Savings	2.5	3.9	1.0	1.3	2.8	4.7	3.2	5.3	1.8	4.0	1.3	0.6
Fixed Capital Formation	0.0	2.1	1.8	8.7	8.7	7.2	4.7	4.1	3.5	4.4	2.7	1.9
Stock Changes	0.0	0.1	2.9	0.0	0.0	0.0	0.0	0.0	0.0	0.0	0.0	0.0
Other Physical Asset/liability	0.0	0.3	0.3	0.1	−0.9	−0.3	0.0	0.0	−0.6	1.1	0.0	2.3
Net Borrowing	0.0	1.3	−4.0	−7.5	−5.1	−2.2	−1.6	1.2	−1.1	−1.4	−1.4	−3.6
External Finance (Net)		−0.6	2.0	2.6	4.6	1.7	1.8	0.5	0.8	−1.5	−1.8	1.7
Internal Finance (BCB)		−0.7	2.0	4.9	0.4	0.5	−0.2	−1.7	0.2	2.9	3.2	1.9

Source: Author's own estimates based on UDAPE (1997a); (INE 1989b)

Table 3.5 *The accumulation balance for public enterprises (percentage of GDP), continued*

	1985	1986	1987	1988	1989	1990	1991	1992	1993	1994	1995
Current Income	17.7	18.4	14.1	15.9	18.6	18.8	20.2	18.4	16.8	16.4	15.7
Intermediate Consumption	5.8	5.7	4.4	4.1	5.2	4.9	4.6	4.5	4.0	3.7	3.4
Wages and Salaries	2.3	1.1	1.1	1.7	2.5	2.6	2.7	2.8	2.9	2.9	2.1
Indirect Taxes	6.8	9.3	5.7	7.3	7.0	8.5	9.6	8.0	7.8	7.0	6.7
Operating Surplus	2.8	2.3	2.9	2.9	3.9	2.8	3.4	3.1	2.1	2.9	3.5
Net Other Current	0.3	0.8	2.7	0.5	1.7	-0.2	1.0	0.5	0.3	0.4	1.9
Interests	1.3	0.9	0.4	0.4	0.4	0.4	0.4	0.4	0.6	0.6	0.6
Gross Savings	1.1	0.7	−0.3	2.0	1.7	2.6	2.0	2.2	1.3	1.9	1.0
Fixed Capital Formation	1.2	1.5	3.1	2.8	2.9	3.7	3.5	4.0	3.2	2.6	2.2
Stock Changes	0.0	0.0	0.0	0.0	0.0	0.0	0.0	0.0	0.0	0.0	0.0
Other Physical Asset/liability	−0.1	0.0	0.6	0.1	−0.2	−0.3	−0.1	−0.3	−0.4	−0.2	−0.8
Net Borrowing	0.0	−0.8	−3.9	−0.9	−0.9	−0.8	−1.4	−1.6	−1.5	−0.5	−0.5
External Finance (Net)	0.2	0.2	−1.6	0.6	1.3	0.0	0.4	0.1	0.3	−0.6	0.1
Internal Finance (BCB)	−0.2	0.6	5.5	0.3	−0.3	0.8	1.1	1.5	1.2	1.1	0.4

Source: Author's own estimates based on UDAPE (1997a); (INE 1989b)

ernment increased sharply, reaching an annual average equivalent to 6.7 per cent of GDP (43 per cent of total sales). As a result of the various trends followed by these different variables, public enterprise savings ranged between 0.6 and 5.3 per cent of GDP during the late 1980s. (However, although in 1987 when COMIBOL had to make extraordinary payments to the workers dismissed during the company's restructuring process, public enterprise savings stood at –0.3 per cent of GDP.)

New investments by state enterprises were curtailed in 1986, following the introduction of the NEP, falling to as low as 1.5 per cent of GDP. However, they increased to 3.1 per cent of GDP in 1987 when some of the bottlenecks that had constrained external funds disbursements were eliminated. Investments fell to 2.5 per cent of GDP in 1988 and to 2.1 per cent in 1989.

The saving-investment gap of public enterprises narrowed to only 0.8 per cent of GDP in 1986–89; this gap was covered mostly through external finance (although internal finance was still required). It is important to note that in 1987 the private enterprise deficit widened to 3.9 per cent of GDP, owing to unplanned increases in wage payments, delays in payments by Argentina for Bolivia's gas natural exports, and the costs of restructuring COMIBOL. This deficit was financed by more Central Bank credit. At the macroeconomic level, however, adjustment did not take place through inflation. The increased demand generated by the higher deficit (to the extent that the deficit was not financed by increasing domestic credit) was reflected in a fall in reserves (World Bank 1989, p.9).

The vulnerability of public enterprises' total incomes to exogenous shocks was made clear again in 1992 and 1993, when gas export prices dropped. Revenues fell from 20 per cent of GDP in 1991 to 18.4 per cent in 1992 and 16.8 in 1993. Total revenues fell further in 1994 and 1995, but this was a reflection of the fact that some public enterprises had already been transferred to the private sector, as part of the capitalization process. Other expenditures by public firms, such as wages and investment, present the same pattern. Wage payments fell from 2.9 of GDP in 1994 to 2.1 in 1995. Likewise, investment dropped from 4 per cent of GDP in 1992 to 2.2 in 1995.

Finally, public enterprises' gross income and investment levels also fell after 1994. Part of this decline is explained by the fact that investment decisions were postponed until the moment the capitalization process was completed. Moreover, the operations of the capitalized – and effectively transferred to the private sector – public enterprises were no longer recorded as part of the NFPS' balance.

(d) The changes introduced by the structural reforms

As a result of the structural reforms, the behavioural rules that govern public enterprises' adjustment will, without any doubt, experience the most profound changes of all sectors. The capitalization and privatization programmes were designed to achieve efficiency, both by transferring control rights of state-owned companies to the private sector and by introducing competition whenever possible.

The six major state-owned enterprises were included in the capitalization scheme. These were: ENDE (National Electricity Company), ENTEL (National Telecommunications Company), LAB (Lloyd Bolivian Airlines), YPFB (Bolivian Petroleum Company), ENFE (National Railway Company) and EMV (Vinto Smelting Company). Thus far, the first five were capitalized by different strategic investors, with tenders

Table 3.6 Capitalization of Public Enterprises (US$)

Strategic Investor	Capitalized Enterprise	Book Value	Capitalization Value
Dominion Energy	Corani (ENDE)	33 030 000	58 796 300
Energy Initiatives	Guarachachi (ENDE)	35 280 000	47 131 000
Constellation Energy	V. Hermoso (ENDE)	30 750 000	33 921 100
ETI Euro Telecom	ENTEL	130 000 000	610 000 000
VASP	LAB	24 000 000	47 475 000
Cruz Blanca	Red Occidental (ENFE)	29 000 000	13 251 000
Cruz Blanca	Red Oriental (ENDE)	24 000 000	25 853 099
AMOCO Bolivia Petroleum Co.	Chaco S.A.M. (YPFB)	156 300 000	306 667 001
YPF, Perez-Companc, Pluspetrol	Andina S.A.M. (YPFB)	130 400 000	264 777 021
ENRON Bolivia-Shell Overseas	Emp. Transportadora S.A.M. (YPFB)	97 500 000	263 500 000
Total		690 260 000	1 671 371 521

Source: INE (1997)

totalling more than US$ 1.6 billion (see Table 3.6). This amount is due to be invested in these firms in a period of time that varies between five to seven years.

From being state monopolies in most of the sectors they operated in, the capitalized firms will now operate under a new regulatory framework, SIRESE (System of Sectoral Regulation), which was set up with a mandate to oversee the electricity, telecommunications, hydrocarbons, transport, and water services sectors. SIRESE is supposed to act as the independent guarantor of the rights of the state, the private operators, and consumers. It aims to strike a balance between consumer protection and incentives to investment, promoting free competition and transparency.

In summary, during the whole period under analysis (even during the 1970s, a period of high gross incomes), public enterprises consistently presented a saving-investment deficit due to high transfers to the government, undervalued exchange rate, low prices for public services, high interest payments on the external debt accumulated during the 1970s, and high restructuring expenses (in the case of COMIBOL). Finance was obtained from several sources: during the 1970s, external sources financed 76 per cent of public enterprise deficit, while 24 per cent came from domestic sources (Central Bank credit). During the first half of the 1980s, external finance not only fell but also became negative when the external debt acquired during the 1970s had to be repaid. Domestic finance was the only source available to reduce the large deficits. After 1985, public enterprise deficits were substantially reduced, so that domestic finance was controlled but not completely eliminated, and external finance remained at a very low level. With the capitalization of public enterprises, direct foreign investment will be the main source of finance.

3.5 Accumulation Balance Adjustment for Companies

There are no theoretical models in the development economics literature that can be used to explain the behaviour of large companies in developing countries. Such models in principle should explain the microeconomic behaviour of capitalist firms facing the constraints that characterize under-developed economies, as well as taking advantage of the dominant position that they have in LDC markets. In that respect, FitzGerald (1991, p.2) has pointed out that, '...the immense volume of empirical research on the activities of "small" firms in agriculture and industry (which dominate employment) has not been matched by comparable work on the private corporations – despite the evident importance of these in LDC investment, saving, output and exports.'

Bolivia has been no exception to this lack of research on the subject; there has been no systematic empirical research on the operational and financial microeconomic behaviour of the corporate sector. Data for companies' accumulation balances are very limited. Time series for the sector's accumulation balances appear in National Accounts publications (INE 1990) only for the period 1978–89 (see Table 3.7). The lack of theoretical and empirical research on the topic contrasts with the importance of the sector's behaviour in explaining key macroeconomic variables.

It is crucial to assess the microeconomic behaviour of corporate firms and their relationships with the state, private banks and higher-income households to understand many macroeconomic events observed in the Bolivian economy in the last two decades. Events such as the acquisition of the country's large public external debt during the 1970s, the transfer of these resources to the private sector (that is, to private banks, corporate firms and eventually upper-income households), and the uses given to these resources (productive investment, consumption and capital flight) can only be explained by understanding the way companies interact with the state, with the financial institutions and with rich households; and the way these linkages have changed over time in response to external and internal shocks. The most noticeable linkages among these various groups are as follows:

(a) The strong linkages between companies and the state meant the corporate sector had great power to influence government actions. That power was greatly diminished after the 1952 revolution with the nationalization of mining companies and large-scale land reforms, and was not significantly restored until 1971 under the Banzer government (1971–79), when the national capitalist sector regained political power. According to Ladman (1982, pp. 330–1), '...private business was Banzer's strongest element of support' (small and medium-sized mining companies; agricultural, commercial, and petroleum interests of the Oriente). These groups 'helped bring Banzer to power and he utilized policy measures that directly benefited them'.

During the 1980s the entrepreneurs' corporate association emerged as a major political actor, signalling a 'new-right' that subsequently gained considerable influence – but not outright dominance – in the conservative governments of Paz Estenssoro (1985–89) and Paz Zamora (1989–93) (Dunkerley 1992, p.30; Toranzo and Arrieta 1989).

(b) In Bolivia there are strong linkages between corporate firms and upper-income households. In relatively well developed financial markets where company shares are distributed among a large number of shareholders, corporate decisions tend to be relatively independent of household decisions, and are supervised by boards of directors. Firms will choose between retaining profits in order to finance investment or distributing them to shareholders in order to increase the value of the shares in the equity market (Davis and Pointon 1984). In a less developed country like Bolivia, however, equity markets are still in their early stage of development, and shares tend to be concentrated in relatively few hands. Thus corporate investment decisions are influenced by the opportunity costs of alternative assets outside the business (capital flight, for example) in which households can invest available funds.

(c) There are close associations between groups of large firms and commercial banks (Leff 1976). The relationship goes in two directions: firms make large deposits in banks (working capital), and the banks negotiate for foreign credits and provide the firms with preferential lines of credit. When firms and banks belong to such a group, then the bank may even act as the 'treasury department' of a conglomerate (FitzGerald 1991).

In the Bolivian case, there are close linkages between companies, commercial banks and households. Hinojosa (see Mercado 1988) has attempted to sketch these links in a 'map of extreme wealth', in which there is a clear tendency within the Bolivian capitalist sector towards the formation of economic family groups. These groups can generally be identified with a small number of family names. Normally, each group owns middle-size mining firms, commercial import-export enterprises, large factories, agro-industrial firms, insurance companies, and so on. Most important, however, is the fact that in all cases these groups are associated with a bank.

The existence of these institutional linkages between companies and households, banks and the state, is vital for an understanding of some of the macroeconomic events witnessed in Bolivia during the last two and a half decades.

(a) During the 1970s

During the 1970s the Banzer government had the solid backing of the agricultural, commercial, and petroleum interests of the groups from the east of the country (Oriente). He also gained the support of the small- and medium-sized mining companies that had begun to flourish during the second half of the 1960s. According to Ladman (1982, p.330),

> ...The government maintained the allegiance of these groups by carefully providing a favourable economic environment to them [private businesses], with the result of increased output that contributed to the economic boom of the country... There was a 238 per cent increase in the value of agricultural exports between 1971 and 1974. Most of this increase was due to sharp increases in sugar, cotton and mahogany exports, all of which came from the Oriente.
>
> A major means used by the Banzer government to assuage the interests in the Oriente was credit. The real amount of agricultural credit in Bolivia increased 50 per cent over the 1971–74 period, of which an estimated 80 per cent went to the Oriente. Moreover, this credit was loaned at concessionary interest rates that were 6 to 15 interest points below the rate charged for commercial loans. This clearly resulted in a substantial transfer of income to the large commercial farmers of the Oriente. The unwillingness of the government to enforce collection of delinquent loans increased the income transfer substantially, as did the rather severe inflation. With these bargains, it was little wonder that much agricultural credit found its way into other activities such as construction and foreign investments.

Another favoured group during the Banzer government was the medium-sized mining companies. According to Dunkerley (1984, p.226),

> The most marked characteristic of the organisation of mining in this period was the officially-sponsored ascendancy of the 25 larger firms of

> the private sector organised in the 'Asociación de Mineros Medianos' (ANMM). Between 1973 and 1976 the value of COMIBOL's exports rose by 55 per cent while taxes on its operations increased by 99 per cent; over the same period the ANMM's revenues from foreign sales rose by 76 per cent but its taxes by only 26 per cent. Rates of profit as a consequence varied widely, COMIBOL's falling by 107 per cent and the ANMM's growing by 27 per cent. Boosted not only by favourable government treatment but also by price rises for subsidiary minerals in which it had obtained a sizeable share of control (tungsten: 70 per cent; antimony: 100 per cent; copper: 65 per cent), the ANMM increased its labour force by 80 per cent and accounted for a fifth of national mineral production.

Private business was undoubtedly Banzer's strongest element of support. It helped bring him to power and he utilized policy measures that directly benefited it. The development strategy adopted during the period of Banzer's government was based on favouring the private corporate sector to the detriment of public enterprises. According to that strategy, the private sector was supposed to become the engine of Bolivian economic development. Private investment, however, did not react accordingly, but decreased sharply in 1973–74. According the World Bank (1985b, p.5), 'In spite of the unprecedented degree of political stability in the 1970s, private entrepreneurs did not find investing in Bolivia an attractive proposition'. Although the government issued policy statements encouraging foreign and domestic private sector entrepreneurs to invest in Bolivia, new private investment flows failed to materialize. During 1971–81, foreign private investment was at some US$20 million per year, while Bolivia's capital investment abroad (and unrecorded imports) amounted to some US$150 million per year. Some authors attribute the lack of response by private investors to the favourable economic and political environment created by the government, to the lack of indigenous entrepreneurial capacity.

According to Baran (1968, p.236), however, the entrepreneurial capacity problem in less developed countries does not depend on the supply of entrepreneurial capacity as much as on the uses given to that capacity within the existing economic and social order. Thus the Bolivian entrepreneurial sector was highly uncertain about the country's economic future, so that the risk factor weighed heavily on their decisions. They became involved in short-term unproductive activities that were nevertheless very profitable (such as import activities and real-estate speculation). Other authors (Devlin and Mortimore 1983, p.224) maintain that other factors that negatively affected private investment during that period were: a change in the real interest rate from negative in 1974 and 1975 to positive during 1975 and 1976. They also suggest that private investment was crowded out by public investment after 1974, since the large increase in public investment in 1975 was almost immediately followed by a reduction in private investment.

(b) During the first half of the 1980s

The economic decline that began at the end of the 1970s brought about far less favourable conditions for the corporate sector. The economic recession of the early 1980s greatly reduced gross corporate incomes (from 39.5 per cent of GDP in 1978 to only 26.9 per cent in 1981, and partially recovering to 30.6 per cent in 1984). The export sector was the worst hit ; the undervalued official exchange rate greatly reduced export profitability. As a consequence, between 1980 and 1985, mineral exports by the medium-scale mining companies fell by 26 per cent, while agro-industrial exports went down by 70 per cent. Conversely, the sectors that benefited from the gap between the official and parallel exchange rates were those which were able to obtain foreign exchange at the official rate. The gainers within the private sector included importers whose applications were accepted by the Central Bank.

As a reflection of the much lower levels of income and activity, companies cut down some of their expenditures: intermediate consumption went down from an amount equivalent to 20.5 per cent of GDP in 1978 to 15.5 per cent in 1984. Within the same period, wage payments were cut from 8.3 per cent of GDP to 7.5 per cent. During the same period, indirect tax payments (net of subsidies) reflected the erosion of the value of tax revenues due to high inflaction; these indirect tax payments declined from 1.9 per cent of GDP to 0.2 per cent, while direct tax payments by companies dropped from 0.9 per cent of GDP to only 0.2 per cent.

Interest payments by companies increased sharply during 1981 and 1982; however, they reduced again in 1983 as a result of the 'de-dollarization decree'.

Distributed profits remained quite stable during the 1978–84 period (around 3.3 per cent of GDP), perhaps showing that shareholders tried to maintain stable levels of personal income.

During the economic crisis of the early 1980s corporate fixed investment fell as a percentage of GDP from 4.6 per cent in 1980 to 2.3 per cent in 1985, suggesting a serious deterioration in the value of their capital stock. The deterioration in the investment climate derived from both the worsening perception of the risk of investing in the country and the fear of expanded state intervention. Moreover, the policy of rationing foreign exchange through administrative schemes implemented in 1982 did not work efficiently. The allocation of foreign exchange was erratic. No clear guidelines were stated and applications for foreign exchange had uncertain and irregular outcomes. Priority in the allocation of foreign exchange was given to debt-servicing, so that it became increasingly unlikely that foreign exchange would be used for investment purposes.

Some observers maintain that, in the face of the far less promising perspectives for agro-industrial growth, the elite rural groups turned their attention towards '...a carefully-planned expansion of another "non-traditional export": cocaine' (Bascopé 1982, pp.56, 67). With experience in the international export of commodities, such as cotton in the early 1970s, members of the agro-industrial capitalist groups in the Oriente were strategically positioned to enter the expanding illicit international markets for cocaine in the late 1970s. Having benefited from the rural modernization and state protection of the past two decades, this group enjoyed a number of comparative advantages that enabled them to seize the lucrative drug-related opportunities. The ownership of private ranches and commercial farms provided a strong base from which to exercise both economic and political power over local public officials charged with keeping vigilance. Farms located in isolated and protected areas provided safe landing strips for small aircraft. The Oriente's powerful elite groups had the means and experience to acquire cheap labour, international business connections and capital for the basic investment in transport, and the infrastructure, equipment and inputs for the clandestine laboratories (Bascopé ibid).[2]

Table 3.7 *The accumulation balance for companies (percentage of GDP)*

	1978	1979	1980	1981	1982	1983	1984	1985	1986	1989
Total Sales	39.5	33.2	32.6	26.9	30.9	32.5	30.6	34.7	34.5	39.9
– Intermediate Consumption	20.5	16.1	15.7	13.1	17.9	15.9	15.5	18.4	16.3	18.5
– Wages and Salaries	8.3	8.2	7.4	7.8	6.3	7.1	7.5	11.5	6.0	6.6
– Net Indirect Taxes	1.9	1.8	(0.5)	(0.2)	(0.5)	0.1	0.2	(0.8)	1.0	1.0
Operating Surplus	8.7	7.1	10.1	6.1	7.3	9.4	7.3	5.5	11.1	13.8
– Other Current	0.3	0.2	0.3	0.3	0.3	0.3	0.3	0.3	0.2	0.0
– Direct Taxes	0.9	1.1	1.0	0.9	0.1	0.5	0.1	0.1	0.1	0.4
– Interests	0.6	0.6	0.9	2.1	0.4	1.0	0.4	0.2	1.3	0.3
– Dividend	3.7	3.4	3.4	3.0	3.1	3.1	3.1	(0.9)	1.0	3.7
Gross Savings	3.2	1.8	4.5	(0.2)	1.5	4.5	3.4	4.4	8.5	9.4
– Fixed Capital Formation	2.7	4.1	4.6	5.1	1.0	2.6	3.1	2.3	2.3	2.9
– Stock Changes	1.9	(0.1)	0.2	1.8	0.1	0.8	2.7	1.5	0.8	(0.2)
Other Physical Asset/liability	0.0	0.0	0.0	0.2	0.5	0.1	0.5	0.3	0.3	0.0
Net Borrowing	1.4	2.2	0.2	7.3	0.1	(0.9)	1.8	(0.3)	(5.1)	(6.7)

Sources: INE (1989b, 1990). 1. After 1989, INE did not publish separate national accounts for companies and households

(c) *After 1985*

After 1985, the NEP gave to the private sector (and especially to the entrepreneurial sector) the leading role in the process of economic development. The strong support for the NEP by the entrepreneurs' corporate association (CEPB) and the participation of prominent businessmen occupying key posts in government ratified the emergence of the CEPB as a major political actor that gained considerable influence.[3] The design and implementation of the NEP itself was conducted by a prominent local businessman, Sanchez de Lozada (Toranzo and Arrieta 1989).

Key economic measures within the NEP were directed at promoting larger private activities such as: the development of an investment code that would insure private investment against uncompensated nationalizations, guarantee a stable long-term tax regime, and simplify administration; the development of a mining and hydrocarbons code that would facilitate joint ventures; and the not yet implemented privatization of the public enterprises.

The foreign exchange policy under the NEP was also aimed at promoting private export activities; the devaluation of the official foreign exchange in 1985 and the subsequent policy of export tax rebates for non-traditional exports had a considerable positive effect on Bolivia's private exports (agro-industry and mining). As a result, gross corporate incomes increased from 30.6 per cent of GDP in 1984 to 39.9 per cent in 1989. However, despite all the measures aimed at promoting it, private investment showed no significant sign of recovery until 1989. Following annual declines of 22 per cent during the early 1980s, private investment continued to fall between 1985 and 1989, but at reduced rates of 3 per cent on average. In the late 1980s, the share of corporate investment in GDP remained at around 2.9 per cent. According to a survey of 80 enterprises in all major productive sectors (see Mierau-Klein and Page 1991, p.17), the major constraints on investment (in decreasing order) were: high interest costs, inadequate infrastructure, insufficient purchasing power of the domestic currency, pressures from imports and/or smuggling, the high costs of non-labour inputs, economic and political uncertainty, and too many regulations and red tape.

In the 1990s, the maintenance of the market oriented policies initiated in 1985, and the consolidation of price stability and macroeconomic equilibrium, regained the entrepreneurial sector's confidence in the economy and in the macroeconomic model. Besides, the interest rate slowly but continuously decreased between 1990 and 1996, and the spread between the international and the domestic interest rates narrowed. The response of the entrepreneurial sector to these relatively favourable conditions has been mixed. On the one hand, companies' investments have become more dynamic, boosted by private foreign direct investment. Between 1989 and 1996, foreign investment increased fifteenfold. On the other hand, private entrepreneurial investment has been confined to few sectors.

The agro-business in the Santa Cruz area and jewellery in La Paz were among the most rapidly growing export sectors of the economy. Investments and rapid export growth were also significant in the gold mining sector, and there was an isolated history of success in textiles.

(c) The changes introduced by the structural reforms

The structural reforms are expected to substantially increase the private sector role in the economy. As explained above, the capitalization of the public enterprises has transferred a large proportion of the Bolivian productive capacity to private hands. The new institutional system, created in order to regulate private activity, is expected to increase the confidence of private investors, not only in the capitalized sectors but also in the other sectors of the economy. However, whether the new business environment created by the reforms will succeed in promoting greater private investment and economic growth, will depend on other crucial factors such as private competitiveness, road infrastructure, greater labour productivity, and a greater 'animal-spirit' of local entrepreneurs.

In summary, the accumulation balance behaviour for companies has exhibited very specific features, compared to the other sectors of the economy. These adjustment rules have also undergone important changes over the periods examined. These features are summarized below:

The determination of gross corporate profits tends to vary depending on the particular sector in which the companies operate. Companies produce for domestic as well as for export markets. In the case of export activities (mining and modern agriculture), the mark-up is determined endogenously depending on external prices, the exchange rate and unit costs of production. The mark-up rate for companies that sell in domestic markets depends, in theory, on the degree of monopoly they enjoy in that particular sector. Companies tend to have relatively strong oligopolistic positions in the nontradable sectors (such as construction and services). However, in the tradable goods sector (for example, manufacturing), companies have not enjoyed such positions since they have always faced the competition of external production brought into the country as contraband (before the NEP) and as legal imports after the liberalization of the external sector under the NEP. In these sectors, the 'single-price' law tends to apply and the mark-up rate becomes an endogenous variable.

Direct tax payments, on the other hand, depend on the tax rate and on company profits. Distributed profits tended to remain rather stable over time. A plausible explanation is that shareholder households try to ensure relatively stable sources of income that would allow them to lead comfortable lifestyles.

Several variables have been tested in order to obtain an investment demand for companies. Econometric tests gave the following results (see Appendix 3.4):

(a) Government investment lagged by four periods was shown to have a significant crowding-in effect on company investment. Such a long lag can be justified on the basis of the long periods that public projects took to complete. The estimated crowding-in coefficient was 0.19; this variable was significant at the 88 per cent level.
(b) Public enterprise investment lagged by one period, in contrast, tends to have a strong crowding-out effect on company investment. The crowding-out coefficient is much stronger (–0.77).
(c) The accelerator term in the company investment demand function was shown to have a significant positive correlation with company investment. The estimated coefficient was significant at the 100 per cent level.
(d) The opportunity cost of company investment in physical capital was captured by the real international interest rate, which had a negative effect on company investment demand. This variable was significant at the 87 per cent level.
(e) Bank credit to companies correlated positively with investment. Credit was significant in explaining company investment at the 98 per cent level (coefficient = 0.12).

Finally, companies' access to bank credit has been rather flexible. Over the whole period analysed, companies have enjoyed a privileged access to bank credit, which has tended to adjust to the financial requirements of the non-financial private sector.

3.6 Households

This section discusses the variables that determine consumption, savings, investment and financial behaviours of households. Available time series for the accumulation balance for households are presented in Tables 3.8 and 3.9, taken from the National Accounts. However, National Accounts figures have complete time series only for the period 1978–86, so that data for the period 1970–77 were taken from R. Morales (1985), who conducted estimates of the income structure of Bolivian households for the years 1970–83. The methodology developed by Morales (ibid. p.125)[4] was used here to derive estimates for the years 1987 and 1988, while those for 1989 were taken from the 1989 SAM (UDAPE 1990d).

Based on these data, the consumption, savings and investment functions were tested econometrically (see Appendix 3.5). The explanatory variables used in estimating each of these functions were selected based on the most relevant hypotheses on consumption, savings and investment behaviour. The explanatory variables included in the consumption function were: (a) the real interest rate, which, according to the neoclassical hypothesis is positively correlated with the level of savings and negatively correlated with consumption; and (b) the shares of wages, profits of family-based units, and distributed profits in total GDP. These variables are aimed at capturing shifts in income distribution, which, according to the post-Keynesian hypothesis, are the key determinants of consumption and savings.

The results show that shifts in income distribution are quite significant in explaining consumption and savings, in terms of both the statistics and the theory. The estimate for the average propensity to consume out of wages was very close to 1, and that out of household profits 0.84. Both coefficients were significant at the 100 per cent level. The propensity to consume out of distributed profits was much lower (0.20) and was not statistically significant. The real interest rate, on the other hand, was significant from the statistical point of view, but the sign of the coefficient was positive rather than negative.

Conversely, the income category with the highest average propensity to save, according to the econometric results, relates to 'distributed profits', which was significant at the 90 per cent level. The propensity to save out of 'operating surplus' income was much lower, and was significant at the 96 per cent level. The propensity to save out of wages exhibited a negative coefficient (–0.23) that was significant only at the 75 per cent level. The real interest rate was again significantly correlated with savings from the statistical point of view, but the correlation was not positive; on the contrary, the highest levels of household savings occurred when the real interest rate was at its most negative point.[5]

Distributive shifts also provide a more convincing explanation of household consumption-saving behaviour in Bolivia when other elements are brought into the analysis. The figures in Table 3.1 imply that during 1971–73, when economic policy was focused on stabilizing the economy, a foreign-exchange devaluation in 1972 and its resulting price increases, plus a substantial reduction of state subsidies on a range of basic goods and services in 1973, brought about a reduction in household incomes from 84.6 per cent of GDP in 1971 to only 76.7 per cent in 1974. On average, real wages in 1974 were 16 per cent lower than the level observed in 1971, so that the share of wages in total GDP went down from 37 to 32 per cent. The share of profit earnings by family-based units in total GDP also fell as the direct result of much higher rates of growth of disposable incomes of other sectors vis-à-vis those attained by household-based firms. Peasant incomes, for instance, deteriorated due to price controls on most peasant products imposed under the 1972 stabilization package. As a result, household consumption fell sharply from 75 per cent of GDP in 1971 to 67 per cent in 1974. Conversely, household savings increased from 6.2 per cent of GDP in 1971 to 8.2 per cent in 1974. This would imply that income reductions were not evenly distributed among households, but were biased against households with higher propensities to consume.

Starting from 1975, the share of wages in total GDP recovered, reaching around 35 per cent of GDP in 1977, whereas profit incomes diminished even further when adverse weather conditions reduced the agricultural output and incomes. As a consequence, household incomes as a whole remained at a very low level during that period. Consumption, however, did recover after the low level achieved in 1974, most likely as a result of higher wage earnings. The lower levels observed in total household incomes coupled with higher levels of consumption, brought about an increase in households' average propensity to consume. As a result, household savings fell sharply during most of the second half of the 1970s.

During the early 1980s, household incomes increased to an average of 86 per cent of GDP. That increase was mostly explained by a much higher level of non-corporate profits, which rose to almost 47 per cent of GDP, as a result of increased revenues from the production of coca and unrefined cocaine. Wages remained rather depressed during that period, except for 1984 when they reached their highest point (43 per cent of GDP) as a result of large wage concessions by the government. Income structure in the household sector experienced substantial changes, which in turn brought about changes in consumption behaviour. The share of wage incomes in GDP dropped to an equivalent of less than 40 per cent, while that of non-corporate profits went up to 54 per cent. Distributed profits from companies also dropped from 4 to 3 per cent. As a result of these income shifts, household consumption contracted substantially from more than 70 per cent of GDP in the 1970s to only 65 per cent in the early 1980s. The average propensity to consume fell to only 0.76, implying that distributional shifts favoured those households with much lower propensities to consume. Household savings, which represented around 5 per cent of total GDP in 1978, increased sharply during the first half of the 1980s, reaching their highest levels in 1984 and 1985 when they accounted for 31 and 39 per cent of GDP, respectively. Besides the positive effect of coca revenues, increased household savings were also very much a reflection of the large transfer of income that took place in the early 1980s from the public to the private sector. Direct tax payments by households, for instance, fell from 2.1 per cent of GDP in 1978 to only 0.1 per cent in 1984. Wage payments by the public sector (government and public enterprises), on the other hand, increased from an amount equivalent to 14.4 per cent of GDP in 1978 to 21.5 in 1984. Indirect tax payments fell from 12.9 per cent in 1978 to 5 per cent in 1984. As a result, the overall current balance of the non-financial public-sector moved from a 7.2 per cent of GDP surplus in 1978, to a 13.2 per cent of GDP deficit in 1984. Since the availability of external savings was quite limited during that period, large public sector deficits were matched by equivalent private sector surpluses.

After the stabilization programme, the public sector moved again to a current account surplus (7.6 per cent of GDP in 1986 and 2.4 per cent in 1989). Tax payments increased to 10.7 per cent in 1986 and to 12.9 per cent in 1989. Public sector wage payments fell to 7 per cent of GDP in 1986 and 8 per cent in 1989 when the government froze public sector wages and undertook massive layoffs. In addition, wage rules in the private sector were made more flexible, so that the share of wages in total GDP went down to 24 per cent in 1986 and remained at that low level. Household savings fell to around 4.7 per cent of GDP in 1986 and remained at that level throughout the late 1980s.

The pattern of fixed capital formation by households, on the other hand, was stable during most of the 1970s but became highly unstable during the 1980s. During the 1970s, fixed capital formation stood at an average of 3.7 per cent of GDP, but during the early 1980s it fell steadily, to just 0.5 per cent in 1984, as a result of the chaotic economic conditions that greatly damaged the investment climate. After the 1985 stabilization programme, household investment recovered to 3.1 per cent of GDP in 1986, only to fall again to 1.6 per cent of GDP in 1989. Household investment showed a significant negative correlation with the real international interest rate, indicating the opportunity cost of investing in physical assets. Another variable that also proved to be significant in explaining household investment was a lagged value of the same variable, which indicates that the construction of household dwellings in Bolivia usually takes more than one year (see Appendix 3.6).

Stock changes, on the other hand, were markedly negative in 1982 and 1983 (–5 and –5.6 per cent of GDP, respectively). Drastic reductions in agricultural stocks due to adverse weather conditions largely explain this negative performance. As a result, rural households' investment was negative in those years.

During most of this period, households showed consistent saving-investment surpluses. During the first half of the 1980s, as a result of the drastic decapitalization of the public sector, these surpluses reached unprecedented levels (36 per cent of GDP in 1985). Such surpluses were most likely used in the acquisition of financial assets, both domestic (currency and bank deposits) and external (capital flight).

In summary, the above discussion demonstrates that consumption, savings and investment decisions by households do not depend exclusively on the level of the real interest rate.On the contrary, in the Bolivian case, the relation between the real interest rate and the other three variables moved in quite different directions to what neoclassical theory would predict. Shifts in the distribution of income among wages, operating surpluses and distributed profits seem to provide a far more relevant and coherent explanation of consumption and savings behaviour.

Interest rate differentials, however, together with inflationary expectations and distributional shifts, play an important role in determining the ways in which the financial portfolios of households are reshuffled.

In order to define a household demand function for currency and for bank deposits, it is necessary to make two prior assumptions:

(i) Currency and bank deposits in the accumulation balance equation for households are expressed in terms of flows representing the differences between each asset stock at the beginning and the end of the period. However, household demand for most financial assets is essentially a demand for stocks rather than for flows. Flows tend to reflect only those changes in the households' portfolio structure that arise from changes in preferences for the various assets available. Therefore, bank deposits and currency demand functions have to be defined in terms of stocks; the flow in the accumulation balance is calculated as the difference between the initial and final stocks of an asset.

(ii) Data on the demand for currency and bank deposits exist only for the private sector as a whole. However, since different income categories, namely wages, household operating surpluses and distributed profits, can be included as explanatory variables in the asset demand functions, then it is possible to estimate individual financial asset demand functions for each household category; to do so, it is necessary to impute to the asset demand functions of the various household categories, the corresponding parts of the estimated asset demand function ascribed to the particular income categories, which, in turn, are associated with different household groups. In this way, the demand for currency and bank deposits out of wage earnings and household operating surpluses can be allocated to rural and lower-urban households, while that part of the asset demand out of dividends can be allocated to upper-income households.

> The part of asset demand that is attributed to interest rate differentials and to inflationary expectations can be allocated to the upper-income households' asset demand function, since this particular group has access to information and is in a better position to adjust its portfolios in response to changes in these variables.

According to econometric tests, household demand for currency (see Appendix 3.7) proved to be significantly negatively correlated with the real domestic interest rate (which measures the opportunity cost of holding currency) and with the current rate of inflation. Besides, since currency is usually associated with transactions, currency demand was shown to have a significant positive correlation with total household wage-earnings and with distributed profits. Household operating surpluses showed a positive correlation with currency demand, but not a significant one.

Bank deposits, on the other hand, were divided into two groups: demand deposits and quasi-money. This distinction was made bearing in mind that demand for each of these two types of assets obey essentially different motives and therefore are explained by different variables.

Demand deposits, for instance, are, first of all, more related to transaction motives, so that income shifts were included as explanatory variables for this asset demand function. Second, since demand deposits do not yield interest, the interest rate yield from other types of asset (such as the real international interest rate) should negatively influence holdings of demand deposits. Third, since demand deposits are not indexed to price changes, inflationary expectations (p) should tend to discourage demand for them. The econometric results of the demand function for demand deposits for households are presented in Appendix 3.8.

Household demand for quasi-money (time and savings deposits) was more associated with portfolio decisions (the allocation of wealth among a portfolio of assets including money); therefore, the explanatory variable included in the quasi-money demand function for households is the real domestic interest rate (ir). This variable was shown to be significant at the 98 per cent level. From the income categories, only distributed profits were significant in explaining changes in the demand for quasi-money (at the 90 per cent level). Econometric results for the

Table 3.8 *Accumulation Balance Structure for Households (percentage of total household incomes)*

	1971	1972	1973	1974	1975	1976	1977	1978	1979	1980	1981	1982	1983	1984	1985	1986	1987	1988	1989
Wages	44.2	44.7	40.6	42.2	43.7	44.2	45.5	43.1	42.9	43.1	39.6	38.8	38.9	46.8	31.8	32.3	33.8	35.4	37.0
Operating Surplus	50.2	51.1	53.6	52.8	51.5	51.2	50.2	52.1	52.7	52.2	56.8	54.8	59.7	51.5	51.3	63.9	62.7	61.3	60.0
Dist. Prof, interest	4.4	3.7	4.8	4.5	4.4	4.3	4.0	4.5	3.6	2.7	3.3	6.5	-0.3	-2.0	7.9	0.0	n.a.	n.a.	0.0
Net Other Current	1.1	0.5	0.9	0.5	0.4	0.3	0.3	0.3	0.9	2.0	0.3	-0.2	1.6	3.8	9.0	3.8	3.5	3.3	3.0
Total Income	100.0	100.0	100.0	100.0	100.0	100.0	100.0	100.0	100.0	100.0	100.0	100.0	100.0	100.0	100.0	100.0	100.0	100.0	100.0
Direct Taxes	3.1	3.1	1.8	1.2	1.1	1.0	1.1	1.5	0.9	0.4	0.9	0.2	0.2	0.0	0.0	0.4	0.6	0.8	1.1
Con- sumption	89.6	90.1	87.4	88.0	93.5	91.3	93.7	92.3	85.3	84.6	83.5	82.3	81.3	66.1	61.6	93.3	94.2	93.9	93.2
Gross Savings	7.3	6.8	10.8	10.8	5.5	7.7	5.3	6.1	13.8	15.0	15.6	17.5	18.6	33.9	38.3	6.3	5.2	5.3	5.7
Gr. Fixed Capital Formation	4.5	4.1	5.1	4.9	5.5	4.9	4.5	5.1	4.5	3.1	2.8	2.5	1.1	0.5	1.0	4.1	3.5	3.4	2.1
Stocks Changes	1.1	1.9	1.5	-1.3	1.9	-0.5	-0.1	1.3	1.7	-0.5	-0.6	-6.1	-6.9	-2.4	2.4	2.2	1.0	-0.3	-2.0
Oth.Phys. Asset/liability	0.0	0.0	0.0	0.0	0.0	0.0	0.0	-0.4	-0.7	0.6	0.1	-0.5	-0.7	-0.8	-0.3	-0.9	0.0	0.0	0.0
Net Borrowing	1.8	0.8	4.3	7.2	-1.9	3.2	0.9	0.1	8.3	11.9	13.3	21.7	25.0	36.6	35.3	0.9	0.7	2.2	5.5

Sources: INE (1989b, 1990)

Table 3.9 *Accumulation Balance Structure for Households (percentage of GDP)*

	1971	1972	1973	1974	1975	1976	1977	1978	1979	1980	1981	1982	1983	1984	1985	1986	1987	1988	1989
Wages	37.4	36.0	32.7	32.4	34.0	35.0	35.0	32.8	33.9	34.1	32.2	31.5	31.7	43.1	32.3	24.1	26.3	27.0	27.9
Operating Surplus	42.5	41.1	43.2	40.5	40.1	40.5	38.6	39.6	41.6	41.3	46.2	44.5	48.6	47.5	52.1	47.7	48.6	46.8	45.3
Dist. Prof, interest	3.7	3.0	3.9	3.5	3.5	3.4	3.1	3.4	2.8	2.2	2.7	5.3	-0.2	-1.9	8.0	0.0	0.0	0.0	0.0
Net Other Current	1.0	0.4	0.7	0.4	0.3	0.3	0.2	0.3	0.7	1.6	0.3	-0.1	1.3	3.5	9.1	2.8	2.7	2.5	2.3
Total Income	84.6	80.6	80.5	76.7	77.9	79.1	76.9	76.0	79.0	79.1	81.3	81.1	81.5	92.2	101.5	74.7	77.6	76.2	75.6
Direct Taxes	2.6	2.5	1.4	1.0	0.8	0.8	0.8	1.2	0.7	0.3	0.8	0.2	0.1	0.0	0.0	0.3	0.5	0.6	0.9
Con- sumption	75.8	72.6	70.3	67.5	72.8	72.2	72.0	70.1	67.3	66.9	67.8	66.7	66.2	61.0	62.5	69.6	73.1	71.6	70.5
Gross Savings	6.2	5.5	8.7	8.2	4.2	6.1	4.1	4.7	10.9	11.9	12.7	14.2	15.1	31.3	38.9	4.7	4.1	4.1	4.3
Gr. Fixed Capital Formation	3.8	3.3	4.1	3.7	4.3	3.9	3.5	3.9	3.5	2.4	2.3	2.0	0.9	0.5	1.1	3.1	2.7	2.6	1.6
Stocks Changes	0.9	1.5	1.2	-1.0	1.5	-0.4	-0.1	1.0	1.3	-0.4	-0.5	-5.0	-5.6	-2.3	2.4	1.7	0.8	-0.2	-1.5
Oth.Phys. Asset/ liability	0.0	0.0	0.0	0.0	0.0	0.0	0.0	-0.3	-0.5	0.4	0.1	-0.4	-0.5	-0.7	-0.3	-0.7	0.0	0.0	0.0
Net Borrowing	1.5	0.7	3.4	5.5	-1.5	2.5	0.7	0.1	6.6	9.4	10.8	17.6	20.4	33.7	35.8	0.7	0.5	1.7	4.1

Sources: INE 1989b, 1990

quasi-money demand function for households are presented in Appendix 3.9.

Although both the introduction of different income categories into the analysis and consideration of income shifts among these categories help to understand the behaviour of key variables of the accumulation balance for households (consumption and savings, as well as demand for different financial assets), there are still important institutional differences within each income category that are not captured by the time series available. Wage earnings, for instance, include earnings by skilled and unskilled workers, who are likely to have different saving-investment behaviours. Household profit earnings, on the other hand, include earnings by peasant producers of traditional goods, peasant and small-scale producers of coca and unrefined cocaine, and small-scale firms in urban areas. The saving-investment behaviours of household groups in these income categories are likely to differ substantially.

The rest of the chapter analyses the institutional differences among household categories that determine particular trends in their accumulation balance adjustments. Accumulation balance adjustments for the three main household groups included in the SAM are analysed separately: upper-income and lower-income urban households, and rural households.

3.6.1 Upper-urban households

Modelling of the accumulation balances for upper-income urban households is relatively difficult. Unlike peasant and urban informal sector households, the microeconomic behaviour of upper-urban households in developing countries has not been properly studied. No serious attempts have been made either to develop theoretical models, or to conduct empirical studies on how rich households adjust to the external shocks.

National Accounts statistics only comprise time series on the accumulation balance for households as a single group, without differentiating consumption, investment, domestic asset acquisition, and so on, for the household categories defined in the SAM. Nevertheless, household incomes appear to be categorized according to the incomes attributed to the various factors of production, namely wages, household operating surpluses and dividends. As explained above, since these factor income classes can be associated with different household categories, it is possible to estimate individual functions (such as consumption-savings, demand for money, investment, capital flight, and so on) econometrically for each factor income category and consequently for each household group. This procedure is particularly useful since it enables all the key functions for the different household groups, which are at the core of their accumulation balance adjustments, to be defined.

Within the SAM framework, the social groups included in the 'upper-income household' category were: (a) small-scale producers in activities other than commerce, (b) skilled wage-earners, and (c) owners of companies (rentiers). These income categories form a far from homogeneous household group. It includes members of the upper class, which can be associated with what FitzGerald (1991, p.5) defines as '..the relatively small number of "rentier" (or "capitalist") households, who receive substantial dividends from firms, and are the owners of the equity (as well as most of land and assets abroad)…', and members of the middle class. In principle, however, these groups have in common, albeit with different intensities, a much stronger position within society and can have more effective control over their income and consumption levels. In that respect, Romero (1982 p.314) has pointed out that in Bolivia:

> …the diversity and hierarchies of the various functional components of the middle class have become obvious in relation to power and privilege. Yet, even those groups farthest from the centres of decision, due to apparently more neutral organizations in relation to power, have had sufficient survival capacity and influence to achieve advantages beyond their economic sphere. For example, they have gained advantages in better public services, health, and general living conditions superior to those of the poorer classes. In part, this can be attributed to the use by the middle class of systems of social communication to generate currents favourable to their interests.
>
> It is the middle-class groups, together with the upper classes, who monopolize the advantages of urban development. Almost all the housing with running water, electricity, and public sewers is located in the principal cities, and, within these cities, in the downtown and residential areas with middle and higher income levels. Moreover, the various urban sectors have, in general, better living conditions, as measured by these standards, than those of the rural population. This has occurred

> and has been maintained by the state's constant directing of resources to urban rather than rural areas in an effort to contribute to the political and economic stability in urban centres.

During the 1970s, upper-income urban households benefited from the economic boom and from the large resource transfers from the state. As discussed previously, the large volume of credit allocated to the private sector during the 1970s greatly exceeded the capacity of private companies to use them productively. Therefore, these resources somehow found their way to finance unrecorded imports and capital flight. The middle-class groups (such as government bureaucrats, technocrats in the private and public sectors and transporters) also benefited from the development strategy of that period in that the military government tried to build a much wider base by gaining their support. As Dunkerley (1984, p.227) has pointed out,

> The short-run commodity booms prompted …an expansion in the size and average income of the professional middle class (state spending on services quadrupled), and — in line with the need to accommodate and cater to the new consumerist aspirations of this stratum — a rise in urban construction. While Santa Cruz grew outwards, La Paz expanded both outwards and upwards, with the progressive emergence of ugly but prestigious tower-blocks populated by young middle class escaping the constraints as well as the support structure of their parental homes. Those who directed and funded this activity built themselves opulent suburbs, such as Calacoto and Cota Cota in La Paz, where a conspicuous and competitive consumption was concretised on a scale that would be the envy of many European executives. With the advent of cocaine these redoubts of the elite were supplemented with even more extravagant examples of spacious, arriviste architecture.

During the 1980s, the benefits received by middle-class households were reduced significantly once the state faced far more severe financial constraints, but they were still in a better position to negotiate preferable salaries and benefits compared with other household groups. In addition, certain groups within the middle class benefited enormously from the drugs trade. For instance, besides the rural capitalist groups, another major group in this drug-trafficking power structure was a sector of the Bolivian military which entered the illicit trade in the late 1970s and early 1980s under the leadership of General García Meza and Colonel

Arce Gómez. During the military's 14 years in political power, military officers were able to carve out various economic interests through public land grants, bank credits, and timber and mineral rights concessions from the state. With well-organized political protection, private guards, financial resources, outposts, private landing strips and aircraft, trucks and access to abundant cheap labour, this military group, similar to the other strategically placed elite group, possessed comparative advantages for seizing the lucrative opportunities of the illicit drugs trade.

In summary, upper-income households enjoyed a strong position in Bolivian society that allowed them not only to maintain high living standards but also to accumulate external assets in offshore banks (capital flight). During the 1970s, the main sources of finance for capital flight were the external loans obtained by the public sector that were transferred to the private sector mainly through credit. During the 1970s, coca proceeds became the paramount source of foreign exchange for the country as external credit shrank; therefore, coca-generated foreign exchange overtook external credit as the main source of foreign exchange used by upper-income households in order to finance their accumulation of foreign assets abroad.

In summary, from the discussion of the accumulation balance for capitalist households, it is clear that upper-urban households most of the time enjoyed a relatively strong position to adjust their incomes to desired levels of consumption and investment. Thus it is more likely that the variables on the uses-of-funds side of the balance equation are determined first, and that some of the variables on the sources-of-fund side tended to adjust through different mechanisms.

First, household investment demand essentially comprises the construction of dwellings. As discussed before, household investment has been shown to be significantly correlated (a) positively with a lagged value of the same variable, and (b) negatively with the real international interest rate.

According to econometric results (see Appendix 3.6), the lagged value of investment demand has a very strong positive effect while the real international interest rate has a significant negative effect on household investment. Bank credit however seems not to be significant in explaining upper-urban household investment demand.

Household demand for currency and bank deposits, on the other hand, depends on their current incomes, as well as on the interest rate of alternative assets and inflationary expectations (see Appendices 3.7, 3.8 and 3.9).

The last component on the uses-of-funds side of the balance equation for upper-income households comprises the amount of foreign exchange deposited in offshore banks or held within the country (capital flight).[6] In both cases, capital flight comprises that foreign exchange that did not enter the economy's formal financial channels. According to some estimates, capital flight amounted to US$82.8 million per year during the 1970s and US$413.3 million per year during the 1980s. As explained before, capital flight was financed from different source over the two decades, as the country's access to foreign exchange switched from official sources (banks and official creditors during the 1970s) to unofficial sources (coca proceeds during the 1980s). There is agreement among authors that during both periods capital flight can partly be explained by the fact that Bolivia received amounts of foreign exchange that the country was unable to absorb. Following this line of reasoning, capital flight is determined as the variable that closes the external balance and will be explained in more detail in the following chapter.

The savings of upper-urban households depend on current incomes (that is, distributed profits, dividends, interest earnings and other types of property rent, as well as on the salaries earned by skilled workers in the public and modern private sectors) and on current expenditures (consumption and direct tax payments).

Household incomes comprise dividends and wages earned by skilled wage-earners. As discussed above, dividends tended to remain relatively unchanged, showing the desire to secure constant flows of income to finance sophisticated lifestyles. Wage earnings, on the other hand, depend on the wage rate for skilled workers, which tends to be highly indexed to inflation, and on the level of employment.

Consumption by capitalists is not likely to act as the sink variable in the overall balance equation for the sector. Upper-urban households try to maintain levels of consumption according to their social position and secure finance later. An aggregated consumption function for households was estimated (see Appendix 3.5). As in the case of demand functions for financial assets, different income categories were included in that consumption function, enabling the identification of which part of total household consumption can be attributed to capitalist households.

Finally, upper-urban households seek to stabilize their levels of current income by maintaining a steady flow of distributed profits from companies in the case of rentiers (or by negotiating higher wages in the case of skilled workers), and by obtaining finance through increased bank credit. However, bank credit to households was rather limited over the periods under analysis, representing at most an amount equivalent to only 5.5 per cent of bank portfolios over the whole period. In fact, most of the domestic credit acquired by the private non-financial sector came in the form of loans to firms. However, there is evidence that companies did not always use those loans to finance productive investment within the firm, but to finance activities other than those for which the loans were obtained. As Torrico (1982, p.271) notes, '...loan delinquency was very high. By 1975, 47 per cent of BAB [Bolivian Agricultural Bank]'s portfolio was in arrears mostly due to heavy delinquency experienced in cotton, soya-beans and beef cattle in the Oriente. The State Bank also experienced heavy delinquency. A consequence was that the credit institution lost considerable income and lending capacity...'.

3.6.2 Lower-urban households

To construct a behavioural model for the accumulation balance for lower-urban households this section first attempts to identify the most relevant institutional features of the behaviour of urban households both from a theoretical perspective and from the point of view of the Bolivian reality.

In general, urban-poor households comprise "unskilled" wage-earners working in the private (companies) and public (government and state enterprises) sectors; and the self-employed in the so-called informal sector.

There is a tendency in most developing countries towards what has been called a deproletarization of the labour force, or the informalization of the economy. Past experiences in developing countries in general and in Bolivia in particular, have demonstrated that job generation by the modern sector of the economy is not sufficient to absorb the increasing labour surpluses of urban areas (Carbonetto 1985). This surplus is the result of a combination of factors: on the one hand, the relatively small sizes of incorporated firms, and the labour-saving technology they use, reduce labour absorption within the entrepreneurial sector, and on the other, the rapidly increasing labour supply, stimulated by strong migratory flows from rural to urban areas. Workers who are unable to find jobs in the modern sector seek alternative sources of employment and income in a wide variety of activities, including small household-based production and trade units.

The concept of an urban informal sector (UIS) (PREALC 1978, Sethuraman 1976) has been widely adopted in developing countries to explain the behaviour of this heterogeneous group of economic activities in urban areas which provide alternative employment for the urban poor. Following the ILO/PREALC approach, Sethuraman (1981, p.17) defines the informal sector as consisting of '...small-scale units engaged in the production and distribution of goods and services with the primary objective of generating employment and income to their participants notwithstanding the constraints on capital, both physical and human, and know-how'. In the same vein, FitzGerald and Vos (1989, p.48) give a more comprehensive definition of such non-corporate enterprises:

> This category embraces a wide range of activities by peasants, artisans, petty traders and so on, and which take place in competitive markets. Their main source of income is the profit earned in the small enterprise, including the imputed incomes of their own-account worker and the family labour he or she employs. Consumption, production, savings and investment decisions take place within the same unit on the basis of the total household income. Their investments largely take the form of purchasing equipment or expanding labour employment in order to enhance production and income. This investment is limited by available resources, which typically consists of their own surplus income (savings) plus credit from informal money lenders and some rationed amount of government credit channelled through state-owned development banks. Their main relation to the formal banking system, if any, is as depositors.

This approach to the urban informal sector has been challenged by many authors on the grounds that the informal economy is not always a set of survival activities performed by destitute people on the margins of society. According to Castells and Portes (1989, p.12), '...studies in both advanced and less developed countries have shown the economic dynamism of unregulated income-generating activities and the relatively high level of income of many informal entrepreneurs, sometimes above the level of workers in the formal economy'.

The urban informal sector in Bolivia, however, is largely linked to material survival, in contrast with findings of research elsewhere (see Uribe-Echeverría 1991). In those case studies, productive industrial capital articulates with a wide series of informal activities. In the case of Bolivia, such connections are absent. Although some productive activities can be found within the urban informal sector, the liberalization of customs regulations and the growth in contraband has eroded long-standing informal activities such as the manufacture of low-cost footwear and clothing (Blanes Jimenez 1989). This tendency has accentuated over time due to the economic recession.

Therefore, the ILO/PREALC approach to the informal urban sector is retained as the basic theoretical framework in the modelling of the Bolivian urban informal sector. The main elements of this approach are as follows.

(a) The informal sector represents an employment alternative for workers who cannot be absorbed into the entrepreneurial sector (private or public). The fact that the entrepreneurial and public sectors cannot absorb a large part of the labour force, gives informal employment a structural character. Therefore, UIS units can no longer be regarded merely as temporary alternatives for the urban unemployed. A large proportion of these workers are employed within the UIS, and do not compete for jobs in the organized sector of the labour market (Carbonetto 1985, p.6).

    There is also a cyclical component within UIS employment that is related to the economic activity and aggregate demand fluctuations (ibid, p.7). Although output and employment in some informal activities depend on aggregate demand resulting from income generated in the formal sector (in commerce and services, for example), employment tends to be anti-cyclical vis-à-vis formal sector activity. It increases in times of low activity in the formal sector and declines when this sector expands; therefore, in times of economic recession there is a strong tendency for per capita incomes in informal units to deteriorate (FitzGerald 1976).

(b) The organizational structures adopted by informal economic units essentially respond to household survival strategies. This element distinguishes informal economic units from those operating in the capitalist sector, which mainly follow capital accumulation and profitability criteria (Moller 1980).

The survival objectives that characterize the behaviour of informal units tend to be the same in times of economic boom and of economic recession (Escóbar 1990, p.11). In periods of rapid economic expansion, some informal units can attain some capital accumulation and expand economic activity. However, there is an attitude of risk aversion aimed at guaranteeing the activity's permanence in the long run and consequently the continuity of family consumption. Likewise, in periods of recession, characterized by low income levels and profit margins, informal units tend to stay within the market. Although they are largely underpaid during these periods, they at least secure some kind of income in order to complement the incomes of other family members and therefore satisfy the basic needs of all members of the household.

(c) Another important feature of informal economic units is related to the way they are articulated to the rest of the economy. Normally, informal activities are dependent on entrepreneurial units. First, UIS activities can cover only narrow market segments that are not or are only partially covered by the entrepreneurial sector. These segments expand and contract, depending on the expansion and contraction of formal sector activities. The activities covered by UIS units tend to be located in highly competitive tertiary or service sector activities, ranging from teashops to garbage collection, from street entertainers to shoeshine boys, where sellers deal directly with the buyers of their services. As start-up costs and profit margins are low, these occupations rarely have markets for hired labour. Others cover more complex organizations such as small-scale manufacturers, repair shops, and cheap restaurants, where the need for a division of labour leads to the hiring of wage labour.

Second, UIS are subordinated to the activities of the entrepreneurial sector through generic mercantile relations (purchase and sale of goods and services); and through specific mercantile relations (subcontracting some parts of the productive process). Both types of relations generally imply value transfers from informal to entrepreneurial units. The mechanisms through which these transfers take place are: (1) price differentials against UIS units resulting from the purchase of inputs, materials and services, and low demand for UIS goods and services by the entrepreneurial sector (unequal exchange); (2) UIS engaged in commerce activities contribute to the distribution of commodities produced by the formal sector at very low cost, reducing industrial and commercial capital transport and distribution costs; and (3) by subcontracting parts of the productive process, incorporated enterprises save social benefit payments, depreciation of machinery and equipment, overtime work costs, and so on.

A third form of articulation that also implies a transfer of value to the capitalist sector is related to the labour force reproduction. This can take place in two ways: (1) The existence of the UIS allows capitalists to pay low wages. The possibility that some other family members can contribute to the household's basic consumption with incomes from informal activities, plus the scarcity of waged employment opportunities, force workers to accept low wages in state-run and entrepreneurial sectors. This situation obviously promotes accumulation in the entrepreneurial sector and facilitates government expenditure-reducing policies through the reduction of wages and salaries. (2) Informal units produce goods and services aimed at satisfying the demand of low-income groups (wage earners and other self-employed workers), thus contributing to the overall labour force reproduction.

As mentioned above, over the last two decades there has been a general change in the employment structure of lower-urban households as the importance of the informal sector in the Bolivian economy has increased (see Table 3.10). During the 1970s, employment and income for lower-urban households depended mostly on the formal sector. According to the 1976 census, 46.2 per cent of total urban employment was concentrated in the public and entrepreneurial sectors, while 42.6 per cent depended on family-based units and small-scale enterprises. The employment structure completely changed during the 1980s when economic growth and employment in the formal sector contracted. In 1980, informal employment already comprised 53 per cent of total urban employment, while formal employment fell to 42 per cent. During the economic crisis of the early 1980s, formal employment fell even further, to 38 per cent of the total urban employment, while informal employment increased to 55 per cent. In 1989, after four years of the stabilization and structural adjustment programmes, informal employment increased to 61 per cent while formal employment fell to 34 per cent. This trend further consolidated during the 1990s: in 1995, informal urban employment increased to more than 6 per cent of total urban employment, while formal employment decreased to 32 per cent. These figures show very clearly that a process of 'deproletarization' or 'informalization' of the Bolivian urban labour force has been occurring over the last two decades (Toranzo and Arrieta 1989). The high growth rates of informal employment have been concentrated in family-based units which provided jobs for increasing numbers of urban unemployed, not just for those expelled from the entrepreneurial or small enterprise sectors, but also for new entrants to the urban labour force, mostly unskilled and inexperienced women and young workers.

Informal employment growth has been concentrated in the tertiary sector of the economy. Commercial and service activities have attracted growing numbers of people in recent years; between 1985 and 1995, the proportion increased from 31 to 41 per cent of total urban employment, whereas informal employment in manufacturing maintained its share at about 13 per cent (see Table 3.11).

The rapid growth in informal employment in services, construction and commerce-related activities is associated with much lower levels of

Table 3.10 Urban employment structure: principal cities (percentage of total urban employment)

Sectors	1976[1]	1980[2]	1985[3]	1990[4]	1995[5]
Total	100	100	100	100	100
Formal Sector	46.2	42.0	37.9	34.6	32.5
Public Sector	34.0	24.0	23.7	17.5	12.9
Private Sector	12.2	18.0	14.2	17.1	19.6
Informal Sector	42.6	53.0	55.4	61.4	66.7
Small Enterprises	14.2	17.0	17.5	15.6	21.6
Family-based Units	28.4	36.0	37.9	38.9	39.7
Domestic Services	11.2	5.0	4.6	6.9	5.4

Sources: 1. INE (1978), 2. INE (1980), which covers only the city of La Paz, 3. INE (1988), 4. INE (1995)

Table 3.11 Informal employment by economic activity (percentage of total urban employment)

	1985[a]			1990[b]			1995[b]		
	Small Enterprises	Family-based Units	Total Informal	Small Enterprises	Family-based Units	Total Informal	Small Enterprises	Family-based Units	Total Informal
Manufacturing	6.2	6.9	13.1	4.3	5.8	10.1	5.7	7.6	13.3
Commerce	3	19.9	22.9	2.6	20.2	22.8	6.0	23.3	29.4
Services	3.8	4.7	8.6	4.7	14.6	19.3	3.1	9.0	12.1
Construction	2.5	2	4.5	1.6	2.2	3.8	4.0	2.2	6.1
Transport	2.1	2.4	4.5	1.5	2.4	3.9	1.8	1.8	3.6
Other Activities	2	1.9	3.9	0.7	0.5	1.3	1.0	1.2	2.2
Total	*19.6*	*37.9*	*57.5*	*15.5*	*45.7*	*61.2*	*21.6*	*45.0*	*66.6*

Sources: [a] INE (1988), [b] INE (1995)

income and with an ever increasing subsistence objective pursued by most informal workers. The fairly low levels of capital and skills required to start up most of the informal commercial and service activities explain the preference of informal workers to enter this sector.

On the other hand, the share of transport in total urban employment contracted between 1985 and 1990. These activities normally require working and fixed capital that cannot be secured when the units are working at a subsistence level.

In summary, from the above discussion the importance of differentiating the strictly survival motivations of informal units engaged in service from those engaged in non-service activities becomes clear. Total employment of members of lower-urban households can thus be divided into three groups: those employed in the formal modern sector as wage labourers; the self-employed in non-service activities such as construction and manufacturing; and the self-employed in service and commercial activities.

The breakdown of informal employment into service and non-service activities is aimed at capturing the increasing survival motivation that characterizes the informal units engaged in service and commercial activities as opposed to those working in other sectors (such as manufacturing). Following the rationale of the previous discussion, employment in modern activities is correlated with the activity levels shown by these specific sectors.[7] Based on the data shown in Table 3.11, we can argue that employment in small firms and family-based units engaged in manufacturing and construction (that is, in non-service activities), tend to be pro-cyclical with the activity level in the sector.

Employment in the service and commercial sectors, on the other hand, acts as the sink variable for employment for urban-poor workers. Start-up costs are very low, so that informal labourers who cannot secure jobs in the incorporated firms and small enterprises are forced to undertake commercial and service activities, which constitute their last income alternative.

The total income received by lower-urban households comes from two sources: from wage earnings and from the profits of informal units. Wage earnings depend on the level of employment of unskilled workers in the modern sector (which depend on the activity levels of these sectors) and on the wage rate, which is determined institutionally; that is, the government fixes the minimum national wage rate.

Informal profits depend on the quantities actually sold and on the profit margins which are the difference between the price at which goods and services are sold and the unit costs of intermediate inputs used in production. There are some arguments that support the hypothesis of the existence of fixed mark-up determined in terms of the subsistence strategy of informal units. A number of authors maintain that the incomes of informal units cannot be lower than the minimum required for subsistence; two arguments are used to support this hypothesis (De La Piedra 1986). First, there is price collusion among informal workers, aimed at protecting informal units against increases in the supply of similar goods. Second, the very permanence of the activity would be jeopardized if the income generated were not enough to cover the minimum required for subsistence.

According to Escóbar (1990, p.63), the price collusion mechanism can be detected among informal units operating in Bolivian urban areas. Therefore, the deterioration of the incomes of informal units is principally explained by the sharp reduction observed in their activity levels over the last decade.

Production and income generated by informal units have followed a pro-cyclical pattern vis-à-vis activity in the formal private and government sectors. During the 1970s, informal units expanded following the overall economic boom, and were able to generate surpluses for investment and, consequently, to expand production and employment. The growth of informal units was essentially endogenous, since their own surpluses were not complemented with additional resources from the financial system. After 1978, when the formal economy started moving into a recession, informal units contracted. This obviously affected their capacity to generate surpluses for investment, so that production and employment in non-service sectors contracted. After the NEP was implemented, income and activity in the formal sector adjusted downwards. The outcome was a sharp reduction in income and employment in non-service informal units. Informal employment in commercial and service activities, on the other hand, increased sharply while average incomes fell. As Escóbar (ibid, p.2) points out: '...each new vendor that starts his activities in the streets and markets, can only generate a small income taking clients from other street vendors'. As a result, the already very low average income of all informal workers has fallen even further.

This type of employment is essentially adopted as a means of material survival, so that the capacity of informal units to generate income for investment almost disappears.

The access of lower-urban households to bank credit is very limited. A survey of small-scale firms and family-based units carried out by CEDLA (1989) demonstrated that low capitalization level of informal units,[8] their low capacity to compete in the markets, and the low or non-existent profit margins they can obtain severely limit their access to credit.

Based on the previous discussion, we can argue that given the limited access of lower-urban households to other sources of funds, their savings capacity largely determines investment. The savings capacity of informal units will increase when the levels of activity and income are higher. Under these circumstances, informal units can expand investment and productive capacity. On the other hand, savings would almost disappear when incomes are so low that they can only cover consumption. However, in recessions savings cannot be negative given the low capacity of lower-urban households to obtain finance from other sources.

According to household surveys carried out by the National Statistics Institute (INE) in 1987 and 1989, the proportion of workers with incomes lower than, or very close to the cost of the basic family food basket[9] was 54 per cent in 1987 and 70 per cent in 1989 (INE 1989a). A survey carried out by CEDLA (1989)[10] indicated that the bulk of informal workers interviewed complained that their current income levels could cover only the direct cost of production, family consumption and in some cases the reposition of capital, leaving no net savings for reinvestment. Therefore, investment acts as the closure for the accumulation balance for lower urban households.

3.6.3 Rural households

The ways in which rural households adjust their balances in response to external shocks have tended to vary over the last two decades. During the 1970s, rural households adjusted to external shocks in a rather passive fashion. Their lack of access to credit, low productivity, weak competitive positions in goods and labour markets, coupled with restrictive development policies have tended to undermine the sector's potential, and output remained largely stagnant. Rural households did not benefit from the relatively large capital flows that entered the country in the 1970s. Between 1975 and 1979, the output of traditional crops fell by 7 per cent; as a result, incomes investment and consumption steadily deteriorated.

During the 1980s the situation for peasant households engaged in the production of traditional crops such as potatoes and maize did not change substantially. The constraints faced by rural households during the 1970s were aggravated by the severe economic crisis of the early 1980s. Moreover, agricultural output fell by 41 per cent in 1983 and by 13 per cent in 1989 due to extremely adverse weather conditions, and incomes, consumption and investment contracted even further.

Starting from 1980, however, a number of Bolivian peasants became engaged in the booming production of coca and unrefined cocaine, making this the most profitable crop for peasants. Between 1979 and 1989 the production of coca leaves expanded by more than 500 per cent. Coca growers enjoyed substantial increases in their income and consumption levels. However, as will be discussed in the following sections, peasants benefited only marginally from the windfall gains from coca since the bulk of the surpluses were extracted from them by international drug traffickers.

3.6.3.1 Institutional features

In order to gain a better insight into the main equilibrating mechanisms in the accumulation balance for rural households, it may be useful to define more clearly the institutional characteristics of peasant households, both from a theoretical point of view and from the perspective of the Bolivian reality.

In the process of constructing an economic definition of peasant households, Ellis (1988, p.4) has identified the most important features that characterize peasants, both as a social group and as an economic unit of production and consumption:

(a) Peasants as a social group are always part of a larger economic system (Wolf 1966), in that they participate in exchange with the larger system, and that their production is exposed in some degree to market forces. The inputs and outputs of peasant farms are subject to valuation by the wider market at prevailing prices, even if households participate in markets for only a small proportion of their requirements. This characteristic can be found in Bolivian rural societies. Although household production has subsistence objectives, Bolivian peasants are related to the markets somehow. As Romero (1982, p.305) points out: 'Few of the farm families are completely self-sufficient; the majority are oriented, in varying degrees, toward some production for the market'. Besides, peasants depend on the markets for goods such as sugar, salt and cooking oil.

(b) Peasants are subordinated to other economic groups. The idea of subordination implies unequal social or cultural status, coercion of one social group by another, and unequal access to political power. Most relevant for us is that it also implies the economic domination of peasants by other social groups. Urioste (1989, p.17) argues that '...peasant societies in Bolivia, specially those settled in the highlands, can be considered as being the object of domination by other groups, specially by those settled in urban areas'.

The economic and political system in which the peasant must operate often serves to his disadvantage and keeps him in an an economic situation that inhibits the growth of his income level. An example within this system is the typical marketing system for basic foodstuffs in rural areas. Here the peasant is subjected to middlemen and low product prices, both of which contribute to the exploitation of the peasant, with its consequent negative influence on the conditions of peasant life. This exploitation exists because of the conditions of production in which the peasants of the altiplano and the mountain valleys work, and because of the minimal pressure peasants are able to exert on the political decision centres. The fact that the middlemen virtually control local markets is not, in itself, a sufficient explanation of the mechanisms by which part of the peasant wealth passes to other sectors of society. In many cases the middleman has been replaced by cooperatives or other marketing structures. The low product prices, however, have been maintained. The level of prices for traditional products reflects not only market supply and demand, but also, in large measure, the government's policy of keeping food prices low in order to benefit the urban consumer. The weak position of peasants in the power structure has not enabled them to effectively counteract the urban pressures on the government to maintain low prices.

(c) Peasants are not a uniform (homogeneous) set of farm families all with the same status and prospects within their communities. On the contrary, peasant societies are always and everywhere typified by internal differentiations along many lines. In Bolivia there are three distinguishable peasant groups: first, a group where subsistence farming predominates; second, a group where subsistence farming is mixed with market-oriented farming; and third, a group of peasants engaged in the production of coca and its by-products.

The first group consists of various small communities and ex-haciendas located principally on the southern and central high plains or altiplano. The small size of farms, poor quality of land, rudimentary technology of production, and difficult communications have contributed to a very low level of productivity in the zone. Furthermore, the soil has been severely exhausted by intensive use, and in any given year, two-thirds of the land has to be kept idle to allow soils to regenerate. Most farmers cultivate low-productivity small farms to produce staples and vegetables (potatoes, maize, beans, quinoa, and so on). They have poor links to markets and credit institutions, and sell on average less than 30 per cent of their output (World Bank 1990).

The major efforts of these peasants are directed to the bare survival of the family unit. Their extreme marginality often means that collective peasant action takes the form of a withdrawal from modern society. The result of this decision is the abandonment of all efforts to learn in terms of the larger social medium, and the limitations of aspirations to the narrow community framework. The maintenance of traditional values and roles works against economic advancement for these peasants and for their participation in the national society; in fact it tends to lead to an increase in their marginality. (Romero 1982, p.305)

The second group includes the majority of peasants located in the regions of the mountain valleys and altiplano, where land reform was introduced. The predominant crops grown by this second group are traditional: potatoes, barley, quinoa, wheat and corn. Livestock and poultry production is also common. Production techniques, which continue to be quite archaic, are labour intensive and usually use only animal power.

The family is the principal unit of production. Except on rare occasions, paid workers are not employed, and the traditional forms of labour sharing and cooperation are sufficient to satisfy farm labour requirements even in periods of high demand. Despite the low productivity levels, relatively favourable weather and soil conditions allow two-crop farming in the region. Production often covers the needs of the national market for many basic foodstuffs.

The third group of peasants comprises those engaged in the production of coca and unrefined cocaine. Given the special conditions in which these activities are developed, this group has a completely different saving-investment behaviour from that of other peasants. However, they cannot be regarded as a non-peasant socioeconomic group.

(d) Peasants are farmers since they obtain their livelihoods from the land, mainly by the cultivation of crops, although livestock may have varying degrees of importance within their farm system. The small-farm sector in Bolivia represents over 95 per cent of the rural population and produces approximately 80 per cent of the value of all agricultural crop production.

(e) Peasants, as farmers, have access to the resource of land as the basis of their livelihood. An important attribute of peasants worldwide is the significance of non-market criteria in the allocation of land. In Bolivia, the size of landholdings of farmers practising traditional agriculture range from half a hectare in the vicinity of Lake Titicaca and the Cochabamba Valley, to 15–25 hectares in some of the drier areas of the altiplano and mountain valley regions. Approximately 55 per cent of the properties in these zones are less than 5 hectares in size, and more than two-thirds of them are fewer than 10 hectares. The relatively small sizes of farms in traditional agriculture are largely the result of the land reforms implemented in 1953, which broke up large estates and parcelled them out to landless peasants (Whitaker and Wennergren 1982; J.A. Morales 1990).

(f) It is generally agreed that reliance on family labour is a defining economic characteristic of peasants. In Bolivia, family labour is used intensively in land preparation, seeding, insect and weed control, livestock management, and harvesting, and in domestic activities such as spinning and weaving. Labour is the most important of all productive factors and is supplied almost exclusively by the family, augmented by traditional community labour pools.

(g) Bolivian agriculture mainly comprises small farms with traditional production technologies and subsistence consumption (World Bank 1990; R. Morales 1984; Urioste 1989a-b; Ministerio de Planeamiento y Coordinación 1989). Traditional production techniques are utilized in most of the small-farm sector; the influences of the ancient Inca civilization and the colonial period are still evident. Primitive ploughs and digging tools, animals or humans for motive power, and indigenous varieties of seeds and animals are common. The family is usually extended, mainly of Quechua or Aymara origin, and adults, especially women, generally speak little or no Spanish.

(h) Perhaps the most popular defining feature of peasants used by economists is the subsistence basis of their livelihood. Subsistence refers to the proportion of farm output that is directly consumed by the household rather than sold in the market. The degree of subsistence is one of the reasons why the integration of peasants into the market economy is only partial.

Bolivian rural households consume a large part of their production. As stated before, only 30 per cent of agricultural output reaches the market. Households' total cash income depends not only on the marketable surplus but also on prices. Since the demand for agricultural products in Bolivia is price-inelastic (elasticity was on average –0.73 during the 1980s), an increase in agricultural output and therefore in marketable surpluses tends to move relative prices against the sector. As a consequence, the cash incomes of rural households fall in relative terms. This, in turn, might lend to a fall in their consumption of goods and services purchased in the market.

This discussion provides the criteria required in order to model the accumulation balance for rural households. For the purposes of this analysis, rural households are divided into two groups: peasants engaged in the production of traditional crops, and those engaged in the production of coca leaves and unrefined cocaine. The accumulation balances for these two groups are analysed separately, but the existing socioeconomic links between them are discussed and incorporated in the model.

3.6.3.2 Rural household producers of traditional crops

This category includes peasants who produce traditional agricultural products and have limited or no marketable surpluses; and those who produce traditional agricultural products and, although poor, have some small production surplus.

Barnum and Squire (1979) have developed and applied a model of a farm household that is suitable for explaining the behaviour of Bolivian peasant households, and this is used as a basis for the model of rural households developed in this thesis. The assumptions of the Barnum-Squire model are as follows:

(a) There exists a market for labour so that farm households are able to hire out labour at a given market wage.
(b) The land available to the farm household is fixed, at least during the production cycle under study.
(c) The total labour time available to the household can be allocated either to farm work or to other activities (such as wage labour off the farm).
(d) An important choice for households is that between their own consumption of output and sale of output in order to purchase non-farm consumption needs.

A central feature of the Barnum-Squire model is that it achieves an accurate representation of the multiple goals of the household, the interaction between those goals, and their impacts on the response of the household to changing circumstances. According to this model, rural households have to face a trade-off: to use their available time for farm work or for wage work off the farm, or to produce crops for their own consumption or for sale in the market. Although these trade-offs are included in the Bolivian model for rural households, they are made less flexible in the sense that the alternatives open to small farmers are determined, to a large extent, outside the decision power of rural households.

Given the reliance of peasant households on family labour, it can be taken as the most relevant and representative factor of production (Urioste 1989b). Since labour is the most important input for peasant households, the time available has to be allocated among a number of alternative activities: wage work off the farm, mostly in the modern agricultural sector; activities related to the production of coca and its by-products; and all farm activities, including both those related to the agricultural production, and the investment activities within the farm, such as house building and repair and land improvement. The bulk of this time is used for agricultural tasks, but part is left for other farm duties that can be regarded as investment activities, usually related to house construction and repair, improvements to and preparation of new land to expand future production.[11] Assuming that the number of person-days devoted to investment activities within the farm is proportional to the number of person-days devoted to farming activities, then rural household investment would be proportional to the total person-days devoted to farm activities.

Investment by peasants is not closely linked to markets. Given the low capital intensity of peasant agriculture, investment does not involve machinery and equipment acquisitions, but rather tools created by the peasants themselves. As many authors have pointed out (Whitaker and Wennergren 1982, Urioste 1989b), the level of investment in fixed capital, animals, machines, building, and irrigation infrastructure is relatively low, and much of what does exist has been created with heavy labour inputs. Livestock production is a principal subsistence activity of much of the small-farm sector but does provide some income from commercial sales. Livestock is raised on native ranges, generally with no modern management. The results are depleted ranges and inferior animals.

Total production is determined by the number of person-hours devoted to farm activities. However, weather conditions constitute a variable that has played a very important role in determining agricultural output in Bolivia.

The second trade-off faced by rural households is related to the decision to produce for their own consumption or for sale in the market. Urioste (ibid, p.146) found that half of the total production by rural farmers in the northern highlands of Bolivia is used for their own consumption. Furthermore, taking into account the amount of output used for seed, rural households consume as much as 70 per cent of their production. Consequently, the activities of the bulk of rural people are subsistence-oriented, only partially involved in the market economy (Whitaker and Wennergren 1982). J.A. Morales (1990) however, argues that the marketed surpluses are to some extent responsive to agricultural price changes, but production is not necessarily elastic. All these arguments may imply that self-consumption by rural households is mainly determined by their own subsistence needs, but it is also slightly responsive to the sector's relative prices vis-à-vis manufacturing prices. This model of agricultural production was also adopted by UDAPE (1990c, p.126). Due to lack of data, however, the elasticity coefficient of marketable agricultural surpluses vis-à-vis agricultural price changes is difficult to calculate.

Finally, rural households have to maintain an additional balance, which is that between their monetary incomes and monetary outlays. This budget constraint states that households' total sources of monetary funds have to be equal to their monetary outlays:

Rural households' sources of monetary funds comprise: the proceedings of the agricultural output surplus sold in the market; wage incomes from off-farm work; and loans obtained from banks during the period.

The uses of funds are, basically, the consumption of goods and services purchased in the market, and purchases of intermediate inputs.

The variables included in the sources-of-funds act more as constraints in the accumulation balance for rural households. This statement is supported by a number of arguments:

(a) Agricultural production very often depends on factors that are beyond rural households' control, such as the weather conditions. Monetary incomes also depend on prices that are, most of the time, determined in very fluctuating markets.
(b) Wage incomes depend on modern agricultural activity levels and on a wage rate determined by capitalists in the modern agricultural sector.
(c) Sample survey data show that Bolivian rural households have very limited access to bank credit (Miller and Ladman 1982). An extensive survey of small-farm households in 1977 showed that only 6.7 per cent of farmers used agricultural credit during the agricultural year (Riordan 1977). The major impediments to borrowing are the small scale of operations, as measured by the amount of usable land, borrower's transaction costs that arise from loan paperwork, use of Indian language, remoteness from financial markets, little education and low degree of market integration. This situation has not changed substantially over the last 12 years (World Bank 1990, Schuh 1991). The Bolivian Agricultural Bank (BAB), the only na-

tional credit institution for which the majority of loans are supposed to be directed towards small farmers, '...in reality has provided subsidized credit to powerful friends of (especially) the military governments' (World Bank ibid).

3.6.3.3 Coca-producing rural households

Although the production of coca leaves and the initial stages of cocaine refining are carried out by small farmers, the nature of this activity makes their saving-investment behaviour completely different from those of all other rural households. For this reason, the accumulation balance for coca producers is analysed separately.

First, coca leaf production is labour intensive, so that the quantities produced are closely related to the number of peasants engaged in coca harvesting. Coca leaf production grew by 7 per cent per year during most of the 1970s, and by 26 per cent between 1978 and 1988. This sharp increase was mostly associated with the larger number of people who migrated to coca-producing regions in response to much higher income opportunities offered by coca-cocaine activities vis-à-vis other sectors of the economy. As Healy (1986, p.110) has pointed out, 'The rapidly increasing unemployment and impoverishment of the Bolivian workforce made the comparatively high income opportunities associated with the coca leaf and cocaine boom extremely attractive for the poorest segments of society'.

A 1981 household survey by CERES, a Bolivian social research centre, gives some background on the small farmers producing coca leaf in the tropical Chapare lowlands of the Department of Cochabamba (Flores and Blanes 1984). The survey findings show that most small-scale farmers of the Chapare are former highlanders who resettled and cleared land for food and coca production, and in some cases received land titles from the state. The majority of families came to the tropical Chapare lowlands from neighbouring Cochabamba Valley. Another significant percentage of smallholders migrated from the department of Potos, one of Bolivia's poorest regions.

The study indicates that 62 per cent per cent of these farmers were without lands in their highland home communities prior to migration. Of those who did possess land in their home communities, 50 per cent owned one hectare or less (Flores and Blanes ibid.). These figures underscore the poverty levels that have pushed numerous peasant families into the coca-growing area in pursuit of improved livelihoods over the past 15 years.

Seasonal migration to the lowlands allows highland peasants to complement their low incomes from underpriced highland cash crops with rural wage labour. The temporary migrant farmers work as wage labourers for smallholders who own or control land, or both, in the Chapare. Some members of this group of temporary migrants eventually resettle permanently to grow coca and tropical food crops on their own, but this change only takes place over a number of years.

There are no reliable estimates of the number of people involved in the production of coca. Some estimates are based on the number of hectares and on an estimated labour coefficient per harvested hectare. According to the 1986 Triennial Plan, 15,000 families were engaged in the production of coca leaves in 1978. MACA estimates that during that year, 19,000 hectares were harvested (MACA 1989), producing 38,000 tons of coca leaves (MACA, ibid). According to these figures, the labour productivity coefficient in 1977 was 2.5 tons of coca leaves per worker per year.

Without changing this coefficient, UDAPE (1990b) estimates that in 1987, there were around 60,000 coca growers in the Yungas in the Department of La Paz, and the Chapare region. In that year the total area harvested was 61,000 hectares and total production reached 151,000 tons (MACA, ibid). Likewise, UDAPE (ibid) estimates that in 1989 there were 56,000 coca producers, harvesting 55,700 hectares, with a total production of 139,000 tons.

All of these estimates assume that there is a fixed coefficient between the number of people involved in coca harvesting and the volume of coca actually produced

Another point of concern is related to the way in which coca output is allocated. Part of the production is devoted to traditional uses and part is used in the illegal production of drugs.

Traditional coca leaf production and marketing have been legal for consumption by 1.5 million coca leaf chewers among the rural population, mostly peasants and miners. There are several estimates of traditional coca consumption. UDAPE (ibid) put traditional coca-leaf consumption at 24,000 tons per year, whereas official estimates (Triennial Anti-Narcotics Plan 1987) are much lower, at only around 10,000 tons (10 per cent of total production in 1986). The remainder, which is the bulk of the coca-leaf production, is utilized in the production of cocaine. The seemingly insatiable demand for cocaine in the developed countries has been responsible for driving up both the price and the levels of production of coca leaf (Sage 1989, p.43).

In an effort to even out coca leaf price fluctuations and retain more value from their own labour power, small farmers have increasingly entered the first stages of coca processing and started dealing in coca paste rather than coca leaves.[12] The conversion is a relatively straightforward operation, involving the mixing of leaves, kerosene and lime in a macerating pit lined with polythene. Casual labourers (pisadores) are generally employed to help with the carrying of materials and the barefoot treading of leaves in the pit, although the operation remains firmly at the level of household production (Sage ibid, p.43).

The involvement of small peasants in the illicit processing of coca has brought them large income gains. Flores and Blanes (1984) found that coca-producing peasants enjoy the highest incomes of the smallholder class in Bolivia. Sage (ibid, p.43) argues that '...the cocaine industry has become "democratized" by allowing small producers to increase their participation and benefit from the higher income deriving from the sale of coca paste'.[13] Therefore, small-scale coca producers have been able to generate large incomes that no other small-scale farming sector in Bolivia has been able to achieve during the national economic recession of the 1980s.

According to many authors, a large part of the potential coca surplus is extracted from peasants; according to Sage (ibid, p.54), '...although the gross incomes of coca producers are potentially high, much of the value generated by the producers' labour is accumulated outside of the region'. There are many ways in which the surplus is extracted from petty producers. Merchant capital, which has performed such an influential role in shaping the character of regional economies, has quickly exploited the possibilities for high profits offered by trading in narcotics, and has come to dominate the Chapare. Thus intermediaries obtain coca paste from producers in exchange for contraband – cars, motorcycles, and domestic appliancesa – a transaction which, though it locks up capital in commodities for a longer period, generates the greatest returns from unequal exchange. Sage (ibid, p.44) argues that '... large numbers of merchants and traders operate in the zone. These are involved in buying coca paste, using US dollars or offering automobiles and motorcycles in exchange; selling ingredients for processing operations (kerosene, sulphuric acid, lime, and toilet paper)'.[14]

Besides such ingredients, merchant capital also supplies contraband consumer goods – household appliances, cars and other luxury items such as alcohol, cigarettes, and even foodstuffs; sales of foreign goods are booming while production in the Chapare stagnates – other than cocaine. The declining production of staples has increased the region's reliance upon the market to satisfy its basic food needs. This, together with a rapid monetization of the economy but with the US dollars as the main currency, has fuelled an inflationary cost of living, making the Chapare the most expensive region in Bolivia.

In summary, from this discussion we can argue that rural households essentially secure their social reproduction from the cultivation and primary processing of coca leaves. Despite the appearance of conspicuous consumption, the production process itself is not capitalized and transformed. Once capital acquires the coca paste or base, further refining and movement is accompanied by an exponential rise in prices.

The extraction of surpluses from petty producers by merchant capital takes place through relative prices. The price of coca and coca paste received by petty producers is determined by merchants based on the mark-up they want to obtain, given the international price of cocaine and the technical coefficient of transforming coca paste into its more refined stages.

Coca-producers' demand for financial assets has been augmented due to the increased foreign exchange earnings derived from coca production. During the 1980s, within the Chapare region, there was a marked increase in the monetization of the peasant economy with the US dollar as the main currency, and a breakdown of the reciprocal labour patterns and mutual support structures characteristic of local Andean life (Flores and Blanes 1984).

As discussed previously, income from coca production has been used to buy durable imported consumer goods (such as wrist watches, refrigerators, stoves, motorcycles, radios, bicycles and other products previously considered 'luxury items', such as canned beer and imported L&M brand cigarettes) and speculative purchases that have little impact on national production (Flores and Blanes 1984).

On the other hand, in spite of large surpluses extracted from peasants, there is still some surplus left to finance household investment. One measure of the increased income, purchasing power and peasant consumption preferences is truck sales. During a six-month period in 1981, 300 large trucks were purchased by peasant smallholders in the Chapare (Flores and Blanes 1984, p.90). Bolivian peasants regard trucks as a means of upward mobility: ownership brings both social status and a way to escape from reliance on farming as a way of life and precarious means of support. Flores and Blanes (ibid., p.190) also note that 'Income from coca production has been used for land and housing investment'.

3.7 Conclusions

The main conclusion of this chapter is that the approach followed by 'neostructuralist' authors (FitzGerald and Vos 1989) to the study of macroeconomic adjustment in developing countries, where different economic agents, facing different constraints and pursuing different objectives, interact through the different markets, is quite relevant and more useful in gaining an understanding of the Bolivian economy compared with other theoretical approaches (such as the neoclassical approach).

The analysis in this chapter demonstrates that in the Bolivian case, there are different groups that face different constraints, their economic activities are motivated by essentially different objectives, and, therefore, their microeconomic behaviours are ruled by different institutional factors. This diversity of objectives and institutional settings has determined particular adjustment rules in response to the external shocks to the Bolivian economy over the last two decades. These adjustment rules did not remain unchanged over time, however, but tended to vary as some institutional factors were modified by external forces as well as by changes in the direction of economic policy.

For instance, over the period under analysis, small-scale activities tended to be subsistence-oriented. They were mainly located in the agricultural and urban informal sectors (such as handicraft manufacturing and petty trading), and faced relatively competitive markets for their products. Their activities were restricted by price policies implemented by government, lack of access to formal credit, and a generally unfavourable income distribution. For these sectors, investment depended very much on their capacity to generate savings, which was rather limited given their subsistence income levels (prior savings approach). In the case of peasants, there were no differences between saving and investment decisions since both tended to be determined simultaneously in a Ricardian fashion. During the 1980s, however, a group of peasants started receiving large revenues from the production of coca and cocaine. Although large surpluses were extracted from them by merchants who control the final stages of drug processing and distribution, this group of peasants experienced large increases in their levels of income, consumption and investment.

Companies, on the other hand, were motivated more by objectives such as to increase local market share and/or profit maximization. Their activities were concentrated in export agriculture, mining, light industry, commerce and financial services. Companies enjoyed oligopolistic positions in markets for nontraded goods. In markets for traded goods they faced external competition, but they could still influence exchange rate policy in order to maximize profits or their share in local markets. Company investment generally led savings; extra savings were secured by: (a) increasing their own savings through higher levels of output (Keynesian case) and/or higher prices that redistributed income from wages to profits (post-Keynesian case); or (b) by obtaining credit from the banking system. Therefore, companies' savings availability tended to adjust to their planned investment. The main constraints that limited companies' investment were the reduced size of domestic markets, import competition and the general lack of confidence in the country's long-term viability, which acted as a powerful deterrent to the expansion of investment during the 1970s. During the first half of the 1980s company investment decisions were hampered by the uncertain political and economic climate, as well as by the lack of foreign exchange to import capital goods as postulated by the two-gap approach. After 1985, the high real interest rate discouraged company investment (neoclassical position). However, company investment also was inhibited by the lack of adequate public infrastructure (structuralist position).

Over the whole period, capitalists received resources beyond their capacity to invest them productively within the country. Therefore, these excess resources were taken out of the country (capital flight). During the 1970s, these resources were the counterpart of the large public external debt that was built up, as resources were transferred from the public to the private sector through domestic credit. During the 1980s on the other hand, capital flight was financed largely by the proceeds from the sale of coca.

Public enterprises, for their part, controlled natural resource export activities (minerals, oil and gas), energy, transport and some heavy industry. Over the last two decades, the objectives of public enterprises have very often been subordinated to national goals and to power group interests. As a consequence, large surpluses have been extracted from public enterprises, mainly through highly undervalued exchange rates and heavy taxation, to be used by the state to finance public investment in other sectors of the economy, or to expand credit to the private sector. During the 1970s, the expansion of credit to the private sector failed to promote private investment and eventually went to finance capital flight. Although public enterprises in general had no problems in obtaining external finance, their investment was inhibited by the heavy financial drain imposed on them through taxation and the overvalued exchange rate, and by the external debt that had to be repaid during the 1980s, thus limiting the availability of foreign exchange to pay for imports of capital goods.

Government activities, on the other hand, were focused on the provision of public goods (roads, infrastructure, schools, hospitals, and so on) in order to provide support for private sector activities. During the 1970s, the government had no major problems in finding finance for investment; extra savings were obtained from the surpluses from public enterprises, and from domestic and external borrowing. During the early 1980s, however, when external credit dried up and public enterprise surpluses were greatly reduced, the government had to reduce spending. The main constraints faced by the government during that period were the lack of foreign exchange to finance imports of capital goods, and the large macroeconomic imbalances created by the need to finance the fiscal deficits. After 1985, the binding constraint on government investment was the priority given to achieving fiscal budget equilibrium under the NEP.

Appendix 3.1 The Consumption Function for the Government

The government's consumption function was tested econometrically:

$$G = g_1.G(-1) + g_2.\Delta F_{GV} + g_3.\dot{p}$$

where:

$G(-1)$ = government consumption in the previous period (millions of 1989 bolivianos)

ΔF_{GV} = capital inflows received by the government within the period (millions of 1989 bolivianos)

$\dot{p}$ = inflationary expectations (percentage change).

The results obtained were as follows:

LS // Dependent Variable is G
SMPL range: 1973–89
Number of observations: 16

Variable	Coefficient	Std. Error	T-Stat.	2-Tail Sig.
$G(-1)$	1.0284528	0.0331001	31.071003	0.000
ΔF_{GV}	0.5841606	0.3244238	1.8006099	0.095
$\dot{p}$	-0.0771238	0.0358126	-2.1535385	0.051

R-squared	0.757009	Mean of dependent var.	2221.943
Adjusted R-squared	0.719729	S.D. of dependent var.	526.1338
S.E. of regression	278.5383	Sum of squared resid.	1008586
Durbin-Watson stat.	1.879208	F-statistic	20.25986
Log likelihood	–111.1148		

Appendix 3.2
The Investment Function for the Government

The government's investment demand function was tested econometrically:

$$I_{GV} = z_1.I_{GV}(-1) + z_2.\Delta F_{GV}$$

where:

$I_{GV(t-1)}$ = government investment in the previous year (millions of 1989 bolivianos)

ΔF_{GV} = external capital flows received by the government within the period (millions of 1989 bolivianos).

The results obtained were as follows:

LS // Dependent Variable is I_{GV}

SMPL range: 1973–89

Number of observations: 16

Variable	Coefficient	Std. Error	T-Stat.	2-Tail Sig.
$I_{GV(t-1)}$	0.5440983	0.2006004	2.7123494	0.017
ΔF_{GV}	0.6602900	0.2941833	0.2941833	0.041

R-squared	0.477726	Mean of dependent var.	495.5968
Adjusted R-squared	0.440421	S.D. of dependent var.	304.1896
S.E. of regression	227.5491	Sum of squared resid.	724900.3
Durbin-Watson stat.	1.927750	F-statistic	12.80586
Log likelihood	–108.4726		

Appendix 3.3 The Investment Function for Public Enterprises

The public enterprises' investment demand function has been tested econometrically:

$$I_{SE} = z_0 + z_1.I_{SE}(-1) + z_2.\Delta F_{SE}$$

where:

$I_{SE}(-1)$ = public enterprise investment in the previous year (millions of 1989 bolivianos)

ΔF_{SE} = external capital inflows received by public enterprises within the period (millions of 1989 bolivianos).

The results obtained were as follows:

LS // Dependent Variable is I_{SE}
SMPL range: 1975–89
Number of observations: 15

Variable	Coefficient	Std. Error	T-Stat.	2-Tail Sig.
Const.	163.77337	110.08817	1.4876564	0.163
$I_{PE(t-1)}$	0.5891793	0.1810830	3.2536422	0.007
ΔF_{PE}	0.5948706	0.2876380	2.0681222	0.061

R-squared	0.715235	Mean of dependent var.	605.9487
Adjusted R-squared	0.667774	S.D. of dependent var.	372.4070
S.E. of regression	214.6517	Sum of squared resid.	552904.5
Durbin-Watson stat.	1.494405	F-statistic	15.07002
Log likelihood	–100.1458		

Appendix 3.4
The Investment Function for Companies

The investment demand function for companies was tested econometrically:

$$I_{CP} = h_0 + h_1.\Delta L_{PB.CP} + h_2.ir^* + h_3.(GDP/KAP) + h_4.I_{GV}(-4) + h_5.I_{SE}(-1)$$

where:

$\Delta L_{PB.CP}$ =	domestic commercial bank credit to companies (in millions of 1989 bolivianos)
ir^* =	international interest rate (percentage)
GDP/KAP =	capacity utilization (accelerator term)
$I_{GV}(-4)$ =	government investment with a four-year lag (in millions of 1989 bolivianos)
$I_{SE}(-1)$ =	public enterprise investment in the previous year (in millions of 1989 bolivianos).

The results obtained were as follows:

LS // Dependent Variable is I_{CP}
SMPL range: 1976–89
Number of observations: 14

Variable	Coefficient	Std. Error	T-Stat.	2-Tail Sig.
Const.	–7091.1404	854.02513	–8.3031988	0.000
$\Delta L_{PB,}$	0.1212694	0.0385870	3.1427534	0.014
i*	–21.707062	12.666321	–1.7137622	0.125
GDP/KAP	272.32278	30.823618	8.8348742	0.000
$I_{GV(t-4)}$	0.1913867	0.1127293	1.6977539	0.128
$I_{SE(t-1)}$	–00.7715798	0.1315652	–5.8646184	0.000

R-squared	0.925905	Mean of dependent var.	512.9266
Adjusted R-squared	0.879595	S.D. of dependent var.	224.7442
S.E. of regression	77.98495	Sum of squared resid.	48653.22
Durbin-Watson stat.	2.327871	F-statistic	19.99378
Log likelihood	–76.93905		

Appendix 3.5
The Consumption Function for Households

The consumption function for households was tested econometrically:

$$C_{HH} = c_1.WAG + c_2.OS + c_3.DIV + c_4.ir$$

where:

WAG = total wage earnings (in millions of 1989 bolivianos)
OS = total households' operating surplus (in millions of 1989 bolivianos)
DIV = total distributed profits to households (in millions of 1989 bolivianos)
ir = domestic real interest rate (percentage).

The results obtained were as follows;

LS // Dependent Variable is C
SMPL range: 1970–89
Number of observations: 15

Variable	Coefficient	Std. Error	T-Stat.	2-Tail Sig.
WAG	1.0441313	0.1614834	6.4658720	0.000
OS	0.8423830	0.1125628	7.4836717	0.000
DIV	0.2048099	0.3682178	0.5562194	0.589
Ir	31.512236	4.1436685	7.6049123	0.000

R-squared	0.523098	Mean of dependent var.	10035.91
Adjusted R-squared	493.2664	S.D. of dependent var.	714.2775
S.E. of regression	2.162007	Sum of squared resid.	2676429.
Durbin-Watson stat.	–111.9737	F-statistic	6.118713
Log likelihood			

Appendix 3.6
The Investment Function for Households

The investment demand function for households was tested econometrically:

$$I_{HH} = f_0 + f_1.I_{HH(t-1)} + f_2.i^*$$

where:

$I_{HH(t-1)}$ = household investment in the previous year (in millions of 1989 bolivianos)

i^* = international interest rate (percentage).

The results obtained were as follows:

LS // Dependent Variable is I_{HH}

SMPL range: 1971–89

Number of observations: 16

Variable	Coefficient	Std. Error	T-Stat.	2-Tail Sig.
Const.	236.21474	95.443100	2.4749273	0.028
$I_{HH(t-1)}$	0.4869669	0.1981467	2.4576081	0.029
i*	–22.651264	9.9475238	–2.2770756	0.040

R-squared	0.725329	Mean of dependent var.	320.5282
Adjusted R-squared	0.683072	S.D. of dependent var.	143.2321
S.E. of regression	80.63451	Sum of squared resid.	84525.01
Durbin-Watson stat.		F-statistic	17.16466
Log likelihood			

Appendix 3.7 Currency Demand Function for Households

The currency demand function for households was tested econometrically:

$$CU_{HH} = \Pi_0 + \Pi_1.\underline{\wp} + \Pi_2.i_r + \Pi_3.WAG + \Pi_4.DIV + \Pi_5.OS$$

where:

$p =$	current rate of inflation (percentage change)
$i_r =$	real domestic interest rate (percentage)
WAG =	total wage earnings by households (millions of 1989 bolivianos)
DIV =	total distributed profits to households (millions of 1989 bolivianos)
OS =	households' operating surpluses (millions of 1989 bolivianos)

The results obtained were as follows:

LS // Dependent Variable is CU_{HH}

SMPL range: 1971–89

Number of observations: 15

Variable	Coefficient	Std. Error	T-Stat.	2-Tail Sig.
Const.	–731.02672	559.92075	–1.305589	0.224
p	–0.0812864	0.0183291	–4.434819	0.002
i_r	–7.018230	1.1534233	–6.084696	0.000
WAG	0.2742419	0.0473014	5.7977587	0.000
DIV	0.2234373	0.0858219	2.6034996	0.029
OS	0.0538707	0.0677819	0.7947663	0.447

R-squared	0.961775	Mean of dependent var.	1007.412
Adjusted R-squared	0.940539	S.D. of dependent var.	366.9680
S.E. of regression	89.48360	Sum of squared resid.	72065.84
Durbin-Watson stat.	2.163045	F-statistic	45.28987
Log likelihood	–84.86372		

Appendix 3.8
The Demand-Deposit Demand Function for Households

The demand-deposit demand function for households was tested econometrically:

$$DP^{d}_{HH} = \Pi_0 + \Pi_1.\dot{p} + \Pi_2.i_r + \Pi_3.WAG + \Pi_4.DIV + \Pi_5.OS$$

where:

$\dot{p}$ =	inflation within the period (percentage change)
i_r =	real domestic interest rate (percentage)
WAG =	total wage earnings by households (millions of 1989 bolivianos)
DIV =	distributed profits to households (millions of 1989 bolivianos)
OS =	household operating surpluses (millions of 1989 bolivianos).

The results obtained were as follows:

LS // Dependent Variable is DPHH

SMPL range: 1971–89

Number of observations: 15

Variable	Coefficient	Std. Error	T-Stat.	2-Tail Sig.
Const.	–510.90253	474.10658	–1.0776111	0.309
p	–0.1013542	0.0155200	–6.5305623	0.000
i_r	–1.7240571	0.9766482	–1.7652797	0.111
WAG	0.1251031	0.0400519	3.1235251	0.012
DIV	0.4566702	0.0726687	6.2842747	0.000
OS	0.0384403	0.0573935	0.6697666	0.520

R-squared	0.923218	Mean of dependent var.	417.4218
Adjusted R-squared	0.880561	S.D. of dependent var.	219.2404
S.E. of regression	75.76923	Sum of squared resid.	51668.79
Durbin-Watson stat.	2.566176	F-statistic	21.64301
Log likelihood	–82.36827		

Appendix 3.9
The Quasi-Money Demand Function for Households

The quasi-money demand function for households was tested econometrically:

$$QM_{HH} = \Pi_0 + \Pi_1.DP_{HH(t-1)} + \Pi_2.i_r + \Pi_3.DIV + \Pi_4.OS + \Pi_5.WAG$$

where:

$QM_{HH(t-1)}$ stock of quasi-money demanded by households in the previous year (in millions of 1989 bolivianos)
i_r = real domestic interest rate (percentage)
DIV = distributed profits to households (in millions of 1989 bolivianos)
OS = total household operating surpluses (in millions of 1989 bolivianos)
WAG = total wage earnings by households (in millions of 1989 bolivianos).

The results obtained were as follows:

LS // Dependent Variable is QM_{HH}
SMPL range: 1971–89
Number of observations: 15

Variable	Coefficient	Std. Error	T-Stat.	2-Tail Sig.
Const.	140.12916	1168.4982	0.1199224	0.907
QM(−1)	0.8110306	0.1589785	5.1015111	0.001
i_r	6.6626810	2.0809723	3.2017154	0.011
WAG	0.2675171	0.1406000	1.9026819	0.090
DIV	0.0158347	0.1378584	0.1148623	0.911
OS	0.0025207	0.1021115	0.0246854	0.981

R-squared	0.826383	Mean of dependent var.	1006.306
Adjusted R-squared	0.729930	S.D. of dependent var.	351.3310
S.E. of regression	182.5807	Sum of squared resid.	300021.4
Durbin-Watson stat.	2.421504	F-statistic	8.567671
Log likelihood	−95.56077		

Notes

1. R. Morales (1985, p.176) estimated the distribution of income among households, companies, financial institutions, public enterprises and government for the years 1970–83. The methodology is described in R. Morales (ibid, p.125).

2. Since National Accounts allocate to 'households' the operating surpluses arising from the coca business, the figures appearing in the accumulation balance for companies do not include coca proceeds (Table 3.6). This procedure is maintained in this book; incomes from coca are therefore included directly as part of the accumulation balance for upper-income households.

3. According to Dunkerley (1992, p.30) 'It has been suggested that economic developments over the previous decade had encouraged the emergence of a "new entrepreneur" – a beneficiary of the expansion of agro-business and cheap credit under Banzer, bolstered by the relative strengthening of private mining (ANMM) and banking (ASOBAN), better educated and less overtly "political" than the generation that had arisen in the 1950s…' Leading businessmen became active militants in the main political parties, but presented themselves first and foremost as entrepreneurs.

4. The methodology utilized contains, in each case, observed variables which are the totals of the columns (x_i) and the totals of the rows (x_j) of an unknown matrix X (which elements x_{ij} are to be estimated). We assume that there is another reference matrix X_0 (with known elements $x_{0i,j}$), that 'informs' on the structure of matrix X, but has different values for the totals of the rows and columns.

   The unknown values of matrix X are estimated by minimizing the Euclidian distance between both matrices, subject to the constraint imposed by the totals of the rows and columns of the unknown matrix (i.e. x_i and x_j) (see R. Morales, ibid). In formal terms, this problem is set up in the following way:

minimize: $\sum\left(x_{ij}-x_{0\,ij}\right)^2$

s.t. $$\sum_i (x_{ij}) = x_{.j}$$

$$\sum_j (x_{ij}) = x_{i.}$$

5. In 1984 and 1985, household savings reached 31 and 39 per cent of GDP, respectively. Real interest rates, however, were as low as –89.5 and –97.5 per cent in those two years.

6. This was a common practice during the hyperinflationary period.

7. The employment absorption coefficients by sector are calculated on the basis of the SAM's values in the base year.

8. Given that informal establishments are often no larger than booths or stands (Blanes Jimenez 1989), their capacity to offer collateral is very limited. The urban informal sector in Bolivia is closely linked to material survival.

9. The structure of the family basic basket, considered as reference, is that agreed between the CBO (Central Obrera Boliviana) and the government in November 1985. The cost of this basket was updated by the CET (Centro de Estudios del Trabajo) to June 1986 and May 1988. CEDLA updated the basket to June 1989, utilizing changes in the consumer price index (CPI).

10. This survey was based on interviews with around 100 small-scale firms and family-based units working in the manufacturing and service sectors in La Paz.

11. M. Urioste (1989a) found that peasant households in the north of the highlands, where 14 per cent of the rural population is concentrated, use almost half of their time in agricultural activities. The rest of the time is devoted to activities such as house repairs.

12. Although coca prices have been high, they have also been subject to severe fluctuations from week to week, the result not only of the logic of supply and demand but of the campaigns of repression occasionally mounted by the state.

13. The involvement of small producers in the primary processing stage admirably suits the interest of those fractions of capital that concentrate upon the more technical – and more lucrative – downstream refining and marketing operations. The on-site reduction of bulk, transforming 500 kg of leaves to 2.5 kg of paste, facilitates collection and transport.

14. The sale of ingredients used in the manufacture of coca paste requires little capital investment, but provides high rates of return from exorbitant mark-ups. In May 1985, for example, one litre of kerosene in the city of Cochabamba cost 5,000 pesos, whereas in the Chapare it retailed at 200,000–300,000 pesos; toilet paper, which is used as a filter and drying material and for which function it absorbs 60 per cent of national toilet paper production, cost 110,000 pesos per roll in the city, but over ten times that price in the markets of the Chapare (Healy 1986).

4 Financial Balances

4.1 Introduction

The previous two chapters concentrated on the adjusting mechanisms that brought equilibrium to the accumulation balances for all the economic agents. These discussions demonstrated that the adjusting rules tended to be essentially different for each agent, and that the adjustment mechanisms tended to vary from period to period in response to external shocks and to changes in domestic policy. However, in order to have a full and coherent version of the whole economy, we still need to analyse and specify adjustment for the financial sector balance; this is carried out in this chapter.

Section 4.2 provides a general description of the Bolivian financial system.

Section 4.3 discusses the mechanisms that brought adjustment to the financial sector over the different periods. To provide a clear picture of how Bolivian financial institutions reacted to external shocks, separate analyses are presented for the Central Bank and for the rest of the financial system. The discussion helps to identify the key stylized facts that characterized the sector's behaviour over the three periods analysed. This section argues that the main role of the financial system over the last two decades has been to provide finance to the formal sector of the economy (the public and corporate sectors). Finance was secured from various sources whose importance varied over the three periods: external sources, domestic deposits and credit creation by the Central Bank. These stylized facts are later incorporated in the behavioural models constructed for the Central Bank and the private commercial banks. Section 4.4 discusses the interest rate determination. Finally, section 4.5 presents some concluding remarks.

4.2 The Structure of the Bolivian Financial Sector

A key economic feature that differentiates developed and developing countries is the structure of the financial system. Agénor and Montiel (1996) highlight some of these characteristics:

> The menu of assets available to private savers in developing countries from the formal financial system is often limited to cash, demand deposits, time deposits, and government securities acquired in a primary market. In addition to being limited in scope, the financial system is also limited in size and geographic distribution. Many private individuals thus have limited access to commercial banks, which are by far the dominant organized financial institutions – often operating under oligopolistic market structures and a high degree of concentration. Other specialized institutions exist, but they typically conduct a very small portion of total financial intermediation in the economy. Secondary securities and equities markets are either nonexistent or very limited in scope, so that bank credit and internally generated funds provide the bulk of financing for private firms. Commercial banks often operate under a large array of government-imposed restrictions. These include binding legal ceilings on lending rates, high reserve and liquidity ratio requirements, and restrictions on their portfolio composition designed to direct resources toward favored sectors. . . More generally, informal modes of financial intermediation tend to arise in response to government regulations.

Most of these features are important characteristics of the Bolivian financial system. In 1997, the Bolivian banking system comprises 17 commercial banks, of which 13 are national and 4 are of foreign origin. Financial operations are concentrated in few large banks; 54 per cent of total deposits and 53 per cent of loans are in the hands of the 4 largest banks. Bank operations are also geographically concentrated; 94 per cent of total deposits and 86 per cent of total loans are concentrated in the country's three main cities: La Paz, Cochabamba and Santa Cruz.

Specialized bank operations were discontinued in 1992, as part of the governmental policy aimed at withdrawing the state from commercial banking activities.

A particular feature of the Bolivian banking system is the high degree of dollarization; 89 per cent of total deposits and total loans are dollar denominated.

4.3 Financial Balances

During the 1970s, the Bolivian economy experienced a rapid process of financial deepening. The total liquidity of the economy (measured by M2) expanded in real terms by 98 per cent between 1972 and 1978 (see Table 4.1) and the number of commercial banks operating within the country increased from 13 to 19.

The increased capital inflows allowed the banking system to accumulate foreign exchange reserves (net reserves increased more than three times in real terms), which in turn helped the banking system to expand its credit.

Between 1972 and 1977 the amount of domestic credit directed to the private sector increased in real terms by 145 per cent, while that directed to the public sector went down by 50 per cent. In 1977, more than

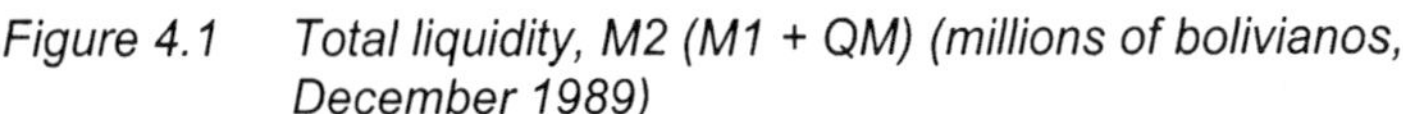
Figure 4.1 Total liquidity, M2 (M1 + QM) (millions of bolivianos, December 1989)

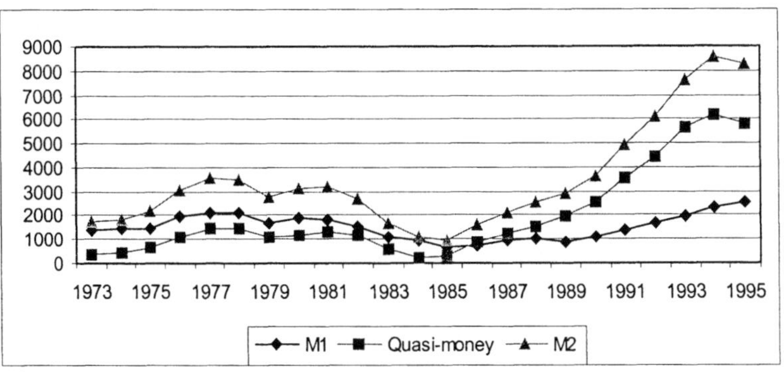

Sources: World Bank 1985b, BCB (a; various issues)

80 per cent of the total credit made available by the banking system was directed to the private sector, more specifically, to private companies and households (see Ramos 1980, p.164).

In addition to the availability of external resources, the banking system's loanable resources were increased through a sharp expansion in the volume of deposits made by the public. The amount of quasi-money (savings accounts and time deposits) increased in real terms by 261 per cent between 1973 and 1977 (Figure 4.1). That expansion was encouraged by the positive real interest rates prevailing at that time and because new banking system regulations were introduced authorizing financial transactions in foreign currency and in local currency with maintenance of value.

During 1978–82, the amount of capital inflows fell sharply. Net foreign reserves fell in 1978 and became negative in 1979. In order to offset the contractionary effects of this reduction in reserves on economic activity, monetary policy became very flexible. The amount of domestic credit expanded in real terms by almost 16 per cent as the government began increasingly to finance its deficit by resorting to Central Bank credit. Net credit to the public sector rose by 130 per cent in real terms in the pre-hyperinflation period (1978–82). In order to absorb the liquidity

Figure 4.2 Interest rates (percentage)

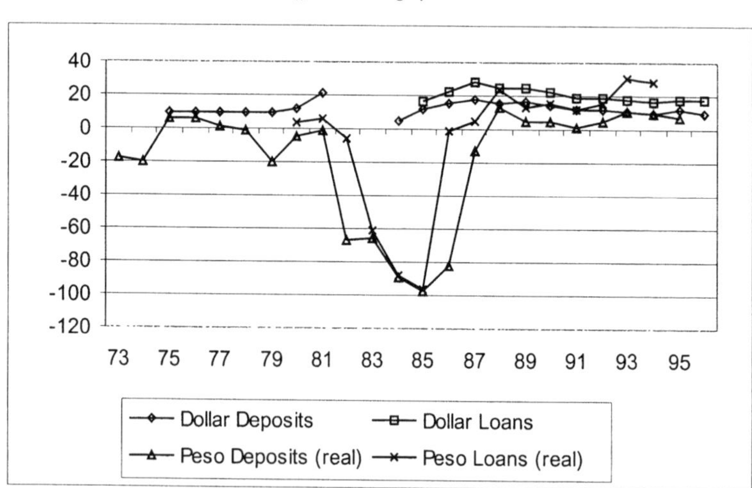

Sources: World Bank 1985b; BCB (a; various issues)

created by the increased finance to the public sector and to avoid inflationary pressures, the annual interest rate on dollar-denominated deposits was increased by the Central Bank from 9.3 in 1979 to 11.5 in 1980 and to 21.5 in 1981 (Table 4.2). This measure had the desired effect: the demand for quasi-money, which had fallen in 1979, expanded by 21 per cent between 1979 and 1982.

In 1982, as the economic crisis worsened, a process of financial dis-intermediation began, which greatly reduced recorded financial assets within the economy. Interest rate and exchange controls, in conjunction with hyperinflation, resulted in strongly negative ex post deposit and lending rates, reducing the attractiveness of domestic assets (Figure 4.2). Between 1980 and 1985, total liquidity (M2) in the economy fell by 69 per cent in real terms, demand deposits by 87 per cent, and quasi-money by 74 per cent. The dedollarization decree in 1982 converted all foreign currency contracts into pesos at the official, highly undervalued exchange rate. Those with dollar accounts in Bolivian banks suffered huge losses, exacerbating a decline in confidence in the banking system and leading to a sharp increase in the share of foreign currencies in domestic assets (Afcha 1989, p.12). The stock of money in real terms fell sharply, despite the huge expansion in the nominal value of this variable.[1] These two apparently contradictory phenomena can be satisfactorily reconciled only by bringing into the analysis the dwarfing effect of hyperinflation on the real value of the stocks of assets at the beginning of the period that were not protected against inflation (currency and deposits, for example). As can be seen in Table 4.3, during the period of relatively low inflation (1973–81) the total liquidity of the economy, as a percentage of GDP, increased from 14.4 to 19.6; this represented an average increase equivalent to 0.5 per cent of GDP per year. The average increase in the money stock in nominal terms as a percentage of GDP (see Table 4.4) averaged 3.9 per cent between 1974 and 1981, implying an average loss in the real value of existing stocks of 3.4 per cent of GDP per year (see Appendix 4.1). In 1982, the authorities induced an expansion in liquidity equivalent to 17 per cent of GDP. This expansion caught the public off guard and liquidity expanded in real terms by 5.4 per cent of GDP.

Between 1982 and 1985, the total liquidity of the economy in real terms dropped from 24.8 to only 10 per cent of GDP, representing an average reduction equivalent to 4.8 per cent of GDP per year. However,

Table 4.1 *Total liquidity outstanding at 31 December (bolivianos of December 1989)*

	1973	1974	1975	1976	1977	1978	1979	1980	1981	1982	1983	1984
Net Foreign Reserves	290	959	609	921	1010	296	–284	–334	–825	–2 204	–404	11
Net Domestic Credit	2 420	1 703	2 188	2 947	3 365	4 098	3 995	2 214	4 213	4 654	2 942	1 533
– Public Sector	1 116	208	401	692	557	953	1 313	1 681	1 716	2 196	1 735	808
– Private Sector	1 304	1 495	1 787	2 255	2 809	3 145	2 682	533	2 497	2 458	1 207	725
CDs BCB												
Other Accounts	–948	–817	–655	–840	–836	–888	–944	–43	–227	207	–864	–443
	0	0	0	0	0	0	0	0				
Sources of M2	1 762	1 845	2 143	3 028	3 539	3 505	2 766	1 838	3 161	2 656	1 674	1 101
									0	0	0	0
Money (M1)	1 371	1 418	1 484	1 932	2 115	2 081	1 672	1 904	1 834	1 525	1 102	910
– Currency	972	925	972	1 199	1 329	1 399	1 189	1 265	1 160	1 049	785	793
– Demand Deposits	399	493	512	733	786	682	483	639	674	476	317	117
Quasi–Money	391	426	659	1096	1 424	1 424	1 094	1 184	1 328	1 132	572	191
Uses of M2	1 762	1 844	2 143	3 028	3 539	3 505	2 766	3 089	3 161	2 656	1 674	1 101

Source: Author's own estimates, based on BCB (a; various issues)

Table 4.1 *Total liquidity outstanding at 31 December (bolivianos of December 1989), continued*

	1985	1986	1987	1988	1989	1990	1991	1992	1993	1994	1995
Net Foreign Reserves	229	837	651	546	230	579	749	725	722	827	1 102
Net Domestic Credit	648	884	1 760	2 547	3 901	4 724	5 849	8 519	10 712	11 917	10 430
– Public Sector	–721	–1 023	–743	–225	524	687	639	1 644	1 954	1 909	421
– Private Sector	1 369	1 907	2 502	2 772	3 376	4 037	5 210	6 875	8 758	10 008	10 009
CDs BCB											
Other Accounts	93	–137	–274	–574	–1 248	–1 671	–1 685	–3 143	–3 819	–4 210	–3 236
Sources of M2	970	1 584	2 136	2 519	2 882	3 633	4 914	6 101	7 614	8 534	8 297
	0	0	0	0	0	0					
Money (M1)	664	731	925	1 025	907	1 076	1 375	1 655	1 967	2 344	2 523
– Currency	581	592	723	787	642	695	716	763	813	1 020	1 091
– Demand Deposits	83	139	202	238	265	380	659	892	1 154	1 324	1 432
Quasi–Money	306	853	1 211	1 494	1 975	2 557	3 539	4 446	5 647	6 190	5 774
Uses of M2	970	1 584	2 136	2 519	2 882	3 633	4 914	6 101	7 614	8 534	8 297

Source: Author's own estimates, based on BCB (a; various issues)

Table 4.2 *Interest rate and inflation (percentage)*

	1973	1974	1975	1976	1977	1978	1979	1980	1981	1982	1983	1984
Interest Rate[a]												
Dollar Deposits[b]			9.3	9.3	9.3	9.3	9.3	11.5	21.5			5.0
Peso Deposits	11.7	11.7	11.7	11.7	11.8	11.8	16.0	18.0	23.0	32.0	45.0	140.0
Dollar Loans[b]												
Peso Loans								27.9	32.0	45.0	69.0	157.0
Consumer Price Index (Percentage change)	34.8	39.0	6.0	5.5	10.5	13.5	45.5	23.9	25.1	296.5	328.5	2 177.2
Real Interest Rate[c]												
Peso Deposit	–17.1	–19.6	5.4	5.9	1.2	–1.5	–20.3	–4.8	–1.7	–66.7	–66.2	–89.5
Peso Loan								3.2	5.5	–63.4	–60.6	–88.7

Notes: [a] End of the period. [b] Dollar lending and deposits were prohibited by the 1982 dedollarization decree. [c] Comparing the interest rate and the rate of change in the consumer price index for equivalent period.

Sources: World Bank (1985b); UDAPE (1997b)

Table 4.2 Interest rate and inflation (percentage), continued

	1985	1986	1987	1988	1989	1990	1991	1992	1993	1994	1995	1996
Interest Rate[a]												
Dollar Deposits[b]	11.2	14.9	17.8	15.8	16.1	14.6	11.4	11.7	10.2	9.6	11.3	8.9
Peso Deposits	110.0	33.4	32.7	27.8	20.8	20.5	19.0	24.0	19.7	15.8	21.7	16.8
Dollar Loans [b]	16.8	22.0	28.5	24.4	24.4	22.3	19.1	18.6	17.9	16.2	17.8	17.1
Peso Loans	232.1	64.8	43.2	39.6	39.4	38.9	37.9	58.8	59.6	52.7	51.8	62.6
Consumer Price Index (Percentage change)	8 170.5	66.0	10.7	21.5	16.6	18.0	14.5	10.5	9.3	8.5	12.6	8.0
Real Interest Rate [c]												
Peso Deposit	–97.5	–82.3	–13.5	13.1	4.6	5.1	1.4	4.7	10.4	9.8	7.2	
Peso Loan	–96.0	–0.7	4.2	23.1	13.4	15.5	11.6	15.1	27.5	30.9	28.3	

Notes: [a] End of the period. [b] Dollar lending and deposits were prohibited by the 1982 dedollarization decree. [c] Comparing the interest rate and the rate of change in the consumer price index for equivalent period.

Sources: World Bank (1985b); UDAPE (1997b)

Table 4.3 *Total Liquidity (outstanding at 31 December of each year as percentage of GDP)*

	1973	1974	1975	1976	1977	1978	1979	1980	1981	1982	1983	1984
Net International Reserves	2.4	6.5	3.9	5.4	5.7	1.6	–1.9	–2.1	–5.1	–20.6	–4.4	0.2
Net Domestic Credit	19.8	11.6	13.9	17.3	18.9	22.2	26.2	18.5	26.2	43.5	32.1	24.1
– Public Sector	9.1	1.4	2.6	4.1	3.1	5.2	8.6	14.0	10.7	20.5	19.0	12.7
– Private Sector	10.6	10.2	11.4	13.2	15.7	17.1	17.6	4.5	15.5	23.0	13.2	11.4
CDs BCB												
Other Accounts	–7.7	–5.6	–4.2	–4.9	–4.7	–4.8	–6.2	–0.4	–1.4	1.9	–9.4	–6.9
Sources of M2	14.4	12.6	13.7	17.7	19.8	19.0	18.1	16.1	19.6	24.8	18.3	17.3
Money (M1)	11.2	9.7	9.5	11.3	11.9	11.3	11.0	11.9	11.4	14.2	12.0	14.3
– Currency	7.9	6.3	6.2	7.0	7.4	7.6	7.8	7.9	7.2	9.8	8.6	12.4
– Demand Deposits	3.3	3.4	3.3	4.3	4.4	3.7	3.2	4.0	4.2	4.4	3.5	1.8
Quasi–Money	3.2	2.9	4.2	6.4	8.0	7.7	7.2	7.4	8.2	10.6	6.3	3.0
Uses of M2	14.4	12.6	13.7	17.7	19.8	19.0	18.1	19.3	19.6	24.8	18.3	17.3

Sources: World Bank (1985b); BCB (a; various issues); UDAPE (1997b)

Table 4.3 *Total Liquidity (outstanding at 31 December of each year as percentage of GDP), continued*

	1985	1986	1987	1988	1989	1990	1991	1992	1993	1994	1995
Net International Reserves	2.4	4.7		3.7	1.5	3.8	4.5	4.3	4.2	4.6	6.1
Net Domestic Credit	6.8	5.0		17.2	26.1	30.7	35.4	50.1	62.1	66.3	55.3
– Public Sector	–7.6	–5.8		–1.5	3.5	4.5	3.9	9.7	11.3	10.6	0.2
– Private Sector	14.4	10.8		18.7	22.6	26.2	31.5	40.4	50.7	55.7	55.1
CDs BCB											
Other Accounts	1.0	–0.8		–3.9	–8.4	–10.8	–10.2	–18.5	–22.1	–23.4	–17.8
Sources of M2	10.2	9.0		17.0	19.3	23.6	29.7	35.8	44.1	47.5	43.6
Money (M1)	7.0	4.1		6.9	6.1	7.0	8.3	9.7	11.4	13.0	13.9
– Currency	6.1	3.4		5.3	4.3	4.5	4.3	4.5	4.7	5.7	6.0
– Demand Deposits	0.9	0.8		1.6	1.8	2.5	4.0	5.2	6.7	7.4	7.9
Quasi–Money	3.2	4.8		10.1	13.2	16.6	21.4	26.1	32.7	34.4	29.7
Uses of M2	10.2	9.0		17.0	19.3	23.6	29.7	35.8	44.1	47.5	42.6

Sources: World Bank (1985b); BCB (a; various issues); UDAPE (1997b)

Table 4.4 *Changes in Total Liquidity[a] (as percentage of GDP) and inflation (percentage change year-end to year-end)*

	1974	1975	1976	1977	1978	1979	1980	1981	1982	1983	1984
Net International Reserves	5.1	−1.9	2.0	1.0	−3.2	−3.2	−0.7	−3.5	−18.6	1.2	0.4
Net Domestic Credit	−0.3	3.7	5.1	3.9	6.1	7.7	1.6	8.9	33.5	20.3	22.0
– Public Sector	6.9	3.8	6.3	6.6	7.8	12.9	23.1	23.7	16.5	13.4	11.5
– Private Sector	3.8	2.4	3.3	4.3	3.6	3.4	−8.2	11.3	17.1	6.9	10.5
CDs BCB											
Other Accounts	−0.9	0.7	−1.3	−0.4	−0.8	−2.2	4.4	−1.1	2.5	−10.0	−6.4
Sources of M2	**3.9**	**2.6**	**5.8**	**4.5**	**2.1**	**2.3**	**5.4**	**4.3**	**17.4**	**11.5**	**16.1**
Money (M1)	2.9	0.9	3.1	2.1	1.2	1.6	3.5	1.9	9.9	8.2	13.5
– Currency	1.5	0.6	1.6	1.4	1.2	1.5	1.9	0.9	7.1	5.9	11.9
– Demand Deposits	1.4	0.3	1.5	0.7	−0.1	0.1	1.6	1.0	2.9	2.2	1.6
Quasi–Money	1.0	1.6	2.8	2.4	0.9	0.8	1.9	2.4	7.4	3.4	2.6
Uses of M2	**3.9**	**2.6**	**5.8**	**4.5**	**2.1**	**2.3**	**5.4**	**4.3**	**17.4**	**11.5**	**16.1**
Inflation	**39.0**	**6.0**	**5.0**	**10.5**	**13.5**	**45.5**	**23.9**	**25.1**	**296.5**	**328.5**	**2177.2**

Notes: [a] Changes include revaluation of existing assets.
Sources: World Bank (1985b); BCB (a; various issues); UDAPE (1997b)

Table 4.4 *Changes in Total Liquidity[a] (as percentage of GDP) and inflation (percentage change year-end to year-end), continued*

	1985	1986	1987	1988	1989	1990	1991	1992	1993	1994	1995
Net International Reserves	2.4	4.0	–0.6	0.1	–1.6	2.5	1.5	0.3	0.3	0.9	2.0
Net Domestic Credit	6.8	2.8	5.3	7.4	11.5	9.2	10.4	18.9	16.9	11.4	–2.9
– Public Sector	–7.3	–3.3	1.1	2.6	4.8	1.6	0.2	6.3	2.6	0.6	–9.1
– Private Sector	14.1	6.1	4.2	4.8	6.7	7.6	10.2	12.7	14.3	10.8	6.2
CDs BCB											
Other Accounts	0.6	–1.1	–1.3	6.7	–5.1	–4.0	–1.4	–9.5	–5.5	–3.8	2.8
Sources of M2	**9.8**	**5.7**	**3.4**	**–5.1**	**4.8**	**7.7**	**10.5**	**9.7**	**11.8**	**8.4**	**1.9**
Money (M1)	6.9	1.9	1.4	1.6	0.2	2.0	2.6	2.4	2.6	3.0	2.4
– Currency	6.1	1.4	1.0	1.1	–0.2	1.0	0.7	0.7	0.7	1.5	1.0
– Demand Deposits	0.8	0.5	0.4	0.5	0.4	1.0	2.0	1.7	2.0	1.5	1.4
Quasi–Money	2.9	3.8	2.0	3.5	4.6	5.7	7.9	7.3	9.2	5.5	–0.6
Uses of M2	**9.8**	**5.7**	**3.4**	**5.1**	**4.8**	**7.7**	**10.5**	**9.7**	**11.8**	**8.4**	**1.8**
Inflation	**8170.5**	**66.0**	**10.7**	**21.5**	**16.6**	**18.0**	**14.5**	**10.5**	**9.3**	**8.5**	**12.6**

Note: [a] Changes include revaluation of existing assets.
Sources: World Bank (1985b); BCB (a; various issues); UDAPE (1997b)

the average increase in liquidity in nominal terms was equivalent to 12.5 per cent of GDP per year. Thus, the average loss in the real value of existing financial stocks during the period of hyperinflation was as high as 17.3 per cent per year (equivalent to the average stock of money existing prior to the hyperinflation). That means that, during the years of high inflation (1984, 1985 and even 1986), the stocks of money outstanding at the end of the period were virtually equivalent to the money created within the period, since the real value of existing stocks at the beginning was reduced to negligible levels by hyperinflation.

In 1985 the NEP instituted fundamental reforms of financial regulations. Supreme Decree 21060 abolished all controls on interest rates and authorized financial transactions in foreign currency and in local currency with maintenance of value. Reserve requirements on foreign currency were lifted; those on local currency were changed to 10 per cent on savings deposits and 50 per cent on sight deposits. Domestic residents were permitted to borrow and lend abroad. A number of directed credit schemes at subsidized interest rates were eliminated.

As a result of all these measures and once inflation was brought down, domestic credit and reserves started to recover. Financial liberalization and the end of hyperinflation brought about an immediate increase in recorded financial assets. Domestic credit in real terms increased more than fivefold between 1985 and 1989, mostly to the private sector. Net credit to the public sector for most of the period was negative (that is, the amount of public sector deposits in the banking system was larger than the amount of credit they received). Only in 1989 was this tendency reversed, when only 12 per cent of net banking system credit was directed to the public sector.

Much of this credit expansion in 1985–89 was financed by a more than sixfold increase in bank deposits (in real terms) as funds were repatriated to take advantage of high interest rates, with some switching from informal to formal financial intermediaries. The share of financial assets denominated in foreign currency increased after 1985; foreign currency deposits equalled 55 per cent of total bank liabilities to the private sector in 1989 compared with 29 per cent in 1986. The availability of foreign deposits certainly increased the supply of capital to the Bolivian economy by providing depositors with an asset that was less subject to the risk of devaluation. However, the large share of dollars in the financial system reduced the government's ability to extract seigniorage, severely limiting the flexibility of fiscal policy. The availability of foreign currency deposits meant that the government had to finance its deficit with foreign credit (credit from the domestic private sector was limited) or risk a rapid increase in inflation. Foreign-currency denominated deposits, particularly since the bulk were short term, may have been more sensitive to changes in perceptions of government policy than boliviano deposits, and thus were more likely to result in a decline in confidence. The growing share of bank deposits denominated in foreign currency thus increased the risk that banks could suffer abrupt changes in their deposit levels, increasing the potential for instability. Finally, net foreign reserves held by the banking system recovered from negative levels in 1979–83 to positive levels during 1985–89.

During the 1990s, the total liquidity of the financial system increased very rapidly. Bank deposits rose from a level equivalent to 15 per cent of GDP in 1989 to 37.6 per cent in 1995. As a result, the interest rates for dollar denominated deposits went down from 14.6 per cent to 11.3 per cent during the same time period. More than 90 per cent of the deposits were expressed in dollars, showing the low confidence on financial assets expressed in Bolivianos. This is also reflected in the low demand for currency, which stood at levels between 4 to 5 per cent of GDP during the period. The stability attained and the high levels of interest rates explain the rapid increase in deposits.

The higher levels of deposits went to finance higher levels of domestic credit and accumulation of foreign reserves in the banking system. Total portfolio rose from a level equivalent to 26 per cent of GDP in 1989 to 55 per cent in 1995. Most of the finance was directed to the private sector. Net reserves on the other hand, rose from 1.5 per cent of GDP in 1989 to 6.1 per cent in 1995.

In summary, the changes in the financial sector adjustment over the three periods under study originated in the external environment due to external shocks and the introduction of new regulations on the functioning of the financial system. During the 1970s, financial intermediation deepened as the level of domestic credit rose sharply (mostly directed to the private sector). This finance came through increased deposits due to high real domestic interest rates prevailing at that time, and higher levels of external borrowing by the banking system. During the first half of the 1980s, financial intermediation fell sharply when confidence in the financial system slumped, inflation mounted, and the real value of domestic financial assets fell significantly. Although credit to the private and public sectors expanded, high rates of inflation dwarfed the real value of non-indexed financial stocks, as can be seen in Table 4.1. Credit expansion by the banking system was financed through money creation when foreign exchange reserves were exhausted and external credit was refused. After 1985, bank credit started to recover in real terms through a significant increase in the amount of domestic financial assets (mostly quasi-money) attracted by higher real interest rates. Increased deposits also helped the financial system to accumulate reserves.

During the 1990s, further reforms were introduced to the financial sector, aimed at reducing the government involvement on financial activities. Three public banks were closed between 1991 and 1992: Banco Agricola (BAB), Banco Minero (BAMIN), and the Bolivian State Bank (BANEST).

At the end of 1994, two private banks (Banco Sur and Banco Cochabamba) were liquidated by the Superintendence of Banks, because of their poor financial and management conditions. The two banks presented increasing levels of overdue portfolio, high levels of loans to related groups, and low capital to assets ratios. These were, in fact, problems that were common to most of the commercial private banks. In order to sort out these problems, the Central Bank Law was passed in 1995. It obliged banks to increase their capital to asset ratios from 8 to 10 percent, to apply Basel standards for asset evaluation, and to eliminate lending to related parties over a period of three years. To support commercial banks to adjust to the new tighter regulations, the Central Bank has set up a special fund (FONDESIF) from which banks can borrow fresh capital from new owners or through merger; to replace or strengthen management; and to write off or provision nonperforming loans.

The 1995 Central Bank Law focuses the Central Bank functions on maintaining macroeconomic stability and the purchasing power of the Boliviano. The Central Bank cannot buy new debt certificates issued by non-financial public institutions and can only carry out open market operation by trading treasury bonds of previously existing debt. The law also grants more autonomy to the Central Bank, by establishing that the president and the directors will be elected by congress for a period of eight years. Furthermore, a new nonbank financial intermediary (NAFIBO), a joint venture of the government and private investors, takes over from the Central Bank the lending of development funds to commercial banks.

In order to gain a better understanding of how the financial sector adjusted to external shocks over the past two decades, as well as how the reforms redefine the way the Bolivian financial system operates, sections 4.3.1 and 4.3.2 analyse the accumulation balances adjustments for the Central Bank and for commercial banks separately, since these two sectors tended to adjust in essentially different ways.

4.3.1 Commercial and specialized banks

The consolidated accumulation balances for the commercial and specialized banks (the banking system excluding the Central Bank) show that their main function was to direct resources obtained from different sources (Central Bank credit, private deposits and external credit) to the private non-financial sector (companies and households). During the whole period under analysis, about 75 per cent of commercial bank portfolios were held in the form of credit to the private sector (see Table 4.5).

Between 1973 and 1979, the outstanding bank finance to the non-financial private sector increased as a proportion of GDP, from 10.3 to 17.3 per cent (see Table 4.7), as a reflection of the process of financial deepening experienced by the Bolivian economy. The sectors that benefited the most from the increased volumes of commercial bank credit were industry, agriculture and commerce; these sectors secured 80 per cent of the total credit made available during that period.

There is a big contrast between the amounts of credit directed to the corporate and non-corporate sector during those years. In the case of industry, for instance, 45 per cent of the total credit went to the corporate sector, while handicraft producers received only 1.2 per cent. The same occurred in the case of credit to the agricultural sector. The Banco Agrícola de Bolivia (BAB, the Agricultural Bank of Bolivia), which granted around 60 per cent of total agricultural credits during that period, allocated about 75 per cent of that credit to activities controlled by large capitalist groups in the east of the country: cotton, sugar-cane and cattle (Devlin and Mortimore 1983, p.192). In the case of commerce, most of the credit was directed to the import trade, which is mainly controlled by large corporations.

Table 4.5 *Structure of new credit made available by commercial banks (percentage)*

	Commerce	Industry	Handcraft	Construction	Agriculture	Exports	Individuals	Other	Services	Mining	Total
1974	9.0	37.2	1.6	1.1	37.9	–5.3	1.3	15.9	0.0	1.3	100
1975	26.3	25.4	4.3	7.8	34.2	3.4	5.6	–24.4	0.0	17.6	100
1976	19.8	35.9	–0.4	2.9	9.9	14.4	6.0	1.0	0.0	10.3	100
1977	18.3	59.5	1.1	1.8	13.7	–10.2	1.8	13.7	0.0	0.3	100
1978	17.1	68.0	0.0	6.1	5.4	–1.5	2.0	3.6	0.0	–0.6	100
1979	5.9	44.0	0.4	6.3	14.5	4.0	1.3	21.0	0.0	2.7	100
1980	4.9	–22.8	8.7	7.8	44.0	10.6	11.1	17.2	0.0	18.7	100
1981	35.4	31.3	–0.8	11.5	9.7	–1.9	13.4	–1.7	0.0	3.1	100
1982	15.9	36.0	0.2	6.9	17.1	2.0	3.7	9.1	0.0	9.2	100
1983	12.4	35.3	0.6	6.1	22.0	–1.3	5.0	8.0	0.0	11.9	100
1984	10.8	32.2	0.5	5.2	28.4	0.2	4.1	7.0	0.0	11.7	100
1985	10.6	32.7	0.8	2.8	23.2	0.4	7.6	12.2	0.0	9.5	100
1986	14.2	24.6	0.7	4.7	34.1	0.4	6.8	10.5	0.0	4.0	100
1987	20.8	29.6	0.8	2.2	22.3	0.4	7.1	13.1	0.0	3.7	100
1988	11.7	23.2	–1.4	–0.4	36.3	–0.7	–12.3	–21.4	59.0	6.0	100
1989	16.0	24.0	–0.2	7.1	39.0	–0.1	–1.5	–2.3	6.8	11.3	100
1990	32.3	19.2	n.a.	2.9	2.7	n.a.	n.a.	2.5	36.1	4.3	100
1991	25.9	19.6	n.a.	6.0	5.7	n.a.	n.a.	4.9	36.7	1.3	100
1992	26.5	23.1	n.a.	8.2	10.3	n.a.	n.a.	2.8	27.0	2.0	100
1993	41.1	15.4	n.a.	19.3	20.9	n.a.	n.a.	2.7	–2.8	3.3	100
1994	–0.2	22.5	n.a.	–8.3	–9.1	n.a.	n.a.	2.1	97.4	–4.5	100
1995	21.4	13.8	n.a.	4.2	20.9	n.a.	n.a.	–1.5	35.6	5.6	100
1996	27.2	5.5	n.a.	–3.1	8.9	n.a.	n.a.	2.6	58.6	0.3	100
Average											
1974–80	14.5	35.3	2.2	4.8	22.8	2.2	4.1	6.9	0.0	7.2	100
1981–85	17.0	33.5	0.2	6.5	20.1	–0.1	6.8	6.9	0.0	9.1	100
1986–90	19.0	24.1	0.0	3.3	26.9	0.0	0.0	0.5	20.4	5.9	100
1991–96	23.7	16.6	n.a.	4.4	9.6	n.a.	n.a.	2.3	42.1	1.3	100

Source: BCB (a; various issues)

The credit expansion of the 1970s was financed by increased time and savings deposits by the public (quasi-money), which went up from an amount equivalent to 1 per cent of GDP in 1974 to 2.4 per cent in 1977, as a result of a series of regulations introduced to promote domestic savings. In 1974, through Supreme Decree 11302, the state guaranteed the maintenance of the value of peso-denominated savings deposits in relation to dollar-denominated deposits. This increase in deposits made it unnecessary for the commercial banks to resort to Central Bank credit, which was utilized only marginally during that decade (it increased by an amount equivalent to 0.6 per cent of GDP per year). These modest expansions were further reduced by the required bank reserves in domestic currency, which increased by an amount equivalent to 0.4 per cent of GDP per year. In fact, the ratio between bank reserves and total deposits remained stable between 1974 and 1981, at around 0.4.

Commercial banks also resorted to external borrowing as a means of financing their operations (Hinojosa and Espinoza 1983), also facilitated by a series of decrees that tended to promote their access to external sources of finance. According to statistics from their own financial statements, between 1973 and 1982, the commercial banks' external debt increased from US$30.9 million to US$221.7 million, representing average annual increases of 48 per cent. The bulk of these credits were short-term; between 1973 and 1978 short-term loans to commercial banks increased by 56 per cent while long term loans rose by 40 per cent per year on average (Table 4.6).

During the 1970s, the government introduced a series of regulations on commercial bank operations in order to direct the external loans to productive activities. Supreme Decree 12766 (August 1975) established that banking system loans financed with the banks' own resources or with funds obtained domestically and abroad should be channelled to activities within the country, in specific fixed proportions: 75 per cent minimum to productive sectors and 25 per cent maximum to commerce and individuals. In addition, Central Bank Resolution 4896 stated that at least 80 per cent of the contingent operations for financing imports should be used for the purchase of capital goods and inputs for the productive sector, and for necessities.

By 1977, however, it was evident that the increasing inflow of foreign capital was not being directed to the economy in forms appropriate to finance economic development, given that a large proportion of the loans received were short-term. To correct that tendency, the government established a 10 per cent reserve requirement on external credits obtained by commercial banks (Decree 14677). The reserve requirement did not apply, however, if the terms at which the credit was obtained were longer than two years, or if the domestic commercial bank allocated the credit either to productive sectors (also at terms longer than two years) or to export activities.

There is strong evidence that, in practice, the external credits obtained by commercial banks were not invested in productive activities, but were used to finance luxury imports and capital flight (Devlin and Mortimore 1983; Ramos 1980; Rivas 1989; Lopes 1983). According to Hinojosa and Espinoza (ibid., p.59),

> the cost and term conditions at which the external resources were obtained, were not adequate for financing longterm economic development.... Besides, it was evident that external inflows benefited activities related to importing commerce and to the commercial banks themselves which experienced an extraordinary expansion during that period. Commercial banks, therefore, did not fulfil the investment requirements of the productive sectors because, in essence, banks were not prepared to operate on those terms and to assume the risks involved in these projects.

With regard to the lack of effectiveness of the legal regulations in directing bank operations, Hinojosa and Espinoza (ibid., p.46) argue that 'the monetary authorities did not strictly apply the penalties established by the law because of the actions of associations or power groups, the easing of bank supervision systems, or the direct involvement of authorities in illegal operations'.

Between 1978 and 1979, bank deposits by the public went up but at a much lower pace than during the 1973–1977 period, as confidence in the financial system diminished; these deposits amounted to only 0.6 per cent of GDP per year during these two years. In order to offset the much lower levels of deposits, the monetary authorities approved an increase in the interest rate for dollar – as well as for peso-denominated deposits, and deposits increased by amounts equivalent to 3.3 per cent of GDP per year during 1980 and 1981. Commercial bank credit, which had slowed down during 1979–80, expanded at a much faster pace after 1981.

Table 4.6 Commercial banks external debt (outstanding at the end of the period) (in millions of current US$)

	Short Term	Long Term	Total
1973	14.7	16.2	30.9
1974	28.9	21.3	50.2
1975	39.7	34.6	74.3
1976	40.6	60.0	100.6
1977	80.9	70.0	150.9
1978	136.0	85.8	221.7
1979	106.9	161.3	268.1
1980	83.6	145.2	228.8
1981	93.3	166.2	259.4
1982	94.2	147.8	242.0
1983	76.9	136.2	213.2
1984	90.8	121.7	212.5
1985	75.5	149.8	225.3
1986	79.6	129.3	208.8
1987	70.4	50.6	121.0
1988	57.5	41.9	99.4
1989	13.1	43.8	56.9
1990	26.3	41.3	67.6
1991	43.9	63.4	107.3
1992	98.6	70.2	168.8
1993	231.0	93.0	324.0
1994	333.3	146.1	479.4
1995	397.4	148.3	545.7
1996	420.5	138.1	558.7
Average			
1973–75	27.8	24.0	51.8
1976–80	89.6	104.5	194.0
1981–85	86.1	144.3	230.5
1986–90	49.4	61.4	110.8
1991–96	254.1	109.9	364.0

Sources: BCB (a; various issues)

During the first half of the 1980s, the access of commercial banks to external credit disappeared. In 1980 interest payments were around US$40 million, and for the first time since 1971 external flows became negative. Between 1979 and 1985 the commercial banks' outstanding external debt fell, on average, by almost 3 per cent per year, but its importance in terms of commercial bank liabilities increased dramatically as devaluation increased the domestic value of the outstanding external debt vis-à-vis other non-indexed liabilities (such as Central Bank credit). Table 4.7 shows that the outstanding long-term external debt in the balance for the commercial banks went up from an equivalent of 2.7 per cent of GDP in 1981 to 8.3 per cent in 1985.

Despite the lower levels of external credit during the first half of the 1980s, commercial bank credit expanded substantially (by an amount equivalent to 9.1 per cent of GDP per year), implying a major transfer of resources to the non-financial private sector (see Tables 4.8 and 4.9). Again, the sectors that benefited the most from this credit were commerce, private industry and agriculture. In the case of agricultural credit, the government attempted to redirect credit to peasants, especially after the 1983 drought severely affected peasants' output and income.

The finance for commercial bank credits during the first half of the 1980s came from credits obtained from the Central Bank, which increased by an amount equivalent to 3.7 per cent of GDP per year, and from deposits made by the public, which despite the acute decline in the real value of deposits, increased in nominal terms by an amount equivalent to 4.6 per cent of GDP. Although the interest rate on bank loans was negative during this period, banks found other mechanisms to profit from the economic crisis (Afcha 1989, p.25). As the World Bank (1989, p.48) pointed out,

> ...paradoxically, the hyperinflation may not have greatly damaged banks' profitability. While the shrinking of the money supply (in real terms) cut their volume of business, banks were well situated to take advantage of the possibilities for profitable arbitrage inherent in the system of financial controls. For example, banks (or their customers) could profit from subsidized credit available from the Government and the opportunity to convert pesos into foreign currency at the official exchange rate. Banks also developed strategies for increasing profits in a high inflation environment. Many branches were opened to encourage deposits, on which banks paid highly negative rates.

The active participation of commercial banks in speculative activities has also been highlighted by R. Morales (1985, p.21), who argues that they accumulated exchange reserves in amounts that greatly exceeded their foreign-exchange-denominated liabilities. According to Morales, that was possible only because banks could intervene in the parallel exchange market and because, although credit operations were stipulated in foreign exchange, disbursements were done in domestic currency. Both cases meant that eventually banks utilized the domestic-currency-denominated deposits of their customers for the purchase of foreign exchange. The differences, resulting from the foreign exchange modifications applied to the difference between banks' foreign-exchange-denominated assets and liabilities, represented a supplementary net profit to the banks.

The commercial banks also benefited from non-indexed Central Bank credit; in contrast with foreign credit, the proportion of Central Bank credit in the balance for the commercial banks fell from 5.2 per cent of GDP in 1982 to 4.5 per cent in 1985, even though during that period Central Bank credit had expanded by an average of 3.7 per cent of GDP per year. This obviously represented a large transfer of resources from the Central Bank to commercial banks through no-indexed credits.

Finally, in order to support commercial banks that had suffered a substantial increase in overdue loans, the reserve requirements were initially reduced; but later, with the deepening of the fiscal imbalances in 1983, they were increased again. In 1984 the reserves-deposits ratio was on average around 0.6.

After 1985, despite the very high real interest rates that followed the stabilization and liberalization programme, commercial bank credit expanded by amounts equivalent to 3.8 per cent of GDP per year. Once inflation had been brought down, these increases also brought about a recovery in the real value of outstanding commercial bank credit by more than fourfold between 1984 and 1989. This tendency was reinforced by the fact that, after 1985, banks were authorized to provide indexed credit.

During this period, bank credit was again directed to commerce, private industry and particularly agriculture. When agricultural exports expanded, once more, favourable conditions were established for the sector under the NEP.

The recovery in the value of bank assets, however, may be understating the weakness of their portfolios since the level of overdue loans excludes non-performing loans that are refinanced continually by the banks. Because the banks are not permitted to accrue interest on loans, even one day overdue, there is a strong incentive to refinance these (World Bank 1989, p.50).

After 1985, and once inflation was brought down, banks (or their customers) could no longer benefit from speculative activities. As the World Bank (ibid, p.50) commented,

> ...Adjustment to disinflation proved to be difficult for many banks. With low rates of inflation and liberalized deposit rates, the large network of bank branches was no longer profitable. Employment in the formal banking sector has declined sharply. Stabilization also ended the real estate boom, reducing the market value of banks' capital. The sharp change in relative prices lowered profits in many enterprises with large debts to the major banks. Uncertainty over economic prospects also greatly increased the share of short term liabilities in banks' deposits, which increases the risk and limits the amount of long-term lending the banks can do. Banks thus experienced a general deterioration in the quality of their portfolios and profits.

After the stabilization programme the government introduced measures to strengthen banking supervision. For instance, new regulations aimed at strengthening bank portfolios require banks to increase their collateral on outstanding loans. This measure is also expected to help reduce the concentration of bank loans that is almost an institutional characteristic of their portfolios. As the World Bank (ibid, p.51) noted, 'A large proportion of banks' assets have been lent with no guarantees beyond personal signatures, in many cases to people with financial interests in the bank'.

After the introduction of the NEP, bank operations were financed mainly by Central Bank credit and by impressive increases in dollar-denominated deposits, which rose in response to the higher real interest rates. Central Bank credit expanded by an amount equivalent to 2.5 per cent of GDP per year; dollar-denominated deposits increased by an amount equivalent to 3 per cent of GDP per year between 1986 and 1989. Dollar-denominiated deposits had been illegal prior to the stabilization programme; in 1989 they constituted around 80 per cent of total banking system liabilities. This demonstrated the continued lack of con-

Table 4.7 *Commercial and specialized banks (outstanding balances at the end of the year as percentage of GDP)*

	1973	1974	1975	1976	1977	1978	1979	1980	1981	1982	1983	1984	1985
Assets	**12.5**	**11.0**	**12.5**	**16.6**	**18.1**	**17.9**	**18.3**	**17.8**	**17.7**	**25.2**	**15.9**	**10.7**	**12.4**
Net Foreign Reserves	–0.6	–1.0	–1.0	–0.7	–1.8	–2.9	–2.0	–0.8	–0.9	–3.6	–2.0	–2.6	–2.9
Bank Reserves	2.8	2.2	2.7	4.3	4.7	4.0	3.0	3.5	3.4	6.2	4.8	2.0	1.0
Credit to the Private Sector	10.3	9.8	10.8	13.0	15.2	16.7	17.3	15.1	15.1	22.7	13.1	11.3	14.3
Credit to the Public Sector													
Liabilities	**12.5**	**11.0**	**12.5**	**16.6**	**18.1**	**17.9**	**18.3**	**17.8**	**17.7**	**25.2**	**15.9**	**10.7**	**12.4**
Deposits	6.7	6.5	7.6	11.1	12.5	11.6	10.5	11.1	12.1	14.8	9.7	4.8	4.1
– Demand Deposits	3.4	3.5	3.3	4.4	4.4	3.8	3.2	3.9	4.1	4.4	3.4	1.8	0.9
– Quasi-money	3.3	3.0	4.3	6.6	8.1	7.9	7.3	7.2	8.0	10.4	6.2	3.0	3.2
Central Bank Credits	4.2	3.0	3.8	3.2	3.5	3.6	3.2	3.2	3.1	5.2	3.7	4.2	4.5
Long Term External Debt	1.3	1.0	1.4	2.2	2.2	2.3	4.4	3.0	2.7	7.4	4.8	4.7	8.3
Other Accounts (Net)	0.3	0.5	–0.4	0.2	–0.1	0.4	0.1	0.5	–0.2	–2.2	–2.2	–3.0	–4.6

Sources: World Bank (1985b); BCB (a; various issues); UDAPE (1997b)

Table 4.7 *Commercial and specialized banks (outstanding balances at the end of the year as percentage of GDP), continued*

	1986	1987	1988	1989	1990	1991	1992	1993	1994	1995	1996
Assets	**11.0**	**14.3**	**20.1**	**26.2**	**28.9**	**33.9**	**40.2**	**46.9**	**48.9**	**50.7**	**54.6**
Net Foreign Reserves	–0.7	–0.6	–0.3	1.0	0.5	0.2	–0.5	–3.0	–4.4	–4.8	–4.7
Bank Reserves	1.0	1.3	3.2	4.6	4.4	5.0	4.5	5.1	3.7	4.5	5.0
Credit to the Private Sector	10.6	13.5	17.1	20.7	24.0	28.7	36.3	44.8	49.4	49.7	50.3
Credit to the Public Sector				–0.1	–0.1	–0.1	-0.1	-0.1	0.1	1.3	3.9
Liabilities	**11.0**	**14.3**	**20.1**	**26.2**	**28.9**	**33.9**	**40.2**	**46.9**	**48.9**	**50.7**	**54.6**
Deposits	5.9	7.6	10.7	13.7	17.5	23.1	28.2	34.8	34.5	35.6	40.9
– Demand Deposits	0.8	1.1	1.5	1.6	2.3	3.6	4.7	5.9	6.5	7.1	8.4
– Quasimoney	5.1	6.5	9.2	12.1	15.2	19.5	23.5	28.9	28.0	28.5	32.4
Central Bank Credits	4.0	5.3	7.7	7.0	6.6	5.9	7.3	6.5	9.1	11.3	9.4
Long Term External Debt	2.8	1.1	0.9	1.0	0.9	1.2	1.3	1.7	2.5	2.3	2.0
Other Accounts (Net)	–1.8	0.2	0.8	4.4	3.9	3.6	3.4	3.9	2.8	1.5	2.2

Sources: World Bank (1985b); BCB (a; various issues); UDAPE (1997b)

Table 4.8 *Commercial and specialized banks (changes in the outstanding balances as percentage of GDP)**

	1974	1975	1976	1977	1978	1979	1980	1981	1982	1983	1984	1985
Total Assets	**3.5**	**2.9**	**5.6**	**4.0**	**2.4**	**3.4**	**4.4**	**3.5**	**18.4**	**9.0**	**9.7**	**12.3**
Net Foreign Reserves	–0.6	–0.1	0.2	–1.2	–1.3	0.4	0.7	–0.3	–3.3	–1.0	–2.5	–2.9
Bank Reserves	0.6	0.8	1.9	1.0	0.0	–0.4	1.3	0.7	4.8	3.1	1.7	0.9
Credit to the Private Sector	3.6	2.2	3.5	4.1	3.7	3.4	2.4	3.1	16.9	6.9	10.5	14.2
Credit to the Public Sector												
Total Liabilities	**3.5**	**2.9**	**5.6**	**4.0**	**2.4**	**3.4**	**4.4**	**3.5**	**18.4**	**9.0**	**9.7**	**12.3**
Deposits	2.5	2.0	4.4	3.1	0.9	0.9	3.3	3.3	10.2	5.6	4.2	4.0
–Demand Deposits	1.5	0.3	1.5	0.7	–0.1	0.1	1.5	1.0	2.8	2.2	1.6	0.9
–Quasi-money	1.0	1.7	2.9	2.4	0.9	0.8	1.8	2.3	7.3	3.3	2.6	3.2
Central Bank Credits	0.5	1.2	–0.2	0.8	0.6	0.3	0.9	0.5	4.0	2.3	4.0	4.5
Long Term External Debt	0.2	0.6	0.9	0.3	0.4	2.5	–0.3	0.3	6.3	2.7	4.4	8.3
Other Accounts (Net)	0.3	–0.8	0.5	–0.2	0.5	–0.2	0.4	–0.6	–2.1	–1.6	–2.9	–4.6

Note: * Changes including revaluation of existing assets.
Source: Table 4.7

Table 4.8 *Commercial and specialized banks (changes in the outstanding balances as percentage of GDP)*, continued*

	1986	1987	1988	1989	1990	1991	1992	1993	1994	1995	1996
Total Assets	**7.0**	**4.6**	**6.6**	**9.1**	**7.4**	**10.5**	**10.8**	**11.3**	**7.2**	**7.0**	**9.4**
Net Foreign Reserves	0.3	0.0	0.3	1.2	–0.3	–0.2	–0.7	–2.5	–1.7	–0.9	–0.4
Bank Reserves	0.7	0.5	2.0	1.9	0.6	1.5	0.1	1.1	-0.9	1.2	1.0
Credit to the Private Sector	6.0	4.2	4.4	6.1	7.0	9.3	11.4	12.6	9.6	5.6	6.0
Credit to the Public Sector				–0.1	0.0	0.0	–0.1	0.0	0.2	1.2	2.8
Total Liabilities	**7.0**	**4.6**	**6.6**	**9.1**	**7.4**	**10.5**	**10.8**	**11.3**	**7.2**	**7.0**	**9.4**
Deposits	4.6	2.4	3.5	4.6	6.2	9.0	8.1	9.8	3.6	4.7	9.2
–Demand Deposits	0.5	0.4	0.4	0.4	0.9	1.8	1.6	1.7	1.3	1.3	2.1
–Quasi-money	4.1	2.0	3.1	4.3	5.3	7.2	6.6	8.1	2.3	3.5	7.1
Central Bank Credits	2.6	1.8	2.6	0.5	0.8	0.5	2.2	0.1	3.2	3.2	–0.7
Long Term External Debt	0.1	–1.4	–0.1	0.2	0.1	0.5	0.2	0.5	1.0	0.1	0.0
Other Accounts (Net)	–0.3	1.8	0.5	3.8	0.3	0.5	0.2	0.9	–0.6	–1.0	0.9

Note: * Changes including revaluation of existing assets.
Source: Table 4.7

fidence of economic agents in the financial system and ultimately in the continuation of the economic programme as a whole. Some authors identify bank behaviour as a key factor in the 'dollarization' of the economy. Srivastava (1991, p.35) maintains that

> while the market for dollar assets has been quite active as banks have competed aggressively for the previously hoarded dollars, at the same time the banks have almost neglected the domestic currency assets. This has prompted the extensive dollarization of the financial sector which can pose severe problems for monetary policy management. In addition it also may contribute to the credibility problem if the banks' behaviour has a significant signalling role in the public's perception of the success of the stabilization programme.

Another characteristic that highlights the level of uncertainty and the lack of confidence in the financial system is the fact that the bulk of bank deposits were short-term and therefore more likely to result in a further decline in confidence. This aspect, together with the high degree of dollarization, rendered bank deposits unsuitable for financing long-term development projects.

The commercial banks' loanable funds expanded further as reserve requirements were substantially reduced after 1985. As a result, the banks' reserves-deposits ratio went down to 0.35, but in 1989 it increased again because banks found it attractive to invest part of their portfolios in certificates of deposit issued by the Central Bank, which were paying close to market interest rates. New external loans for the commercial banks were not substantially resumed under the NEP, even though efforts were made to reduce arrears.

During the 1990s, the level of deposits in commercial banks rose from 17.5 per cent of GDP in 1989 to 40.9 per cent in 1996. In 1994, total deposits outstanding in commercial banks decreased as a percentage of GDP, because the Superintendence's intervention in the two banks affected the public's perception about the financial system's solvency. As a result of the increase in deposits, commercial banks' lending to the private sector rose from a level equivalent to 24 per cent of GDP in 1990 to more than 50 per cent in 1996. Lending to the public sector on the other hand only became important in 1995, when commercial banks shifted part of their portfolio to public debt certificates. Central Bank's finance to commercial banks increased by 3.2 per cent of GDP per year in 1994 and 1995, because the Central Bank absorbed the liabilities of the two banks that were closed at the end of 1994. Although the law does not explicitly establish a deposit insurance mechanism, the liabilities of the banks that went bankrupt in the last seven years were completely absorbed by the Central Bank. This has prevented banks from being more closely supervised by depositors, because depositors' savings remain unaffected by the banks' errors.. This has generated a 'moral hazard' type of problem, and solvency has become meaningless as a parameter for competition between banks (UDAPE 1997a).

Commercial banks' reserves in the Central Bank increased not only due to the compulsory reserve requirements, but also because banks invested part of their assets in interest-yielding Deposit Certificates (CDs) issued by the Central Bank.

In summary, although there were substantial changes in the way commercial banks obtained resources and transferred them to the private sector, some institutional characteristics of commercial bank behaviour have greatly affected the allocation of credit.

First, apart from Central Bank credit, commercial banks have consistently resorted to short-term sources of finance. During the 1970s they contracted short-term external loans, and under the NEP, short-term dollar-denominated deposits became the banks' main source of finance. This factor has prevented banks being an effective means for mobilising resources to finance long-term development projects.

Second, the Bolivian commercial bank market is highly concentrated, with just six banks (the five major private commercial banks) holding 64 per cent of total deposits and 63 per cent of total capital (UDAPE 1997a). The result is an oligopolistic financial system where the interest rate and the level of deposits are determined by the banks themselves rather than through competition (Apt and Schargrodsky 1995).

Third, over the whole period, commercial bank credits were highly concentrated in few customers who very often had financial interests in the banks.

Fourth, Central Bank credit to the financial system, even under the stabilization programme, has expanded continuously, suggesting a tendency to adjust to the financial needs of the commercial banks. The expansion in Central Bank credit to commercial banks to pay for the deposits of the two banks that were closed at the end of 1994 further supports this argument. However, the Central Bank can also absorb commercial banks' excess liquidity, as happened when commercial banks invested part of their portfolio in Deposit Certificates issued by the Central Bank.

Finally, the reforms to the financial system introduced during the 1990s will change the adjustment behaviour of commercial banks in two basic ways: the capital to assets ratio will be increased to 10 per cent and lending to related parties will be eliminated.

4.3.2 The Central Bank

For most of the period under analysis, the Central Bank has fulfilled its functions as banker to the government and the commercial banks. Central Bank credit to the public and private sectors has contracted or expanded depending on the availability of other alternative sources of finance to these two sectors (see Table 4.9).

Between 1974 and 1977, Central Bank credit contracted on average by an amount equivalent to 0.8 per cent of GDP per year. During those years, non-financial public institutions resorted to external borrowing and to their own surpluses to cover their financial needs; commercial banks on the other hand, tended to use deposits made by the public as well as foreign credit. Between 1978 and 1981, however, Central Bank credit expanded on average by amounts equivalent to 3.4 per cent of GDP per year as foreign capital inflows to the non-financial public institutions were halted. The sources of finance used by the Central Bank to fund this credit expansion were: short-term external credit (50 per cent), reserves (17 per cent) and currency creation (33 per cent). Very clearly, during that period the country started experiencing problems in obtaining long-term foreign finance and increasingly had to resort to domestic sources (printing money).

Between 1982 and 1984, credit to the public sector grew on average by an amount equivalent to 14 per cent of GDP per year, and to the private sector by 3.1 per cent of GDP per year. Credit expansion to the private sector, however, was offset by the much higher levels of reserves that commercial banks were required to maintain during that period. The expansion of Central Bank credit was mostly financed through money creation, which increased by an amount equivalent to 8.8 per cent of GDP per year.

Table 4.9 *Central Bank (changes in the outstanding balances as percentage of GDP)**

	1974	1975	1976	1977	1978	1979	1980	1981	1982	1983	1984	1985
Total Assets	**1.8**	–0.1	**1.7**	**1.6**	**1.2**	**0.5**	**2.0**	–0.4	**1.0**	**15.0**	**17.4**	**1.9**
Net Foreign Reserves	5.9	–1.8	1.9	2.2	–1.9	–3.9	–1.9	–2.5	–15.1	2.2	3.0	5.3
Net Credit to Public Sector	–4.2	1.3	1.9	–0.4	2.6	3.6	4.4	2.2	16.3	13.3	11.4	-7.3
– To Government	–2.0	–1.1	–2.6	–0.1	1.7	3.6	2.7	1.9	–3.8	1.6	–1.4	-14.3
– To Public Enterprises	–2.2	2.4	4.5	–0.3	0.8	0.0	1.6	0.4	20.0	11.7	12.8	7.1
Net Credit to Private Sector	0.1	0.4	–2.0	–0.2	0.6	0.8	–0.4	–0.2	–0.1	–0.5	3.1	3.9
– Gross Credit	0.5	1.2	–0.2	0.8	0.6	0.3	0.9	0.5	4.0	2.3	4.0	4.5
– Deposits	0.4	0.8	1.9	1.0	0.0	–0.5	1.3	0.7	4.2	2.7	0.9	0.6
Total Liabilities	**1.8**	–0.1	**1.7**	**1.6**	**1.2**	**0.5**	**2.0**	–0.4	**1.0**	**15.0**	**17.4**	**1.9**
Currency	1.7	0.6	1.7	1.4	1.3	1.6	1.9	0.9	7.6	6.2	12.6	6.3
Long-term External Debt	0.2	0.1	–0.3	0.0	0.5	–0.3	0.5	1.1	5.3	16.8	17.8	13.5
CDDs												
Other Accounts Net	–0.1	–0.8	0.3	0.2	–0.6	–0.8	–0.4	–2.4	–12.0	–8.1	–13.0	–17.9

Note: *Changes including revaluation of existing assets.
Sources: World Bank (1985b); BCB (a; various issues); UDAPE (1997b)

Table 4.9 Central Bank (changes in the outstanding balances as percentage of GDP), continued*

	1986	1987	1988	1989	1990	1991	1992	1993	1994	1995	1996
Total Assets	**2.2**	**1.9**	**2.8**	**3.2**	**3.9**	**0.9**	**6.4**	**2.9**	**7.3**	–4.6	**0.7**
Net Foreign Reserves	3.6	–0.6	–0.2	–2.7	2.5	1.6	0.9	2.8	2.5	2.7	4.9
Net Credit to Public Sector	–3.4	1.1	2.4	4.4	1.5	0.2	5.7	2.3	0.4	–7.5	–3.3
– To Government	–1.1	–1.3	1.4	1.5	0.8	–0.3	8.4	1.9	0.4	–5.2	–3.5
– To Public Enterprises	–2.2	2.4	0.9	2.9	0.7	0.5	–2.7	0.4	0.0	–2.3	0.2
Net Credit to Private Sector	1.9	1.4	0.7	1.5	-0.1	-0.9	–0.2	–2.2	4.4	0.2	–0.9
– Gross Credit	2.6	1.8	2.6	3.7	1.3	0.6	–0.3	–0.2	3.7	1.3	0.2
– Deposits	0.7	0.4	2.0	2.2	1.4	1.5	–0.1	2.0	–0.7	1.1	1.1
Total Liabilities	**2.2**	**1.9**	**2.8**	**3.2**	**3.9**	**0.9**	**6.4**	**2.9**	**7.3**	–4.6	**0.7**
Currency	1.4	1.1	1.2	-0.1	0.9	0.6	0.7	0.5	1.4	1.0	0.4
Long-term External Debt	1.3	2.3	3.1	4.8	3.4	2.2	2.4	2.1	2.9	–4.4	–0.4
CDDs									2.6	–2.1	–0.2
Other Accounts Net	–0.5	–1.4	–1.4	–1.6	–0.4	–1.9	3.3	0.3	0.4	0.9	0.8

Note: *Changes including revaluation of existing assets.
Sources: World Bank (1985b); BCB (a; various issues); UDAPE (1997b)

In 1983, the Central Bank's net external reserves increased by 9.3 per cent as a share of GDP, but only because the external debt was converted from short- to long-term when the Bank failed to honour its repayment commitments.

During the period of hyperinflation the weight of foreign debt in the Central Bank's balance increased substantially even though external finance had been stopped. The outstanding debt rose from 5.7 per cent of GDP in 1980 to 24.2 per cent in 1985, mostly as a result of the revaluation of the external debt, which, unlike most Central Bank assets, was 100 per cent indexed to the exchange rate. This brought about a large de-capitalization of the Central Bank, whose net wealth fell on average by 11 per cent of GDP per year.

Immediately following the 1985 stabilization programme, most efforts were concentrated on controlling credit expansion to the public sector. The surpluses generated by the state oil company YPFB were used to cover the rest of the public sector deficit and even increase deposits in the Central Bank so that new credit to the public sector was negative in net terms. The ratio between the total credit to the public sector and the total reserves and deposits held by the public sector in the Central Bank (which between 1974 and 1984 had fluctuated between 1.3 and 1.6), was reduced to 0.8. Between 1985 and 1986, Central Bank credit to the public sector contracted, in net terms, by an amount equivalent to 5.4 per cent of GDP per year. These credit contractions helped the Central Bank to expand credit to the financial system by an equivalent of 2 per cent of GDP per year, and to accumulate reserves by an amount equivalent to 4.7 per cent of GDP at its peak in 1986. Money creation was drastically reduced to only 1.4 per cent of GDP per year.

Starting from 1987 and once the stabilization programme was under way, Central Bank credit to the public sector expanded by an amount equivalent to 2.3 per cent of GDP per year. This was financed mostly by external borrowing, which increased by 2.1 per cent of GDP per year. Gross credit to the private sector increased by an equivalent of 2.4 per cent of GDP. The Central Bank also began to issue debt instruments, largely certificates of deposit (CDs) that paid close to market rates of interest, in order to absorb excess liquidity from the financial system. By 1989 most CDs were held by commercial banks (commercial bank deposits in the Central Bank increased by an amount equivalent to 1.3 per cent of GDP). Finally, money creation was maintained at a very low level (1 per cent of GDP per year in 1977 and 1988) and was made negative in 1989 by an amount equivalent to 0.1 per cent of GDP.

During the 1990s, the Central Bank considerably reduced its finance to the public sector. The total credit outstanding to the NFPS diminished from an equivalent of 35 per cent of GDP in 1990 to only 11.4 per cent in 1996. Although NFPS' deposits in the Central Bank also experienced a sizeable reduction, in net terms credit went down by 6.9 per cent of GDP between these two years. This reflects a general macroeconomic policy aimed at reducing Central Bank involvement in the finance of the NFPS' deficits. On the other hand, the level of outstanding Central Bank credit to commercial banks shrank by 1.8 per cent of GDP during the same period of time. This restrictive monetary policy allowed the Central Bank to accumulate foreign exchange reserves by an amount equal to 11 per cent of GDP.

In summary, the Central Bank has, for most of the time, performed its function as the government's banker and lender of last resort to the commercial banking system. Earlier discussions showed that Central Bank credit acted as the closing variable for the accumulation balances for the commercial banks, government and public enterprises. The degrees to which these three economic agents resorted to Central Bank credit have varied depending on the availability of other sources of finance (external credit in the case of the government and public enterprises, and external credit and domestic deposits in the case of the commercial banks). In this way, the use of Central Bank finance was insignificant during the 1970s, extensive during the first half of the 1980s, and moderate during the second half of the 1980s and the first half of the 1990s.

The ways in which the Central Bank has funded credit expansions has varied drastically over the different periods. During the 1970s, the Central Bank mostly resorted to its own reserves to increase finance. These reserves were enlarged by the external resources made available to the country. Between 1980 and 1985, money creation was mostly used; monetary policy was confined exclusively to financing the public sector deficit. During the second half of the 1980s, the Central Bank's main source of finance was the expansion of commercial bank deposits, which increased in response to the close-to-market interest rates paid by, and lower risk attached to the certificates of deposit issued by the Central Bank (see Table 4.9). The reforms to the financial system introduced during the 1990s strengthened Central Bank autonomy and considerably limited the Central Bank's finance to the NFPS.

4.4 Interest Rate Determination

Before the introduction of the NEP in 1985, the nominal interest rate in Bolivia was determined by the Central Bank.

Between 1970 and 1979, interest rates paid on savings deposits were maintained at a fixed 11.75 per cent per year. Between 1973 and 1974, relatively high rates of inflation resulted in negative rates of interest. During the years of relatively low inflation (1975–77), interest rates were positive in real terms, albeit very low. Alternative domestic assets (such as the dollar-denominated deposits authorized in 1975) yielded lower nominal interest rates, and since the exchange rate was kept fixed, in real terms the yields were even lower still.

After 1979 inflation and devaluation increased sharply. Peso-denominated deposits became less attractive, and the public switched to dollar-denominated deposits paying higher nominal interest rates and, with repeated devaluations, even higher real interest rates.

After the 1982 dedollarization decree, the monetary authorities were unable to maintain positive real interest rates. Although the nominal rates were increased up to 140 per cent in 1984, hyperinflation transformed these into highly negative rates ranging from –66.2 per cent in 1983 to –97.5 per cent in 1985.

Under the 1985 stabilization and financial liberalization programmes, interest rate controls were lifted, real interest rates rose to extremely high levels, but nominal interest rates declined steadily. However, inflation fell much more rapidly, and real interest rates (comparing nominal interest rates with inflation over the same period) remained above 15 per cent during the rest of the decade. The persistence of high interest rates in the second half of the 1980s has been interpreted in a number of ways.

(a) The World Bank (1989, p.53) argues that despite considerable progress in reducing inflation and the government's commitment to a liberalized economic environment, public confidence in the maintenance of the new policy regime remained low. Thus, financial institutions had to offer high interest rates to compensate for the perceived risk involved in holding domestic assets.

(b) The degree of competition in the Bolivian banking system is regarded as very low (World Bank, ibid.; UDAPE 1991, p.21). With only six banks controlling 65 per cent of total deposits, some observers argue that the major banks fix both deposits and interest rates, and competition is largely carried through advertising to increase market shares.

(c) The persistent government deficit is continuously financed through open-market operations that pay high interest rates, and the interest rates paid by the Central Bank are regarded as references for the interest paid or charged by other banks. The validity of this argument was demonstrated in 1991, when the Central Bank decided to halve the interest paid on its CDs and the rest of the financial system followed.

During the 1990s, the large increase of deposits in the banking system tended to reduce interest rates. The interest rate paid on dollar denominated deposits decreased from 14.6 per cent in 1990 to 8.9 per cent in 1996. This caused a reduction in the country's implicit risk premium (the difference between dollar denominated interest rates and the LIBOR) to 3 percentage points, compared with spreads above 6 percentage points in 1990. On the other hand, the interest rate on dollar denominated loans also experienced a significant reduction, from 22.3 per cent in 1990 to 17.1 in 1996 (see Table 4.2). However, the current levels are still high, which discourage investment. Spreads however have tended to increase during that period.

There are different explanations for the persistence of high interest rates after stabilization: high country risk (Ramirez and De la Viña, 1992), low credibility of macroeconomic policies and stabilization (Antelo, 1994), existence of strong oligopolies in the Bolivian financial system (Apt and Schargrodsky, 1995).

In summary, before 1985 the interest rate was customarily determined by the Central Bank, and the real interest rate was determined endogenously depending on the rate of inflation. After 1985, when interest rate controls were lifted, the real interest rate increased rapidly as inflation was brought under control. During the 1990s however, the increase in bank deposits brought about a reduction in the interest rate.

4.5 Conclusions

The aim of this chapter was to discuss adjustment for the financial sector of the Bolivian economy over the last two and a half decades, thus completing the analysis of the whole economic system with a full picture of macroeconomic adjustment.

An understanding of the mechanisms and institutional factors that ruled adjustments for the financial balances was considered particularly important since the relationship between the closures of the financial sector is very closely connected to and almost overlaps with the overall closure at the macroeconomic level. That was not the case with supply-demand balances for productive sectors, nor with the accumulation balances for individual economic agents whose adjustments, although having macroeconomic implications, were mostly visualized at the sectoral level.

The findings of this chapter further confirm the soundness of the approach adopted in this research to understanding macroeconomic adjustment in a developing economy. Institutional factors other than the price mechanism largely determined adjustment in the financial sector in the Bolivian economy over the period analysed. In addition, these institutionally determined adjustment mechanisms have not been the same over the whole period, but have tended to vary over time depending on the external environment and on the direction of domestic policy.

Section 4.2 argued that the interest rate mechanism did not play a significant role in bringing adjustment to the Bolivian financial sector during the whole period studied. During the 1970s and early 1980s, the interest rate was determined administratively, and most of the time led to negative real interest rates. Financial adjustment therefore occurred through financial flows, largely conditioned by institutional factors that played major roles in the allocation of credit and resource mobilization. For instance, sectors with connections with financial institutions and influence over the design of the monetary policy, such as the government, public enterprises and corporate sector, had relatively easy access to credit), while others, such as peasants, had very limited access to or were completely excluded from financial markets. Even after the financial liberalization introduced in 1985, the interest rate mechanism failed to be effective in bringing adjustment to financial markets. The interest rate remained at a very high level during most of the post-stabilization period. Financial flows therefore again played a fundamental role in bringing equilibrium to the financial sector.

The ways in which resources were mobilized also depended on institutional settings. The sources used by the financial system to finance credit expansions tended to vary over time, depending on the relative amounts of resources available from each of these sources (external credit, deposits, and money creation). Resorting to these alternative sources had different implications for the closure at the macroeconomic level. Deposits were associated with higher interest rates, money creation with higher rates of inflation.

The reforms implemented during the 1990s introduce substantial changes to the way the financial system operates. These measures are aimed at enhancing the autonomy of the Central Bank, limiting the NFPS' capacity to resort to the Central Bank's credit in order to finance its deficits, and strengthening the supervision of financial institutions in order to eliminate lending to related parties.

Appendix 4.1 Inflation, Financial Stocks and Financial Flows

Inflation greatly distorts financial balances and therefore financial statistics, so that researchers must be cautious when analysing financial time-series in periods of inflation, because their conclusions could be greatly distorted if the effects of inflation are not properly understood or identified. For example, in periods of high inflation, there is a tendency for the *stock* of money supply (M/P) to fall in real terms. This is explained in terms of the inflation tax that makes people shift away from money to other assets that are better protected against inflation.

High inflation, however, is always accompanied by large increases in the money supply in nominal terms. ($M_t - M_{t-1} > 0$). Whatever the rate of inflation, it is not possible to say that the *flow* of money during that period is negative, even in real terms, thus ($(M_t - M_{t-1})/P_t > 0$). At most it tends to be zero when inflation is very high.

How, then, is it possible that the *stock* of money in real terms falls if the *flow* in real terms is positive (or in the extreme case zero)? This can only be explained in terms of the devaluation effect of inflation on existing stocks. The negative change in the *stock* of real money ($M_t/P_t - M_{t-1}/P_{t-1}$) can be decomposed into: (a) a positive *flow* ($(M_t - M_{t-1})/P_t$) that tends to be smaller for high rates of inflation, and (b) a negative revaluation of existing stocks that tends to be highly negative when there are large changes between P_t and P_{t-1}. Thus:

$$M_t/P_t - M_{t-1}/P_{t-1} = ((M_t - M_{t-1})/P_t) + (1/P_t - 1/P_{t-1}).M_{t-1}$$

Note

1. Although the stocks of money in real terms fell sharply, it is not accurate to argue that during that period there were negative changes in the flows of bank credit, currency, bank deposits or other stocks of domestic assets; on the contrary, there were huge expansions in the nominal values of all these monetary variables and at most (in the extreme case of hyperinflation) we could expect a close to zero change in the amount of real balances (when very high inflation erodes nominal changes in asset stocks almost instantaneously), but never negative.

5 Supply-Demand Adjustments Employment and Income Distribution

5.1 Introduction

External shocks have also influenced the processes of adjustment in the supply-demand balances in the Bolivian economy during the 1970s, 1980s and first half of the 1990s. The discussion in this chapter will help to identify some general characteristics of the country's long-term economic performance.

This chapter highlights the heterogeneous nature of supply-demand adjustments in a developing economy such as Bolivia. Sectoral market clearing mechanisms in developing economies vary depending on the institutional features that govern sectoral adjustments. Some sectors are dominated by oligopolistic structures, and prices are determined through a mark-up over the cost of production. These sectors operate with excess capacity or inventories, so that excess demand is cleared through increased output. Other sectors are more competitive and excess demand is cleared through price changes. Supply in these sectors is fixed in the short term. Sectors that produce for export markets are price takers and foreign markets will take all output produced by these sectors. These features obviously provide additional support for the argument in this book that a more disaggregated approach to macroeconomic analysis is needed.

Section 5.2 concentrates on the discussion of the clearing mechanisms that characterized adjustment in the supply-demand balance of each sector. Aspects such as market structures, price formation, supply and demand compositions are analysed for the key productive sectors of the Bolivian economy. A summary of the most relevant market clearing mechanisms is given for each productive sector during each period of time analysed. The expected changes in sectoral adjustment, brought about by the structural reforms of the 1990s, are also discussed. Section 5.3 addresses the long-term changes observed in the factor income distribution. These changes will help to identify the main variables that determine distributional shifts among factors of production and eventually among households and the other institutional economic agents whose accumulation balances were discussed in Chapter 2. Finally, section 5.4 presents some concluding remarks.

5.2 Supply-Demand Balance Adjustments

The adjustments of economic activities followed different patterns in response to external shocks. Excess demand adjustment in the various markets for goods and services took place through a combination of changes in the following mechanisms: output, prices, exports and imports.

Table 5.1 presents the annual average growth rates by sector during five selected periods. It also presents the changes that these different growth rates produced on the GDP structure in constant values.

(a) During the 1970s

During the period 1971–75, the economy experienced rapid economic growth (6.8 per cent per year on average) fuelled by an oil and gas export boom, increased government spending and capital inflows; the oil and gas sector grew on average by more than 27 per cent per year. Bolivia also made an attempt to develop its precarious manufacturing sector, which grew at 6.8 per cent per year.

Between 1976 and 1980, the country was still receiving large capital inflows, but average annual growth fell to only 2.9 per cent. Growth was mostly concentrated in the nontraded sector: electricity grew on average at more than 7 per cent per year, transport and communications at 8.9 per cent, banking at 8.5 per cent and public services at 4.4 per cent. The two most important export sectors remained largely stagnant during this period: hydrocarbon production fell by 6.5 per cent per year, and mining output by 2.3 per cent.

Table 5.1 *Average GDP growth rate and GDP structure in real terms*

	Average Growth Rate					GDP Structure					
	1971-75	1976–80	1981–85	1986–90	1991–95	1970	1975	1980	1985	1990	1995
Agriculture	5.6	2.2	3.1	1.1	3.5	15.5	14.6	14.1	17.6	17.7	16.3
Mining	3.4	–2.6	–10.3	10.4	4.3	12.3	10.3	7.8	4.9	5.1	6.6
Hydrocarbons	27.0	–6.5	0.8	1.9	3.8	3.8	6.8	4.1	4.7	4.8	4.6
Manufacturing	6.8	4.8	–5.4	4.5	3.9	18.0	18.1	19.8	16.4	17.8	18.5
Construction	5.9	1.2	–5.5	0.1	6.9	5.3	5.1	4.6	3.8	3.4	3.8
Energy	7.3	7.6	4.3	3.7	8.4	0.9	1.0	1.2	1.6	1.7	2.2
Transport and Communication	9.9	9.0	4.1	4.8	5.7	4.3	5.0	6.6	8.9	9.7	11.0
Commerce	3.9	1.7	0.8	5.8	4.2	8.9	7.7	7.3	8.1	9.2	9.8
Banking	13.0	8.5	–6.3	–3.7	6.8	4.8	6.3	8.0	6.3	4.9	5.3
General Government	8.6	4.4	–1.4	–3.0	2.1	11.8	12.9	13.9	14.3	11.9	10.1
Ownership of Dwellings	3.4	3.3	0.7	0.2	1.6	7.1	6.1	6.2	7.1	6.9	5.8
Other Services	3.5	2.9	–2.2	3.9	1.9	7.3	6.2	6.3	6.1	7.1	6.0
GDP at m.p.	6.8	2.9	–2.0	2.1	3.9	100.0	100.0	100.0	100.0	100.0	100.0

Sources: INE (1997); World Bank (1985b); UDAPE (1997a)

Table 5.2 GDP structure in nominal terms

	1970	1975	1980	1985	1990	1995
Agriculture	18.1	18.6	18.9	29.3	16.7	15.9
Mining	9.3	6.5	10.6	2.0	6.5	5.4
Hydrocarbons	1.0	4.8	5.6	9.9	4.7	1.7
Manufacturing	14.5	13.4	15.0	12.1	18.5	19.6
Construction	4.1	4.1	3.8	4.3	3.3	3.3
Energy	1.4	1.0	0.7	0.9	1.8	4.2
Transport and Communication	7.5	7.4	6.1	10.7	10.2	11.5
Commerce	17.6	19.1	11.1	10.9	9.7	9.7
Banking	1.4	2.0	6.0	6.7	4.6	4.0
General Government	8.0	8.7	10.8	6.3	11.0	12.2
Ownership of Dwellings	8.8	7.5	8.4	4.0	6.5	5.1
Other Services	8.3	7.1	3.0	3.0	6.6	7.5
G D P at m.p.	100.0	100.0	100.0	100.0	100.0	100.0

Sources: INE (1997); World Bank (1985b); UDAPE (1997a)

(b) Between 1980 and 1985

The net resource transfers to the country fell sharply and eventually became negative as the external debt-service burden increased. As a result, Bolivia made large resource transfers abroad (US$530 million between 1982 and 1984). This large resource drain had an extremely severe stagflationary impact on the economy; prices as measured by the GDP deflator rose by 171 per cent in 1982, 280 per cent in 1983, 1,497 per cent in 1984, and 12,364 per cent in 1985, while real GDP fell by 1.8 per cent per year. The worst-hit sectors were mining, banking, manufacturing and construction, which reduced their activity levels on average by 10.2, 6.3, 5.4 and 5.5 per cent per year, respectively, and government services by 1.4 per cent per year. Agriculture and hydrocarbons showed low growth rates (3.1 and 0.8 per cent per year respectively), while electricity production expanded by 4.3 per cent per year. Agricultural production contracted sharply in 1983 due to adverse weather conditions. However, this negative behaviour was reversed in the following two years. Part of this recovery was explained by the sharp increase in the production of coca. The level of services, however, remained practically unchanged.

(c) After the 1985 NEP

In 1986, the year after the introduction of the stabilization programme, GDP fell by 3 per cent. This negative behaviour was the result not only of the contractionary impact of the stabilization programme itself, but also of the collapse of the international tin market in October 1985. The price of tin fell by 40 per cent, making most of the Bolivian mines unprofitable, and mining output contracted by 27 per cent. The construction sector was worst hit by the recessionary impact of the stabilization plan; it decreased by 21 per cent. Government services fell by 16 per cent, due to the restructuring imposed on the public sector. Agricultural output fell by 4 per cent, but again this was due to adverse weather conditions.

However, over the whole period under the stabilization and structural adjustment programmes (between 1986 and 1995) GDP growth was positive. Starting from 1986, the country resumed its relations with international financial institutions and foreign capital again began to flow into the economy. Between 1986 and 1990 output grew at 2.1 per cent per year on average. During this period, the mining sector recovered after its extremely poor performance in the previous five years (mining output grew by 10.4 per cent per year). Hydrocarbon output grew by 1.9 per cent per year, manufacturing by 4.5 per cent and electricity by 3.7 per cent. Between 1991 and 1995, the yearly average GDP growth rate increased to 3.9 per cent.

Since supply-demand adjustments for the different activities also came through price changes, the full impact of the combined quantity and price adjustments is reflected in their nominal shares of GDP. This structure is presented in Table 5.2. It is interesting to analyse the large shifts that took-place in the structure of the Bolivian GDP. The share of agriculture of GDP, for instance, stood at 18 per cent during the 1970s. By 1985, however, due to huge price distortions, it increased to 29 per cent; and during the post-stabilization period its weight in total GDP slowly decreased, reaching 15.9 per cent in 1995. The weight of hydrocarbons, on the other hand, was very low in 1970 (less than 1 per cent of GDP). Due to the oil and gas boom, it increased to 9.8 per cent in 1985, and decreased afterwards when export prices and volumes were revised downwards, within the terms of the gas export contract signed with Argentina.

From this preliminary analysis, it seems that the various economic activities tended to adjust to the external shocks following different patterns. The markets for each productive sector seem to have distinctive institutional features (such as price formation, market structure and production functions), which determined the specific sectoral adjustment to the changing patterns followed by capital inflows and other external shocks. The following sections analyse in depth the supply-demand balance adjustments for key economic activities during the 1970s, 1980s and first half of the 1990s.

5.3 Agricultural sector

5.3.1 Modern agriculture

Modern agriculture comprises all agricultural activities on relatively large-scale holdings, using modern techniques and producing for export markets. Markets for both inputs and products are relatively well developed, and the products of this large-farm sector are all marketed (Whitaker and Wennergren 1982, p.239). Modern agriculture activities are mostly located in the eastern lowlands of the country, in the departments of Santa Cruz and Beni. These producers are highly organized and generally have good access to agricultural research and extension services, in which they participate directly. The main problems they face are inadequate clearing methods, inadequate production systems, incorrect use of machinery resulting in the compacting of soil, blockage of natural watercourses, and lack of permanent roads for access to export markets.

The predominant products are cotton, sugar cane, soy beans, wood and beef cattle.

The behaviour of the corporate agricultural sector in Bolivia has been very unstable in the last two and a half decades.

During the 1970s, Bolivia experienced an agricultural export boom in products such as sugar, cotton, soy beans and beef, partly in response to the favourable external market conditions at the beginning of the decade. During the 1970s, a large proportion of public expenditure was allocated to support the development of large-scale commercial

Table 5.3 *Average yearly growth rate of modern agriculture's selected products*

	1971–75	1976–80	1981–85	1986–90	1991–95
Soya bean		26.4	22.5	17.0	30.7
Sugar cane	10.0	3.6	2.3	0.2	3.0
Cotton	34.0	−20.9	−7.1	−14.2	50.2
Total	13.6	−1.2	7.1	8.0	24.2

Sources: World Bank (1985b); INE (1997); BCB (c; various issues)

agriculture in the Santa Cruz region. One element of this plan involved granting credit via the Banco Agrícola de Bolivia (Agricultural Bank of Bolivia, BAB) to operators of relatively large farms in the lowlands. A second major programme area was to improve the processing and marketing of agricultural products, including sugar, rice, dairy products, and vegetable oils carried out by the Corporación Boliviana de Fomento (Bolivian Development Corporation, CBF). The combined BAB and CBF programmes accounted for 85 per cent of all public sector resources allocated during 1971–73.

The elite rural groups that benefited the most from the government's policies included owners of large cattle ranches and merchants (for example, exporters of cattle, rubber and Brazil nuts) in the eastern department of Beni, and the agro-business elite (whose wealth and income derived primarily from sugar cane, cotton, soy beans, cattle production, commerce and agro-industries such as sugar and rice mills) in the Santa Cruz region.

The agricultural export boom took place on the farms and in the agro-industries of the Santa Cruz area (Ladman 1982). This economic group benefited from favourable pricing, export, credit, marketing and investment policies of the Bolivian state during this period. US-financed road-building, agro-industrial and land clearance projects demonstrated strong foreign support for this rural modernization strategy.

As a result of these favourable conditions, modern agricultural output increased on average by more than 13 per cent per year between 1971 and 1975. Although activity levels fell during the second half of the 1970s, average output was 10 per cent higher than in 1970–73.

Table 5.4 Average yearly exports of modern agriculture's selected products (US$ million)

	1971–75	1976–80	1981–85	1986–90	1991–95
Cotton	20.2	12.9	2.3	4.6	15.9
Brazil Nuts		2.4	1.6	7.6	14.1
Rubber		4.3	2.3	2.1	0.3
Meat and Cattle	1.6	1.24	1.1	15.3	4.3
Timber	19.8	24.1	9.4	34.7	62.9
Soya bean		6.9	5.1	31.5	88.1
Sugar		47.6	7.0	14.1	26.8
Leather		4.7	1.3	14.5	12.7

Sources: World Bank (1985b); INE (1997); BCB (c; various issues)

Between 1980 and 1985, the sector remained largely stagnant, as most of the favourable market and credit conditions disappeared, and output fell by 15 per cent. An overvalued exchange rate, and exchange rate controls imposed by the government in 1982, served to reduce agricultural exporters' competitiveness by more than 40 per cent. As a result, exports dropped by 47 per cent.

After 1985, the sector experienced much higher rates of growth, as the NEP placed special interest on promoting non-traditional exports and a more realistic exchange rate policy was implemented. Relative prices improved by almost 40 per cent for agricultural exporters. To provide compensation for duties paid on imported inputs, in 1987 the government introduced a flat 10 per cent rebate known as CRA (Certificado de Reintegro Arancelario) to exporters of non-traditional products. In 1991, this rebate was abolished and replaced by a duty drawback system. Output and exports increased by 42 and 83 per cent between 1985 and 1989, respectively. The production of soy beans increased very rapidly in the last fifteen years. Soy production went up from 38,000 metric tons in 1980 to 100,000 in 1985, and to almost 900,000 tons in 1995. As a result, export earnings jumped from US$7 million in 1980 to US$126 million in 1995. Other export products that also performed well during this last period are timber and sugar.

In summary, over the period under analysis, agro-industry exports proved to be responsive to external prices, exchange rate policy, internal price stability and export incentives. Econometric tests show that during the 1970s, agricultural exports in a given year were responsive to the relative price prevailing in the previous year (the elasticity coefficient being 1.8). During the 1980s, agro-industry exports became more elastic to relative prices in the current year, but the elasticity coefficient fell to 1.2. In both periods, relative prices proved to be significant in explaining changes in export volumes.

There are two additional factors that contributed to the agro-industry export boom. The first was government investment in infrastructure. The export boom of the 1970s for instance, was the result of the Bolivian government's plan to develop the lowlands implemented after the 1952 revolution.[1] The second contributing factor was the duty preferences given to Bolivian exports within the Andean Group.

5.3.2 Traditional agriculture

Traditional agriculture includes production of labour-intensive agricultural units (excluding coca production), namely peasant units engaged in traditional subsistence farming, mainly in the central highlands of the country, producing staple foods to satisfy domestic demand. As the Bolivian government pointed out (Ministry of Finance, 1996) 'These producers use precarious dry farming methods (only a few regions are irrigated, amounting to less than 75,000 has.), have very limited access to new technological packages, institutional credit, technical assistance, markets for materials (seed) and other production support services. Moreover, access to the basic services of education, health, and potable water is poor or non-existent. Their products have a restricted market, primarily because of lack of roads and the distance from markets, causing inconstant prices and uncertainty. The main crops are: potatoes, corn, wheat, barley and quinua'.

Traditional agriculture's output (excluding the production of coca leaves) remained largely stagnant over the last two and a half decades for most traditional crops (such as potatoes, maize and wheat).

Between 1971 and 1975, this sector's output increased by 30 per cent (5.4 per cent per year on average). In 1976 and 1977, due to adverse weather conditions, output dropped by 7.7 and by 13 per cent and remained at that level until the end of the decade.

Table 5.5 Average growth rate of modern agriculture: selected products

	1971–75	1976–80	1981–85	1986–90	1991–95
Wheat	6.9	–0.5	4.3	–6.0	18.0
Rice	11.8	–5.5	12.7	4.1	4.5
Maize		4.7	7.6	–6.0	5.1
Potato	5.0	–1.2	–0.5	–4.2	0.7
Yucca		–5.1	11.4	5.3	-9.5
Oats			6.4	–1.9	–4.5
Tomato	4.6	–13.4	–1.4	7.0	1.4
Corn			–6.1	0.0	3.6
Onion			2.1	1.6	3.8
Orange	4.4	5.0	–14.9	15.4	3.3
Grape			-5.8	1.0	1.2
Banana	3.5	–8.9	7.3	8.4	-5.1
Alfalfa			–6.0	–9.2	–1.9
Coffee			7.3	4.2	-6.6
Total	5.4	–2.8	2.8	–1.6	1.0

Sources: World Bank (1985b); UDAPE (1997a); INE (1997); BCB (c; various issues)

During the 1980–89 period, production in the traditional agricultural sector presented a very uneven pattern. Between 1980 and 1982, output grew by 18 per cent (5.8 per cent per year on average). In 1983, however, production experienced a 40 per cent drop due to extremely adverse weather conditions; an unprecedented drought in the highlands of the western part of the country (altiplano) caused substantial crop losses of cereals and tubers. 1984 saw a partial recovery, which, however, was not sustained in 1985. Very heavy rains again fell on the altiplano in early 1986 causing Lake Titicaca to rise and flood large areas of the fertile lakeshore; 40,000 people were made homeless and crop losses were estimated at US$50 million. As a result, output dropped by 7 per cent. In 1989, adverse weather again caused further output contractions, this time by 13 per cent. As a result of these adverse shocks, traditional agricultural output in 1989 was just below the 1975 level.

During the first half of the 1990s output remained largely stagnant, growing on average at 1 per cent a year.

In summary, traditional agriculture's output has been heavily influenced by adverse climatic conditions, especially in 1977, 1983, 1986 and 1989, and has remained largely stagnant over the period under study. Output grew on average by 0.8 per cent per year during the 1970s, by 1.1 per cent during the 1980s and by 1 per cent in the first half of the 1990s.

There is widespread consensus among writers (World Bank 1990; Whitaker and Wennergren 1982; Ministry of Finance 1996), about the basic problems that have restricted the development of a stronger agricultural sector in Bolivia: (a) an extremely limited and deficient scientific base for the sector; (b) lack of human capital at both the general and technical-scientific level of training; (c) deficient basic infrastructure, such as local roadways and irrigation systems; (d) lack of efficient rural credit systems; and (e) lack of a sustainable management of natural resources.

On the other hand, the rate of growth of demand for food far exceeded that of domestic agricultural production. On average, the population increased at about 2.1 per cent as measured by the 1976 and 1992 population census, resulting in a direct increase in demand of at least the same magnitude.[2] A consequence of the greater growth in demand than in production was an upward pressure on food prices. Before 1985, the government introduced a number of policies aimed at maintaining low, fixed prices for basic food products in order to protect consumers. These restrictions brought about the emergence of black markets when food was in short supply.

Traditional agricultural prices are determined in relatively competitive and atomistic domestic markets. Once marketable output supply has been determined after the harvest period, it remains fixed in the short term (within the year). Thus, prices and therefore rural households' profit margins adjust in order to balance the marketable surplus to the nominal value of urban household demand. Thus, rural-urban terms of trade (vis-à-vis manufacturing prices, for example) is inversely correlated with agricultural output levels. The fact that demand for agricultural products is price inelastic[3] means that an increase in supply brings about a large reduction in prices and consequently a deterioration of peasant incomes.

5.3.3 Coca

By far the most lucrative agricultural products are coca and its illicitly produced by-products, namely coca paste and unrefined cocaine. Fine-tuned over the millennia to the Andean ecosystem, the coca leaf is considered a 'wonder crop' (Plowman 1986). In the Chapare region it grows relatively well on poor soils, has few problems with blight and pests, yields four to five harvests annually and offers a much higher and more stable economic rate of return from land and labour investment than any other Bolivian cash crop in the highlands or lowlands (Healy 1986, p.127). The coca sector comprises both the traditional harvest of coca leaves (including that for customary local consumption) and the illicit production and export of coca by-products as part of the illegal international drug trade.[4] In Bolivia, coca is grown in the subtropical and tropical regions of the departments of Cochabamba and La Paz and covers about 60,000 hectares. Of this production, 12,000 hectares is intended for traditional consumption. The other 48,000 hectares are cultivated to produce leaves that are first converted into coca paste, and then into cocaine for export. In the Chapare region there are 80,000 coca producers, and a further 30,000 in Yungas and Santa Cruz regions.[5] Elementary cocaine refining is a labour-intensive activity. The technology is simple, easy to master, and provides peasant farmers with benefits from their land and labour investment in addition to their basic agricultural production.

Since the mid-1970s the booming demand of the international drug trade has transformed this traditional activity into one that provide at least part of their income to between 48,000 and 61,000 rural families (UDAPE 1990b, World Bank 1992). Coca leaf production increased from 6,000 metric tons in 1970 to 48,000 in 1980, and to 140,000 tons in 1990. The traditional domestic consumption is estimated to be only 14,000 tons.[6] National Accounts estimates report that during the 1990s, coca production has reduced by almost 3 per cent a year on average.

Table 5.6 Average growth rate of coca production

	1971–75	1976–80	1981–85	1986–90	1991–95
Coca	14.5	32.7	21.7	1.7	-2.8

Sources: MACA 1989; INE 1997; BCB (c; various issues)

The price offered to coca leaf growers is sensitive to the foreign demand for cocaine (Healy 1986, p.129). Although the price in 1989 (of $100 per 100 lbs. of leaves) was well below that offered in the early 1980s, it still made coca a much more lucrative crop than cocoa, coffee or nuts (UDAPE 1990b, p.4; Flores and Blanes 1984).

According to estimates, at the end of 1987 the value added of the coca-cocaine industry was approximately US$1.1 billion—equivalent to 15 per cent of GDP. Corresponding estimates for 1991 are US$320 million (6 per cent of GDP) (UDAPE 1990b). This illustrates the still significant, although substantially reduced, importance of the sector. It has been commonly assumed that approximately one-third of this value is retained by factors of production in Bolivia. As such, in recent years the industry's actual contribution to the economy has been estimated at 2 per cent of GDP.

Although difficult to quantify, most studies suggest that the importance of coca-cocaine in the economy has declined since 1988. Some of this decline is explained by government programmes to curtail coca production[7], but part of the decline is explained by price decreases.

In summary, during the period under analysis, coca output has been demonstrated to be quite responsive to changes in price and profitability. Econometric tests (see Appendix 5.2) show that relative price changes (the price of coca relative to prices of other traditional agricultural products) were significant in explaining the observed rapid increase in coca output. Coca production can react very quickly to price increases because of the particular characteristics of the coca plant. As Sage (1989) has pointed out, 'Coca is part of a diversified cropping system that fits well both into the environment and the agricultural cycle of small-farm households without being too demanding of labour. As it is harvested four times per year it provides a regular source of income to meet household expenditure.'

Local producers have entered the cocaine refining processes, since they entail only rudimentary technology, little infrastructure and no large investments[8]. A minor part of total coca production (about 10 per cent) was used for traditional consumption.

External prices for coca by-products are determined in external markets, although Bolivia's coca production may affect international cocaine prices, given its importance in the total production of raw material. Domestic prices of coca, on the other hand, are linked to changes in the world's demand for and supply of cocaine, which can lead to large mismatches in domestic markets.

5.4 Mining

Mining production is carried out by the state-owned Corporación Minera de Bolivia (COMIBOL), medium-scale private companies and a large number of small-scale mining cooperatives (Cariaga 1982). They produce tin, antimony, tungsten, zinc, bismuth, copper, gold and silver for export.

The smelting industry, on the other hand, includes the state-owned Vinto high-grade tin smelter, which is currently run at one-quarter of its capacity, a low-grade smelter that has been closed, the Karachipampa lead-zinc smelter plant, which is out of operation due to a lack of raw materials, and the Palca tin volatilization plant, which operates only sporadically (Cariaga ibid).

The importance of mining in the Bolivian economy has greatly decreased over the last two decades (see Tables 5.1 and 5.2). Between 1975 and 1980, mining represented between 10 and 12 per cent of GDP, employed around 4 per cent of the country's labour force, and provided between 60 and 70 per cent of all foreign exchange. After the overnight collapse of the tin market in October 1985, the share of mining in total GDP fell to 2 per cent, in total employment to 2 per cent, and in total foreign exchange earnings to 39 per cent. By 1995, the share of mining in total GDP was 5.4 per cent and in total exports 43 per cent.

In 1977, Bolivia had more than 15 per cent of the world tin production capacity, 6 per cent of the world smelting capacity, and 12 per cent of the known tin reserves. Compared with other major tin producers (Malaysia, Thailand and Indonesia), Bolivia's production is characterized by high cost and low efficiency, resulting from the complexity of the mineral concentrates obtained and the decreasing ore reserves. These constraints put Bolivia in a disadvantaged position to compete in world markets.

Between the nationalization of the tin mines in 1952 and the implementation of the NEP in 1985, some 65 per cent of Bolivia's mineral production was in the hands of COMIBOL, the state-owned holding company created to operate the nationalized mines. Of the remainder, some 25 per cent were operated by medium-sized, privately owned, mining companies, and the balance of 10 per cent was in the hands of 2,000–4,000 small private operating units. The performance of all three categories of producers has been hampered by long-term structural problems and by sharp fluctuations in international prices of metals.

In an unpublished economic analysis of Bolivia in 1977, the World Bank noted that COMIBOL, since its creation in 1952, has experienced a multitude of problems due to its excessive centralization, the slow erosion of its capital assets, its inefficient use of labour, and excessive welfare benefits for its employees. According to the World Bank analysis, most of COMIBOL's mines were de-capitalized and were operating with very low levels of ore reserves. Operational costs were rising as mines became progressively deeper and the ore grades mined deteriorated. ...COMIBOL's equipment was already depreciated and technically obsolete at the time of nationalization [1952] and no significant new investment has been carried out until recently. Investment has been channelled mainly into ore processing (including volatilization) which has succeeded in increasing recovery ratios in spite of the falling mineral content of ores.

However, in spite of these various adverse conditions, during the 1970s COMIBOL managed to expand its production, especially in 1974–78, in response to the favourable world market conditions prevailing at that time, which were reflected in higher prices for producers.

Between 1979 and 1983, output remained stagnant. From 1984 onwards the sector experienced a huge contraction. The problems faced by COMIBOL were exacerbated by the general economic environment and by labour unrest; as a result, COMIBOL's production in 1985 was 50 per cent below its 1980–82 level.

Under the NEP, COMIBOL's functions were decentralized and personnel levels reduced in an attempt to cut public expenditure.[9] After the 1985 collapse of tin prices, the company was restructured, its labour force reduced to around 6,500 (compared with 27,500 in 1985) and many mines were closed. Some were given over to mining cooperatives whose members were drawn from those made redundant.[10] As a result, COMIBOL's output between 1985 and 1987 fell by 84 per cent. During the period 1988–91, COMIBOL's output partially recovered, due to higher prices for zinc. In 1989, for the first time, zinc export revenues were higher than tin export values. Between 1991 and 1995 however,

Table 5.7 Mining production (yearly average growth rates)

	1973–80	1981–85	1986–90	1991–95
COMIBOL	–2.3	–11.7	–3.9	–17.5
Medium-scale	–1.3	–7.0	12.1	18.1
Small-scale	–2.3	–4.3	32.2	–3.1

Sources: World Bank (1985b); INE (1997); BCB (c; various issues)

production plummeted by almost 70 per cent, again largely due to low international metal prices.

The output of the medium-sized privately owned mines, on the other hand, remained largely stagnant over most part of the period under analysis. Before the NEP was implemented, the sector suffered from the general deterioration in the investment climate. Medium-sized mining companies chose to keep low profiles for fear of becoming targets of nationalization. Their exploration efforts were also limited by the fact that the government withheld as 'fiscal reserves' (areas where concessions were only granted by special decree) the most promising areas. After the NEP was implemented and after the introduction of the mining code in 1991, foreign investment in the mining sector increased substantially. More than 30 well-known international private enterprises[11] invested in the sector around US$290 million after 1990. As a result, medium-scale firms' production more than doubled between 1991 and 1995. Output growth, however, was concentrated in non-traditional minerals such as gold and zinc.

The third sector in the mining industry embraces both individual prospectors and the larger cooperatives. After 1985, the ranks of the co-operatives were swollen by miners made redundant by COMIBOL and the medium-sized private companies; Catavi, for most of this century the largest tin mine in the world, was closed and turned over to these new prospectors. Mining conditions are primitive, returns very low and state benefits minimal, yet this sector sold half the recorded tin production in 1989. In that year, production in this sector was around 200 per cent higher than in 1980, and has increased the share of small-scale mining in the sector's output from an average of 12 per cent between 1973 and 1985, to 39 per cent between 1986 and 1989. However, between

1990 and 1995, this sector remained largely stagnant and production fell by 3 per cent a year on average.

In summary, since Bolivia is a 'price-taker' in the international metal markets, exports depend on the country's existing productive capacity. From the analysis above, it follows that mining production behaved differently in each of the three sub-sectors, according to particular factors. (i) COMIBOL's output has been limited by a continuously depreciating capital stock, but has been responsive to price fluctuations within the limits imposed by its installed capacity (see Appendix 5.3 for an econometric specification of COMIBOL's production function). (ii) The output of medium-scale mines has shown relatively more stable growth rates over the whole period. Econometric tests (see Appendix 5.4) show that the sector's output is significantly explained by the medium-scale mining firms' existing physical capital, although output does not appear to be very responsive to relative price fluctuations. Investment by medium-sized mining enterprises, to increase its productive capacity, was sensitive to macroeconomic conditions and to the degree of protection that the existing legal framework provides to private investment. (iii) The output of the small-scale mines tends to be correlated with the number of people working in the sector, since the technology used is more labour intensive.

5.5 Oil and Gas

In the 1970s, the discovery of hydrocarbon fields indicated the possibility of sizeable petroleum and gas deposits. Between 1970 and 1973 crude oil production increased by 95 per cent. Between 1970 and 1976 the gross profits of YPFB, the state-owned oil company, rose from US$18.3 million to US$96.4 million, and would have been appreciably greater had the domestic price not been kept low, increasing domestic consumption and restricting export capacity. In 1976 YPFB exported 8 million barrels of crude for US$112.6 million and sold 6.6 million barrels to the domestic markets for US$64.3 million (Dunkerley 1984, p.223). YPFB also had to pay large royalties to the local governments, so that an increasing proportion of the corporation's investment had to be financed through foreign loans. The greater part of this investment was directed towards expanding and modernizing refinery capacity in line with the expectations of the government's 1975–80 development plan to increase production from 40,000 to 180,000 barrels per day. In fact, although refinery capacity was increased to 70,000 barrels per day, production never exceeded the 1973 peak of 47,000 barrels per day.

By the middle of the decade it was evident that the existing wells were becoming depleted. Between 1971 and 1977 YPFB and the private companies spent a total of US$120 million on exploration but found reserves of only 20 million barrels of oil and 50 million cubic feet of gas. Between 1973 and 1980 oil production fell by 50 per cent to a level just sufficient to cover domestic demand. As a result, petroleum exports were halted in 1980.

Between 1980 and 1985 oil production fell by a further 12 per cent. In 1986, Bolivia was virtually self-sufficient in oil, with a production of 19,000 barrels per day (including the production of natural gasoline). That year oil output reached its lowest level over the whole period under analysis.

Starting from 1987, oil production started to recover, and reached 31,700 barrels a day in 1990. From 1991, Bolivia reinitiated its oil exports, which reached US$60 million in 1995.

Natural gas, on the other hand, has made an increasingly important contribution to export earnings as sales of oil have diminished. Gas exports have been dominated by the arrangement Bolivia has had to export gas to Argentina, Bolivia's main customer for gas, which is fed through a 526-km pipeline. Bolivia began exporting natural gas in 1972. Natural gas prices steadily increased until 1982. In 1985 earnings from gas amounted to about US$373 million, or 60 per cent of total exports, as against only US$67 million (10.5 per cent) in 1977. Since then the value of natural gas exports has almost halved (although the volume has remained the same): in 1995 sales contributed 7.8 per cent of Bolivia's official export earnings (compared with 36 per cent in 1987 and 44 per cent in 1982).

The price has been falling, and an agreement signed in 1987 effectively pegged prices to world market prices. A new agreement reached in 1992 reduced the price of natural gas by almost 60 per cent and maintained the volume of exported gas. In 1995 the price was about US$1.272 per 1000 ft3, compared with US$3.320 in 1987.

Official estimates put Bolivia's natural gas reserves at 1.1 trillion ft3, enough to cover local demand as well as exports to Argentina and Brazil until the year 2013.

In 1995, Yacimientos Petrolíferos Fiscales Bolivianos (YPFB), the state oil company, accounts for about 68 per cent of total crude production and for 78 per cent of total natural gas output (INE 1997); private foreign oil companies operating under licence account for the remainder. YPFB owns and operates the country's refineries, which have a total capacity of 74,000 barrels per day (b/d), far above the production of crude oil which is around 29,000 b/d .

Two events will greatly impact upon the hydrocarbon sector's performance in the future: the capitalization of YPFB and the construction of the gas pipeline to Brazil. By mid-1997, part of YPFB was capitalized in three separate parts, while the state retained ownership of the refinery and distribution branches of the industry. Enron-Shell purchased the transportation sector of YPFB, which included the agreement to invest in the completion of the natural gas pipeline to Brazil. Two exploration units were sold, one to a consortium of YPF, Perez Companc and Pluspetrol Bolivia, and the other to Amoco Petroleum Company. The construction of the gas pipeline to Brazil will demand a minimum investment of US$2 billion, of which US$350 million will finance the construction of that part of the pipeline that lies on Bolivian territory. The completion of the pipeline is expected by the end of 1998 and will represent to the country between US$100 and US$200 million a year as additional export revenues.

In summary, the natural gas supply-demand balance is mostly demand-driven. Natural gas export quantities together with prices are fixed under long-term contracts signed with the customers. Natural gas reserves are sufficient to supply the volumes agreed under these contracts.

The supply-demand balance for petroleum and its derivatives, on the other hand, is very much supply-determined. If production exceeds domestic demand, then excess supply is exported. During the 1970s, when production was well in excess of domestic absorption, Bolivia was able to export crude oil. During the 1980s, production fell to levels just adequate to satisfy domestic demand (some imports were required when output fell below these levels). Domestic demand is mostly for refined petroleum, at a level of around 20,000 barrels per day. When production rose during the 1990s, oil exports resumed.

Crude oil production has been limited by lack of investment and has fallen over time owing to well depletion, obsolete machinery and inadequate exploration activity. Econometric tests (see Appendix 4.5) showed that crude oil production is significantly explained by the sector's existing capital stock, especially if existing oil reserves are included.

The country's refinery capacity, on the other hand, is well above actual domestic demand, and so does not represent a bottleneck in the production of refinery products. Domestic prices are fixed by government as a policy variable.

5.6 Manufacturing

According to various studies (R. Morales 1984; E. Cobas 1987; World Bank 1989; J. Espejo et al. 1988; Ministerio de Planeamiento y Coordinación 1989), the Bolivian manufacturing sector can be characterized as follows:

(a) It is mainly engaged in import substitution and is relatively underdeveloped. Individual plants are small and dispersed. About half of industrial workers are self-employed or employed as family workers in small-scale household firms.
(b) Inadequate infrastructure, lack of transport facilities and the competition of foreign-produced manufactures are serious obstacles to further expansion. Manufacturing firms operated with increasingly large volumes of unutilized productive capacity during the 1980s.
(c) Nondurable consumer goods, such as food, beverages, tobacco and textiles, account for about 60 per cent of manufacturing activity, while handicrafts and intermediate goods account for the remainder.
(d) Production is primarily directed to satisfy basic consumer demand in domestic markets, and exports are undermined by the low competitiveness of local production and lack of export promotion policies.
(e) The manufacturing sector depends heavily on imported intermediate inputs, which imposes a constraint on output expansion.

The Bolivian manufacturing sector is concentrated in the following productive sectors: fresh and processed meat, dairy products, grain mills and bakeries, other food manufactures, beverages, tobacco, textiles, clothing, and leather products, wood and wood products, paper and paper products, chemical products, non-metallic minerals, machinery and equipment, and other manufactures.[12]

The manufacturing sector increased its share in total GDP from 13 per cent in 1975 to about 15 per cent in 1980, reduced again to only 12 per cent in 1985, and steadily increased afterwards to 18.5 per cent in 1990 and to 19.6 per cent in 1995.

During the period 1971–75, manufacturing output[13] increased on average by almost 6 per cent a year, a large share of which can be attributed to the large investment undertaken by the state-owned Corporación Boliviana de Fomento (CBF). The corporation's activities were concentrated on a reduced number of important projects (capacity expansion of the Guabirá and Bermejo sugar refineries, various projects to produce dairy products, PIL, the pottery and earthenware factory FABOCE, the edible oils factory Villamontes, a flat glass factory, and expansion of the cement factory FANCESA). Within the Quinquennial Plan (1976–80) CBF's investments were sizeable and represented one-third of total public sector investment during that period (Devlin and Mortimore 1983, p.204). Although these projects brought about significant increases in the domestic production of sugar, alcohol, dairy products, pottery and earthenware, edible oils and cement, practically all of them were poorly conceived and badly executed (too large and too costly) and, in general, reflected the influence of suppliers rather than adequate project appraisal. Most projects suffered delays, sometimes of several years, and operated at very low capacity utilization levels.

According to National Accounts statistics, between 1980 and 1985 manufacturing output contracted by 6 per cent a year. Almost all manufacturing sectors experienced substantial contractions during that period. These reductions, as measured by the Manufacturing Physical Volume Index (INVOFIN), were: textiles and leather (–15 per cent a year); wood and wood products (–10.7 per cent a year); paper, products and printing (–12 per cent a year); chemicals (–6.4 per cent); metallic products and machinery (–18.9 per cent); and non-metallic minerals (–5.3 per cent). Only the production of food, beverages and tobacco experienced a relatively small contraction (-1.7 per cent a year over the period). According to a World Bank survey of 59 large enterprises operating in manufacturing, supply-side constraints were the key determinants of the severe deterioration in capacity utilization, to which lack of demand appears to have been subordinated. Among the most important constraints were lack of primary inputs, lack of foreign exchange, strikes, and lack of spare parts (see also Mierau-Klein and Page 1991, p.4).

The capacity utilization rate declined continuously during the economic crisis of the early 1980s. According to World Bank calculations it was 51 per cent in 1983 and 46 per cent in 1984 and 1985.

In contrast with the experience of other adjusting economies, however, no further deterioration in capacity utilization from the low levels attained by 1985 occurred following the implementation of the adjustment package. Capacity utilization rates in fact improved to 55 per cent in 1986 and 60 per cent in 1987 and 1988. Between 1985 and 1990, the average growth rate of the manufacturing sector was 5.8 per cent a year on average.

According to the World Bank survey, by 1988, supply-side constraints had become almost negligible, and import competition and lack of demand had become the most frequently quoted constraints. Almost 70 per cent of respondents in manufacturing activities pointed to demand-side constraints impeding additional sales (due either to competition from imports or insufficient domestic purchasing power). Imports

Table 5.8 Manufacturing production (yearly average growth rates)

	1971–75	1976–80	1981–85	1986–90	1991–96
Food, beverage and tobacco	7.9	6.4	–1.7	4.4	7.4
Textiles and leather	-0.6	-5.6	–15.8	–4.0	7.3
Wood and wood products	10.7	–1.7	–10.7	3.4	0.3
Paper, products and printing	14.6	6.2	–12.1	9.7	–1.4
Chemicals, plastics	11.2	7.1	–6.4	0.3	14.0
Non-metallic minerals	12.8	2.7	–5.3	15.4	6.8
Metalic products and machinery	25.8	8.7	–18.9	21.7	0.3
Others*					84.2
Total	*5.8*	*2.1*	*-6.0*	*5.8*	*4.9*

Note: * Mostly jewellery
Sources: World Bank (1985b); INE (1997); BCB (c; various issues)

and/or smuggling were identified as the most important competitors by almost 50 per cent of manufacturing firms.

During the 1990s, manufacturing output increased by almost 5 per cent a year. Due to price stability, a favourable exchange rate policy, and tax incentives, manufacturing exports were amongst the fastest growing activities of the economy. The production of jewellery, for instance, grew at more than 80 per cent a year on average, bringing about a remarkable increase of its share in total exports, from zero in 1991 to 6.6 per cent in 1995. Agro-industry exports also showed positive trends.

In summary, first of all, the economy generated productive capacity in some basic manufacturing sectors during the 1970s because of the specific development strategy applied by the government aimed at industrializing the country. Competition from imported goods (mostly contraband) prevented a faster growth of manufacturing output.

Secondly, during the first half of the 1980s manufacturing output growth was mainly constrained by lack of foreign exchange necessary to import intermediate inputs due to the external crises faced by the country.

Thirdly, competitive imports, on the other hand, responded to relative price changes over the 1970s and second half of the 1980s. During the first half of the 1980s, however, coca surpluses played a more important role in determining the volume of competitive imports (mostly luxuries).

Finally, for the most part of the period under analysis, manufacturing exports played a less important role in explaining the behaviour of manufacturing output. However, during the first half of the 1990s they tended to increase faster, due to price stability, a favourable exchange rate policy and tax neutrality.

5.7 Electricity

In 1989 the total installed generating capacity was 566 MW, of which thermal power accounted for 46 per cent and hydroelectric for 54 per cent. The state-run Empresa Nacional de Electricidad (ENDE) owns about 80 per cent of installed capacity, while the other 20 per cent is owned by private mining companies.

The electricity production sector increased its share of GDP from 0.94 per cent in 1970, to 1.20 per cent in 1980, to 1.70 per cent in 1990, and to 2.16 per cent in 1995. This increase is explained by a 100 per cent expansion in consumption during the period 1971–80, a 46 per cent growth between 1980 and 1990, and a 49 per cent increase between 1990 and 1995.

Between 1970 and 1979, installed capacity increased from 261.3 to 421.3 MW. At the end of 1984 installed capacity was 566 MW, of which thermal power plants accounted for 46 per cent and hydroelectric plants for 54 per cent. At the end of 1995 installed capacity was 804.5 MW. Electricity consumption increased by 7 per cent per year between 1970 and 1979, comprising increases in consumption by households of 7 per cent, by manufacturing of 13 per cent and by mining of 3.6 per cent.

During the 1980s the sector continued to grow, but at a slower pace (2.6 per cent per year). The near-collapse of the mining economy in the mid-1980s depressed consumption by that sector by 30 per cent between 1985 and 1989. Other types of electricity consumption increased steadily over the same period: households increased 11 per cent, industry 18 per cent, and commerce 73 per cent. Estimated average demand is about 70 per cent of installed capacity, so there is enough excess capacity to respond to demand increases.

Prices were determined by the government over the whole period. From 1974 until 1978, electricity prices followed overall price increases in the economy, but between 1979 and 1981 prices deteriorated significantly when adjustments were postponed. In 1982 there was a considerable price increase. During the hyperinflationary period however, prices deteriorated sharply since electricity price adjustments were almost 100 per cent behind the overall price level of the economy. Under the NEP, prices were adjusted to more competitive levels, but relative prices of electricity are still very low compared with those prevailing during the 1970s.

5.8 Construction

Between 1970 and 1980, the share of the construction sector in total GDP was on average 4.4 per cent, and absorbed around 5.5 per cent of the labour force. Between 1970 and 1976, the sector grew at an average rate close to 6 per cent per year, and absorbed 45 per cent of the gross fixed capital formation, financed mostly through external credit (R. Morales 1984, p.27). During that period, more than 55 per cent of public sector investment demand was concentrated in construction and public works. The country's inadequate physical infrastructure (partly) explains the efforts undertaken in this direction. Besides, construction (mostly housing) comprised more than 45 per cent of private investment. There is agreement (Ramos 1980; Dunkerley 1984; Rivas 1989) that during the 1970s, a large part of the external credits acquired by the country was used to finance the construction of luxury buildings rather than to expand the country's productive capacity.

The construction sector was one of the worst hit by the economic crisis of the early 1980s. Between 1980 and 1985 the sector's activity level fell by 20 per cent and by a further 12 per cent in 1986. Between 1980 and 1985, total fixed investment had fallen by 23 per cent.

After 1986, however, the construction sector output again showed positive growth rates as investment (mostly public) showed some signs of recovery. According to National Accounts estimates, construction output grew by 20 per cent between 1987 and 1990. During the first half of the 1990s, the sector's output grew at the same rate as total investment (by almost 50 per cent).

In summary, construction output is very much linked to the level of public and private investment demand. Econometric tests show that both private and public investment are significant in explaining the sector's output behaviour.

Because construction is essentially a nontraded sector, prices tend to be determined according to a fixed mark-up over variable costs of production (BCB 1983).

5.9 Services

The Service sector includes the following activities: commerce; transport and storage; communications; finance, insurance and business services; ownership of dwellings; and community, social and personal services.

5.9.1 Private Services

Data on the service sector are quite limited. National Accounts estimates of the output of different service activities are not based on direct observations, but greatly rely on the assumption that service sector output tends to follow the trend determined by the activity levels of other productive sectors.[14] The rationale for this assumption is that the various types of service (such as transport and commerce) are to a large extent regarded as activities complementary to those in the primary and secondary sectors (R. Morales 1985, p.33).

National Accounts figures indicate that private services as a whole grew at an average rate of 5.6 per cent per year during the 1970s. The sector activities that exhibited faster growth were financial services, transport and communications and commerce, demonstrating the emphasis given to the development of tertiary activities during the 1970s described by many observers (Ramos 1980, p.212; Rivas 1989, p.213).

According to National Accounts statistics, the growth of service activities reversed between 1980 and 1985 when output fell by 1.4 per cent a year on average. Financial service output dropped by 3.0 per cent a year as formal financial intermediation reduced and most international banks left the country. The chaotic economic conditions prior to August 1985 greatly reduced recorded financial assets within the economy.

After 1985, service sector output recovered, growing at 1.3 per cent per year between 1985 and 1990. Commerce and transport and communications were the fastest growing activities, with around 3.5 per cent growth each per year. During the 1990s, growth accelerated to 4.1 per cent a year. The large growth observed in total deposits in the formal financial system, brought about a large increase in financial activities (11.5 per cent on average over the last five years). Commerce, transport and communication maintained their growth rates similar to those presented by the productive activities.

Table 5.9 *Services output (yearly average growth rates)*

	1970–75	1976–80	1981–85	1986–90	1991–95
Commerce	3.8	1.9	–3.6	3.0	4.3
Transport, Storage and Communication	9.9	9.6	4.4	4.4	5.5
Financial Services	12.8	6.6	–3.0	–1.6	11.5
Ownership of Dwellings	3.4	3.5	1.2	1.1	1.5
Government Services	8.6	5.9	–1.8	–1.0	2.2
Other Services	4.9	1.7	–3.7	0.6	4.2

Sources: World Bank (1985b); INE (1989b, 1996)

The share of services in total GDP remained relatively constant at around 50 per cent during the last two and a half decades. On the other hand, employment in the services sector increased by 30 per cent between 1978 and 1989, and its share in total employment remained relatively constant, fluctuating around 13 per cent.

One of the main features of the Bolivian economy's development pattern observed over the last years is the fast growth observed in informal activities, especially in service sectors such as commerce. However, informal services showed a much lower share in total value added and a much larger share in total employment. According to UDAPE estimates, the share of informal service activities in GDP increased from less than 4 per cent in 1978, to 4.6 per cent in 1989. Informal employment, however, was two and a half times higher in 1989 than in 1978, accounting for 18 per cent of total employment in 1989. This big gap between the growth rates of informal value-added vis-à-vis informal employment, brought about a sharp reduction in the average incomes of informal workers.

In summary, output of services activities has tended to follow the pattern observed in other productive activities, such as agriculture, manufacturing, imports.

Since the Bolivian service sector is largely nontraded, it does not have to face international competition. Prices of services tend to be determined through a fixed mark-up over variable costs.

On the other hand, the output of informal services tends to be pro-cyclical vis-à-vis the activity levels of other sectors. However, the sector's employment tends to be anti-cyclical. Given the particular characteristics of the sector (such as low entrance investment requirements), the sector's output is absolutely demand-driven and adjusts to the level of demand.

The prices of informal services, on the other hand, are determined according to the minimum required for informal household subsistence. There are two arguments upon which that hypothesis is grounded (De La Piedra 1986). First, there is a price collusion among informal workers, aimed at protecting informal incomes; second, the very existence of the activity would be jeopardized if the income earned dropped below the minimum required for subsistence.

5.9.2 Public Services

This sector corresponds to the SNA category public administration and defence (major group 910 ISIC). It comprises: general public services; defence; general administration of economic policies and services; health policies and services; social security and assistance; and housing and community development policies and services.

The output of government services rose steadily during the 1970s (by around 7 per cent per year). During most of that period, government access to external finance guaranteed and promoted a higher level of government involvement in economic activity.

When external finance was sharply reduced in 1982, public sector activities went down in real terms. Between 1983 and 1986, public administration's value added declined by 19 per cent in constant terms, although government expenditures increased by more than 5000 times in nominal terms. This decrease is explained both by the fact that public inflationary expectations became rational during the hyperinflationary period, and by the government's inability to obtain resources from the private sector through seigniorage.

Between 1986 and 1995 (once the austerity programme was introduced and price stability was attained), the real value added of government services increased by almost 2 per cent a year, in real terms.

The share of government services in total employment fell from 12 per cent in 1985 to 8 per cent in 1989.

5.10 Employment and Income Distribution

The different patterns observed in sectoral adjustment, has brought about considerable shifts in the country's employment structure and income distribution among the various socioeconomic groups. This section discusses the most important shifts observed in this regard over the last two and a half decades.

5.10.1 Employment

The share of agriculture in total employment has decreased from 48 per cent in 1970 to 37 per cent in 1989. This sharp reduction is largely explained by the natural tendency of the agricultural sector in a developing economy to reduce its importance in the generation of GDP and employment to other sectors of the economy.

The mining sector also reduced its share in total employment absorption. During the 1970s, mining absorbed about 5 per cent of employment. During the 1980s, because of the deep crisis suffered by the mining sector, employment absorption by the sector reduced to less than 2 per cent in 1989.

Manufacturing shows an increased participation in employment generation. During the 1970s manufacturing share in total employment became more important due to the basic industrialization process that the country experienced during that decade. Because of the acute crises of the early 1980s, manufacturing employment reduced to 9.7, and started to recover during the second half of the 1980s, after the stabilization programme was implemented.

The importance of commerce and finance in the generation of employment is exhibited by the employment increases these sectors generated; from absorbing only 7.7 per cent of jobs in 1970, at the end of the 1980s they accounted for almost 16 per cent of total employment.

Table 5.10 *Employment Structure*

	1971	1975	1980	1985	1989
Agriculture	48.0	45.7	42.0	38.6	37.9
Mining	5.2	5.1	3.3	2.5	1.7
Hydrocarbons	0.6	0.8	0.3	0.4	0.4
Manufacturing	8.7	9.0	12.8	9.7	10.3
Construction	3.9	5.5	5.1	3.1	4.6
Electricity	0.4	0.4	0.8	0.9	0.8
Transport and Communication	5.8	5.8	4.7	5.2	5.6
Commerce and Finance	7.7	7.8	11.2	14.2	15.9
Other Services	19.7	19.7	19.7	25.4	22.9
Total Employment	100.0	100.0	100.0	100.0	100.0
Unemployment Rate	9.1	5.1	9.4	9.4	7.0

Sources: World Bank (1985b); INE (1989a)

5.10.2 Income distribution

Unfortunately the quality of data on income distribution in Bolivia is scarce and it is difficult to obtain consistent data that could provide good insights about trends over time. The 1976 and 1992 national census and the household surveys provide the key source for the estimation of income distribution conditions, although data before the stabilization is not comparable with more recent information. However, in this section we refer to these sources of data in order to analyse income distribution conditions at different points in time.

A 1976 income distribution was initially elaborated by the Musgrave Mission based on labour and demographic statistics. Later, in 1979, PREALC carried out a new estimation for 1976, based on Musgrave's methodology, but complemented with the results of the 1976 census (see PREALC 1979).

Based on the 1976 census, it was calculated that 80 per cent of all Bolivians were poor in 1976. A household was defined as poor if its income could cover only 70 per cent or less of the cost of a basic needs basket.[15] Among the poor, two subcategories were identified: the very poor whose incomes could cover 80 per cent or less of the basic needs food basket, and the extremely poor who could cover only 30 per cent or less of the basic food basket (R. Morales 1984, p.51; World Bank 1990 p.9). Of the 20 per cent extremely poor, more than 95 per cent are non-salaried agricultural workers (PREALC 1979, p.4).

Time series on rural earnings are virtually non-existent, but agricultural production has fallen over time, especially for the crops grown by the small highland farmers, indicating that there has been a sharp reduction in peasant incomes. INE has estimated peasant incomes based on the value added in agricultural production for a series of products. These estimates indicate that while agricultural incomes have increased overall, this was exclusively due to increases in the value of coca production.

The main commodities produced by peasants have shown a continued decline, with an extremely low value in 1983 due to a severe drought. If the 1980–82 average is taken as the base, the real value added from potatoes (the main source of income for highland farmers) dropped by more than 5 per cent per year up to 1987. Vegetable and maize production fell by 1 per cent per year. Maize and most vegetables are produced in the valleys region by small farmers. In summary, there

Figure 5.1 *Internal terms of trade (agriculture vis-à-vis manufacturing) (base year 1990 = 100)*

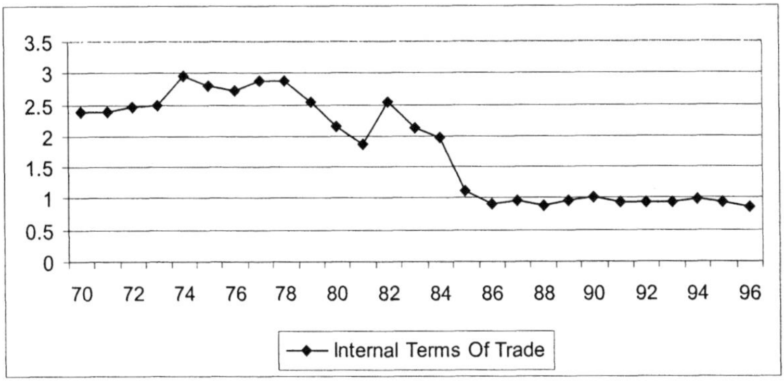

Source: Author's estimates based on: World Bank 1985b; INE 1997

is strong evidence that earnings of rural smallholders have fallen in real terms, except for those who have taken part in the coca boom. Additionally, the internal terms of trade of the traditional agricultural sector, vis-à-vis the manufacturing, have decreased over time (see Figure 5.1). They experienced an increase in 1983, when the prices of food increased sharply, due to the food shortages caused by the adverse climate conditions lived that particular year. After the 1985 stabilization programme, the internal terms of trade seem to have stabilized, however at a lower level than that observed during the 1970s.

Real wages reduced over time, especially during the 1980s. In 1983 the official minimum monthly wage, converted into dollars at the free market rate, was US$42. In December 1985, it was US$16. Although it has since recovered, the dollar equivalent was still only 20 per cent in early 1990 compared with November 1982, when the minimum wage was instituted. In fact, many unskilled workers are still paid less than the official minimum wage rate.

During the 1970s nominal wages were able to adjust to price changes, but in the 1980s this situation completely reversed. Real wages and salaries were eroded by inflation and by the freeze imposed under the New Economic Policy (see Figure 5.2). They fell by 8 per cent in 1981 and by 27 per cent in 1982. The sharpest reductions however, occurred after the stabilization programme in 1985, when real wages dropped by 64 per cent that year and have since remained at that level.

Figure 5.2 *Real wage rate and real minimum wage rate indexes (base year 1982 = 100)*

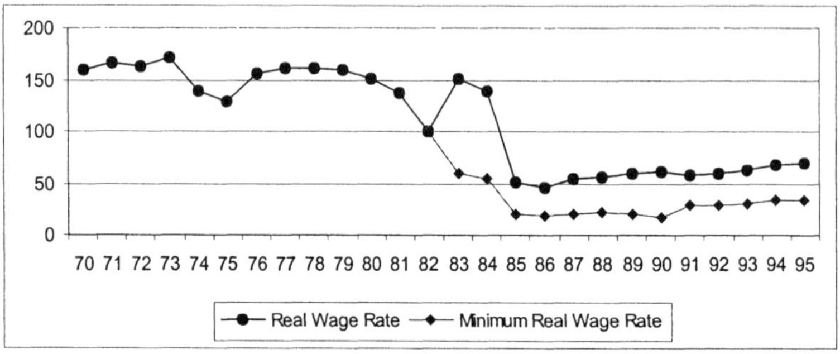

Source: Author's estimates based on World Bank 1985b; INE 1997

As a result of the erosion of the value of real wages and of employment reductions, the share of skilled wage-earnings in total income fell from 21 per cent in 1976 to 18 per cent in 1989. In 1982, a minimum wage rate was established, which also has shown a decreasing tendency in real terms.

The household survey data for 1989 and 1993 indicate that real wage incomes dropped by about 8 per cent in the period between those years. Wages recovered in more recent years, showing a 3 per cent increase between 1993 and 1995, consistent with a drop in the unemployment rate.

From 1980 to 1988, self-employment grew in the major urban areas. According to World Bank (1990) estimates, between 1982 and 1988 the share of self-employment in total mining employment grew from 16 to 20 per cent, and in total manufacturing from 59 to 68 per cent.

5.11 Concluding Remarks

This chapter further confirms the advantages of a disaggregated approach to macroeconomic adjustment in a highly heterogeneous developing economy. The supply-demand balances for the most important economic activities showed highly differentiated adjustment behaviours during the periods under analysis.

Institutional factors other than purely relative price mechanisms largely dominated adjustment in each of the supply-demand balances.

By including these individual institutional features, a much deeper understanding was gained of key macroeconomic processes such as output and shifts in relative price behaviour and income distribution among the different factors of production, and eventually among the various economic agents.

Appendix 5.1
Traditional Agricultural Output

The following function was selected for traditional agricultural (TA) output. The econometric results obtained were the most realistic of all the functions tested from the economic and statistical points of view.

$$X_{TA} = \forall_1 . X_{TA(t-1)} + \forall_2 . N_{TA} + \forall_3 . \Theta$$

where:

X_{TA} = Traditional agricultural output (millions of 1980 Bolivianos),

N_{TA} = Number of people working in the sector,

Θ = Dummy variable representing weather conditions.

The econometric results obtained were as follows.

LS // Dependent Variable is X_{TA}

SMPL range: 1971–89

Number of observations: 19

Variable	Coefficient	Std. Error	T-Stat.	2-Tail Sig.
Q	-377.89553	59.947280	-6.3037978	0.000
XTA(t-1)	0.5803521	0.1315144	4.4128399	0.000
NTA	1.2694822	0.3411518	3.7211655	0.002

R-squared	0.604967	Mean of dependent var.	1853.047
Adjusted R-squared	0.555587	S.D. of dependent var.	217.8168
S.E. of regression	145.2060	Sum of squared resid.	337356.7
Durbin-Watson stat.	1.810941	F-statistic	12.25145
Log likelihood	–119.9122		

Appendix 5.2
Coca Production

The following equation was tested econometrically for coca output:

$$X_{CO} = 8_0 + 8_1.X_{CO(t-1)} + 8_3.((e^P.PW_{CO})/PD_{TA})$$

where:

X_{CO} = Coca output in millions of 1989 Bolivianos,

$((e^P.PW_{CO})/PD_{TA})$ = Coca price relative to those of TA products.

The econometric results obtained were as follows.

LS // Dependent Variable is XCO

SMPL range: 1971-89

Number of observations: 9

Variable	Coefficient	Std. Error	T-Stat.	2-Tail Sig.
$(e^P.PW_{CO})/PD_{TA}$	10.747648	4.0627857	2.6453888	0.033
$X_{CO(t-1)}$	1.0116253	0.0295122	34.278201	0.000

R-squared	0.990263	Mean of dependent var.	370.1109
Adjusted R-squared	0.988872	S.D. of dependent var.	271.6960
S.E. of regression	28.66066	Sum of squared resid.	5750.033
Durbin-Watson stat.	1.744533	F-statistic	711.9259
Log likelihood	–41.83926		

Appendix 5.3 Mining Output (COMIBOL)

Separate production functions were estimated for COMIBOL and the medium-scale mining sector output. The equations tested for COMIBOL's output were:

$$\log(X_{CMB}) = (_0 + (_1.\log(X_{CMB(t-1)})) + (_2.\log(K_{CMB(t-1)}) + (_3.\log((e.PW_{MN})/P_{GDP})$$

where:

X_{CMB} = COMIBOL's output in millions of 1989 Bolivianos,

$K_{CMB(t-1)}$ = COMIBOL's capital stock in the previous period,

$(e.PW_{MN})/P_{GDP}$ = Price of mining products relative to GDP deflator.

The econometric results obtained were as follows.

LS // Dependent Variable is log(XCMB)
SMPL range: 1971–89
Number of observations: 16

Variable	Coefficient	Std. Error	T-Stat.	2-Tail Sig.
$\text{Log}(X_{CMB(t-1)})$	0.7887557	0.1543716	5.1094600	0.000
$\text{Log}(K_{CMB(t-1)})$	0.1897383	0.1149119	1.6511629	0.123
$(e.PW_{MN})/P_{GDP}$	0.5247284	0.2523741	2.0791691	0.058

R-squared	0.990263	Mean of dependent var.	370.1109
Adjusted R-squared	0.988872	S.D. of dependent var.	271.6960
S.E. of regression	28.66066	Sum of squared resid.	5750.033
Durbin-Watson stat.	1.744533	F-statistic	711.9259
Log likelihood	–41.83926		

Appendix 5.4 Mining Output (Medium-Scale Companies)

The production function for medium-scale mining companies tested was:

$$\log(X_{MM}) = *_0 + *_{1.}\log(X_{MM(t-1)}) + *_{2.}\log(K_{MM(t-1)} + *_{3.}\log((e.PW_{MN})/P_{GDP})$$

where:

X_{MM} = Medium-scale firms' output in millions of 1989 Bolivianos,

$K_{MM(t-1)}$ = Medium-scale firms' capital stock in the previous period,

$(e.PW_{MN})/P_{GDP}$ = Price of mining products relative to GDP deflator.

The econometric results obtained were as follows.

LS // Dependent Variable is log(XMM)

SMPL range: 1971–89

Number of observations: 13

Variable	Coefficient	Std. Error	T-Stat.	2-Tail Sig.
$\text{Log}(X_{MM(t-1)})$	0.4151216	0.2266816	1.8312981	0.097
$\text{Log}(K_{MM(t-1)})$	0.5209132	0.2030773	2.5650983	0.028
$(e.PW_{MN})/P_{GDP}$	0.1336575	0.1075879	1.2423101	0.242

R-squared	0.562290	Mean of dependent var.	5.693304
Adjusted R-squared	0.474748	S.D. of dependent var.	0.136475
S.E. of regression	0.098909	Sum of squared resid.	0.097831
Durbin-Watson stat.	1.955878	F-statistic	6.423087
Log likelihood	13.33532		

Appendix 5.5
Oil Production

The equation for the hydrocarbon sector's production function that gave the most realistic results, from both economic and statistical points of view, was the following:

$$\log(X_{HD}) = {}_{v0} + {}_{v1} \log(K_{HD})$$

The results obtained were as follows.[16]

LS // Dependent Variable is $\log(X_{HD})$
SMPL range: 1974–89
Number of observations: 16

Variable	Coefficient	Std. Error	T-Stat.	2-Tail Sig.
Const.	4.0239627	1.0677960	3.7684750	0.002
Log(K_{HD})	0.3728599	0.1435639	2.5971696	0.022
Ar(1)	0.5566038	0.2757240	2.0186988	0.065

R-squared	0.806862	Mean of dependent var.	6.750027
Adjusted R-squared	0.777149	S.D. of dependent var.	0.149506
S.E. of regression	0.070577	Sum of squared resid.	0.064755
Durbin-Watson stat	1.619048	F-statistic	27.15470
Log likelihood	21.37481		

Notes

1. During these years, most major public investment projects were part of the government's plan to develop the lowlands and were sponsored by official multilateral and bilateral agencies. Brazil financed the Santa Cruz-Sao Paulo railroad, which linked a previously isolated region of Bolivia to the Atlantic seabord; similarly, USAID financed the road link between Santa Cruz and Cochabamba, already linked to La Paz; and Argentina financed a rail link between Santa Cruz and Jujuy, thus linking Santa Cruz to Buenos Aires.

2. During the 1970s, it is estimated that GDP per capita grew at 1.8 per cent per year. The United Nations Food and Agricultural Organization has estimated the income elasticity of demand for the farm value of all food to be 0.6 in Latin America. Assuming the income elasticity is the same in Bolivia, demand increased by approximately 1.08 per cent per year because of increases in per-capita incomes. The total increase in demand from rising population and per-capita incomes was 3.8 per cent. Therefore, excess demand for agricultural products increased by around 3 per cent per year during the 1970s. During the 1980s, output grew on average by 1 per cent per year. In the same period, average per-capita incomes fell by 0.4 per cent per year. As a result, demand for agricultural products increased by approximately 2.4 per cent per year. Thus excess demand grew by 1.4 per cent per year.

3. An econometric estimate of the price-demand elasticity for TA products was 0.6 (using pooled data for the whole period).

4. Three stages can be identified in the processing of coca leaf into cocaine products: past, base and hydrochloride (US Embassy 1990; UDAPE 1990b).

5. There are no reliable figures on the economic dimensions of coca-cocaine activities. A number of estimates have been made, but they differ considerably. The most elaborate estimates on the size of the coca industry in 1989 were made by UDAPE (1990b) and by the US Embassy (1990). Although both studies used similar methodologies, there are strong differences in the level of some basic information, namely prices, area harvested, yield, and unit costs. The main results of the two studies are compared in the table.

Size of the coca industry (1989)

	UDAPE	US Embassy
Coca leaf		
Hectares Cultivated	55 753[a]	38 250[b]
Yield (MT leaves/Hect.)	2.5	1.4
Production (MT)	139 238	55 233
Price (US$/Kilo)	1.2	1.4
Costs (US$/Kilo)	0.2	0.7
Value Added (million US$)	169.6	39.1
Paste		
Yield (Kg leaf/Kg paste)	0.01	0 01
Production (MT)	1 224	556
Price (US$/Kilo)	160.0	160 0
Costs (US$/Kilo)	136.1	146.0
Value Added (million US$)	29 2	7.9
Base		
Yield (Kg base/Kg paste)	0 50	0 25
Production (MT)	617	139
Price (US$/Kilo)	700 0	700 5
Costs (US$/Kilo)	342 9	650 4
Value Added (million US$)	220.4	7.0
Hydrochloride (HCL)		
Yield (Kg HCL/Kg base)	0.32	0 91
Production (MT)	222	126
Price (US$/Kilo)	2 200	1 605
Costs (US$/Kilo)	1 068	923
Value Added (million US$)	251.7	86 0
Total Value Added Industry (million US$)	629.5	139.9

Notes: a. Includes areas harvested in the Yungas, Chapare and Santa Cruz regions; based on field estimates by MACA (UDAPE 1990b).
b. Only includes area harvested in the Chapare region, based on satellite imaging data provided by NAU (US Embassy 1990).

The US Embassy's study only includes coca production in the Chapare region, whereas the UDAPE study includes production in the Chapare, Yungas and Yapacani regions. Since both institutions had access to almost the same sources of information, their studies do not present substantial differences in the prices utilized for the various stages in the coca production. However, the Embassy's study consistently utilizes higher unit costs and lower yield coefficients than those used by UDAPE. This obviously reduces the value added at each stage in the coca-cocaine production chain, as can be observed in the table above.

The National Accounts study estimates the coca industry's value added at US$500 million, although no explicit distinction is made between the different processes where this value added is generated. Since there is no conclusive true figure for the value added by the coca industry, this study uses the National Accounts estimates in order to maintain consistency with other macroeconomic figures. However, UDAPE's structure is used to distribute coca's value added among the social groups engaged in the coca economy.

The value added generated in the first two stages (coca leaves and paste) accrues to Bolivian nationals (that is, peasants), so that its impact on the domestic economy is strong. On the other hand, the value added in the later stages of production (base and HCL), is associated more with foreign factors of production (international drug traffickers), so that it is more likely to leave the country and thus have little impact on the domestic economy (UDAPE, ibid, p.12; US Embassy, ibid, p.1).

6. There are 1.5 million coca leaf chewers in Bolivia. A much higher percentage of the Bolivian population regularly consumes the coca leaf for daily sustenance than is involved in the production, transport, marketing, processing and trafficking of coca and its derivatives. Indeed, 87 per cent of the inhabitants of small towns and rural communities use the coca leaf for some 40 different health remedies (Carter 1981, p.129).

7. Government efforts towards curtailing coca production are based on a three-pronged strategy: (i) interdiction efforts at the intermediary level of the coca-cocaine chain; (ii) an eradication programme started in 1989, where farmers voluntarily destroy their plantations for monetary compensation; and (iii) the alternative development investment project which provides alternative employment to farmers potentially involved in coca production (World Bank 1992).

8. 'Cocaine can be manufactured in the back of a truck, in an adobe hut or even in the middle of a cane field ... the physical requirements of this technology can be diffused quite rapidly to the rural producers and throughout the small- and medium-sized merchant population' (Healy 1986).

9. Between 1981 and 1985 COMIBOL added almost US$720 million to the public deficit.

10. The COMIBOL output level seems to be highly correlated with international metal prices. A regression run between the company's output index as a dependent variable and a weighted international metal price index as explanatory variable, gives a R2 = 0.71. According to this regression, the price elasticity of COMIBOL's output is 2, and is highly significant (t = 5.7).

11. Among the most important foreign firms that invested in the mining sector are: RTZ, Barrick Gold, Battle Mountain, Takla Star, Da Capo, Corrientes Resources, Echo Bay, Auspac Gold, Renison Goldfields, Billiton and Orvana.

12. In the 1995 SAM, the production of basic metals and oil refinery were grouped together with mining, and oil and gas activities, respectively. In the SNA however, they belong to the manufacturing sector (major division 3 ISIC).

13. Excluding hydrocarbon refining and metal processing that were included in the oil and gas and mining sectors, respectively, within the SAM framework.

14. National Accounts estimates of the value added of private services are themselves obtained endogenously using a Leontief-type model (INE 1990).

15. The basic needs basket used was developed by the Latin American branch of the International Labour Office (PREALC).

16. The initial regression estimated showed first-order autocorrelation, which was corrected using the Cochrane-Orcutt technique, also sometimes called 'first-order autoregressive correction'.

6 The Analytical Framework of this Book

6.1 Introduction

The discussion in the first three chapters of this book demonstrated that the different socioeconomic groups (government, public enterprises, companies, households and banks) have followed different adjustment patterns, in reaction to the external shocks and policies. The fluctuating pattern followed by capital inflows and by the country's terms-of-trade throughout the last two decades and a half, and the stabilization policies and structural reforms implemented, affected each of the groups in a different fashion. Very often, the policies were designed to change the behavioural rules of a specific agent (for example, the popular participation reform, the reforms to the financial system and the capitalization of public enterprises). The various adjustment patterns followed by groups have determined the direction of adjustment at the macroeconomic level. Thus, macroeconomic adjustment in Bolivia has been the outcome of sectoral adjustments and of the interactions among the different agents through the diverse markets in which they operate.

The reduced-SAM model presented in this chapter attempts to provide a more subtle and plausible interpretation of macroeconomic adjustment in Bolivia. This attempts to achieve this in four ways.

(a) By explicitly separating formal from informal activities in the productive sector. This separation is crucial in the Bolivian case because the relative expansion or contraction of these activities have completely changed the structure of the economy in terms of income, investment, employment, fiscal revenues, foreign exchange earnings, capital flight and so on.

(b) By including separate accumulation balance adjustments for different economic agents (companies, households and government), which tend to be essentially different because they are ruled by different institutional settings (such as objectives, constraints in the different markets they face, bargaining power and access to finance).

(c) Closures in the reduced-SAM model are differentiated by periods of time that are defined according to prevailing external and internal conditions.

(d) The reduced-SAM model incorporates balances for all sectors of the economy (supply-demand balances, accumulation balances, and balances for the external and financial sectors); therefore, macroeconomic equilibrium is obtained simultaneously through the interaction of all sectoral balances.

Section 6.2 provides a general explanation of the SAM framework, which is then used to characterize the structure of the Bolivian economy. The disaggregation introduced in the different accounts is explained. The reader is frequently referred to previous chapters for the justifications of the grouping criteria adopted. Section 6.3 introduces the various balances that, as highlighted above, are crucial to explain macroeconomic adjustment. The accumulation balances for the different economic agents (households, companies and government); the external balance, the financial balances, and the supply-demand balances are defined in algebraic terms. In this way, all the possible adjustment mechanisms for each balance are clearly identified. The balances expressed in algebraic terms are utilized in section 6.4 to analyse sectoral and macroeconomic adjustment during the three time periods studied (the 1970s, the first half of the 1980s, and following the 1985 NEP). The sectoral adjustment mechanisms set up by the structural reforms of the 1990s are also outlined in this section. Sectoral adjustments in each of these time periods are discussed in sections 6.4.1, 6.4.2, 6.4.3 and 6.4.4, respectively. For justifications for the adjustment mechanisms selected, for the different balances and for the different time periods, the reader is referred, in each case, to Chapters 2, 3, 4 and 5, where full references and detailed discussions of the adjustment mechanisms are provided. Summaries of how economic adjustment took place during each of the three time periods and how the structural reforms are expected to modify sectoral adjustments, are provided, specifying very clearly which variables are considered as endogenous, exogenous, policy variables and fixed parameters. Finally, the most important conclusions are outlined in section 6.5.

6.2 The Reduced-SAM Based Model for the Bolivian Economy

The reduced-SAM model is aimed at setting up a framework for the algebraic formulation of the main hypotheses of this research. The degree of disaggregation does not go beyond what is strictly necessary in order to facilitate the algebraic formulation of the hypotheses.

Although most of the variables included within the reduced-SAM model, are treated with a much higher degree of disaggregation in the SAM presented in Appendix A (where the full 1995 SAM is developed), in Appendix B (where the structure of the CGE model is explained), and in Chapters 1 to 3 (where the adjustment mechanisms for each balance are discussed in detail) the reduced-SAM model developed in this chapter maintains the essence of the approach followed throughout the rest of the book.

The main characteristics of the reduced-SAM model are: it differentiates adjustment mechanisms for the various balances, it differentiates adjustment mechanisms over time, and it considers macroeconomic adjustment as being determined jointly by the interactions of all sectors.

6.2.1 General outline of the system

The reduced-SAM basic structure comprises the standard accounts categories reflecting general accounting procedures (Pyatt and Round 1984). These account categories are also included within the 1995 SAM framework:

(1) Productive activities
(2) Factors of production
(3) Current accounts for economic agents (institutions)
(4) Current account for the rest of the world (ROW)

(5) Capital accounts for economic actors (institutions)
(6) Capital account for the rest of the world
(7) Financial accounts.

Table 6.1 gives a schematic presentation of this structure. The first class of accounts identifies the receipts and disbursements by ‘‘activities’. In row 1 are the receipts: the proceeds of sales to other economic activities (that is, intermediate demand) and to institutions (that is, consumption and investment), and of exports. These are balanced by the ‘outgoings’, or the costs of production, in column 1: payments between activities as intermediate sales, payments made to factors of production during the production process (value added), indirect tax payments made to government, and the costs of imported intermediate inputs.

The second class of accounts shows, in row 2, the income distribution to factors and, in column 2, how this income is appropriated by the various institutions according to their factor endowments.

The third class of accounts shows the sources and uses of current income by institutions. In row 3, there are three income items: factor income, transfers among institutions (such as direct tax payments, social security payments, distributed profits), and net current transfers from the rest of the world (ROW). Column 3 shows how institutions allocate their incomes: expenditures on the consumption of locally produced and imported goods, outlays due to the redistributive processes, and savings.

The fourth kind of accounts presents the sources and uses of funds by institutions. The sources are displayed in row 5: own savings, credit from external sources and credit from the domestic financial system. The uses of funds by economic agents are shown in column 5: they go to finance physical investment, the acquisition of external financial assets (namely capital flight, foreign exchange reserves and external debt payments), and the acquisition of domestic financial assets.

The transactions between the country and the ROW are recorded in accounts 4 and 6. The current transactions are displayed in row and column 4. Row 4 shows receipts by the ROW due to imports and net factor payments. These are balanced by payments from the ROW (column 4). The origins of these payments are exports, the current transfers to local institutions from ROW. The difference between receipts and payments constitutes the current account balance, and is shown as a transfer from

Table 6.1 SAM for the Bolivian economy

		1		2			3			4	5			6	7		
		ACTIVITIES		FACTORS			INSTITUTIONS CURRENT				INSTITUTIONS CAPITAL				FINANCIAL		
		Formal	Informal	Wages	Formal Profits	Informal Profits	Com-panies	House-Holds	Govern-ment	Rest of the World	Com-panies	House-Holds	Govern-ment	Rest of the World	Central Bank	Commercial Bank	TOTALS
ACT	Formal Informal	INTERMEDIATE DEMAND					FINAL DEMAND (CONSUMPTION)			EXPORTS	FINAL DEMAND (INVESTMENT)						TOTAL DEMAND
FACTOR	Wages Profits F. Profits I.	DISTRIBUTION OF VALUE ADDED TO FACTORS															TOTAL FACTOR INCOME
CURRENT	Companies Households			DISTRIBUTION OF INCOME TO HOUSEHOLDS					NET SUBSIDIES	TRANSFERS							TOTAL INCOME OF INSTITUTIONS
	Government	IMPTOS INDIRECTOS					DIRECT TAXES										
	Rest of the World	INTERMEDIATE IMPORTS DEMAND					INTEREST				IMPORTS OF CAPITAL GOODS						CUR. ACC. (DEBIT)
CAPITAL	Companies Households Government						SAVINGS BY INSTITUTIONS				FLOWS OF FUNDS						TOTAL INVESTMENT FINANCE
	Rest of the World									EXT. SAV.							
FIN.	Central Bank Commercial Banks																
TOTALS		TOTAL SUPPLY		REDISTRIBUTED FACTOR INCOME			USE OF DISPOSABLE INCOME OF INSTITUTIONS			CURR. ACC. (CREDIT)	TOTAL INVESTMENT (FINANCIAL AND PHISICAL)						

the ROW current account to the ROW capital account as ‘external savings’.

The capital transactions with the ROW are displayed in column and row 6. Column 6 shows the total capital inflows received from the ROW. The uses made of these inflows appear in row 6. They go to finance the current balance of payments deficit, the acquisition of external financial assets by economic agents and by financial institutions.

Finally, the financial accounts show the sources and uses of funds to financial institutions. Row 7 presents the sources of these funds: total acquisition of financial assets by non-financial agents, total foreign credit, and total credit conceded among financial institutions. These totals are balanced by the uses made of these funds, displayed in column 7: credit to non-financial institutions, and the acquisition of foreign financial assets.

6.2.2 Relevant breakdown of accounts

This section discusses the breakdown in the reduced-SAM for Bolivia that is relevant to this research.

The most important characteristic of the SAM approach is that it presents data in a disaggregated manner. It extends information far beyond the detail of traditional National Accounts and embraces classifications that are capable of tracing the essential interconnections throughout the economic system. The choice of disaggregation must obviously depend on both its analytical value and on the availability of data to sustain it. This stage is crucial for the uses that can be made of a SAM.

The broad classes of accounts can be disaggregated into the following:

(a) Productive activities can be classified according to the sector in which they operate (such as agriculture, manufacturing and mining), according to the type of commodity they produce (tradables as opposed to nontradables); according to their technological or institutional characteristics (small-scale or large-scale, formal or informal, public or private, and so on) and/or according to the type of market in which they operate, whether competitive flexi-price market or oligopolistic fix-price market.

(b) The breakdown of income distribution across factors of production can differentiate income that remunerates the use of labour services (wages) from the income that pays for the use of capital by households and other institutions. Since these factor services are heterogeneous, separate accounts can be specified. For instance, capital can be disaggregated to distinguish ownership (private or public), or the legal status of the firm (formal or informal).

(c) The breakdown of institutions or economic actors can single out economically relevant individuals and institutions into groups related to functional categories of income distribution, namely households (including non-corporate enterprises), private (corporate) enterprises, public enterprises, and the government (central and local).

Once the incomes received by these economic agents have been identified, their saving-investment patterns can be equally well distinguished within the SAM framework. Different economic actors tend to consume and save different proportions of their incomes; in some cases income is devoted to the consumption of necessities, while in others, the proportion consumed is small and the rest is used to finance imported luxuries. In addition, the proportion saved plus the additional capital transfers from other sectors are invested in different proportions by the various economic agents.

(d) Finally, the breakdown of the financial accounts can single out financial institutions (such as the Central Bank, commercial banks or development banks) according to their main institutional characteristics.

In this section, the six account categories presented in section 6.2.1 are disaggregated into more detailed structures. The disaggregation chosen attempts to reflect the heterogeneous nature of the Bolivian economy that emerged from the debates on the country's macroeconomic behaviour over the last two and a half decades. The main features that reflect the heterogeneous nature of the Bolivian economy are as follows:

- a segmented productive structure with a growing informal sector;
- a high level of dependence of the economy on the external sector;
- a high level of state participation in economic activity;
- a segmented financial system;

- differentiated accumulation behaviour for the various institutions and social groups; and
- disparate access to credit by the various economic institutions and social groups.

The reduced-SAM is presented in Table 6.2. The disaggregations for each of the accounts are now discussed.

(i) *Productive activities*

All productive activities are grouped in two broad categories, formal and informal.

(a) The activities in the 'formal' sector are those controlled by corporate (including state-owned) enterprises. The categories included here are: modern agriculture, mining, hydrocarbons, manufacturing, construction, electricity, modern services and government services. Their common characteristics are:
   - They use relatively capital-intensive technology and wage labour.
   - They operate in oligopolistic markets and therefore set prices through mark-ups over their costs of production.
   - Production in these sectors is relatively more responsive to demand changes because there exist reserves of productive capacity.
   - Corporate enterprises operate mostly in export activities (such as mining, oil, and agro-industry).

(b) The activities within the informal sector are: traditional agriculture, coca production and informal services in urban areas. The main characteristics that distinguish the informal sector are:
   - They operate in relatively more competitive markets; depending on the level of buyer demand, prices therefore adjust in order to clear excess demand.
   - Output responses to changes in aggregate demand in these sectors are quite limited because production is generally constrained by structural factors and bottlenecks.

(ii) *Factors of production*

Factors of production have been grouped into three categories: wage labour, corporate profits, and non-corporate profits by household-based firms in the informal sector:

(a) Wage labour comprises two categories (skilled and unskilled); the main sources of income are fixed wages.
(b) Corporate profits comprise those profits by companies and public firms within the formal sector.
(c) Non-corporate profits comprise incomes of small peasants in rural areas, and by small-scale producers and informal workers in urban areas.

(iii) Institutions

In the reduced-SAM, the institutions have been divided into three categories: companies, households, and government.

(a) Companies include private corporations and public enterprises.
(b) Households include the three household categories identified in chapter 3: rural, lower-urban and upper-urban.
(c) Government includes the central and local governments.

(iv) Financial accounts

This set of accounts shows the role of financial institutions as financial intermediaries. All the capital transactions among different economic actors are carried out through the financial system. The reduced-SAM distinguishes separate accounts for the Central Bank and for commercial banks.

6.2.3 Outline of the model for the Bolivian economy

The structure of the reduced-SAM appears in Table 6.2.

(a) Column 1 shows the cost structure for formal activities. It comprises: wage payments ($w.b_f.X_f$), imported inputs ($e.P^M.a_m.X_f$) and corporate profits (R_f). Row 1 shows the allocation of total production by the formal sector, as follows: intermediate inputs, which are demanded by informal activities ($P_f.a.X_i$); final consumption by households ($P_f.C_f$) (e.g. agro-industrial products); final government consumption, which is concentrated in formally produced goods and services ($P_f.G$); exports of mining, hydrocarbons and agro-industrial products ($e.P^E.E_f$); investment demand by households ($P_f.(1-\Theta).I_h$), mostly for the construction of dwellings; and invest-

Table 6.2 *Reduced SAM model for the Bolivian economy*

			1	2	3	4	5	6	7	8	9	10	11	12	13	14	15	
			ACTIVITIES		FACTORS			INSTITUTIONS CURRENT				INSTITUTIONS CAPITAL				FINANCIAL		TOTALS
			Formal	Informal	Wages	Formal Profits	Informal Profits	Com-panies	House-Holds	Govern-ment	Rest of the World	Com-panies	House-Holds	Govern-ment	Rest of the World	Central Bank	Commercial Bank	
1	ACTI	Formal		$P_f . a . X_i$					$P_f . C_f$	$P_f . G$	$e . P_f^E.E_f$		$P_f.(1\text{-}\theta).I_H$	$P_f . I_G$				$P_f . X_f$
2		Informal							$P_i . C_i$		$e_p . P_i^E.E_i$		$P_i.\theta . I_H$					$P_i . Xi + e_p . P_i^E.E_i$
3	FACTOR	Wages	$w. b_f . Xf$															W
4		Profits Formal	Rf															Rf
5		Profits Informal		Ri														Rj
6	CURRENT	Companies				$\Gamma . Rf$												$\Gamma . Rf$
7		Households			$w. b_f . Xf$		Ri	DP										Y_H
8		Government				$(1 - \Gamma) . Rf$		$t . \Gamma . Rf$										GR
9		Rest of the World	$e\ P^M . a_m . Xf$					$e . i^* . F_{pb}$	$e_p . P^M . C_m$	$e . i^*.(F_G+F_{CB})$		$e. P^M . I_C$						$e . P^M . M$
10	CAPITAL	Companies						S_C									$\Delta L_{PB . C}$	SF_C
11		Households							S_H								$\Delta L_{PB.H}$	SF_H
12		Government								S_G					$e. \Delta F_G$	$\Delta L_{CB.G}$	ΔB_G	SF_G
13		Rest of the World									S_E		$e_P . \Delta CF_H$			$e . \Delta FR_{CB}$	$e . \Delta FR_{PB}$	$e . \Delta F$
14	FIN.	Central Bank											ΔCu_H		$e . \Delta F_{CB}$		ΔRe_{PB}	ΔLB_{cb}
15		Commercial Banks										ΔDep_C	ΔDep_H		$e . \Delta F_{PB}$	$\Delta L_{CB.PB}$		ΔLB_{PB}
		TOTALS	$P_f . X_f$	$P_i . X_i + e . P^E X_i$	W	Rf	Ri	$\Gamma . Rf$	Y_h	$S_g + GE$	$S_e+e.P^E.E$	UF_C	UF_H	UF_G	$e . \Delta F$	ΔAS_{CB}	ΔAS_{PB}	

ment demand by government ($P_f.I_g$), which is concentrated in capital goods produced domestically (such as the construction of infrastructure).

(b) Column 2 shows the cost structure of informal activities: the acquisition of inputs produced by the formal sector ($P_f.a.X_i$), and profits, which are the difference between the market value of total production and total input costs (R_i). The allocation of total production by informal activities appears in row 2: production from agriculture (staple foods), manufacturing (handicrafts) and informal services, consumed by households ($P_i.C_i$) (this consumption also includes subsistence consumption by peasant households); exports by informal activities, mostly coca and its by-products ($e_P.PE_i.E_i$); and informal construction (self-construction), which constitutes the gross fixed capital formation for poor households ($P_i.\theta.I_h$).

(c) Row 3 shows that wage incomes ($w.b_f.X_f$) originate from formal activities. Column 3 shows that those incomes are eventually received by households.

(d) Row 4 shows that non-corporate profits (R_i) originate from informal activities. Column 4 indicates that households are the final recipients of those profits.

(e) Row 5 shows that corporate profits (R_f) arise from formal activities. Column 5 shows the share of those profits that constitutes income for companies ($\Gamma.R_f$); the other part, which comes from public enterprise operations, is appropriated by government ($(1-\Gamma).R_f$).

(f) Row 6 indicates that the only source of income for companies is the corporate profit earnings resulting from private company operations ($\Gamma.R_f$). Column 6 shows the use that companies make of their gross profits: tax payments to government ($t.\Gamma.R_f$), distributed profits to household owners of shares (DP), interest payments on the private external debt ($e.i^*.F_{pb}$), and the remaining constitutes retained profits which are company savings (S_c).

(g) Row 7 shows the total sources of household incomes: wage earnings ($w.b_f.X_f$), non-corporate profit earnings (R_i) and the distributed profits from companies (DP). Column 7 shows the uses households make of these incomes. Part of them are used to finance consumption of food ($P_i.C_i$), of goods and services produced by the formal sector ($P_f.C_f$) and of imported consumption goods ($e_P.P^M.C_m$). The remainder constitutes household savings (S_h).

(h) Row and column 8 display current government transactions. Row 8 shows government revenues: public enterprise profits ($(1-\Gamma).R_f$) and tax payments by companies ($t.\Gamma.R_f$). Column 8 indicates that these incomes go to finance government consumption ($P_f.G$) and interest payments on the external public debt ($e.i^*.(F_g + F_{cb})$). The remainder comprises government savings (S_g).

(i) Row and column 9 show the current transactions with the rest of the world. Row 9 shows the ROW's receipts from: import payments, i.e. intermediate imports ($e.P^M.a_m.X_f$), imports of consumption goods ($e_P.P^M.C_m$) and of capital goods ($e.P^M.I_c$), and from interest payments on the public and private external debt, ($e.i^*.(F_g + F_{cb})$) and ($e.i^*.F_{pb}$), respectively. Payments from the ROW are shown in column 9. They comprise exports by formal activities ($e.P^E{}_f.E_f$), and by informal activities ($e_P.PE_i.E_i$). The difference between payments to and payments from the rest of the world comprises external savings (S_e).

(j) Row and column 10 display the accumulation balance for companies, that is, the equilibrium between companies' sources and uses of funds. Row 10 shows the sources of funds available to companies: own savings (S_c) and credit obtained from commercial banks within the period ($\Delta L_{pb,c}$). The uses made of these funds appear in column 10: investment in imported capital goods such as machinery and equipment ($e.P^M.I_c$), and new deposits in commercial banks (ΔDep_c).

(k) Row and column 11 show the accumulation balance for households. The sources of funds in row 11 consist of: own savings (S_h) and loans from commercial banks ($\Delta L_{pb,h}$). The uses of funds shown in column 11 include: household investment in capital goods produced by the formal sector ($P_f.(1-\Theta).I_h$); household investment in goods produced within the same household (e.g. self-construction) ($P_i.\Theta.I_h$), to finance capital flight ($e^P.\Delta CF_h$), changes in the stock of currency (ΔCu_h) and bank deposits (ΔDep_h) held by households.

(l) Row and column 12 display the accumulation balance for the government. The sources of funds (row 12) are: the government's own savings (S_g), foreign credits obtained within the period ($e.\Delta F_g$), new credit from the Central Bank ($\Delta L_{cb.g}$), and government bonds (ΔB_b). The uses of these resources appear in column 12; they mostly comprise government investment in locally produced capital goods ($P_f.I_g$) such as infrastructure.

(m) Row and column 13 show the capital transactions with the rest of the world. Column 13 displays receipts from the ROW; they mostly comprise capital inflows received by the government ($e.\Delta F_g$), by the Central Bank ($e.\Delta F_{cb}$) and by commercial banks ($e.\Delta F_{pb}$). The uses made of these resources appear along the row. Part of these flows goes to finance the country's current account deficit (S_e), another part is used to increase foreign exchange reserves in both the Central Bank ($e.\Delta FR_{cb}$) and commercial banks ($e.\Delta FR_{pb}$) and the remainder goes to finance capital flight by households ($e^P.\Delta CF_h$).

(n) Row and column 14 present the balance for the Central Bank. Row 14 shows the changes in Central Bank liabilities, which are equivalent to changes in the stock of high-powered money or the monetary base, and represent sources of funds for the Central Bank: currency (notes and coins) (ΔCu_h) demanded by households, external credits obtained by the Central Bank ($e.\Delta F_{cb}$), and changes in the amount of domestic reserves maintained by commercial banks in the Central Bank (ΔRe_{pb}) to meet the demands of their customers for cash and payments made through cheques deposited in other banks. Reserves consist of notes and coins held by the banks — vault cash — and also of deposits held by the Central Bank. Column 14 shows the sources of changes in the stock of high-powered money: credit granted to the public sector within the period (i.e. both to the central government and to public enterprises) ($\Delta L_{cb.g}$), new loans to the private banking system ($\Delta L_{cb,pb}$) and changes in the amount of foreign exchange reserves ($e.\Delta FR_{cb}$).

(o) Finally, row and column 15 present the balance for commercial banks. Along the row there are the sources of funds for commercial banks, which are equivalent to the increases in the banks' liability position. These sources are: deposits made by companies (ΔDep_c) and by households (ΔDep_h), and credit obtained by commercial banks abroad ($e.\Delta F_{pb}$) and from the Central Bank ($\Delta L_{cb.pb}$). Column 15 shows the changes in the asset position of the commercial banks, representing the uses made of the funds available. Part of these funds goes to finance credit to companies ($\Delta L_{pb.c}$), to households ($\Delta L_{pb\,h}$) and to government (ΔB_g); the rest is used to increase foreign exchange reserves ($e.\Delta FR_{pb}$) and domestic reserves (ΔRe_{pb}).

6.3 Sectoral Balances

The reduced-SAM structure comprises all the macroeconomic balances required for a complete specification of the Bolivian economy: the accumulation balance for all economic agents (companies, households and government), the supply-demand balances for all activities (formal and informal), the balances for financial institutions (the Central Bank and commercial banks), and the balance for the external sector.

Macroeconomic adjustment within reduced-SAM model framework can be interpreted by first looking at adjustments in the individual balances at the microeconomic level. The way in which the overall accumulation balance of the economy adjusts thereafter, will be determined by the interaction and aggregation of individual accumulation balance adjustments.

The accumulation balances for households (equation 6.1), for companies (equation 6.2) and for government (equation 6.3) are obtained from rows and columns 10, 11 and 12 of Table 6.2, respectively. The accumulation balances for the Central Bank (equation 6.4) are obtained from row and column 14 and for the private banks (equation 6.5) from row and column 15. Finally, the external balance (equation 6.6) is derived from row and column 13.

$$S_c + L_{pb\,c} \equiv e.P^M.I_c + \Delta Dep_c \tag{6.1}$$

$$S_h + L_{pb\,h} \equiv [(1-\theta).P_f + \theta.P_i].I_h + \Delta Cu_h + \Delta Dep_h + e^P.\Delta CF_h \tag{6.2}$$

$$S_g + e.\Delta F_g + \Delta L_{cb\,g} + \Delta B_g \equiv P_f.I_g \tag{6.3}$$

$$\Delta Cu_h + e.\Delta F_{cb} + \Delta Re_{pb} \equiv \Delta L_{cb\,g} + e.\Delta FR_{cb} + \Delta L_{cb.pb} \tag{6.4}$$

$$\Delta Dep_c + \Delta Dep_h + e.\Delta F_{pb} + \Delta L_{cb\,pb} \equiv \Delta L_{pb.c} + \Delta L_{pb\,h} + \Delta B_g + e.\Delta FR_{pb} + \Delta Re_{pb} \tag{6.5}$$

$$S_e + e^P.\Delta CF_h + e.\Delta FR_{cb} + e.\Delta FR_{pb} \equiv e.\Delta F_g + e.\Delta F_{cb} + e.\Delta F_{pb} \tag{6.6}$$

Adding the above equations gives:

$$S_c + S_h + S_g + S_e \equiv e.P^M.I_c + [(1-\theta).P_f + \theta.P_i].I_h + P_f.I_g \tag{6.7}$$

Rearranging (6.7) we obtain the standard accumulation balance for the whole economy:

$$[P_f.I_g - S_g] + [((1-\theta).P_f+\theta.P_i).I_h - S_h] + [e.P^M.I_c - S_c] \equiv e.\Delta F \qquad (6.8)$$

An important conclusion derived from equations (6.1) to (6.8) is that adjustment at the macroeconomic level can be derived from individual accumulation balance adjustments for all the socioeconomic agents and institutions of the economy at the microeconomic level. The same reasoning, however, cannot be applied the other way around; from an aggregate closure at the macroeconomic level, it is not always possible to ensure consistency in the closures at the microeconomic level. In fact, this research argues that disaggregated analysis is the only way to obtain a plausible picture of how macroeconomic adjustment takes place in a developing economy.

The rest of section 6.3 concentrates on analysing the structure of each of the balances included in the reduced-SAM model. The aim is to identify all possible adjustment mechanisms for each of the balances. This will be particularly useful in section 6.4, where the most relevant adjustment mechanisms for each balance are discussed in light of the macroeconomic events observed in Bolivia during the 1970s, the early 1980s, and the late 1980s.

6.3.1 Accumulation balances

(i) Companies

As discussed above, the accumulation balance for companies is obtained from row and column 10 of the reduced-SAM; thus,

$$S_c + \Delta L_{pb.c} \equiv e.P^M.I_c + \Delta Dep_c \qquad (6.9)$$

Corporate savings, on the other hand, are obtained from row and column 6 of the reduced-SAM:

$$S_c \equiv \Gamma.R_f - [DP + t.\Gamma.R_f + e.i^*.F_{pb}] \qquad (6.10)$$

Formal profits (R_f) are obtained from column 1:

$$R_f \equiv P_f.X_f - [w.b_f.X_f + e.P^M.a_m.X_f] \qquad (6.11)$$

Taking prices in the formal sector (P_f) to be equal to the unit costs of production plus the mark-up (τ) obtained by companies:

$$P_f = (1+\tau).(w.b_f + e.P^m.a_m) \qquad (6.12)$$

Substituting (6.10) and (6.11) in (6.9), dividing the resulting equation by the capital stock of the economy valued at prices of formal sector output (P_f.K) and rearranging, we obtain:

$$(1-z).(1-t).\Gamma.\pi.u_f - q.i^*.f_{pb} + \Delta l_{pb\,c} = (1+\mu).q.P^M.g_c \qquad (6.13)$$

where:

t =	tax rate on corporate profits
z =	share of corporate profits that is distributed to households
π =	share of corporate profits in the total value of formal sector output, ($\pi = \tau/(1+\tau)$)
τ =	mark-up profit rate obtained by companies
g =	(I/K) rate of growth of capital stock
q =	(e/P_f) ratio of the nominal exchange rate to the formal sector output price or the 'real exchange rate'
u =	(X/K) output-capital ratio as an indicator of capacity utilization
f =	(F/K) foreign capital inflows as a proportion of capital stock
l =	(L/K) bank credit available to the economic agent as a proportion of capital stock
μ =	[$\Delta\varepsilon\pi_\chi)/I_c$] desired balance sheet 'portfolio' of financial assets relative to investment
Γ =	proportion of corporate profits owed to private companies.

Equation (6.13) shows that if there is a disequilibrium between company savings and investment (e.g. $I_c > S_c$) adjustment will come through one or a combination of the following adjusting mechanisms:

(a) Corporate savings can increase. First, if they operate in oligopolistic markets, firms can increase savings by expanding their levels of activity when there is excess capacity (u_f) (the Keynesian case), or by fixing higher prices for their output so that the share of profits (π) in total income will be increased (the Kaldorian case). This latter case, of course, depends on the degree of monopoly in which the firms operate. Second, since firms in the formal sector also produce for export markets, they can influence the economic authorities to set a convenient exchange rate. However, since the formal sector output also depends on imported intermediate inputs, they can eventually ask for differentiated exchange rates, a higher rate for exports and a lower rate for imported inputs, in order to maximize profits.

(b) Companies are able to expand their availability of funds through bank loans. The access of companies to bank credit is facilitated because in Bolivia large enterprises are usually organized into groups associated with a bank that can guarantee the required liquidity on the basis of the profits of the group as a whole.

In summary, there are four possible adjusting variables that can bring adjustment to the accumulation balance for companies when there is disequilibrium between investment and savings. These mechanisms are: changes in the output of the formal sector (u_f); changes in the share of corporate profits in the gross value of formal sector output (π); changes in the level of credit obtained from commercial banks within the period ($\Delta l_{pb.c}$); and adjustments in the level of corporate investment (g_c).

(ii) Households

The accumulation balance for households is obtained from equation (6.2):

$$S_h + \Delta L_{pb.h} \equiv [(1-\theta).P_f + \theta.P_i].I_h + \Delta Cu_h + \Delta Dep_h + e^P.\Delta CF_h \qquad (6.14)$$

S_h can be expanded in term of its fundamentals using row and column 7 in Table 6.2. Thus,

$$S_h \equiv [w.b_f.X_f + R_i + DP] - [P_f.C_f + P_i.C_i + e^P.P^M.C_m] \qquad (6.15)$$

Profits by household-based firms can also be written in terms of its basic components:

$$R_i \equiv P_i.X_i + e^P.PE_i.\ E_i - P_f.a.X_i \qquad (6.16)$$

Based on the stylized facts discussed in section 3.6, we can define the following household consumption functions for commodities produced by formal activities (equation 6.17); by informal activities (equation 6.18), and those that are imported (equation 6.19):

$$P_f.C_f = c.[P_i.(1 - ß) - P_f.a)].X_i + \alpha.(1 - \tau_i).e^P.P_i^E.E_i \quad (6.17)$$

$$P_i.C_i = w.b_f.X_f + P_i.ß.X_i \quad (6.18)$$

$$e^P.P^M.C_m = c_m.z.(1 - t).\Gamma.R_f + (1 - \alpha).(1 - \tau_i).e^P.P_i^E.E_i \quad (6.19)$$

(a) Wage incomes tend to be spent entirely on consumption. Consumption is mostly concentrated on the acquisition of staple foods (C_i).
(b) Peasant producers in the informal sector tend to use a large part (ß) of their production for their own consumption (C_i).
(c) Households consume a proportion (c) of their incomes arising from the sale of marketable surpluses.
(d) The propensity to consume out of distributed profits (c_m) tends to be very low. This type of consumption relates mostly to imported goods.
(e) Peasants working in the informal coca sector tend to spend their incomes on purchases of imported and domestic goods; the latter is mostly concentrated on goods produced by the formal sector. In order to simplify the model, the amount consumed by this peasant household group will be equal to the remaining surplus once intermediaries and merchants have secured for themselves a margin τ_i of total gross value of coca output.

Replacing (6.15)–(6.19) in (6.14), dividing the whole expression by the capital stock of the economy (K) valued at formal sector output prices (P_f) and rearranging, we restate it as:

$$[1 - (c + \delta)].[p_i.(1-ß) - a].u_i + [1-(c_m + \lambda).z.(1 - t).\Gamma.\pi.u_f + \tau_i.q_P.PE_i.\varepsilon_i + \Delta l_{pb} = [(1-\theta) + \theta.p_i].g_h + q^P.\Delta cf_h \quad (6.20)$$

where:

p_i = (p_i/p_f) internal terms of trade between informal and formal activities

c = the propensity of households to consume out of non-corporate profit earnings

c_m = the propensity of households to consume out of distributed corporate profits

β =	the proportion of total informal output that is used for self-consumption within households
δ =	$[\Delta Cu_h/(P_i.(1-\beta) - a)]$ coefficient between household demand for currency relative to monetary incomes arising from the sale of marketable informal output surpluses (excluding self-consumption)
λ =	$[\Delta Dep_h/c_2.DP]$ coefficient between household demand for bank deposits relative to their income from distributed profits
τ_i =	profit margin obtained by intermediaries and merchants out of the total gross value of coca output
θ =	share of household investment in goods produced within the same household (e.g. self-construction)
cf =	(CF/K) capital flight relative to capital stock
ε_i =	(E/K) coca exports as a proportion of total capital stock
PE_i =	international prices for coca exports.

Equation (6.30) outlines the balance between household investment and savings availability. Household investment comprises both physical capital (mostly house construction) and financial capital (in this case mostly used to finance capital flight).

In an unbalanced situation, adjustment is likely to come through one or a combination of the following variables:

(a) Households can finance their acquisition of financial and physical assets using their own savings from various sources of income, such as non-corporate profits, distributed profits and coca earnings (as discussed before, there is no saving out of wage incomes) or borrowing from commercial banks.

(b) Savings out of non-corporate profits can increase through an expansion of output (u_i) or through higher prices (p_i) in the informal sector. However, unlike corporate profit-earners, non-corporate profit-earners have little influence on their levels of income, which are largely determined by factors beyond their control. This is so because informal activities take place in competitive markets; therefore prices are set by market forces. In addition, production by peasants and informal urban firms tends to be extremely inelastic, so that production cannot be expanded as a means to achieve higher levels of income. Moreover, prices for inputs demanded within informal activities in the market tend to be fixed by companies that have oligopolistic positions in those markets.

(c) Household savings out of distributed profits can increase through an output expansion in formal activities (u_f); or by increasing the share of corporate profits in the gross value of formal sector output (π).

(d) Savings out of coca revenues can be increased when: the level of exports is increased, coca prices rise in international markets, the foreign exchange rate in the parallel market goes up, or merchants and intermediaries increase their mark-up and extract more surpluses from peasants.

(e) Finally, households can borrow from commercial banks. Available bank credit to households is set on the basis of factors such as expected ability to repay (or the value of collateral). Therefore, access to credit tends to be very limited ($\Delta l_{pb.h}$).

In summary, any imbalance between household savings and investment can be cleared through nine adjusting mechanisms: informal sector output (u_i), prices of informal output (p_i), the share of corporate profits (π), formal sector output (u_f), informal sector exports (ε_i), commercial bank credit obtained within the period ($\Delta l_{pb.h}$), household demand for physical investment (g_h) and for financial investment (Δcf_h) (capital flight), and finally, the value of the exchange rate in the parallel market (q^P).

(iii) Government

The accumulation balance for the government was outlined in equation (6.3):

$$S_g + e.\Delta F_g + \Delta L_{cb\,g} + \Delta B_g \equiv P_f.I_g \qquad (6.21)$$

Government savings can be obtained from row and column 8 in Table 6.2:

$$S_g \equiv (1-\Gamma).R_f + t.\Gamma.R_f - P_f.G + e.i^*.(F_g+F_{cb}) \qquad (6.22)$$

Replacing (6.22) in (6.21) and dividing the equation by ($P_f.K$), we obtain:

$$[(1-\Gamma) + t.\Gamma].\pi.u_f + q.(\Delta f_g - i^*.f_g) + \Delta l_{cb.g} + \Delta b_g = \Omega + g_g \qquad (6.23)$$

where:

$\Omega = (G/K)$ government consumption as a proportion of capital stock.

According to equation (6.23), if government savings and investments are not balanced ex-ante, ex-post adjustment is likely to come through changes in the following variables:

(a) Formal sector output (u_f) and/or the share of corporate profits in the gross value of formal sector output (π) can increase so that the government's tax revenues and public sector profits can be increased.
(b) External borrowing can be increased (Δf_g).
(c) Domestic credit can be obtained from the Central Bank ($\Delta l_{cb,g}$).
(d) Government can issue bonds (Δb_g).
(e) Current expenditures can be reduced so that savings can be increased (Ω).

Therefore, the government's balance adjustment can take place through changes in the values of seven variables: formal sector output (u_f), the share of corporate profits (π), foreign borrowing (Δf_g), domestic borrowing from the Central Bank ($\Delta l_{cb,g}$), bonds issued to the private sector (Δb_g), the level of government expenditures (Ω), and, finally, thc level of government investment (g_g).

6.3.2 Financial balances

(i) Commercial banks

The accumulation balance for the commercial banks was defined in equation (6.4):

$$\Delta Dep_c + \Delta Dep_h + e.\Delta F_{pb} + \Delta L_{cb.pb} \equiv \Delta L_{pb.c} + \Delta L_{pb.h} + e.\Delta FR_{pb} + \Delta Re_{pb} + \Delta B_g \qquad (6.24)$$

Using the notation and relationships already introduced, and dividing equation (6.24) by $P_f.K$,

$$(1-r).[\mu.q.P^M.g_c + \lambda.z.(1-t).\Gamma.\pi.u_f] + q.(1-fr).\Delta f_{pb} + \Delta l_{cb.pb} = \Delta l_{pb.c} + \Delta l_{pb.h} + \Delta b_g \qquad (6.25)$$

where:

$r =$ reserves-deposits ratio for commercial banks

fr = foreign reserves/external debt ratio for commercial banks.

Equation (6.25) shows the balance between the changes in the total assets and total liabilities of the commercial banks, which is equivalent to the balance between their total uses and total sources of funds. In a disequilibrium situation, adjustment can take place through several variables within this balance:

(a) Company demand for bank deposits may change. However, according to specification of company demand for bank deposits within the model, this depends on the changes that occur in company investment demand (g_c).
(b) Holdings of bank deposits by households may change depending on the variables (u_f) and (π) that determine distributed profits.
(c) Commercial bank borrowing both from external sources (Δf_{pb}) and from the Central Bank ($\Delta l_{cb.pb}$) may vary.
(d) Finally, commercial banks can adjust the amount of credit available to companies ($\Delta l_{pb.c}$), to households ($\Delta l_{pb.h}$) and to the government (Δb_g).

In summary, there are eight variables that can bring adjustment to the balance for commercial banks: company investment (g_c), formal sector output (u_f), the share of corporate profits in the gross value of formal sector output (π), foreign credit to commercial banks (Δf_{pb}), Central Bank credit to commercial banks ($\Delta l_{cb,pb}$), commercial bank loans to companies ($\Delta l_{pb,c}$), to households ($\Delta l_{pb,h}$) and to the government (Δb_g).

(ii) The Central Bank

The accumulation balance for the Central Bank was defined in equation (6.5):

$$\Delta Cu_h + e.\Delta F_{cb} + \Delta Re_{pb} \equiv \Delta L_{cb.c} + \Delta L_{cb.g} + e.\Delta FR_{cb} + \Delta L_{cb.pb} \qquad (6.26)$$

Using the notation and relationships already introduced, and dividing equation (6.26) by $P_f.K$,

$$\delta.[p_i.(1-\beta)-a].u_i + r.[\mu.q.P^M.g_c+\lambda.z.\pi.u_f] + q.(\Delta f_{cb}-\Delta fr_{cb}) = \Delta l_{cb.g}+\Delta l_{cb.pb} \qquad (6.27)$$

Equation (6.27) shows balance for the Central Bank. In an ex-ante dis-equilibrium situation, ex-post adjustment can take place through changes in the values of the following variables:

(a) Currency demand out of the non-corporate profit incomes of households may change. As specified in the model, however, this may depend on the level of informal sector output (u_i) and on the prices at which the marketable surpluses of informal output are sold (p_i).
(b) To increase the reserves requirements of commercial banks, the Central Bank can manipulate (increase) the required reserves-deposits ratio as a policy variable (r). Required reserves can also increase through an expansion of bank deposits by companies and by households. These variables depend on corporate investment demand (g_c), on formal sector output (u_f) and on the share of corporate profits in the gross value of formal sector output (π).
(c) The Central Bank can resort to external borrowing (Δf_{cb}) or can reduce part of its foreign exchange reserves (Δfr_{cb}).
(d) Finally, the Central Bank can adjust the amount of credit available to the government ($\Delta l_{cb.g}$) and to commercial banks ($\Delta l_{cb.pb}$).

In summary, nine variables can bring adjustment to the balance for the Central Bank: prices (P_i) and output level (u_i) in the informal sector, corporate investment demand (g_c), formal sector output (u_f), the share of corporate profits in the gross value of formal sector output (π), foreign credit to the Central Bank (Δf_{cb}), the Central Bank's foreign exchange reserves (Δfr_{cb}), Central Bank loans to the government ($\Delta l_{cb.g}$) and to commercial banks ($\Delta l_{cb.pb}$).

6.3.3 The external balance

To move further in the specification of the reduced-SAM model, this section concentrates on the specification of the balance adjustment for the external sector. The balance was outlined in equation (6.6):

$$S_e + e^P.\Delta CF_h + e.\Delta FR_{cb} + e.\Delta FR_{pb} \equiv e.\Delta F_g + e.\Delta F_{cb} + e.\Delta F_{pb} \qquad (6.28)$$

Replacing S_e with its fundamentals we obtain

$$e.P^M.a_m.X_f + e.i^*.(F_g+F_{cb}+F_{pb}) + e.P^M.I_c + e^P.P^M.C_m$$
$$- (e.P^E{}_f.E_f + e^P.PE_i.E_i) + e^P.\Delta CF_h + e.\Delta FR_{cb} + e.\Delta FR_{pb}$$
$$\equiv e.\Delta F_g + e.\Delta F_{cb} + e.\Delta F_{pb} \qquad (6.29)$$

Using the notation and relationships already introduced, dividing the whole expression by $P_f.K$ and rearranging, we obtain

$$q.[P^M.(a_m.u_f+g_c) + i^*.(f_g+f_{cb}+f_{pb}) - P^E{}_f.\varepsilon_f + \Delta fr_{cb}$$
$$- (1-fr).\Delta f_{pb} - \Delta f_{cb} - \Delta f_g] + q^P.[(c_m.z.\pi.u_f)/q^P$$
$$- (1 - (1-\alpha)(1-\tau_i)).PE_i.\varepsilon_i + \Delta cf_h] = 0 \qquad (6.30)$$

The external balance, as presented in equation (6.30), comprises both official and unofficial transactions. In an ex-ante unbalanced situation, ex-post adjustment can take place through several adjusting mechanisms operating in the informal or parallel foreign exchange market. The transactions that take place in the official market, which appear in the upper part of equation (6.30), are:

(a) Levels of imports of intermediate and capital goods may vary. This will obviously depend on the levels of formal sector output (u_f) and on the level of corporate investment (g_c).
(b) Levels of formal sector exports can change (ε_f).
(c) Accumulation of foreign reserves by the banking system (Δfr_{cb}).
(d) Net capital inflows received by commercial banks (Δf_{pb}), the Central Bank (Δf_{cb}) and by the government (Δf_g).

In the lower part of equation (6.30) the unofficial transactions are valued at the parallel foreign exchange rate. These adjusting mechanisms are:

(a) Imports of consumption goods, which are defined within the model, depend on distributed profits from companies to households. Therefore they are conditioned by the levels of formal sector output (u_f) and of the share of corporate profits in the gross value of formal sector output (π).
(b) Coca exports can change (ε_i). This variable would affect export earnings as well as imports of consumer goods.
(c) The acquisition of foreign assets by households (capital flight) can also close the balance (Δcf_h).

(d) Finally, the value of the exchange rate in the parallel market can change in order to adjust the external balance as a whole (q^P).

In summary, there are 11 variables that can adjust the balance for the external sector: u_f, π, ε_f, ε_i, g_c, Δf_g, Δf_{cb}, Δf_{pb}, Δfr_{cb}, Δcf_h and q^P.

6.3.4 Supply-demand balances

Finally, for a complete specification of the whole macroeconomic system, we need to determine the adjustment for the supply-demand balance of all the economic activities included in the reduced-SAM model, both formal and informal.

(i) The formal sector

The supply-demand balance for formal activities is obtained from row 1 in Table 6.2:

$$P_f.X_f \equiv P_f.a.X_i + P_f.C_{fh} + P_f.G + e._{PEf}.E_f + P_f.(1-\theta).I_h + P_f.I_g \tag{6.31}$$

After dividing equation (6.31) by $P_f.K$, replacing the already defined relationships and rearranging terms, we obtain

$$u_f = [a+c.(p_i.(1-\beta) - a)].u_i + \alpha.(1-\tau_{CO}).q^P.PE_{CO}.\varepsilon_{CO} + \Omega + q.PE_f.\varepsilon_f + (1-\theta).g_h + g_g \tag{6.32}$$

Equation (6.32) says that total supply in formal activities must be equal to total demand. Any disequilibrium between supply and demand will be cleared through the following mechanisms.

(a) Formal sector output (u_f) may increase and accommodate to the level of demand.
(b) Informal sector output may change and reduce or increase the demand for intermediate inputs (u_i).
(c) Demand out of non-corporate profit earnings may vary if informal sector output (u_i) or relative prices (p_i) change.
(d) Demand arising from coca proceeds may vary if there is a change in coca export volumes (ε_i) and/or in the value of the exchange rate in the parallel market.
(e) Government demand can change (Ω).

(f) Exports of goods and services produced by formal activities can change (ε_f).
(g) Demand for capital goods produced by the formal sector can change if government and/or household investment demands vary.

In summary, there are nine variables that can adjust the supply-demand balance for the formal sector: u_f, p_i, u_i, ε_i, Ω, ε_f, g_h, g_g and q^P.

(ii) The informal sector

The supply-demand balance for informal activities is obtained from row 2 in Table 6.2:

$$P_i.X_i + e^P.P_i^E.E_i \equiv P_i.Ci_h + e^P.P_i^E.E_iE_i + P_i.I_h \qquad (6.33)$$

Inserting the already defined consumption functions into (6.33), dividing the whole expression by $P_f.K$, and rearranging terms, we obtain

$$(1 - \beta).u_i = [(1-\pi\text{-}q.P^*.a).u_f]/p_i + g_h \qquad (6.34)$$

According to (6.34), if there is an excess demand in the informal sector demand-supply balance, adjustment will come through the following mechanisms:

(a) Informal sector output can change (u_i) and accommodate to the level of demand.
(b) Household consumption out of wage incomes can change as a result of: first, changes in the levels of informal sector output, which affect wage employment and therefore total wage incomes; second, an increase in the share of corporate profits in the gross value of formal sector output (π) due to a higher mark-up rate, will reduce real wages and therefore consumption; third, the same effect occurs when a devaluation of the official exchange rate (q) increases the share of imported intermediates in the gross value of formal sector output; and fourth, an increase in the price of informal sector output (p_i) reduces demand in real terms.
(c) Finally, adjustment can take place through changes in household demand for capital goods produced within the informal sector (g_h) (e.g. self-construction).

In summary, there are five variables that tend to adjust the supply-demand balance for the informal sector: u_i, u_f, g_h, π and p_i.

6.4 Macroeconomic Adjustment in Bolivia within the Reduced-SAM Model

In the previous section, the overall structure of the reduced-SAM model for the Bolivian economy was specified. The structure of the eight balance equations was outlined and the possible adjusting variables for each balance were identified. In total, 25 adjusting variables were distinguished as possible closures for the eight balances that make up the model. Therefore, 17 variables still need to be specified: (i) exogenous variables, (ii) those determined through specific behavioural equations, (iii) policy variables, and (iv) model constraints. In this way the system will be fully determined with an equal number of balances and closures.

The aim of this section is to identify the most relevant closures within the reduced-SAM model during the periods under study. As discussed in the Introduction, adjustment in the Bolivian economy has tended to vary from period to period as a result of external shocks and domestic policies. Three sub-periods were clearly identified: (i) the 1970s, when the country benefited from a relatively abundant flow of foreign resources; (ii) the first half of the 1980s, when external flows through official channels were drastically reduced while unofficial foreign exchange earnings increased significantly; and (iii) the second half of the 1980s, when the country's economic development strategy was completely changed under the NEP. Furthermore, the reforms introduced in the 1990s redefine the adjustment closures for some of the sectors, namely the government, public enterprises, the Central Bank and private banks.

A general assumption in the following analysis of adjustment within the reduced-SAM model is that external shocks are beyond the country's control. Variables such as capital inflows, external interest rates and terms of trade are therefore taken to be exogenous.

6.4.1 Adjustment during the 1970s

The 1970s were characterized by the accumulation of a large external debt by the public sector, by increased state involvement in economic activity, by large transfers of resources to the private sector through bank credit, and by the rapid accumulation of external assets by the private sector (capital flight) (World Bank 1985b; Ramos 1980; Ladman 1982; Dunkerley 1984). The patterns of adjustment of sectoral balances during the 1970s were as follows.

6.4.1.1 *Companies*

Four possible adjusting variables can bring equilibrium to the accumulation balance for companies: changes in formal sector output (u_f); changes in the share of corporate profits in the gross value of formal sector output (π); credit obtained from commercial banks within the period ($\Delta l_{pb.c}$); and adjustments in the level of corporate investment (g_c).

According to many authors, the accumulation balance for companies showed a favourable situation during the 1970s (Ramos 1980; Dunkerley 1984; Hinojosa and Espinoza 1983). Companies had access to funds out of their own savings, facilitated by favourable external prices for export commodities. In addition, companies enjoyed large financial flows from domestic financial institutions as a deliberate policy of the economic authorities to increase private participation in economic activity (Devlin and Mortimore 1983; Torrico 1982).

Adjustment in the accumulation balance for companies to the wider availability of funds partly came in the form of higher levels of fixed capital formation. Corporate investment was mainly allocated to the agro-export industry and to the construction sector (Dunkerley 1984; García-Rodriguez 1982).

In summary, during the 1970s, corporate investment demand was not constrained by the availability of savings. Companies that wished to undertake any profitable (or unprofitable) investment project could find finance either from their own increased profits or through bank credit made available by financial institutions.

To capture the investment-leading-savings position adopted by companies during that period, the adjustment in the accumulation balance can be described as follows:

(a) Corporate investment was determined by their investment demand (g_c). According to an econometric test carried out within this research (see Appendix 5.4), g_c was positively correlated with the amount of bank credit received within the period ($\Delta l_{pb,c}$), lagged government investment ($g_{g(-t)}$) (the crowding-in effect; World Bank 1985b), and activity levels in the formal sector (u_f) (the accelerator effect); it was negatively correlated with the international interest rate (i^*) and public sector investment demand (g_{pe}) (the crowding-out effect, Devlin and Mortimore 1982). Thus,

$$g_c = g0 + g1(\Delta l_{pb,c}, g_{g(-t)}, u_f, i^*, g_{pe}) \qquad (6.35)$$

(b) During the 1970s, corporate savings could be expanded by increasing the level of capacity utilization (u_f) (the Keynesian case). This adjustment mechanism is discussed later within the demand-supply balance for the formal sector.

(c) Finally, the adjusting variable that acts as the main closure for the accumulation balance for companies is the level of credit obtained from commercial banks ($\Delta l_{pb.c}$). Corporate access to bank credit was facilitated because large businesses in Bolivia are organized into large groups associated with a bank that can guarantee the required liquidity on the basis of the profits of the group as a whole (Hinojosa and Espinoza 1983; Torrico 1982).

6.4.1.2 Households

Nine possible adjusting variables in the accumulation balance for households were identified in section 6.3: informal sector output (u_i), prices of informal output (p_i), the share of corporate profits (π), formal sector output (u_f), informal sector exports (ε_i), commercial bank credit obtained within the period ($\Delta l_{pb.h}$), household demand for physical investment (g_h) and for financial investment (Δcf_h) (capital flight), and finally, the value of the exchange rate in the parallel market (q^P).

During the 1970s, households' investment demand was sharply restricted by the availability of savings and other sources of finance (Romero 1982). Therefore, in an ex-ante unbalanced situation between investment demand vis-à-vis planned savings (e.g. $S_i < I_i$), ex-post adjustment would most likely come through a reduction of investment to the availability of savings ($S \rightarrow I$). This savings-constrained condition is reflected in the model in the following ways:

(a) Household investment demand (g_h) is selected as the final adjusting variable for the accumulation balance for households (the Ricardian case).

(b) Household incomes arising from wage earnings and informal sector profits are assumed to be spent entirely on consumption, since these incomes are assumed to be at the subsistence level (Urioste 1989b; R. Morales 1984). Actually, households whose main sources of income are wage earnings and non-corporate profits have no power to improve their earnings, because of their inflexibility to expand output levels in the activities they control (u_i) (the informal sector), and because they are unable to improve their internal terms of trade (p_i), since P_i is determined in highly competitive, atomistic markets and P_f is fixed by capitalists using a mark-up based on their oligopolistic position in the markets they control.

(c) The bank loans available to households ($\Delta l_{pb.h}$) are defined as a constraint within the balance, to reflect the limitations of households in obtaining more loans from the domestic financial system due to credit rationing or restrictions imposed by bank rules on collateral (Torrico 1982).

(d) The variables u_f and π that determine consumption out of distributed profit incomes are determined within the accumulation balance for the formal sector.

(e) Finally, coca exports (ε_i) were not significant during the 1970s (Healy 1986).

6.4.1.3 The government

Adjustment in the accumulation balance of the government can occur through changes in the values of six variables: formal sector output (u_f), the share of corporate profits (π), foreign borrowing (Δf_g), domestic borrowing from the Central Bank ($\Delta l_{cb,g}$), the level of government expenditure (Ω), and, finally, the level of government investment (g_g).

During the 1970s, the accumulation balance for the government represented a favourable situation (World Bank 1985b). The state had relatively wide access to external and domestic funds, an important part of which came from the government's own savings. This was possible because the favourable tendency of state-owned enterprise income increased government tax revenues. In addition, the government enjoyed relatively easy access to foreign credit. Resort to domestic financial sources (Central Bank credit) was unnecessary because the state became a surplus sector. The large amount of resources available during the 1970s therefore allowed the government and public sector enterprises to expand investment without facing major financial constraints. The unconstrained savings situation enjoyed by the public sector is captured within the model in the following ways:

(a) Government consumption (Ω) and investment demand (g_g) are defined as being determined through specific demand functions. Econometric tests carried out within this research show that government consumption was positively correlated with both government consumption in the previous period (Ω_{t-1}) and capital inflows received by the government, and was negatively correlated with the rate of inflation (p) (see Appendix 3.1):

$$\Omega = f(\Omega_{t-1}, \Delta f_g, p) \tag{6.36}$$

Government investment, on the other hand, showed a positive correlation with government investment in the previous period $g_{g(t-1)}$, and with capital inflows received by the government (Δf_g) (see Appendix 3.2):

$$g_g = f(g_{g(t-1)}, \Delta f_g) \tag{6.37}$$

(b) Foreign capital inflows to the government (Δf_g) are considered to be exogenous to the model, following Devlin's argument that, during the 1970s, Bolivia experienced a supply-led indebtedness (Devlin 1986); besides, the variables (u_f) and (π) that determine government incomes are resolved within the demand-supply balance for the formal sector. The closing variable in the balance for the government therefore has to be the amount of credit it obtains from the Central Bank ($\Delta l_{cb,g}$) (Lehwing 1989).

6.4.1.4 The commercial banks

Seven variables were identified as possible closures for the balance for the commercial banks: company investment (g_c), formal sector output (u_f), the share of corporate profits in the gross value of formal sector output (π), foreign credit to commercial banks (Δf_{pb}), Central Bank credit to commercial banks ($\Delta l_{cb,pb}$), commercial bank loans to companies ($\Delta l_{pb,c}$) and to households ($\Delta l_{pb,h}$). Most of these variables have been defined elsewhere in the model; thus, the two variables available for bringing adjustment to the balance for the commercial banks are:

(a) Foreign capital inflows to the commercial banks (Δf_{pb}), which as in the case of the government are taken to be exogenously determined (Devlin 1986).
(b) The accumulation balance for the commercial banks therefore adjusts through credit from the Central Bank ($\Delta l_{cb.pb}$) (Lehwing 1989).

6.4.1.5 The Central Bank

Nine variables were identified as possible closures for the balance for the Central Bank: relative prices (p_i) and output level (u_i) in the informal sector, investment demand by companies (g_c), formal sector output (u_f), the share of corporate profits in the gross value of formal sector output (π), foreign credit to the Central Bank (Δf_{cb}), foreign exchange reserves held by the Central Bank (Δfr_{cb}), and Central Bank loans to the government ($\Delta l_{cb.g}$) and the commercial banks ($\Delta l_{cb.pb}$). Of these variables, only Δfr_{cb} and Δf_{cb} have not yet been determined elsewhere in the model. Either of these two variables could act as the closure of the balance for the Central Bank in order to reflect the foreign exchange unconstrained situation enjoyed by the Bolivian economy during the 1970s.

(a) Capital inflows received by the Central Bank are considered to be exogenous to the model (Devlin 1986).
(b) The balance for the Central Bank therefore adjusts by reducing or building up foreign exchange reserves (Δfr_{cb}).

6.4.1.6 The external sector

Eleven variables were identified as possible closures for the external balance: u_f, π, ε_f, ε_i, g_c, Δf_g, Δf_{cb}, Δf_{pb}, Δfr_{cb}, Δcf_h and q^P. All of these variables have been determined elsewhere, except capital flight by households (Δcf_h) and the exchange rate in the parallel market (q^P).

(a) During the 1970s, due to the easy availability of foreign exchange to Bolivia, there was no difference between the official and parallel exchange rates. All unofficial transactions in foreign currency were conducted using the officially determined foreign exchange rate (q).

(b) The variable that closes the external balance is therefore $t\Delta cf_h$. This closure reflects the fact that during the 1970s, the foreign exchange available in Bolivia exceeded the country's capacity to absorb and use it productively. As a result, the excess foreign exchange available was used to finance capital flight by the private formal sector (Ramos 1980; World Bank 1985b).

6.4.1.7 *The formal sector*

Nine variables were identified as possible closures for the supply-demand balance for the formal sector: u_f, p_i, u_i, ε_i, Ω, ε_f, g_h, g_g and q^P. Adjustment in the supply-demand balance for formal activities showed the following pattern during the 1970s:

(a) The determination of p_i and u_i is discussed within the closure of the balance for the informal sector (section 6.4.1.8).

(b) Exports from the formal sector demonstrated that they were responsive to relative price changes as nontraditional exports rose in response to terms of trade improvements (World Bank ibid):

$$\varepsilon_f = f(q.P^E) \tag{6.38}$$

(c) The clearing variable in the demand-supply balance for the formal sector is therefore capacity utilization (u_f), since the productive capacity created during the 1970s allowed for output changes in response to excess demand (Ladman 1982b).

6.4.1.8 *The informal sector*

Five variables were recognized as possible closures for the supply-demand balance for the informal sector: u_i, u_f, g_h, π and p_i. Adjustment for informal activities during the 1970s showed the following pattern:

(a) The level of informal output (u_i) (e.g. traditional agricultural output) is considered as a constraint within the model given the structural bottlenecks that characterize informal production (Torrico

1982; Urioste 1989b; R. Morales 1984; Schuh 1991); u_i is therefore assumed to be fixed.

(b) The variable that closes the demand-supply balance of the informal sector therefore has to be p_i.

6.4.1.9 Summary of adjustment mechanisms during the 1970s

The eight balances discussed above describe the adjustment in the Bolivian economy during the 1970s. The eight endogenous variables that were identified as closures for the eight balances of the system were: formal sector activities (u_f), internal terms of trade for informal activities (p_i), investment demand by households (g_h), commercial bank credit to companies ($\Delta l_{pb.c}$), Central Bank credit to commercial banks ($\Delta l_{cb.pb}$), Central Bank credit to the government ($\Delta l_{cb.g}$), capital flight by households (Δcf_h), and foreign exchange reserves held by the banking system (Δfr_{cb}).

The variables considered as constraints or fixed in the model were: informal sector output (u_i), commercial bank credit to households ($\Delta l_{pb.h}$), and the share of corporate profits in the gross value of formal sector output (π).

The variables considered as policy variables were: the nominal exchange rate (e), tax rate (t) and the required reserves/deposits ratio (r).

The variables specified as functions were: formal sector exports (ε_f), government consumption (Ω), and investment demand by companies (g_c) and by the government (g_g).

Finally, the variables considered as exogenous, whose impact we want to evaluate through the model, were: capital inflows to government (Δf_g), to the commercial banks (Δf_{pb}) and to the Central Bank (Δf_{cb}); external prices for formal exports ($P^E{}_f$) and for imports (P^M); coca exports (ε_i); and the international interest rate (i^*).

6.4.2 Adjustment during the first half of the 1980s

The first half of the 1980s was characterized by much lower official export revenues; negative net external capital inflows as debt payments exceeded disbursements of new loans and interest payments increased due to the much higher interest rate; larger fiscal deficits that were financed through money creation; extremely high rates of inflation; increased illegal export revenues due to the coca trade; and a highly segmented foreign exchange market with highly differentiated foreign exchange rates (World Bank 1985b, J.A. Morales 1987a, b; Dunkerley 1992; Healy 1986).

The supply-demand and accumulation balance adjustments under these new conditions are discussed in the following.

6.4.2.1 Companies

During the 1980s, companies became foreign exchange constrained as they found more difficulties in expanding their availability of external resources because of the much lower levels of foreign credit and official export revenues. As a result, output responses in 'formal' activities were restricted by the lack of foreign exchange to finance imports of intermediate inputs (Mierau-Klein and Page 1991), so that their ability to expand corporate savings through increased output was limited. Moreover, companies had to adjust ex-post investment (g_c) to a much lower level determined by the availability of foreign exchange to finance imports of capital goods. As a result, some companies' planned investments did not materialize (Mierau-Klein and Page ibid). The constraint imposed by the foreign exchange gap on formal sector output and corporate investment transformed 'import capacity' into the main closures of the official foreign exchange balance. This is further explained in section 6.4.2.6.

In a situation of ex-ante excess of investment demand vis-à-vis planned savings, however, ex-post equilibrium still came through an expansion of companies' availability of funds. The main mechanisms were:

(a) As inflationary expectations rose, companies increased their share in the gross value of formal sector output (π) by increasing the mark-up rate (τ). This implied a fall in real wages and a consequent reduction in the share of wages in total income (R. Morales 1987b; UDAPE 1990a).

(b) Moreover, given the privileged position enjoyed by companies in domestic financial markets during that period, credit from commercial banks ($\Delta l_{pb.c}$) was assigned freely on demand. It mainly came through private bank loans, which in turn were financed by the Central Bank (Ramos 1989; World Bank 1989). The outcome was a continuous credit expansion that eventually fuelled inflation. Therefore, during the first half of the 1980s, $\Delta l_{pb.c}$ remained as the main closure in the accumulation balance for companies.

6.4.2.2 Households

(a) During the first half of the 1980s, due to higher informal (illegal) export prices (P_i^E) and increased export quantities (ε_i), revenues for households involved in the coca trade expanded sharply (Healy 1986; Naylor 1987). Coca-producing households generated large surpluses. Two groups of people benefited directly from this illegal trade: peasant producers of coca leaves and coca paste, and merchants and traders who organized the production of more refined drugs and smuggled them abroad. Peasants utilized most of their incomes to finance consumption (locally produced and imported) and to acquire some capital goods (such as trucks and houses) (Healy ibid). Merchants most likely used their surpluses to finance capital flight, since they were mostly linked to the international drugs trade (Sage 1989). Capital flight by households (Δcf_h) is determined endogenously within this model, as explained in section 6.4.2.6.

(b) Household earners of non-corporate profits, on the other hand, still faced a very limited access to investable funds. Personal savings were limited by low levels of informal output (u_i) (excluding the production of coca and its by-products) which remained stagnant and even fell sharply in some years, such as 1983, when adverse weather conditions resulted in large reductions in agricultural output (World Bank 1990). In addition, the internal terms of trade for informal sector activities (p_i) were still subject to demand-supply interactions. Bank lending to most household units $\Delta l_{pb.h}$ remained very limited (FUNDES 1990; Urioste 1989b).

(c) Finally, from the above analysis it follows that during the first half of the 1980s, household investment still relied almost entirely on households' capacity to generate their own savings. Therefore, g_h still acted as the main closure in the accumulation balance for households.

6.4.2.3 The government

During the 1980s, in common with companies, the government faced an acute shortage of foreign exchange. Three factors contributed to this situation: (a) a much lower level of export revenues due to the international recession, (b) access to foreign credit stopped and eventually became negative ($\Delta f_g < 0$), and (c) the government started paying interest on the external debt accumulated during the 1970s ($q^o.(i^*.f_g)$).

The foreign exchange gap forced an adjustment in government investment (g_g). Output in activities controlled by public firms (u_f) also had to adjust to the much lower level of foreign exchange available. The combination of these external shocks had negative effects on the fiscal balance:

(a) The fiscal deficit reached unprecedentedly high levels as tax revenues fell as a result of the much lower levels of activity in the formal sector. In addition, as inflation rose, tax revenues deteriorated because taxes were not indexed to inflation (the Tanzi effect) (Tanzi 1982; Sachs 1987; Mann and Pastor 1989).
(b) Government consumption (Ω), on the other hand, did not adjust to the much lower level of government revenues in order to avoid further reductions in economic activity.
(c) The main adjusting variable in the accumulation balance for the government was the amount of Central Bank credit directed to government in order to finance its deficit ($\Delta l_{cb.g}$). This process brought about a continuous increase in the quantity of money in nominal terms. However, the capacity of government to claim real resources from the private sector by financing its deficit through money creation ('seigniorage') ($\Delta l_{cb.g}$), fell sharply as the inflationary expectations of economic agents became more rational. The outcome was hyperinflation (J.A. Morales 1987b; Sachs 1987).

6.4.2.4 The commercial banks

During the first half of the 1980s, the commercial banks played a very active role in providing finance to companies. As discussed previously, $\Delta l_{pb.c}$ was defined as the final closure in the accumulation balance for companies, implying that commercial bank credit adjusted to the requirements of corporate firms. During that period, however, there were several important changes in the way commercial banks financed their operations:

(a) The access of commercial banks to foreign credit (Δf_{pb}) was halted.
(b) Household and company deposits in commercial banks fell in real terms, as inflation and highly negative interest rates made economic agents move their financial assets away from domestic assets and into foreign currency or other highly indexed assets (J.A. Morales 1987b; World Bank 1985b; Afcha 1989).
(c) Therefore, the main source of finance for commercial bank operations was from credit obtained from the Central Bank (World Bank 1985b, 1991). Therefore, $\Delta l_{cb.pb}$ is the most appropriate closure for the accumulation balance for the commercial banks.

6.4.2.5 *The Central Bank*

During the years of hyperinflation (1982–85) the Central Bank was quite passive and accommodating to the financial requirements of the public sector ($\Delta l_{cb.g}$) and to the private financial sector ($\Delta l_{cb.pb}$). The external shocks witnessed during the early years of the decade drastically changed the Central Bank's financial practices. The main changes observed were:

(a) External finance to the Central Bank (Δf_{cb}) was halted, and the heavy burden imposed by the need to service the external debt very quickly exhausted international reserves (fr_{cb}). These two sources of finance, which had been paramount in effecting the adjustment of the 1970s, therefore acted more as constraints during the first half of the 1980s.
(b) As a result of the extremely passive monetary policy adopted by the Central Bank, currency creation became the main mechanism to fund domestic credit expansion. Currency demand by the public, however, fell drastically in real terms, since the hyperinflation represented a heavy tax burden on holders of domestic currency.

6.4.2.6 *The external sector*

A central point in understanding macroeconomic adjustment in Bolivia during the first half of the 1980s is the recognition of the existence of two highly segmented foreign exchange markets: the official and parallel. The foreign exchange control policy implemented in 1982 and the inability of the Central Bank to supply all foreign exchange demanded at the official exchange rate were the causes of this segmentation (World Bank 1985b).

The official exchange market was managed by the Central Bank. Transactions within this market were carried out utilizing the official foreign exchange rate:

$$q.[P^M.(a_m.u_f + g_c) + i^*.(f_g + f_{cb} + f_{pb}) - P_f^E.\varepsilon_f = (1 - fr).\Delta f_{pb} + [\Delta f_{cb} - \Delta fr_{cb}] + \Delta f_g] \quad (6.39)$$

Adjustment in the official exchange market showed the following pattern:

(a) The main official sources of foreign exchange were the revenues from exports by formal companies and public enterprises (ε_f), but these revenues were greatly diminished by lower external prices and the smaller quantities exported.
(b) Foreign borrowing by the government (Δf_g), the Central Bank (Δf_{cb}) and commercial banks (Δf_{pb}) practically disappeared or became negative.
(c) There was a large drain on foreign exchange reserves due to the interest payments on the country's external debt ($i^*.(f_g+f_{cb}+f_{pb})$).
(d) Foreign reserves held by the Central Bank were exhausted (i.e. $\Delta fr_{cb} = 0$).
(e) Therefore, the only variable available as the closure for the balance for the official foreign exchange market was the capacity to finance official imports, namely intermediate inputs ($P^M.a_m.u_f$) and capital goods ($P^M.g_c + P^M.\phi.g_{pe}$). Since a_m is a parameter and P^M is determined exogenously, the variables that actually adjust the balance are u_f and g_c. The extent to which each of these variables adjusted depended on the way the Central Bank allocated foreign exchange across them. This closure is very much in line with the two-gap model approach.

The parallel exchange rate market, on the other hand, operated and adjusted in accordance with market forces:

$$q^P.[(c_m.z.\pi.u_f)/q^P + \Delta cf_h] - (1 - (1 - \alpha)(1 - \tau_{CO})).P_i^E.\varepsilon_i\, 0 = 0 \quad (6.40)$$

(a) The main source of foreign exchange in the parallel market was the increased revenues from illegal exports of coca and its by-products (ε_i).
(b) Most of the foreign exchange demanded in this market was used to finance imports of consumption goods. Demand for imported consumer goods, as defined within the model assumptions, depended on household incomes arising from distributed profits and the proceeds from the sale of coca. These income flows depended on variables determined elsewhere in the model (u_f and π) or on exogenous variables (ε_i).
(c) Therefore, the variable left for adjusting the parallel foreign exchange market is the amount of capital used by households to acquire assets abroad (capital flight) (Δcf_h).

6.4.2.7 *The formal sector*

External shocks greatly changed the means of adjustment in the supply-demand balance for formal activities. As discussed in the previous section, the severe foreign exchange shortage faced by the formal sector during the first half of the 1980s restricted the output responses of formal activities due to the lack of foreign exchange to finance imports of intermediate inputs:

(a) Formal output (u_f), depended on the availability of foreign exchange to finance imports of intermediate inputs; thus it could not freely adjust to changes in demand.
(b) Given the lack of response of output, any excess demand in the supply-demand balance of the formal sector was cleared through price changes via higher mark-up rates (τ), which increased the share of corporate profits in the gross value of formal sector output (π).

6.4.2.8 *The informal sector*

Although informal output expanded during the 1980s, that expansion was exclusively concentrated on coca production and export (ε_i). Domestically sold informal production (u_i), on the other hand, was still highly inelastic, and it contracted substantially when adverse weather conditions devastated traditional agricultural production in 1983.

The internal terms of trade between informal and formal activities (p_i) is therefore retained as the closure for the supply-demand balance for informal activities.

6.4.2.9 Summary of adjustment mechanisms during 1980-85

Nine balances were discussed in this section, one more than those defined for the 1970s, since the external balance in the period 1980–85 was divided into official and parallel. This system, so specified, describes quite well the adjustments in the Bolivian economy during the first half of the 1980s.

Eight endogenous variables were identified as closures in the system: the share of corporate profits in the gross value of formal sector output (π), internal terms of trade for informal activities (p_i), commercial bank credit to companies ($\Delta l_{pb.c}$), investment by households (g_h), Central Bank credit to government ($\Delta l_{cb.g}$), Central Bank credit to commercial banks ($\Delta l_{cb.pb}$), capital flight by households (Δcf_h), and the term ($a_m.u_f+g_c$), which represents the capacity to import intermediate inputs and capital goods. The ways in which the economic authorities allocate resources among these three alternative uses determine the values of u_f and g_c.

Therefore, there is one more variable to be designated as endogenous in order to make the whole system consistent: the obvious candidate is the foreign exchange rate in the parallel market (q^p).

The variables considered as fixed were: informal output (u_i), commercial bank credit to households ($\Delta l_{pb.h}$) and the level of foreign exchange reserves held by the Central Bank (Δfr_{cb}).

The variables considered as policy variables were: the official exchange rate (e^o), the tax rate (t), the required reserves-deposits ratio for commercial banks (r) and government consumption (Ω).

The variable specified as a function was formal sector exports (ε_f).

Finally, the variables considered as exogenous, whose impacts we want to evaluate through the model, were: negative levels of capital inflows to the government ($\Delta f_g < 0$), to the Central Bank (Δf_{cb}) and to commercial banks ($\Delta f_{pb} < 0$), lower external prices for formal exports (P_f^E) and higher prices for imports (P^M), a higher international interest rate (i^*) and, finally, increases in the prices (P_i^E) and volume (ε_i) of illegal exports.

6.4.3 Adjustment following the 1985 New Economic Policy

The purpose of the NEP was to stabilize the economy by reducing inflation and restoring the external balance. However, it was also part of a broader structural adjustment programme aimed at changing the functioning of the entire economy by increasing reliance on the price system, promoting private sector initiative and reducing the influence of the state on production (World Bank 1989, 1991; IMF 1987b; J.A. Morales 1987a, Pastor 1991; Sachs 1987; Dunkerley 1992).

The programme was quite successful in bringing down inflation and maintaining price and exchange rate stability; however, long-term growth proved to be more difficult to attain. Although the foreign exchange constraint was partly removed by the unification of the exchange markets and by restoring relations with foreign creditors, the tight monetary policy imposed did not allow the public sector to execute much needed investment in infrastructure in order to promote private initiative.

Sectoral balance adjustment under the NEP followed the following pattern.

6.4.3.1 Companies

The NEP tried to create the most favourable conditions for the development of the private sector. As a result, the availability of funds for companies was increased, as follows.

(a) Commercial bank credit to companies ($\Delta l_{pb.c}$) was increased as part of the general strategy to promote private initiative. After 1985, once inflation had been brought down, bank credit increased by almost 500 per cent in real terms between 1985 and 1989. In 1989, 88 per cent of total credit was directed to the private sector compared with just 48 per cent in 1985. Therefore, the variable that closes the accumulation balance for companies is the amount of credit from the banking system ($\Delta l_{pb.c}$).

(b) Corporate savings ($\Gamma.\pi.u_f$) benefited from increased profit margins resulting from lower real wages and export incentives and from higher levels of activity once the foreign exchange constraint on production was removed.

(c) Corporate investment, however, did not react significantly to the positive environment that the NEP tried to create with the purpose of providing greater incentives. High real interest rates, the lack of adequate infrastructure to support private investment and the low degree of confidence in the programme prevented companies from expanding their investment demand (World Bank 1991). The high real interest rates paid by the banking system meant that savings and time deposits became highly attractive financial alternatives to productive investment, resulting in a sharp increase in bank deposits as funds were repatriated from abroad to take advantage of high interest rates and as some funds were switched from informal to formal financial intermediaries (World Bank 1989). Thus, corporate investment demand became less foreign exchange constrained and more restricted by its own investment demand functions, which, as discussed previously, were sensitive to the real domestic interest rate and other structural factors such as the lack of adequate infrastructure.

6.4.3.2 Households

The constraints and adjusting variables in the accumulation balance for households did not change substantially under the NEP.

(a) Investment (g_h) continued to act as the closure in the accumulation balance for households, since it remained largely conditional on their capacity to generate own savings. The savings capacity of poor households continued to be extremely limited. Output responses (u_i) to excess demand were quite limited (apart from coca production). Traditional agricultural production continued to suffer from adverse weather conditions (J.A. Morales 1990; UDAPE 1990c; World Bank 1990). The urban informal sector increased significantly only in terms of employment; incomes, however, fell due to the contraction of aggregate demand (Escóbar 1990). As a result, the informal self-employed sector moved to much lower levels of subsistence and their savings and investment capacity became almost non-existent.

(b) Bank credit to households ($\Delta l_{pb.h}$) was still conditional on the availability of collateral and therefore did not play a significant role in the accumulation balance adjustment for households (FUNDES 1990; World Bank 1994).

(c) Peasant household producers of coca continued to enjoy relatively high revenues from the coca by-products trade. However, the price of coca fell due to excess supply, and to compensate for their income losses, these households moved to more advanced stages in the production of refined coca, in an attempt to increase their share in the coca-cocaine value added. The level of coca exports (ε_i) were maintained at those achieved during the first half of the decade (UDAPE 1990b; Dunkerley 1992).

(d) Household demand for time and savings deposits expressed in foreign currency (i.e. certificates of deposits and CDs) responded strongly to the higher real interest rates (i_r). Thus:

$$\mu = f(i_r) \tag{6.41}$$

(e) Capital flight by households (Δcf_h) reversed to some extent when rich households repatriated some capital to take advantage of the much higher i_r. Capital flight determination is discussed later in this section.

6.4.3.3 The government

A paramount element within the stabilization and structural adjustment programmes implemented in Bolivia under the NEP has been the reduction of the fiscal deficit. The measures undertaken were:

(a) Government consumption was substantially reduced.

(b) The tax reform and the more realistic exchange rate policy greatly improved government income compared with the levels observed during the first half of the decade. Government revenues were substantially increased through the tax reforms implemented in 1986.

(c) Interest payments on the external debt ($i^*.f_g$) were renegotiated in order to ameliorate their negative impacts on the fiscal balance and on the balance of payments.

As a result of the above measures, the non-financial fiscal deficit has been reduced significantly (5.1 per cent of GDP in 1989 compared with 20 per cent in 1984). The remaining deficit has been financed largely through Central Bank credit ($\Delta l_{cb.g}$), and it continues to be the ultimate adjusting variable in the balance for the government.

6.4.3.4 *The commercial banks*

The financial liberalization carried out under the NEP had significant impacts on the behaviour of the commercial banks.

(a) The liberalization brought about an increase in the real interest rate. High interest rates and the legalization of dollar deposits boosted deposits, which became the main source of bank finance. As discussed before, μ became a function of the real interest rate paid by banks (i_r).
(b) Foreign finance to commercial banks after the stabilization programme was still at a reduced level ($\Delta f_{pb} = 0$).
(c) Central Bank credit to commercial banks ($\Delta l_{cb.pb}$) expanded quite strongly after 1985, so that $\Delta l_{cb.pb}$ can be retained as the closure of the balance for the commercial banks.
(d) Most of the resources available to commercial banks were used to expand credit to companies ($\Delta l_{pb.c}$), as discussed previously. Commercial bank loans to households ($\Delta l_{pb.h}$), on the other hand, represented only a marginal share of total bank assets.
(e) Commercial banks increased their deposits in the Central Bank to take advantage of the high interest rates paid on time and savings deposits. As a consequence, according to figures published by the Central Bank, although the maximum required reserves-deposits ratio on sight and saving deposits was only 20 per cent in 1986, the average reserves-deposits ratio went up to 37 per cent by December 1989. Thus, in terms of the reduced-SAM model, the parameter r became sensitive to changes in the real interest rate:

$$r = f(i_r) \tag{6.43}$$

6.4.3.5 *The Central Bank*

There were significant changes in the Central Bank adjustment following the financial liberalization:

(a) Since limiting the growth of high-powered money to maintain price stability was among the main objectives of the NEP, the expansion of Central Bank credit to the government ($\Delta l_{cb.g}$) and to the private sector ($\Delta l_{cb.pb}$), had to be compensated through open-market operations carried out by the Central Bank (World Bank 1991). As discussed above, this was reflected in a sharp increase in commercial bank deposits in the Central Bank. Therefore, a plausible closure for the balance for the Bank is through changes in commercial bank deposits in the Central Bank (i.e. a larger value for r). A larger value for r was attained through a higher real interest rate. Therefore, it is the real interest rate (i_r) that brings adjustment to the balance for the Central Bank.

(b) Foreign capital inflows (Δf_{cb}) were limited to those agreed with official international institutions (IMF, World Bank).

(c) A gain in foreign reserves ($\Delta fr_{cb}>0$) was set as a target variable under the agreements with the IMF and World Bank.

6.4.3.6 *The external sector*

(a) As discussed before, under the NEP the foreign exchange balance was unified, as was the exchange rate (i.e. $q = q^P$). For most of the period, the government used the exchange rate as an instrument of inflation control.

(b) Capital flight by households, measured by the item 'net errors and omissions' in the balance of payments, became positive during this period, meaning that household owners of foreign assets abroad repatriated part of these assets in response to higher domestic interest rates. They also switched from informal to formal financial intermediaries (World Bank 1989). At the same time, however, even larger amounts of foreign currency generated through the coca-cocaine business were taken outside the country. Therefore (Δcf_h) is retained as the closure for the external sector balance.

6.4.3.7 *The formal sector*

(a) As discussed previously, the unification of the official and the parallel exchange markets ameliorated the foreign exchange constraint faced by the formal sector during the early 1980s. Formal activities were therefore able to adjust through changes in their activity levels (u_f) in the case of excess demand.

(b) After 1985, however, the most likely case is that u_f adjustments were mostly downwards, since the NEP restricted demand by reducing Ω and g_g. Besides, the fall in real wages under the NEP reduced wage-earners' demand. Moreover, the higher interest rates prevailing after the NEP and the persistent lack of corporate confidence in the continuity of the programme inhibited g_c.
(c) Formal exports (ε_f), on the other hand, reacted positively to the more favourable relative prices resulting from the devaluation of the official exchange rate.

6.4.3.8 *The informal sector*

(a) Output responses (u_i) in the informal sector remained restricted. Therefore, the key adjusting variable in informal markets continued to be the internal terms of trade (p_i).
(b) Informal exports maintained the levels achieved during the first half of the 1980s. International prices for informal exports fell, however, because of excess supply.

6.4.3.9 *Summary of adjustment mechanisms under the NEP*

Eight balance equations were presented in this section, one less than those defined for the period 1980–85, after which the external balance was unified into a single market (see Table 6.3).

Eight variables were identified as balance closures in the system: capacity utilization by formal activities (u_f), internal terms of trade for informal activities (p_i), household investment (g_h), commercial bank credit to companies ($\Delta l_{pb.c}$), Central Bank credit to government ($\Delta l_{cb.g}$), Central Bank credit to commercial banks ($\Delta l_{cb.pb}$), capital flight by households (Δcf_h), and the domestic real interest rate (i_r).

The variables considered as constraints or fixed parameters were: the share of corporate profits in the value of formal output (π), informal output (u_i), commercial bank credit to households ($\Delta l_{pb.h}$), and the level of foreign exchange reserves held by the Central Bank (Δfr_{cb}), which were set as target variables under the agreements signed with the IMF.

The variables considered as policy variables were: the exchange rate (e^o) which was fixed under a 'crawling-peg' system, the tax rate (t), and government consumption (Ω).

The variables specified through behavioural functions were: formal sector exports (ε_f), investment demand by companies (g_c) and by government (g_g), companies' desired balance sheet 'portfolios' of financial assets relative to investment (μ), household preferences for deposits (λ), and the reserves-deposits ratio (r) required of the commercial banks.

Finally, the variables considered as exogenous, whose impacts we wish to evaluate through the model, are: the continuing very low levels of capital inflows to the government (Δf_g), to the Central Bank (Δf_{cb}) and to the commercial banks (Δf_{pb}), much lower external prices for formal exports ($P^E{}_f$) (cf. the 1985 international tin market crisis) and higher prices for imports (P^M), and finally, the reduction in prices ($P^E{}_i$) of illegal exports. The macroeconomic impacts of these exogenous shocks were analysed utilizing an economic system whose functioning was completely changed under the NEP.

6.4.4 Adjustment following the structural reforms in the 1990s

The structural reforms introduced in the 1990s, substantially modified sectoral balance adjustment.

6.4.4.1 Companies

The structural reforms attempted to create the most favourable conditions for the development of the private sector. As a result, the availability of funds for companies was increased, as follows:

(a) The transfer of the public enterprises to the private sector, through the capitalization process, brings significant amounts of foreign direct investment (ΔFDI) to the country. Besides, the new regulatory framework created though the SIRESE law and the sectoral laws provide a favourable environment for investment, by both domestic and foreign private corporations. This provides a boost to companies' investment. This investment, however, might be constrained by the lack of greater government investment in infrastructure.

(b) Due to the increase in foreign investment, companies are likely to enjoy high levels of financial resources availability. Companies may deposit part of these resources in local private banks, in order to accommodate them to their cash flows needs. Thus, companies' deposits in the financial system (ΔDep_c) are likely to be the closure in companies' accumulation balance. Although some companies would still resort to finance from private banks, on aggregate, the level of companies' deposits will be higher than that of bank loans to companies.

6.4.4.2 *Households*

The constraints and adjusting variables in the accumulation balance for households are likely to be the same after the structural reforms.

(a) The poor access to credit by small scale industries ($\Delta l_{pb.h}$), both rural and urban, is considered by many observers to be one of the most important obstacles to this sector's development prospects (World Bank 1996, FundaPro 1997). Therefore, investment (g_h) is likely to act as the closure in the accumulation balance for households in the future.
(b) A higher reliability on other sources of finance, such as households' own savings, will depend on the success of different government strategies to increase the productivity of small-scale enterprises (Ministry of Finance 1996). The education reform is expected to have an impact on productivity in the medium to long term.
(c) The importance of coca proceeds (ε_i), as a major source of income to households, has reduced over time, and, in 1996, their contribution to GDP was estimated at only two per cent of GDP (World Bank 1992).

6.4.4.3 *The government*

The structural reforms of the 1990s have modified government's adjustment rules in different ways.

(a) The popular participation and decentralization laws increased the amount of tax revenues designated to local governments. This introduces rigidities to the management of the government budget at the central level, because, by law, 20 per cent of total tax revenues must be transferred to the regions.

(b) The financial reforms have limited the access of government to Central Bank credit ($\Delta l_{cb\ g}$), reducing the significance of this variable as a closure of the government's balance.
(c) The government has taken measures to reduce its deficit to levels that can be financed by concessional foreign loans (around 2 per cent of GDP in 1995 and 1996).
(d) Taking into account income from taxes and customs duties, as well as contributions from the sale of hydrocarbons, tax revenues have increased from 14.4 per cent of GDP in 1989 to 19.5 per cent in 1996, thanks to the country's greater economic stability, tax reforms and improved efficiency in the administration of tax collection.
(e) Interest payments on the external debt ($i^*.f_g$) were further renegotiated in order to ameliorate their negative impacts on the fiscal balance and on the balance of payments.
(f) The reforms have demanded greater fiscal costs (as in the case of pension reform), which will be financed through a combination of fiscal adjustment and the issue of public bonds (Δb_G). Thus, Δb_G is likely to be the closing variable in government's balance after the reforms.

6.4.4.4 The commercial banks

The financial reforms carried out have changed some aspects of commercial banks' adjustment behaviour.

(a) The newly approved prudential regulatory framework requires commercial banks to comply with a higher asset-to-capital ratio and to eliminate lending to related parties. Commercial banks, therefore, have to increase their own capital in order to mediate the increased amount of resources available to the banking system. Additional capital might come through foreign direct investment.
(b) The trends followed by the financial system in the last years show that the availability of resources to commercial banks increased substantially; first, high real interest rates boosted deposits, which, in turn, reduced interest rate levels; second, commercial banks' foreign borrowing (ΔF_{pb}) increased significantly after 1990; and third, Central Bank credit to commercial banks ($\Delta l_{cb.pb}$) expanded quite

strongly during the 1990s, so that $\Delta l_{cb.pb}$ can be retained as the closure of the balance for the commercial banks.

(c) Most of the resources available to commercial banks were used to expand credit to companies ($\Delta l_{pb.c}$).

(d) Commercial bank loans to households ($\Delta l_{pb.h}$), on the other hand, represented only a marginal share of total bank assets.

6.4.4.5 *The Central Bank*

The financial reforms also introduced significant changes in the Central Bank's adjustment process:

(a) The new Central Bank Law strengthened the Bank's autonomy; maintaining macroeconomic stability became the Central Bank's main priority. This considerably limited the access of the NFPS to Central Bank finance. Before the passage of the law in 1996, the Central Bank had already diminished its involvement in financing the NFPS deficits. The Central Bank's open market operations, aimed at absorbing excess liquidity resulting from the finance of the public sector's deficits, diminished after 1993. In 1995, however, the Central Bank resorted to this mechanism to absorb the excess liquidity created by the credit expansion to the private financial sector, when the two commercial banks were closed in 1994. Thus, with the structural reforms the Central Bank finance to the government ($\Delta L_{cb.g}$) became a constraint in the government's balance. During the 1990s, the outstanding Central Bank credit to the public sector reduced by an amount equal to almost 7 per cent of GDP.

(b) The Central Bank sold to commercial banks part of its stock of treasury bonds and increased its foreign reserves by an amount equal to 11 per cent of GDP after 1990. Thus, foreign reserves is likely to be the closing variable of the Central Bank's balance (Δfr_{cb}).

6.4.4.6 *The external sector*

The increased inflow of foreign exchange due to the capitalization process and the higher levels of foreign direct investment expected are likely to bring about some private capital outflows. Therefore (Δcf_h) is retained as the closure for the external sector balance.

6.4.4.7 The formal sector

(a) The capitalization process will substantially increase investment in formerly owned public enterprises. Thus, productive capacity in these sectors will be significantly expanded. Besides, the capitalization is expected to improve the efficiency of basic services (for example, transport, energy and telecommunications) essential to increase productivity in other sectors. Furthermore, foreign direct investment in sectors other than those that were capitalized is also expected to increase installed productive capacity of formal sector activities. Formal activities' markets are likely, therefore, to adjust through changes in output (u_f) in the case of excess demand.

(b) Formal exports (ε_f), on the other hand, reacted positively to the more stable macroeconomic environment and to more favourable exchange rate policies.

6.4.4.8 The informal sector

(a) Output responses (u_i) in the informal sector are likely to remain restricted. The impacts of the structural reforms (such as education reform and the Strategy for the Productive Transformation of the agricultural sector), aimed at increasing the informal sector productivity, will only be felt in the long term. In the medium term, however, informal output can be considered a function of government investment.

$$u_i = f(g_g)$$

(b) Therefore, the key adjusting variable in informal markets will continue to be the internal terms of trade (p_i).

6.4.4.9 Summary of adjustment mechanisms after the structural reforms

Eight balance equations were discussed in this section (see Table 6.3).

Eight variables were identified as balance closures in the system: capacity utilization by formal activities (u_f), internal terms of trade for informal activities (p_i), household investment (g_h), commercial bank credit to companies ($\Delta l_{pb.c}$), foreign exchange reserves held by the Central Bank (Δfr_{cb}), Central Bank credit to commercial banks ($\Delta l_{cb.pb}$), capital flight by households (Δcf_h), and the domestic real interest rate (i_r).

The variables considered as constraints or fixed parameters were: the share of corporate profits in the value of formal output (π), informal output (u_i), commercial bank credit to households ($\Delta l_{pb.h}$), and Central Bank credit to government ($\Delta l_{cb.g}$).

The variables considered as policy variables were: the exchange rate (e^o), which was fixed under a 'crawling-peg' system, the tax rate (t), and government consumption (Ω).

The variables specified through behavioural functions were: formal sector exports (ε_f), investment demand by companies (g_c) and by government (g_g) companies' desired balance sheet 'portfolios' of financial assets relative to investment (μ), household preferences for deposits (λ), and the reserves-deposits ratio (r) required of the commercial banks.

Finally, the variables considered as exogenous, whose impacts we wish to evaluate through the model, are: the continuing very low levels of capital inflows to the government (Δf_g), to the Central Bank (Δf_{cb}) and to the commercial banks (Δf_{pb}), an increased level of foreign direct investment (Δfdi), external prices for formal exports ($P^E{}_f$) and higher prices for imports (P^M), and, finally, the reduction in prices ($P^E{}_i$) of illegal exports. The macroeconomic impacts of these exogenous shocks

Table 6.3 Summary of adjustments over three periods: the 1970s, 1980–84 and following 1985

	During the 1970s	During 1980-84	After the 1985 Stabilization	After the 1990 Structural Reforms
Balance Closures	u_f, p_i, g_h, $\Delta l_{pb\,c}$, $\Delta l_{cb\,g}$, $\Delta l_{cb\,pb}$, Δcf_h, Δfr_{cb}	π, p_i, g_h, $\Delta l_{pb\,c}$, $\Delta l_{cb,g}$, $\Delta l_{cb\,pb}$, Δcf_h, $a_m.u_f+g_c$, q^P	u_f, p_i, g_h, $\Delta l_{pb\,c}$, $\Delta l_{cb\,g}$, $\Delta l_{cb\,pb}$, Δcf_h, i_r	u_f, p_i, g_h, $\Delta l_{pb\,c}$, Δfr_{cb}, $\Delta l_{cb\,pb}$, Δcf_h, i_r
Constraints or Fixed Parameters	u_i, $\Delta l_{pb\,h}$, π	u_i, $\Delta l_{pb\,h}$, Δfr_{cb}	π, u_i, $\Delta l_{pb\,h}$, Δfr_{cb},	π, $\Delta l_{pb\,h}$, $\Delta l_{cb\,g}$,
Behavioural Equations	ε_f, Ω, g_c, g_g	ε_f	ε_f, g_c, g_g, μ, λ, r	ε_f, g_c, u_i, g_g, μ, λ, r
Policy Variables	e, t, r	e^o, t, r, Ω	e, t, Ω	e, t, Ω
Exogenous Variables	Δf_g, Δf_{pb}, Δf_{cb}, $P^E{}_f$, P^M, ε_i, i*	Δf_g, Δf_{pb}, Δf_{cb}, $P^E{}_f$, P^M, ε_i, i*	Δf_g, Δf_{pb}, Δf_{cb}, $P^E{}_f$, P^M, ε_i, i*	Δf_g, Δf_{pb}, Δf_{cb}, $P^E{}_f$, P^M, ε_i, i*

will be analysed utilizing an economic system whose functioning was completely changed by the structural reforms.

6.5 Concluding Remarks

The approach proposed in this chapter for the study of macroeconomic adjustment in a developing country such as Bolivia provides an insightful understanding of the ways in which the Bolivian economy adjusted to external shocks over the last two decades.

The reduced-SAM model developed and explained in this chapter gives a subtle picture of the adjustment mechanisms that brought ex-post equilibrium to the various balances, and therefore to the Bolivian economy as a whole, during the three periods analysed. The analytical gains obtained through the reduced-SAM model are as follows.

First, by defining a more disaggregated framework, it has been possible to differentiate accumulation balance behaviours for the various social groups and institutions; as a result, the role of income distribution in bringing adjustment can be much more clearly visualized within a consistent and integrated framework. Income distribution is captured at two levels: among factors of production (wages, non-corporate and corporate profits) and among institutions (households, companies, and government). Income distribution is determined by factors such as relative prices, mark-up rates, wage rates, exchange rates, sectoral output (formal vis-à-vis informal), and access to credit (external and domestic).

Second, the model allows for the differentiation of adjustment rules from period to period. The unconstrained foreign exchange situation of the Bolivian economy during the 1970s is captured by the closures of the model selected for that period: the capacity of the formal sector to increase output, the existence of investment demand functions for the government and companies, the capacity of the financial system to adjust by reducing its foreign exchange reserves, and, finally, by defining capital flight as the adjusting variable of the external balance. In this way, any excess of foreign exchange availability vis-à-vis the economy's capacity to absorb it productively goes to finance capital flight.

The segmented condition that characterized the Bolivian external sector during the first half of the 1980s is captured by dividing the external balance into two separate balances, one for the official and the other for the parallel exchange market. With this division the dual situation that characterized sectoral adjustment during that period can be modelled. On the one hand, the government and the formal sector were foreign exchange constrained because of their highly reduced access to foreign exchange; this is captured by allowing the variables u_f, g_f and g_g to adjust the official external balance in two-gap model fashion. On the other hand, households and some companies in the private sector became savings-constrained since the large resources received from foreign exchange revenues from illegal exports were utilized to finance imports of consumption goods and capital flight. This is captured by making g_h the closure in the accumulation balance for households, and Δcf_h the closing variable in the parallel external balance.

The changes introduced in the sectoral adjustment behaviours under the 1985 stabilization programme are captured in the model by changing the balance closures. The unification of the exchange rate market as a means of stabilizing the foreign exchange rate is reflected in the consolidation of the official and parallel external balances into a single balance. The open-market operation policy introduced to sterilize the monetary effects of the fiscal deficit, and the impact that this policy had on the interest rate, are captured by making companies' desired balance-sheet 'portfolios' of financial assets relative to investment (μ) and eventually the real interest rate (i_r) the variable that brings ex-post adjustment to the balance of the banking system.

The further changes introduced in the functioning of the Bolivian economy under structural reforms of the 1990s are captured in the model by modifying the balance closures. The greater autonomy granted to the Central Bank is captured by transforming Central Bank credit to government into a constraint in the government balance. The higher levels of foreign direct investment expected in the following years, due to the capitalization process, are reflected in the more important role that foreign direct investment plays in the companies' balance adjustment. The importance of government investment in the development of the informal sector is captured by making these activities' output a function of government investment.

Third, adjustment and macroeconomic equilibrium within the reduced-SAM model framework are determined by the interactions of all the sectoral balances of the economy. As a result, the interactions among the non-financial, financial and external sectors can be clearly identified and overall consistency of the macroeconomic closure is ensured.

Although the model presented in this chapter provides many elements which explain how adjustment in the Bolivian economy took place over the last two decades, it is still too aggregated, and therefore does not reflect many other structural characteristics that would enhance the analysis if included within the model. For instance, the division between formal and informal productive activities hides many particulars that determine market closures in sectors such as agriculture, mining and hydrocarbons, manufacturing and informal services. Since the outputs produced by these activities satisfy different markets, prices are determined following particular rules. Besides, different sectors have different output response capacities. The category 'companies' masks substantial differences in the accumulation behaviour of private companies and public enterprises.

Chapter 7 presents policy analysis undertaken using a disaggregated CGE model for the Bolivian economy. This will provide a deeper understanding of the adjustment processes discussed in this chapter. The CGE model is analysed in detail in appendix B.

7 Simulation of External Shocks and Policies with the CGE Model for Bolivia

7.1 Introduction

This chapter reports and discusses the results of a number of counterfactual simulation exercises which were carried out through the CGE model constructed and explained in Appendix B. This model is used to assess, numerically, the impact of different external shocks and policy interventions on the economy. There are three groups of simulations exercises that were tested through the model.

First, the impact of three different types of external shocks on the economy and the effects of alternative policy responses to these shocks. The three external shocks tested are: (a) a reduction in the country's terms of trade, (b) an increase in the international interest rate, and (c) a reduction in the flow of external finance received by the country. Each of these shocks will transmit through the system following different patterns. First, terms of trade reductions will tend to decrease export incomes, government revenues, and the profitability of capital in the export sectors. Second, a rise in the international interest rate will increase the fiscal and current account deficits, and will affect financial portfolio decisions of the economic agents, encouraging capital outflows, especially by private agents. Finally, reduced capital inflows will affect the level of foreign exchange reserves, government investment and output.

Although in reality these three types of external shocks have simultaneously impacted upon the Bolivian economy, especially at the beginning of the 1980s, their individual effects are simulated separately through the model. The effects of these shocks are tested and analysed under three policy response alternatives: (a) when no policy response is implemented; (b) when an orthodox stabilization package follows after the shock, consisting of fiscal adjustment through reductions of government expenditures, exchange rate devaluation, and increase in prices of public services; and (c) when a heterodox policy programme is implemented in response to the shock, consisting of increasing taxes to higher income groups, exchange rate devaluation, increasing public investment and reducing government expenditures.

The second type of shock tested through the model is the implementation of a coca-crops reduction programme. Although the importance of illegal coca production has greatly diminished during the 1990s, its contribution to total GDP is still high (2 per cent of GDP). Therefore, a reduction programme of surplus coca crops – coca that is used in the production of drugs – should still have significant impacts on the economy, especially for some macroeconomic variables such as production, employment, income, exports, and foreign exchange earnings.

The third type of shock tested is the occurrence of a significant increase in foreign direct investment inflows to the country. As explained previously, the capitalization of public enterprises is expected to bring about a substantial increase in the amount of foreign direct investment flowing to the country. This massive increase in the foreign investment flows is expected to have significant impacts on the economy, both in the short and long term. In the short term, investment flows will increase capital formation, imports and prices. In the long term, variables such as GDP growth, real wages, and exports are more likely to increase. The effects of the augmented level of capital inflows are tested through the model considering two alternative scenarios of complementary policies: (a) when foreign investment flows are not followed by complementary policies, this means that all the other variables of the model are not changed compared to the values they had in the base-run simulation; and (b) when the shock is accompanied by policies targeted at increasing labour productivity.

The effects of the shocks are analysed over a time horizon of 10 years, the base year being 1995. For this purpose, a base-run simulation is defined and produced through the CGE model. The base run is taken as a benchmark to compare the results obtained in all the simulations considered in this chapter. In this base run, policy variables (such as exchange rate, tax rates, administered interest rates, government consumption) and external variables (such as import and export prices, capital inflows, and world interest rates) are kept constant or are set to follow stable patterns over the time period of the simulation. Section 7.2 discusses in more detail the assumptions adopted and the results of this base-run simulation.

Section 7.3 discusses the results of the first group of simulation exercises, namely the three external shocks and policy responses. Sections 7.3.1 through 7.3.2 briefly discuss the main characteristics of each of the three types of external shocks tested, namely increased capital inflows, lower export prices and higher international interest rates. Section 7.4 discusses the main features of the alternative policy packages that are implemented in response to the shocks and the main criteria by which these policies will be evaluated.

The results of the simulations exercises are reported and discussed in sections 7.5 to 7.8. In these sections, the results of each of the external-shock simulations are tested under the three policy response alternatives, as discussed previously. The simulation results of the first shock, reduced terms of trade, are addressed in section 7.6; the simulation results of the increase in the real international interest rate are analysed in section 7.7, while the simulation results for the diminished foreign finance are examined in section 7.8. The simulation results of the coca crops eradication programme are discussed in section 7.9. These results are compared to the base-run simulation. Section 7.10 discusses the effects of the increased level of foreign direct investment resulting from the capitalization of public enterprises. Section 7.10.1 shows the results of this simulation when no complementary policies accompany the increased inflows of foreign investment, and section 7.10.2 reports the results of this shock when policies aimed at increasing labour productivity are implemented. Finally, section 7.11 presents some concluding remarks.

7.2 Base Run

The RF-CGE model has its own dynamic; this means that even in the case when it is not subject to a particular external shock or policy intervention, it will still exhibit a dynamic trend over time, since some exogenous variables are determined endogenously in the simulations of the previous periods. For instance, output in some sectors is determined by the sector's current physical capital stock, which, in turn, depends on past values for savings, investment and depreciation. Other variables, such as investment, undertaken by government, public enterprises and companies, depend on lagged values of the same variable, bringing about a knock-on effect that passes from one period to the other. Moreover, company investment is crowded-in by past government investment but is crowded-out by public sector investment in previous years. Most of the financial portfolio decisions made by economic agents in a particular period are determined by the agents' current wealth, asset and liability stock values, which, in turn, are determined by past savings, revaluation and net acquisitions of assets and liabilities.

Obviously, the results obtained from the model, once a particular shock or policy is introduced, reflect not only the impacts of the shock and policy applied but also the effects of the model's own dynamic. This could be troublesome, considering that the main objective of the simulations is to identify the impacts of external shocks and policy interventions on the trends followed by key socioeconomic variables. However, it could also be argued that, in reality, shocks and policies work their way through the system in combination with the model's own dynamic forces, so that it is more realistic to look at these impacts by considering a system with its own dynamic.

Although the effects of shocks, policies and the model's own dynamic very often reinforce each other, nevertheless we still wish to concentrate on the individual effects of different shocks and policies. For this purpose, a base-run simulation of the model has been run with no shock or policy. The results obtained therefore show what would be the pattern followed by the different variables only considering the model's own dynamic. Later on, when shocks and policies are introduced, their impacts can be identified by looking at the deviations from the patterns obtained in the basic simulation.

The base run of the dynamic model will be taken as benchmark to compare the results of the simulations. As mentioned above, the base run shows the dynamics of the economy, as represented by the model, when no changes in exogenous variables and base-year parameters occur. Most of the external variables (such as world prices and world interest rates) are kept at their base-year level. The policy variables follow a stable pattern over the time horizon. The exchange rate, for instance, is devalued by 5 per cent a year, and the government spending is allowed to grow by 3.5 per cent per year in real terms.

The results of the base-run simulation are quite satisfactory in that they depict familiar trends in the main variables. This gives us confidence that the model captures the main characteristics of the Bolivian economy well.

The patterns followed by key macroeconomic variables when the system is not subject to external shocks or policy intervention are discussed below.

The base-run simulation captures: first, the high dependency of Bolivia's macroeconomic performance on foreign borrowing, especially on public sector's indebtedness; and second, the fact that government's access to external borrowing will tend to decrease in the long run. The latter is brought into the base-run simulation by exogenously making foreign borrowing by the government continuously decrease over the whole period of the simulation. As a result, the model endogenously produces decreasing growth rates of GDP. Total GDP grows by around 4.3 per cent per year at the beginning of the base-run simulation and by 3.8 per cent at the end.

In the base run, GDP growth rate fluctuates by around 4 per cent. The Bolivian economy has been growing at this rate over the last five years, and it is believed that this rate represents the country's long-term growth rate if the country's current economic structure is maintained. The growth pattern of the base-run simulation is caused mainly by the stable growth observed in private and government consumption. Exports increase at 5 per cent per year and imports at 3.5 per cent. However, investment exhibits decreasing growth rates over time. As a result of the higher growth rates of exports compared to those of imports, the current account deficit declines continuously from 6 per cent of GDP in the base year to 4 per cent in year 10.

The fiscal deficit declines over time because government expenditures grow at a lower pace compared to revenues. Government investment, due to diminished foreign capital inflows, reduces its share in total GDP from 9 per cent in the first year of the simulation to 6.6 per cent of GDP in the tenth year.

Total investment, as a percentage of GDP, presents a very stable pattern, ranging between 15 and 16 per cent of GDP. Domestic savings share in total GDP goes up continuously, increasing from 9 per cent of GDP to 11 per cent of GDP at the end of the simulation period. External savings on the other hand, declines as a share of GDP from 6 per cent of GDP to 4 per cent. This happens because, as explained above, in the base-run simulation external loans – especially those received by government – tend to fall in the long run.

Inflation is stable in the base-run simulation, although it exhibits a slightly increasing tendency over the years. The annual inflation rate fluctuates between 3 and 6 per cent during the whole period of the simulation.

Unemployment steadily increases from 3 per cent of labour force in the first year to almost 5 per cent in the tenth year. This is explained by the lower growth rates exhibited by the economy at the end of the simulation period.

7.3 External Shocks

External shocks can arise from the trade or financial links that the economy maintains with the rest of the world. An unstable world environment can adversely affect developing economies through either international goods markets or international capital markets. Within these broad categories, shocks in the goods market can take the form of reductions in export demand, with a subsequent decline in the price of exports and, in some cases, constraints on the volume of such exports. Alternatively, reductions in the world supply of important commodities can increase the price of some imports into developing countries. Some shocks can be viewed as either import or export shocks. In any case, we can often summarize the net effect of external shocks to both imports and exports by looking at a country's terms of trade, defined as the average price of its exports divided by the average price of its imports (Krugman 1988).

In capital markets, both price and quantity may exhibit a downward trend. Countries that have borrowed extensively on international markets are adversely affected by increases in interest rates. Additionally, an increase in world prices tends to reduce the real value of foreign debt; thus a fall in international inflation amounts to an adverse shock of an increase in international interest rates. A useful summary indicator of the combined effect of interest rates and inflation rates on the burden of debt is the real interest rate.

In addition to changes in the cost of debt, developing countries find themselves constrained by the quantity of borrowing that they can undertake. When countries are dependent on foreign borrowing and are faced with a slow-down in the rate at which they are able to borrow, their economic performance can experience severe recessionary impacts.

We now analyse in more detail each one of these external shocks.

7.3.1 The terms of trade

For most developing countries, the overall effect of external shocks transmitted through the goods market can be summarized by the change in the terms of trade, defined as the ratio of the average price of a country's exports to the average price of its imports. When a country's terms of trade decline, any given volume of exports pays for a smaller volume of imports. To compensate for this decline, a country must do one of three things: increase its export volume, reduce its import volume, or increase the amounts it borrows from abroad.

Although for most LDCs deterioration or improvements in the terms of trade in the past have depended on the business cycle in the industrial countries, they can also be affected by other events that are beyond their control. Many small countries rely heavily on a small number of commodities for export revenues, and fluctuations in the markets for these commodities – which may be largely unrelated to the general world economic trend – can therefore have large impacts on particular developing nations.

7.3.2 The international interest rate

The international borrowing of developing countries is almost entirely denominated in the currencies of developed countries, mostly in U.S. dollars. Thus the principal measure of the cost of debt to LDCs is the interest rate on dollar loans.

An increase in the current interest rate increases the cost of any additional external loans that the country obtains. Whether it also increases the burden of existing debt depends on two factors: whether the debt is at a fixed or floating rate and, if the debt is at a fixed rate, the period to maturation of the debt.

In assessing the ultimate burden of a debt, what matters is not the money value of the debt but the extra exports or forgone imports that will be necessary to generate the foreign currency to repay it. Thus, in assessing the change in a country's debt position over time, we should look not at the change in money value but at the change in the value of the debt in terms of the prices of the country's imports and exports. To put it another way, inflation reduces the real value of a country's debt, and this gain should be subtracted from interest payments in calculating the costs of that debt. The combined effect of interest and inflation rates on the debt burden has to be measured in terms of the interest rate minus the inflation rate: the real interest rate.

7.3.3 Constraints on borrowing

Increases in the cost of the debt are not the only way in which capital markets can be a source of adverse external shocks to national economies. In addition to increases in cost, restrictions on availability have been a major problem for many developing countries.

The characteristic situation is one in which potential lenders lose confidence in a country's ability to repay its debt and become unwilling to lend. If the country has until that point been borrowing extensively, it will abruptly be forced to expand exports or cut imports, processes likely to be costly. The problem is particularly severe if the country already has a large foreign debt and if this debt is of short maturity. As Krugman (1988, p.63) points out, 'To be suddenly forced to meet debt service from current revenues will pose a difficult and in some cases quite literally impossible problem of adjustment. Because crises of confidence usually occur when a country has experienced adverse external shocks, the effect is to compound the problem'.

7.4 Policy Options And Policy Evaluation

7.4.1 Policy alternatives

An adverse shock initially tends to bring about a balance of payments deficit. If possible, the country could first choose to make no adjustment and to compensate for foreign exchange losses by resorting to external finance or by reducing foreign exchange reserves. As mentioned before, however, because crises of confidence usually occur when a country has experienced adverse external shocks, additional external finance might not be available in the quantities required; besides, foreign exchange reserves are limited, and might very soon dry up. In that case adjustment is unavoidable.

The external balance will tend to adjust through lower imports, since exports and external finance cannot be expanded. Lower imports will also have a negative effect on domestic output. As a result, supply is greatly reduced, creating excess demand in the goods market. At this stage, three alternatives are open to the economic authorities.

The first is that the economic authorities take no action and leave the economy to adjust alone (which was the case in Bolivia during the first half of the 1980s). In this case, aggregate demand is not brought into line with the lower levels of supply and adjustment takes place through changes in the nominal value of total supply. This means higher prices (inflation) and large foreign exchange rate depreciation.

The second alternative is that the country adopts an orthodox stabilization programme (Khan and Knight 1981) in line with the IMF and World Bank prescriptions (which is what happened in Bolivia during the second half of the 1980s). The orthodox stabilization programme focuses, in the short term, on controlling aggregate demand and bringing it into line with the lower levels of supply resulting from the shock.

The third alternative, usually termed the heterodox option, calls for avoiding adjustment only on the demand side and suggests measures to increase supply in real terms by removing some of the structural constraints that limit output expansion (Pastor 1987).

The specific policy measures included under the orthodox and heterodox alternatives within the RF-CGE model framework are presented in section 7.5, after a discussion of the criteria by which the alternative policies can be evaluated.

7.4.2 Criteria for policy evaluation

Broadly speaking, the soundness of any economic policy package is judged in terms of its capacity to attain at least the following macroeconomic objectives (Eshag 1983, pp.110):

(a) Sustainable long-term economic growth, eventually leading to economic development. The GDP growth rate is a clear indicator of how successfully this objective is being accomplished. Long-term economic growth prospects can also be evaluated by looking at the share of investment in total GDP.
(b) More equitable income distribution, leading in the long term to the eradication of poverty and the satisfaction of basic needs. The trends followed by real wages and households consumption are indicators of the extent to which these objectives are being realized.
(c) Internal equilibrium, representing a situation when (i) the volume of aggregate effective demand is adequate to ensure the full utilization of productive capacity; and (ii) the general index of domestic prices of goods and services is relatively stable. Therefore, the extent of internal disequilibrium is measured by reference to three indices: first, the unemployment rate; second, the level of capacity under utilization; and third, the rate of price inflation as measured by any price index (GDP deflator or Consumer Price Index).
(d) External equilibrium, which is given by a balanced situation between the country's foreign exchange availability from export revenues, foreign finance, current transfers, and so on, and its foreign exchange requirements to finance imports, payments to foreign factors, external debt payments, and so on. External equilibrium is normally measured in terms of a given balance of payments position. The three most commonly used subtotals are the balance on the current account (visible trade, plus services and non-government transfer payments), the basic balance (the current account, plus official transfers, plus long-term capital movements), and the overall balance (which includes short-term capital movements, errors and omissions; this balance must be matched by a corresponding change in official foreign exchange reserves; (Bird 1984)).

Very often, these various macroeconomic objectives cannot be achieved simultaneously in the short term; therefore the economic authorities have to give priority to some of them, and accept trade-offs in terms of others. The differences of opinion between supporters of orthodox and heterodox policies for macroeconomic stabilization and adjustment strategies have sometimes been regarded as being fundamentally a difference over the relative weights given to the various macroeconomic objectives. Orthodox programmes are often criticized for placing too much emphasis on strengthening the external balance position (Killick 1984a, 1984b); objectives concerning inflation and growth are given secondary preference, while the redistribution of income and wealth are scarcely featured at all.

7.5 Simulation of External Shocks and Policy Options through the RF-CGE Model

The RF-CGE model will help us to evaluate numerically the impacts of external shocks on the Bolivian economy, bringing to the forefront of the analysis the institutional factors that govern adjustment in developing countries, as discussed throughout this book.

The model will be subject to three external shocks: (a) a 10 per cent decrease in the international prices of three of the country's main exports (agriculture, mining and hydrocarbons); (b) a 40 per cent increase in the real international interest rate; and (c) a 40 per cent reduction in the flow of external finance to the government.

In the past, Bolivia has experienced all three types of shock. During the second half of the 1980s, for instance, the overall export price index went down by 20 per cent in 1986 as a result of a 52 per cent reduction in the price of tin following the collapse of the international tin market. Between 1975 and 1979, the LIBOR (London Inter-Bank Offer Rate), the standard for many international loans, averaged 7.8 per cent, but from 1980 to 1984, it averaged 13 per cent, representing a 67 per cent increase. Finally, due to the international debt crisis, between 1980 and 1985, the net capital inflows received by the country were on average 70 per cent lower than those received between 1975 and 1979.

Although the shocks to be simulated through the model are smaller than the actual shocks suffered by the country in the early 1980s, their directions and their effects are the same as those observed in reality. Besides, these shocks are applied to a base year (1995) that had already absorbed the external shocks of the early 1980s and the adjustment policies of the second part of the 1980s and early 1990s. Therefore, the simulation exercises do not try to reproduce what happened in the past, but what would happen if these shocks were to be repeated (with lower intensity in this case).

The effects of these three external shocks are analysed under three policy response alternatives: no policy response, an orthodox stabilization programme, and a heterodox stabilization programme. The specific policy measures included under the orthodox and heterodox policy packages, within the RF-CGE model framework, are discussed in the following.

7.5.1 Orthodox stabilization programme

Orthodox stabilization policies focus on the reduction of excess demand through a combination of 'demand-reducing' and 'demand-switching' policies aimed at controlling aggregate demand and bringing it in line with the lower levels of supply.

Standard orthodox stabilization programs generally comprise a combination of six sets of policies (Balassa 1982): (1) currency devaluation to shift positively the external balance (perhaps accompanied by a unification of previous multiple exchange rates); (2) reduction of the public sector fiscal deficit by modifying existing taxes, instituting new ones, adjusting public sector prices, and reducing consumer and producer subsidies; (3) tighter monetary policy, particularly a reduction in the monetization of the fiscal deficit; (4) reduction of real wages through market mechanisms; (5) an opening of the economy by reducing tariffs and eliminating quotas and export taxes; and (6) rapid decontrol of internal prices.

In terms of the RF-CGE model, the following policy measures have been included as part of the orthodox stabilization programme:

(a) Devaluation in the form of a 10 per cent increase in the nominal value of the official foreign exchange rate.
(b) Increases in the price of public goods in the form of a 10 per cent increase in the domestic prices of hydrocarbons (gasoline) and electricity.
(c) A 10 per cent reduction in the nominal value of government consumption.
(d) Financial liberalization in the form of a 10 per cent increase in the nominal domestic interest rate.

7.5.2 Heterodox stabilization programme

Unlike orthodox stabilization programmes, there is no such a thing as a 'standard' heterodox stabilization package. Since structuralist economists regard macroeconomic adjustment as being essentially determined by each particular country's set of institutional factors, it is more difficult for them to come up with a standard set of policy recommendations that can be generally applied.

However, structuralists give priority to the objectives of growth, employment, income distribution and poverty alleviation. Therefore, heterodox programmes call for avoiding adjustment only on the demand side and suggest measures to increase supply in real terms by removing some of the structural constraints that limit output expansion.

Various structuralist economists have highlighted different actions as ways of removing the supply bottlenecks and other structural rigidities that are causing disequilibria. Government investment in infrastructure is regarded as essential in promoting growth because it crowds-in private investment (Bacha 1990).

Structuralists (Cornia et al. 1987; Foxley 1981) emphasize objectives such as income redistribution and poverty alleviation in order to protect the most vulnerable groups of society during the adjustment. These measures include increased government transfers to the poorest, and specific incomes policies aimed at maintaining real wages.[1]

Other authors focus on specific measures for financing increased government investment and social expenditures. Kalecki (1976, p.98) pointed out the importance of increased taxation of the high-income groups of society as a preferable source of finance, so that the consumption of necessities by the poorest groups is not affected (FitzGerald 1986).

Taking into account all of these criteria, in terms of the RF-CGE model, the following policy measures were included as part of the heterodox stabilization programme:

(a) A 10 per cent increase in the income tax rate applied to companies.
(b) A 15 per cent increase in government investment.
(c) A 10 per cent devaluation. This measure was included because there is a growing consensus among economists about the importance of

maintaining a competitive exchange rate as a necessary (but not sufficient) condition for promoting export growth.

(d) Government expenditures, nominal wages and the domestic interest rate were maintained at their pre-shock levels.

7.6 Shock Resulting from a Reduction in the Terms of Trade

The first shock to be tested through the RF-CGE model is that of a 10 per cent reduction in world prices of three of Bolivia's main commodity exports: agricultural products, mining products and hydrocarbons.

The export price shock is assumed to take place in the first period of the simulation and prices are maintained at that lower level over the rest of the period. The results of the simulations for the three alternative policy scenarios (namely, no policy, orthodox and heterodox policies) are analysed in the following sections.

7.6.1 Terms of trade shock with no policy response

In the short term, a 10 per cent reduction in external prices of the country's main commodity exports has strong recessionary effects on the economy (Figure 7.1a). In the first year after the shock, the GDP growth rate falls by 1.5 per cent of GDP compared to the base-run scenario. The rate of growth of GDP then recovers, but at a lower absolute level of GDP. The reduction in GDP growth rate, during the first year after the shock, is the combined result of decreases in the growth rate of private consumption (by 2.4 percentage points), investment (3.1 per cent), and exports (0.2 per cent). There are various mechanisms through which an export price reduction brings about the above mentioned effects.

The sharp reduction in growth rates of private consumption, in the first year after the shock, arises from a significant contraction in household incomes, which in turn is the result of much lower levels of activity. As output declines in most productive sectors, wage earnings and operating surpluses fall for both small-scale producers and companies (the latter implying lower distributed profits). On the other hand, since domestic agricultural prices are determined in flexi-price markets, households' incomes and consumption also fall due to the lower prices of traditional agricultural products, resulting from the across-the-board demand contraction.

Lower export prices initially reduce income and output in those export activities affected by the shocks. Lower export prices cause a direct reduction in the operating surplus of corporations engaged in export activities, both private and public. This has direct impacts on the corporate sector's financial behaviour and on the fiscal balance, resulting, in both cases, in an expansion of domestic credit. Besides, since output levels in mining and modern agricultural sectors are both price elastic, output growth in these two sectors tend to fall after the shock, bringing about lower levels of activity, wage payments and operating surpluses.

The terms of trade decline has a differentiated effect on the various productive activities. The worst-hit sectors are the export sectors whose output levels are elastic to relative price fluctuations (modern agriculture and mining) and the mark-up sectors whose output adjusts to the lower levels of activity and demand (manufacturing, construction and informal services).

The rates of growth of investment and imports exhibited strong reductions in the short term. Investment growth rate declines due to lower investment levels by households. Households' investment growth rates are slower because of the reduction in household income, which also bring about lower consumption levels. Lower income affects households' savings and investment negatively. Households' investment depends crucially on their own savings because, as explained throughout this book and as specified in the CGE model, households can not obtain funds to amplify their own savings in order to finance investment. Finally, the reduced level of imports is the result of lower levels of consumption and investment.

The fiscal deficit increases by 0.6 of GDP just after the shock takes place, and becomes larger over the years (Figure7.1b). These larger deficits are the result of lower government tax revenues, which arise from the lower activity levels. As a result, domestic finance to the public sector expands from being negative (–1.9 per cent of GDP) in the first year of the simulation to around 0.6 per cent of GDP in the fourth year. In the base run, domestic credit to the public sector was negative during the period of the simulation.

Lower export prices obviously have a direct impact on the balance of payments. As export revenues fall, the current account deficit is higher than that of the base run, during all the years of the simulation. Although the reduced export revenues are compensated by reduced imports, due to the lower level of activity the deficits in the current account of the balance of payments were higher than those observed in the base-run simulation (Figure 7.1b).

The patterns exhibited by savings and investment of the various economic agents resulting from the shock are now described.

Savings by households, companies, public enterprises and government fall, since labour and unincorporated capital profits, export revenues and tax revenues decrease. For the three latter types of agents, the investment-leading-savings approach holds, so that investment remains fairly constant after the shock and even increases in the long term (Figure 7.1d). The combined effect of decreased savings and increased investment as a share of GDP for these three agents brings about an expansion in domestic credit, as highlighted previously. Additionally, households' investment adjusts to the lower level of savings.

Inflation is lower in the first year and 2 percentage points higher in the second year compared to the levels exhibited in the base run (Figure 7.1e). Inflation recovers its initial levels starting from the fifth year. Lower levels of demand initially caused agricultural prices to fall, while prices remain largely unchanged for the mark-up sectors. Obviously, prices for the export sectors also fall as a result of the terms of trade deterioration (as in the cases of mining, hydrocarbons and agriculture).

As a result of the pattern followed by inflation, real wages initially increase compared to the base-run simulation. As inflation goes up, real wages increase at a slower pace, and eventually reach the levels observed in the base-run simulation (Figure 7.1f).

Finally, because of the lower level of activity brought about by the shock, the unemployment rate increases steadily, and is 2 percentage points higher than in the base run, at the end of the simulation period (Figure 7.1g).

7.6.2 Terms of trade shock followed by an orthodox policy package

An orthodox policy package aims to reduce the external imbalances through a combination of 'demand-reducing' and 'demand-switching'

Figure 7.1 *Comparison of key macroeconomic variables behaviour under three policy alternatives, following a 10 per cent export price reduction (deviations from the base-run scenario)*

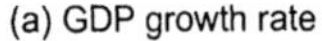
(a) GDP growth rate

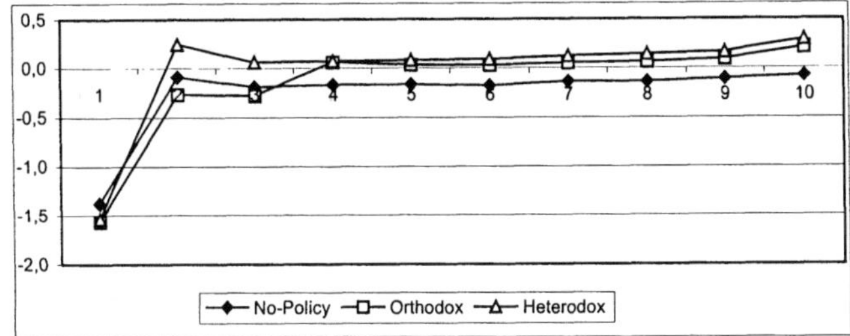

(b) Fiscal deficit (% of GDP)

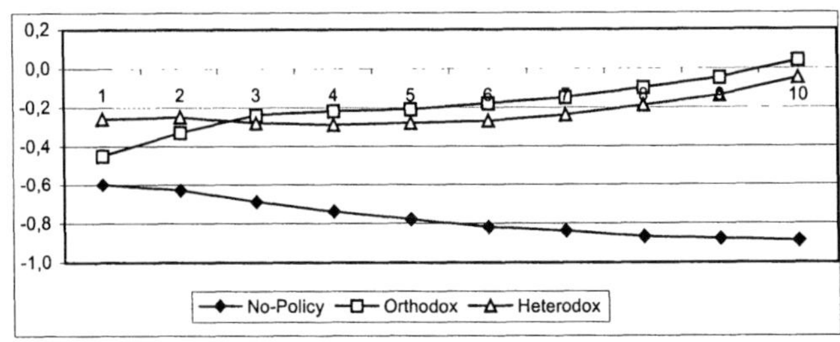

(c.) Current account deficit (% of GDP)

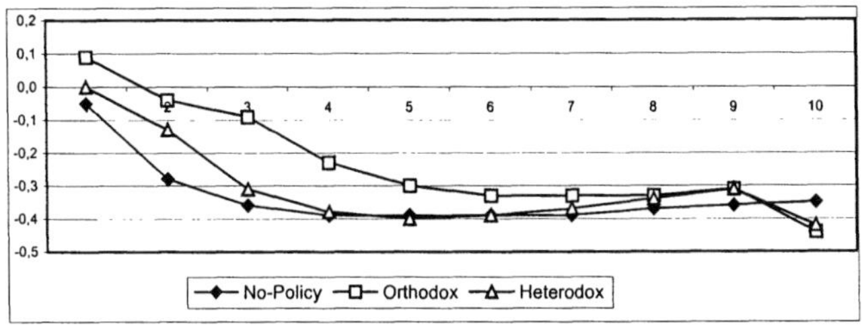

Figure 7.1 Comparison of key macroeconomic variables behaviour under three policy alternatives, following a 10 per cent export price reduction (deviations from the base-run scenario), continued

(d) Total investment (% of GDP)

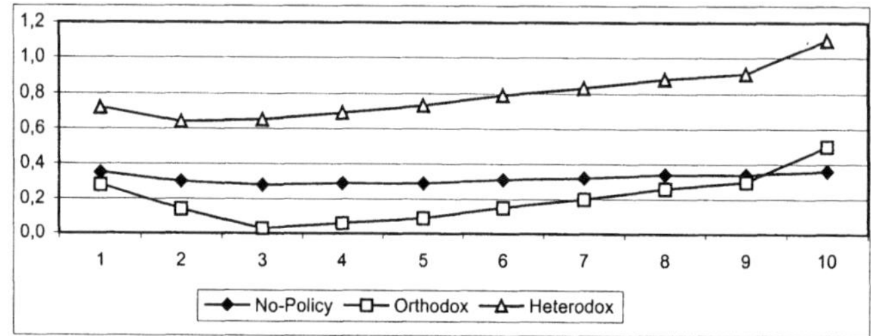

(e) Inflation rate (%)

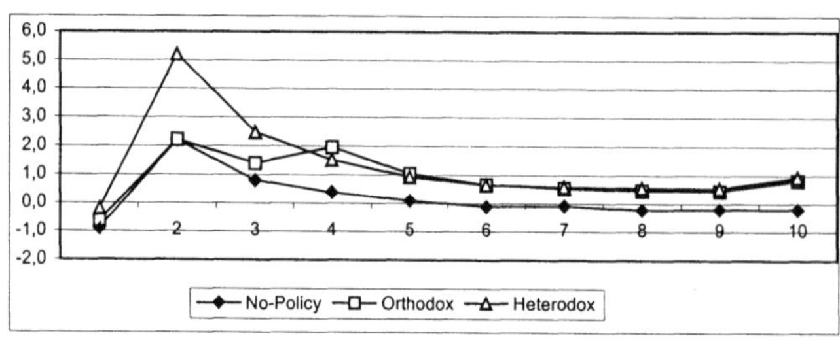

(f) Real wage rate

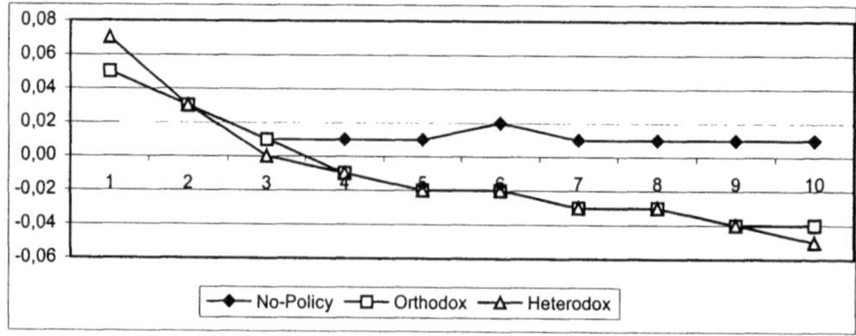

Figure 7.1 *Comparison of key macroeconomic variables behaviour under three policy alternatives, following a 10 per cent export price reduction (deviations from the base-run scenario), continued*

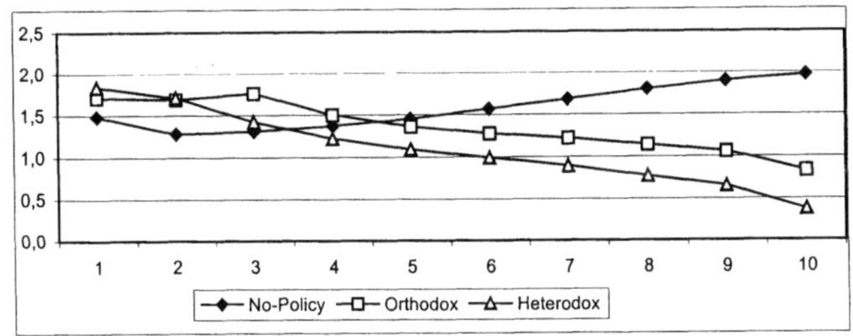

policies. Overall, the orthodox policy package has highly recessionary effects.

The reduction in government consumption and the controls imposed on nominal wages bring about larger contractions in government and households' final demand in addition to those experienced after the shock.

In the short term, devaluation induces an export expansion in sectors such as agriculture, coca, mining, manufacturing and modern services, resulting in a 2.2 per cent increase in total exports. The beneficial effects of devaluation on export profitability are greatly enhanced by the recessionary impact of the orthodox policy package on domestic prices, so that the devaluation of the real exchange rate is larger than in nominal terms.

The positive influence of devaluation on the trade balance is complemented by a higher reduction in imports compared to the shock scenario. Although imports are elastic to relative prices, and therefore devaluation helps to induce lower imports, most of the import contraction has to be attributed to the much lower level of activity.

The investment growth rate becomes more negative (–0.37 per cent in the first years after the external shock and orthodox policy application). This additional reduction may be attributed to the lower levels of investment by households as a result of the contractionary measures applied under the orthodox programme.

The combined effect of the external shock and the policy package affects the various productive sectors of the economy in different ways. There is a very strong recessionary effect on the mark-up sectors; for instance, in the first year, manufacturing output only increases by 1.4 per cent, construction output decreases by 0.4 per cent and informal services decrease by 1.0 per cent. Agriculture, which benefits from devaluation and therefore experiences a partial recovery in its export volumes, suffers a further contractionary effect on output as domestic demand shrinks (the sector's output grows at practically the same rate it grew after the shock). Mining benefits slightly from the devaluation, and output contraction is not as severe as in the case when there is no policy response to the external shock.

Under the orthodox policy package, there is an improvement in the country's balance of payments. The current account deficit, over the whole period, is, on average, 1 per cent of GDP lower than in the no-policy case. In addition, a higher domestic interest rate increases the preference of households for deposits in the domestic financial system; therefore bank deposits over the ten years are around 0.3 per cent of GDP higher than in the no-policy case. These combined effects allow the banking system to increase its foreign exchange reserves by 1.4 per cent of GDP at the end of the simulation period.

The orthodox policy is quite effective in reducing the fiscal deficit. At the end of the simulation period, the fiscal deficit is almost 1 per cent of GDP lower than in the no-policy alternative (see Figure 7.1b). This is the result of lower government expenditures and larger public-sector surpluses resulting from the devaluation and increased prices for public goods and services. As a consequence, the amount of credit directed to the public sector under this alternative policy package falls by around 0.4 per cent of GDP.

Total investment, as a share of GDP, declines after the application of the orthodox policy package, when compared to the no-policy scenario; however, it is still higher than in the base-run simulation. The patterns of individual saving-investment behaviours under the orthodox policy package are as follows. There are improvements in the amounts saved by public sector institutions (state enterprises and government) and a reduction in investment, bringing about a long-term reduction in the fiscal deficit and in the flow of domestic finance directed to the public sector. Conversely, private savings decrease by 0.6 per cent of GDP while investment rises by only 0.2 per cent compared with the no-policy alternative. As a result, the flow of bank credit to the private sector is higher compared to the shock and no-policy scenario.

Deposits in the domestic financial system increase to take advantage of the higher interest rate. Although households reduce their foreign assets in order to finance domestic asset acquisition (capital flight is reduced), it is still necessary for them to resort to increased commercial bank credit to cover the gap between total uses and sources of funds. As a result, domestic credit to the private sector is higher under the orthodox policy package than under the no-policy alternative.

Inflation is higher under the orthodox policy package than under the no-policy alternative, especially after the third year. Although the demand-reducing policies implemented should produce a lower rate of inflation, devaluation has a higher pass-through effect on inflation; thus, the net effect is an increased rate of inflation (see Figure 7.1e).

In addition to the negative effects on output and incomes, the income distribution worsens under the orthodox policy. The real wage rate increases at a much lower pace and is 5 per cent lower at the end of the simulation period compared to the shock-only scenario. Employment, on the other hand, initially worsens under the orthodox policy package. In the long run, however, the unemployment rate is lower than under the shock scenario.

7.6.3 Terms of trade shock followed by a heterodox policy package

The emphasis of the heterodox policy package is to avoid the negative impacts of the external shock on output, long-term growth and income distribution. External balance equilibrium is seen as a constraint rather than an objective in itself.

Under the heterodox policy package, output growth recovers much faster than under the orthodox and the no-policy alternatives (see Figure 7.1a). Private consumption and investment also grow much faster after the implementation of the heterodox policy programme. Investment recovers strongly due to the expansion of autonomous government investment undertaken as part of the heterodox policy measures – by 4.1 per cent, on average, during the initial two years.

Although nominal devaluation is also included as part of the heterodox policy, the response of exports is much more moderate than that observed under the orthodox policy. The explanation for this is that the anti-recessionary bias that characterizes the heterodox policy package brings about relatively large price increases; hence, the same nominal devaluation produces a much smaller devaluation of the real exchange rate. As a result, the initial external export price shock cannot be fully compensated and exports fall by 0.1 per cent.

The anti-recessionary impact of the heterodox policy can be directly disclosed in the behaviour of the construction sector, whose output increases by 3.4 per cent in response to higher government investment. Output in the mark-up sectors (such as manufacturing and modern services), does not fully react to the multiplier effect of increased government investment. Since devaluation has a cost-push effect on prices in these sectors, final demand falls in real terms, limiting larger output expansions.

The heterodox policy is more effective in reducing the fiscal deficit in the short term because of higher tax revenues (see Figure 7.1b). The overall deficit of the consolidated fiscal sector falls to 3 per cent of GDP in the first year of its application (around 0.4 and 0.2 per cent of GDP lower than the levels observed under the no-policy option and orthodox policy, respectively). As a result, domestic credit to the public sector contracts by almost 1 per cent of GDP in the first year and by more than 1 per cent after the eighth year of the simulation.

The current account balance is improved only in the short run under the heterodox policy package; after the fourth year of the simulation, the current account surpluses remain at the same level as that observed with no policy intervention. The anti-recessionary bias of the heterodox policy measures results in larger price increases compared to the other policy alternatives. In the second year of the simulation, inflation stands at 10 per cent (5 percentage points higher than in the base run). Agricultural prices do not fall as sharply as under the orthodox policy, although price increases are observed in some mark-up sectors (manufacturing and modern services in particular).

The heterodox package has a positive impact on total investment, which is more than 1 per cent of GDP higher in the tenth year, compared to the base-run scenario. In relation to sectoral saving-investment behaviours, under the heterodox policy package the following patterns are observed. In the long run, the savings of public sector institutions (the government) show a large increase as a share of GDP (from 6.9 per cent of GDP in the base-year to 8.3 per cent in the tenth year). Public investment, on the other hand, increases to 9.9 per cent of GDP in the first year of the simulation (from 8.9 per cent of GDP in the base-year), and then decreases continuously thereafter to stand at 7.3 per cent of GDP in the tenth year. As discussed previously, as a result of this long term trend in public saving and investment, the initial increase of the public sector deficit reverses and from year nine onwards becomes a surplus.

Private savings and investment, on the other hand, tend to increase in the long run. As a result, the financial requirements of the private sector increase over time. Thus, bank credit to the private sector increases from 2.6 per cent of GDP in the base-year to 5.6 per cent at the end of the simulation period.

Income distribution under the heterodox policy package improves in the short term, compared to the orthodox policy and to the no-policy option. Real wages increase by 7 per cent in the first year of the application of the heterodox policy package, compared to the base-run scenario. In the long run however, the heterodox policy is unable to maintain the increased level of real wages, which suffers a larger deterioration compared to the other policy options. Conversely, the heterodox policy package is more effective in increasing employment in the long run (see Figure7.1g).

7.6.4 Comparison of policies

Compared with the base-run scenario, the 10 per cent reduction in some of the country's export prices has a negative effect on the capacity of the economy to attain some of its macroeconomic goals. Output growth prospects worsen and the current account surplus of the balance of payments is reduced, resulting in a continuous loss of international reserves over the whole period of the simulation.

The orthodox policy package places priority on attacking the external imbalance and therefore on avoiding foreign exchange reductions. The combination of 'demand-reducing' and 'demand-switching' policies successfully brings about a reverse in foreign exchange losses. The external balance improvement, however, is mostly achieved by creating a large contraction in activity. Output contracts even further and income distribution becomes more unequal. Nominal devaluation fails to compensate for the losses in competitiveness caused by the external shock, although this is helped by the created deflation in domestic prices which is created, and which eventually produces a larger devaluation in the real exchange rate. As a result, export expansion is insufficient to boost economic activity. Moreover, higher domestic interest rates also help to restore the external balance.

The heterodox policy programme presents better results in terms of output and employment, since the emphasis of the programme is to reverse the negative impacts of the shock by maintaining aggregate demand. A key factor in the heterodox programme is the increase in taxes on companies. This measure helps the public sector to compensate for income losses due to the shock, and to secure extra finance in order to boost investment. Finally, devaluation proves to be less effective in promoting exports under the heterodox alternative than under the orthodox one. Because the heterodox policy is more inflationary, the same nominal devaluation produces a smaller devaluation in real terms; therefore, gains in export competitiveness tend to be smaller.

7.7 Shock Resulting from an Increase in the Real international Interest Rate

The second shock tested through the RF-CGE model is a 40 per cent increase in the real international interest rate, from 5 to 7 per cent. Again, the external shock is assumed to occur in the first period of the simulation and to stay at that higher level over the rest of the period. The results of the simulations for the three alternative policy scenarios (namely no policy, orthodox and heterodox policies) are analysed in the following.

7.7.1 Increased real international interest rate with no policy response

An increase in the real international real interest rate, in the short and long runs, has a highly negative impact on GDP growth (see Figure 7.2a). The rate of growth of GDP declines by around 0.5 per cent in the second year after the shock, and remains below the growth rate values of

Figure 7.2 *Comparison of key macroeconomic variables behaviour under three policy alternatives, following a 40 per cent increase in the international interest rate (deviations from the base-run scenario)*

(a) GDP growth rate (deviations from base-run)

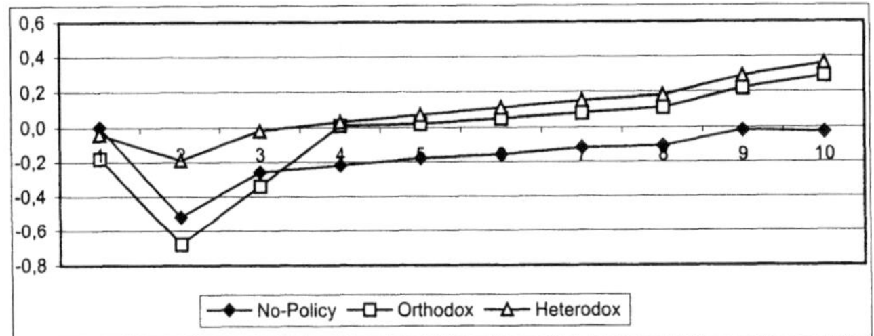

(b) Fiscal deficit (% of GDP)

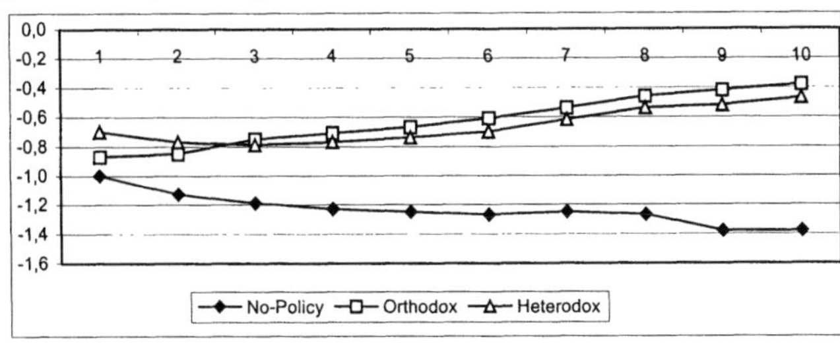

(c) Current account deficit (% of GDP)

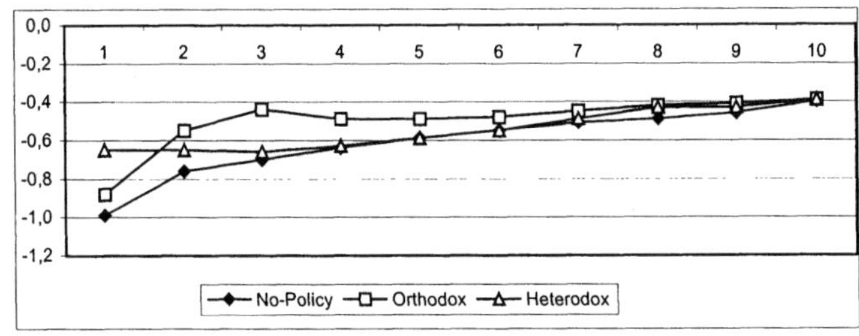

Figure 7.2 *Comparison of key macroeconomic variables behaviour under three policy alternatives, following a 40 per cent increase in the international interest rate (deviations from the base-run scenario), continued*

(d) Total investment (% of GDP)

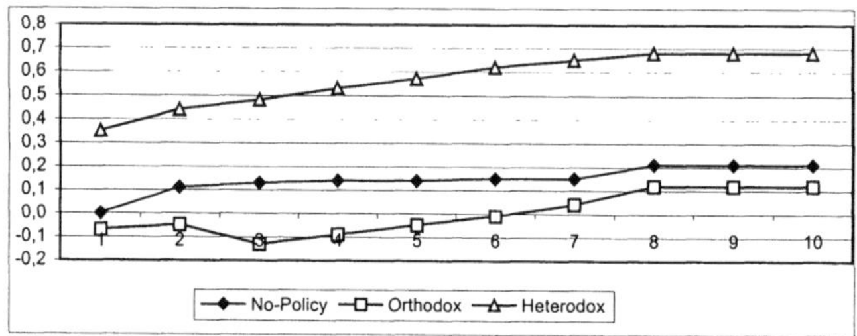

(e) Inflation rate (%)

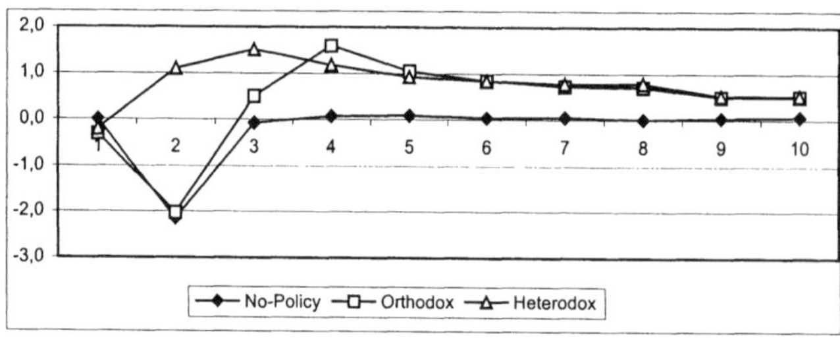

(f) Real wage rate

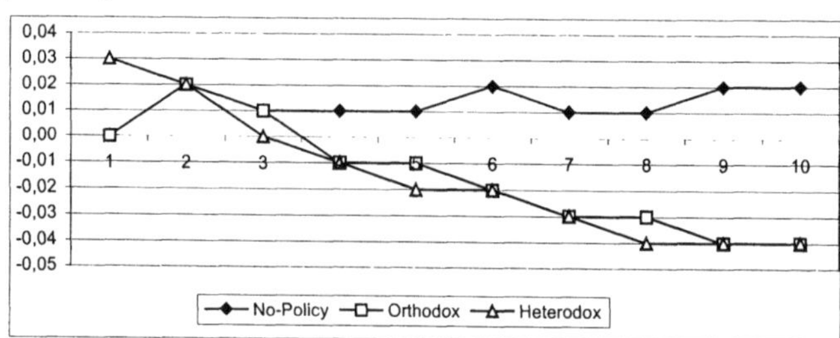

Figure 7.2 Comparison of key macroeconomic variables behaviour under three policy alternatives, following a 40 per cent increase in the international interest rate (deviations from the base-run scenario), continued

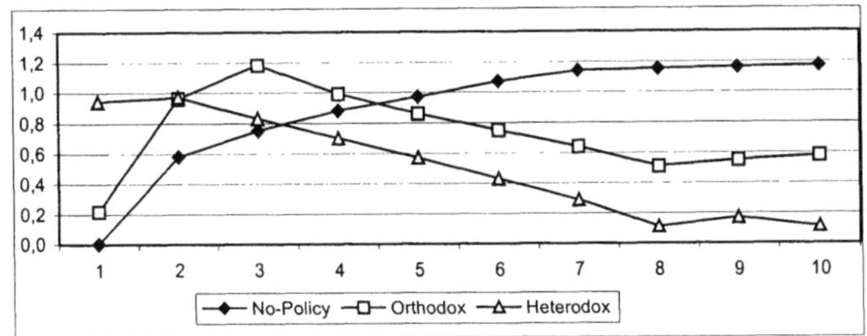

the base-run simulation for the remaining the years. Higher international interest rates bring about a reshuffling of agents' portfolios, increasing deposits abroad and shrinking investment demand. They also reduce government savings by increasing the external debt service burden. Thus, for the same level of foreign finance, the overall saving rate of the economy declines, bringing about a lower level of total investment. As a result, the rate of growth of investment falls by 1.2 per cent during the second year after the shock and continues to fall in subsequent years, all be it at decreasing rates. This is mostly explained by a sharp reduction in investment by companies in rapid response to changes in the profitability of various assets.

In the short and long terms, lower levels of investment have a direct impact on the rates of growth of imports and output in the construction sector. They fall by 1.4 and 1.3 per cent, respectively, during the second year following the shock and at decreasing rates over the subsequent years.

The rate of growth of consumption falls by 1 per cent of GDP, and output levels of the mark-up sectors fall through the multiplier effect initiated by lower investment. Hence, the growth rate of manufacturing output falls by 0.8 per cent and that of informal services by 1.5 per cent.

The consolidated public sector deficit, on the other hand, widens by 1 per cent in the first year of the simulation, mostly as a result of increased government interest payments on its external debt. The deficit increases over the years, and ends up 1.4 per cent of GDP higher than in the base-run simulation (see Figure 7.2b). As a consequence, the flow of domestic credit to the public sector expands by an equivalent amount, since foreign finance remains unchanged.

As the higher international interest rate increases interest payments to the rest of the world, the current account deficit increases by almost 1 per cent of GDP in the first year of the simulation (see Figure 7.2c). The higher deficit persists for most of the simulation period. As a result, the losses of foreign exchange reserves become more acute. Under the shock, international reserves held by the banking system are 3.2 per cent of GDP lower than the level observed at the end of the base-run simulation.

The rate of investment as a percentage of GDP increases slightly, mostly because of the reduced GDP (see Figure 7.2d). In relation to individual accumulation balances, the following patterns are observed. Public sector savings fall because of the increased interest payments. At the same time, investment by government and public enterprises exhibit small increases. The resulting excess of investment vis-à-vis savings is covered by increased Central Bank credit to the public sector.

Savings by companies and households both increase over the long term, and investment declines rapidly. As a result, the private sector generates larger surpluses compared to the base run. Consequently, credit to the private sector halves in the shock scenario vis-à-vis the base run.

Additionally, the level of domestic bank deposits by the private sector does not show substantial changes over the years of the simulation. As a result, foreign exchange reserves held by the banking system decline in the long term.

Inflation in the short term declines as a consequence of the lower activity levels brought about by the shock (see Figure 7.2e). In the long term, however, this trend reverses an inflation exhibited by the rates observed in the base-run scenario. As a result of lower rates of inflation, the real wage rate exhibits greater increases under the shock scenario compared to the base run (see Figure 7.2f). Unemployment, on the other hand, deteriorates sharply as a result of the lower levels of investment and output growth (see Figure 7.2g).

7.7.2 Increased real international interest rate followed by an orthodox policy package

Under the orthodox policy package, the economy shows a more recessionary behaviour in the short term. In the second year following the shock and introduction of the orthodox policy measures, the rate of growth of GDP falls by almost 0.7 percentage points of GDP. The rate of growth of GDP is lower than that observed under the no-policy alternative, because of the very strong bias in the programme for restraining consumption, both by the private and public sectors (see Figure 7.2a). However, in the long term this situation reverses and the economy exhibits higher growth rates, although at a lower absolute level of GDP.

This trend is basically explained by the pattern exhibited by investment, whose growth rate reduces considerably in the short-term. In the long term, however, investment growth partially recovers, at least in comparison to the no-policy option. Private consumption grows at a slightly reduced rate under the orthodox package.

With regard to sectoral behaviour, the combined effects of lower levels of investment and consumption have differentiated impacts on the activities of the various productive sectors. There are considerable reductions in the rate of growth in construction and in the mark up-sectors (manufacturing and services) as a result of the lower investment and consumption demand. The export sectors are less sensitive to devaluation and show growth rates similar to those in the no-policy scenario.

The consolidated public sector deficit reduces considerably under the orthodox policies, as government expenditures are restrained as part of the policy programme. As a result, the flow of Central Bank credit to the public sector is halved. It is important to note, however, that interest payments due to the government's external debt increase as a share of GDP as a result of devaluation.

Under the orthodox policy programme, the external balance performance improves. The current account deficit reduces because of lower imports, due to the contraction in activity and investment. As explained previously, exports are not very responsive to devaluation.

Inflation, which had decreased in the short term under the no-policy alternative, likewise reduces under the orthodox policy package. The initial drop in aggregate demand reduces agricultural prices, which are determined in flexi-price markets. In the long run, however, inflation regains momentum, exhibiting higher rates than in the no-policy scenario.

The implementation of a restrictive orthodox policy package reduces investment, which is lower when compared to the no-policy alternative.

The sectoral accumulation balance behaviours exhibit the following patterns. Government and public enterprise savings, as discussed previously, increase more rapidly than their investment demand, thus reducing the fiscal deficit. As a result, government requires lower, but still positive, flows of Central Bank finance.

A different pattern is observed in the accumulation balance for the private sector. Both private savings and investment decline in comparison with the no-policy option, resulting in higher flows of domestic credit from commercial banks.

Monetary balances show a more contractionary behaviour under the orthodox policy. Total domestic credit is lower than under the no-policy option, and thus gains in foreign exchange reserve are higher.

As a result of higher inflation at the end of the simulation period, real wages decrease under the orthodox programme. The unemployment rate increases in the short term because of lower activity. Employment creation, however, tends to be higher in the long run; starting from the fifth year, the unemployment rate under the orthodox policy package is lower than under the no-policy scenario.

7.7.3 Increased real international interest rate followed by a heterodox policy package

The heterodox policy measures again prove to have the lowest costs of the three policy options in terms of output losses. The rate of growth of GDP falls by 0.2 percentage points in the second year and recover to pre-shock rates over subsequent years. Under the heterodox policy, GDP growth rates are consistently higher than under the no-policy and orthodox policy packages.

Although autonomous government investment expenditures increase as part of the heterodox programme, with the aim of offsetting the recessionary effects of higher international interest rates, the rate of growth of investment is still 1.7 per cent lower than in the base run in the first year following the shock and application of the heterodox policy. Investment exhibits higher growth rates after the first year.

The rate of growth of exports is slightly higher than in the no-policy scenario. The export growth rate increases by 0.7 per cent in the first year of the simulation as compared to the rate observed under the no-policy scenario. This rate, however, is lower than that observed under the orthodox policy alternative. Although devaluation, which is also included as part of the heterodox policy measures, has a positive impact on exports, its effects are not as strong as under the orthodox alternative. This is because, under the heterodox alternative, domestic prices increase much more rapidly, so that the same nominal devaluation produces a smaller depreciation of the real exchange rate.

As a result of the smaller reductions in output and investment, and higher domestic prices, import reductions are not as great as under the no-policy and orthodox policy alternatives.

Sectoral output reacts quite differently under the heterodox policy alternative. Construction output increases at consistently higher growth rates than in the no-policy alternative, closely mirroring investment behaviour. The output growth rate of the mark-up sectors is also higher than in the no-policy option. Output in the exporting activities, on the other hand, grows more quickly than under the no-policy option, but much more slowly than under the orthodox package; this is because of the different real exchange rate depreciations attained under the two other policy options.

The fiscal balance shows more positive results than under the no-policy alternative, in that overall fiscal deficits are reduced as a percentage of GDP, in spite of increased government investment demand. Obviously, this is possible because of higher tax revenues, which are, on average, 0.2 and 0.6 per cent of GDP higher than under the no-policy and orthodox policy alternatives, respectively. Smaller fiscal deficits reduce domestic credit expansion to the public sector to only 0.2 per cent of GDP over the whole period.

In relation to the external sector, the current account balance, under the heterodox policy alternative, presents slightly better results than those obtained under the no-policy alternative. However, these results are not as good as those achieved under the orthodox package. The lower export growth and higher import levels observed under the heterodox policy, when compared to the orthodox scenario, explain that behaviour.

Investment increases under the heterodox policy package, and reaches a level 0.6 per cent higher than that observed in the base run.

The following patterns were observed in the sectoral saving-investment behaviours. Public sector savings increase substantially as income taxes rise. Investment by public enterprises also increases, but at a much slower pace. As a result, the public sector deficit drops faster and the flow of domestic credit to the public sector is thus substantially reduced.

The increased government saving has as a counterpart a decrease in private savings. Corporate savings are lower than those attained under the no-policy alternative because of higher taxation. Household savings fall sharply due to lower government expenditures. Private investment and private bank deposits stay at the same level observed in the no-policy scenario. Additionally, bank lending to the private sector increases compared to the no-policy option. The increase in borrowing by the private sector is explained by the greater financial needs of the private sector due to lower levels of private savings. The sharp decrease in private savings means that it is increasingly necessary for them to resort to additional credit from commercial banks. Thus, the flow of commercial bank credit to the private sector expands at a much faster pace under the heterodox policy package than under the two other policy options.

Under a heterodox policy, the anti-recessionary bias brings about, on average, a 1 per cent increase in the overall price index, as the reduction in agricultural prices is much smaller than under the orthodox package. Employment increases much faster due to higher activity levels; as a result, the rate of unemployment is much lower compared to the no-policy and orthodox policy packages. Real wages show the same pattern as those observed under the orthodox policy; despite the higher price increases observed under the heterodox option, the higher employment levels observed under this policy alternative bring about greater increases in nominal wages, which compensate for higher price increases.

7.7.4 Comparison of policies

The main negative effects of an increased international interest rate are given in terms of lower levels of investment, activity and foreign exchange reserves losses. Output contraction comes mostly in the form of lower investment, as companies and households switch their portfolio decisions in favour of external financial assets. Reserve losses occur mostly as a result of an increased fiscal deficit because of higher interest payments on the public external debt. The increased deficit is financed mainly through Central Bank credit; thus, the Central Bank has to accept some losses in its official exchange reserves.

The orthodox policy again concentrates on reversing reserve reductions by restraining domestic absorption and by promoting exports. Nominal devaluation is shown to be more effective in promoting exports as domestic price deflation brings about an even larger devaluation in real terms. As a result, the Central Bank consistently registers official exchange reserve gains over the whole period. Compared with the no-policy option, levels of output experience larger reductions, as do employment levels. Real wages, on the other hand, improved due to the low inflation levels attained.

The heterodox policy presents better results in terms of output, as the emphasis of the programme is placed on mitigating the negative impacts of the shock by maintaining aggregate demand. Real wages under the heterodox scenario deteriorate compared to the no-policy option, due to higher inflation. Although government investment is explicitly increased as part of the heterodox measures, it can only compensate for a small proportion of the investment reduction induced by the shock. However, investment under the heterodox policy deteriorates to a lesser degree than observed under either the orthodox or no policy options.

7.8 Shock Resulting from a Reduction in Capital Inflows

The last shock analysed through the RF-CGE model is that of a 50 per cent reduction in the level of foreign transfers to the government, both current (i.e. grants) and capital (i.e. lending). As in the cases of the other two external shocks, the reduction in external capital inflows is assumed to take place in the first period of the simulation and to remain at that low level over the rest of the period.

The results of the simulations for the three alternative policy scenarios (no policy, orthodox and heterodox policies) are analysed, respectively, in the following three sections.

7.8.1 Reduced international capital inflows with no policy response

As for the previous external shocks analysed, a reduction in the level of capital inflows has severe stagflationary effects on the economy. In the case that no policy is applied in response to the shock, the rate of growth of output experiences an almost 1 per cent reduction in the second year after the shock (see Figure 7.3a). Output growth remains at a reduced level over the whole period of the simulation. The recessionary effect of lower capital inflows is initially transmitted into the economy through a more than 2 per cent reduction in rate of growth of investment demand. Although lower capital inflows reduce public enterprise and government investment demand, public and private investment become foreign-exchange-constrained because of lower foreign exchange availability. Therefore, the levels of investment undertaken by public and private enterprises fall below those initially intended due to the lack of foreign exchange available to import capital goods.

Additionally, the private consumption growth rate falls by more than 1 per cent during the year following the shock through the multiplier effect of lower levels of investment on incomes.

Exports increase slightly, mostly due to higher hydrocarbon exports. This happens because of the sharp reductions in consumption and activity, which increase the sector's exportable balances. Imports also contract due to lower levels of investment, activity and consumption.

Activity levels in the various productive sectors are affected by the external shock in different ways. The construction output growth rate falls by more than 2.5 per cent due to the lower level of investment demand. The output of some mark-up sectors, such as manufacturing and informal services, also falls as a consequence of lower demand. Manufacturing and modern services output growth rates both fall over the whole period of the simulation because both sectors become foreign-exchange-constrained when the lack of foreign exchange restricts imports of intermediate inputs. As a result, although demand for these sectors' output declined, part of this demand cannot be satisfied, and adjustment takes place through higher prices. Domestic prices for manufacturing and modern services rise during the year following the shock.

The fiscal deficit increases by 0.4 per cent points of GDP due to lower tax revenues (see Figure 7.3b). The fiscal deficit also increases

Figure 7.3 *Comparison of key macroeconomic variables behaviour under three policy alternatives, following a 50 per cent reduction in the level of capital inflows to government (deviations from the base-run scenario)*

(a) GDP growth rate (deviations from base-run)

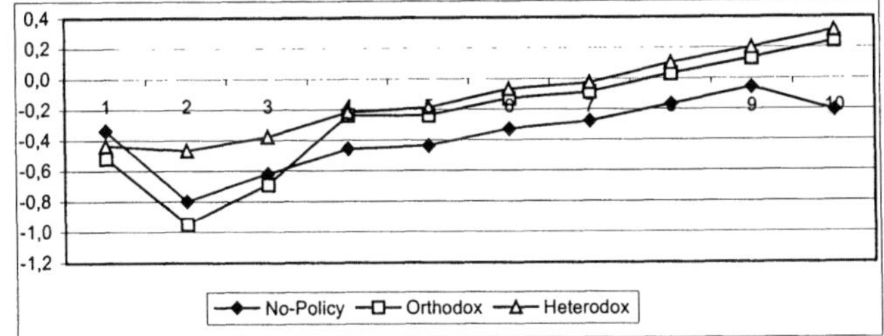

(b) Fiscal deficit (% of GDP)

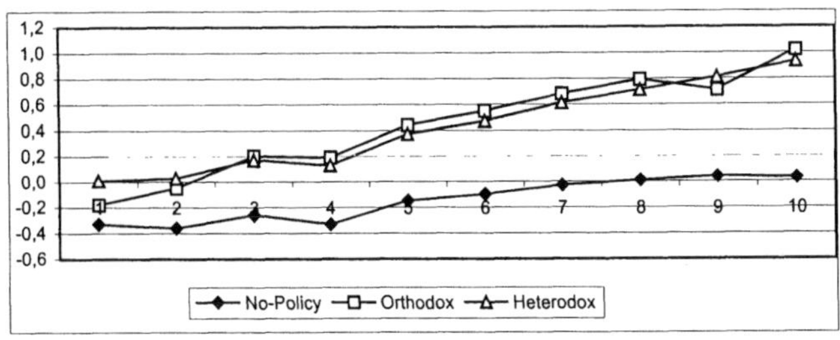

(c) Current account deficit (% of GDP)

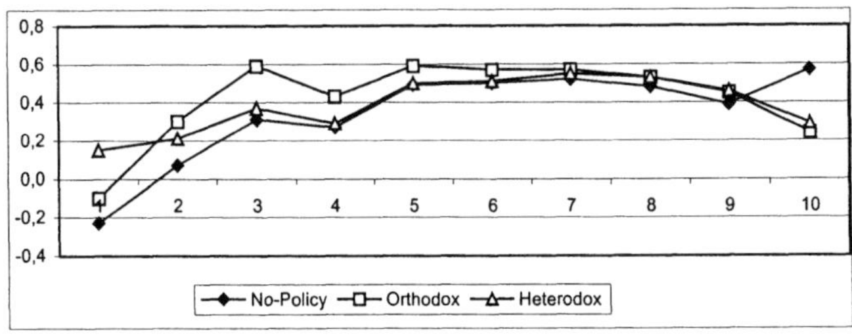

Figure 7.3 *Comparison of key macroeconomic variables behaviour under three policy alternatives, following a 50 per cent reduction in the level of capital inflows to government (deviations from the base-run scenario), continued*

(d) Total investment (% of GDP)

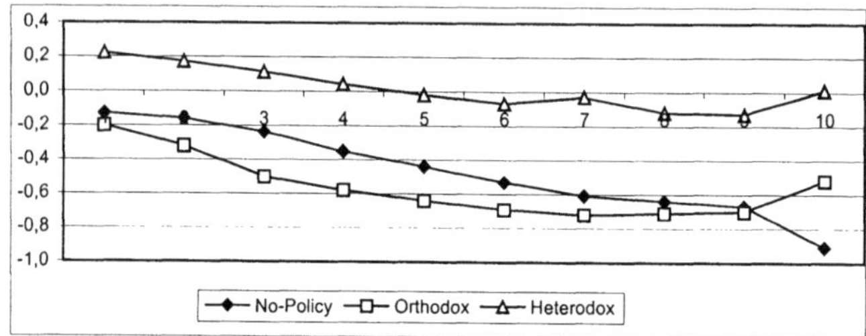

(e) Inflation rate (%)

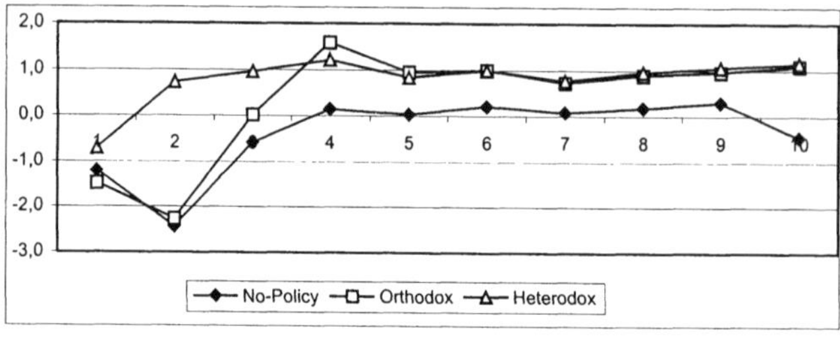

(f) Real wage rate

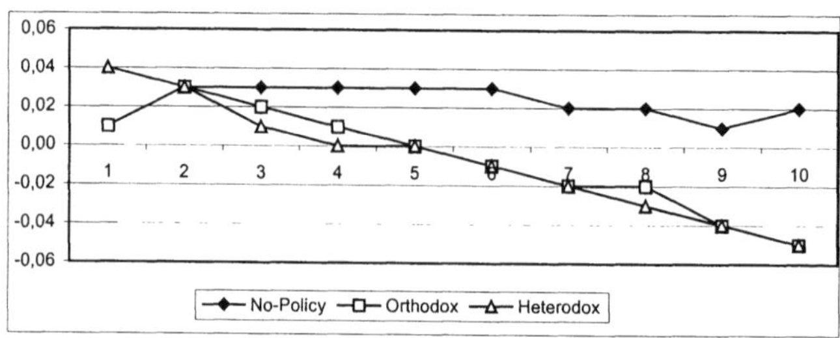

Figure 7.3 *Comparison of key macroeconomic variables behaviour under three policy alternatives, following a 50 per cent reduction in the level of capital inflows to government (deviations from the base-run scenario), continued*

(g) Unemployment rate

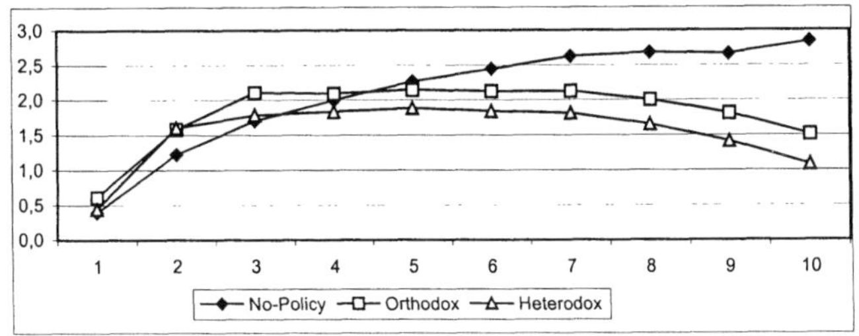

because of the reduced current transfers to the government. These reduced revenues are partially compensated by the lower level of government investment.

The recessionary effect of decreased capital inflows has a positive impact on the current account of the balance of payments. The current account deficit initially increases by 0.1 per cent of GDP (see Figure 7.3c). After the first year there is a noticeable reduction in the current account deficit as a result of increased exports and lower imports. The economy still shows losses in its official foreign exchange reserves, however, since the external shock reduces foreign finance over the whole period.

Total investment declines considerably. At the end of the simulation period, total investment is 1 per cent of GDP lower than the level attained in the base-run simulation.

The sectoral accumulation balance behaviours show the following trends. The consolidated public sector deficit increases by around 0.3 per cent of GDP. There are various explanations for this behaviour. First, government's tax revenues and public enterprises' surpluses are reduced due to a lower level of activity. Second, current foreign transfers to government decline. And third, the reduction in investment does not compensate for the lower levels of income. As a result of the higher fiscal deficit and reduced foreign finance, domestic finance to the public sector increases, on average, by more than 1 per cent over the whole period of the simulation.

Private savings, on the other hand, fall in absolute terms, but increase as a proportion of GDP. Private investment reduces both in absolute terms and as a proportion of GDP. As a result, private deposits in the banking system increase by 1 per cent of GDP and bank lending to the private sector stays at the same pre-shock level.

The inflation rate substantially decreases during the first three years of the simulation (see Figure 7.3e). There are, however, increases in prices for some mark-up sectors: in the manufacturing and modern services sectors, agricultural prices fall significantly because of the recessionary effect of the shock on aggregate demand. The likely explanation for the price increases in the mark-up sectors is that the mark-up rates in these two sectors rise as output responses are limited by the lack of foreign exchange to import intermediate inputs. As a result of lower inflation, the real wage rate improves significantly. Employment, on the other hand, falls sharply under the no-policy option. The unemployment rate increases continuously over the whole period of the simulation (see Figure 7.3g).

7.8.2 Reduced international capital inflows followed by an orthodox policy

Under the orthodox policy package, the contractionary effects of reduced capital inflows on output growth are deepened in the short term but are mitigated in the long term, compared to the no-policy response option.

The rate of output growth is increased starting from the fourth year of the simulation, after a reduction in the first three years. The reduction of investment, consumption and imports under the orthodox programme is more severe in the short term compared to the no-policy alternative. At the same time, export growth slightly increases, since devaluation and price deflation produce a large depreciation of the real exchange rate.

The above tendencies, shown by the different demand components, have differentiated impacts on output growth of the various productive sectors. Overall, however, output growth for the different activities, tends to be lower in the short term just after the application of the orthodox policy package, and higher in the long term, when compared to the no-policy option.

There is an initial reduction in the construction output growth rate, since investment declines in the first years following the application of the orthodox package. In the long run, output in the construction sector grows faster as investment becomes more dynamic. The same trend can be observed in output behaviour of the mark-up sectors (namely manufacturing and informal services). In these cases, the variability observed in the rates of growth of output is linked to the trend followed by private consumption. Hydrocarbon and mining output grow at a slightly higher growth rate compared to the no-policy alternative, as a result of a higher level of exports.

Under the orthodox policy, the overall deficit of the consolidated public sector is reduced, on average, by 1 per cent of GDP compared to the no-policy option. Higher exports help to increase government tax revenues and public enterprise savings. The lower fiscal deficit, which is financed entirely by Central Bank credit as the external finance is curtailled, brings about a 50 per cent reduction in the net domestic borrowing by the public sector.

The current account deficit of the balance of payments also declines considerably under the orthodox policy package, compared to the no-policy option (see Figure 7.3b).

The sectoral accumulation balance behaviours show the following patterns. Although the levels of savings and investment for both government and public enterprises are larger under the orthodox policy programme than those under the no-policy option, savings expand much faster than investment. This brings about a continued reduction in the fiscal deficit and in the flow of Central Bank credit to the public sector. The pattern observed in private saving-investment is completely different. Private savings are lower and investment larger than under the no-policy option. This results in larger private deficits and, consequently, in larger flows of commercial bank credit to the private sector. Additionally, the stock of bank deposits by the private sector at the end of the simulation period reduces by 2 per cent of GDP.

Price increases are initially reduced under the orthodox policy, but the inflation rate increases in the long run. As a result, the real wage rate increases much more slowly than under the no-policy option and decreases compared to the base-run scenario. In the long term, however, employment is higher under the orthodox policy package than under the no-policy alternative.

7.8.3 Reduced international capital inflows followed by a heterodox policy

Although the recessionary effects of diminished capital inflows are much lower under the heterodox policy programme than under either the no-policy or orthodox alternatives, the lower output growth rate brought about by the shock cannot be reversed. The anti-recessionary measures applied under the programme are unable to produce the growth rates which existed prior to the shock, at least until the seventh year of the simulation (see Figure 7.3a). Consumption and investment demand exhibit higher growth rates compared to the no-policy and orthodox scenarios. The same trend is shown by imports, which react to higher investment and consumption demand.

Exports show much more modest growth rates than those exhibited under the orthodox policy measures. Price increases resulting from the anti-recessionary bias embodied in the heterodox policies offset the beneficial effects of the initial nominal devaluation on exports.

The smaller reductions in GDP growth observed following the adoption of the heterodox policy are explained by the less negative behaviour of private consumption compared with either the no-policy or orthodox alternatives. A more equitable income distribution helps to ameliorate the further reductions in consumption and, therefore, in GDP.

Sectoral output behaviour exhibits the following patterns under the heterodox programme: construction shows much higher growth rates because of the increased public investment demand; agricultural output also grows faster than in the orthodox policy package due to higher levels of consumption; and the export sectors, namely mining and hydrocarbons, present slightly lower growth rates of output than those observed under the orthodox alternative due to lower levels of exports. Manufacturing, electricity and services output performances, on the other hand, are less negative than under the orthodox package because of higher levels of consumption.

The heterodox policy package is as effective as the orthodox package in reducing the fiscal deficit. The higher levels of public investment embodied in the heterodox package are compensated by higher tax revenues. As in the orthodox policy option, that part of the deficit that can not be financed by external borrowing is financed through Central Bank credit. Although capital outflows are reduced, official reserve losses cannot be reversed under the heterodox policy alternative, although they are greatly diminished in relation to the levels observed under the no-policy option. Reserve losses occur because of the much lower export revenues.

The sectoral accumulation balance behaviours show the following patterns. There is a large increase in government savings due to higher tax revenues, which help not only to reduce the fiscal deficit substantially and reduce the flow of domestic credit, but also to compensate for the reduction in external finance.

Compared with the levels shown under the orthodox policy, private savings fall much more rapidly than their investment demand; the resulting gap is covered by additional flows of commercial bank credit. The private sector experiences substantial reductions in savings due to higher tax payments. The resulting savings gap is financed mainly by commercial bank credit.

The inflation rate under the heterodox policy alternative is much higher than under the no-policy and orthodox options. Under the heterodox policy alternative prices rise on average by 2 per cent above the rate observed under the no-policy option. The emphasis of this policy on avoiding adjustment through demand restraint alone prevents the agricultural price reductions that occur under the orthodox policy.

Because of the increased inflation observed under the heterodox policy package, real wages increase at much more modest rates than under the no-policy option. However, real wages show the same pattern observed under the orthodox policy option. Higher price increases under the heterodox alternative are compensated by higher increases in nominal wages due to higher rates of growth of GDP and employment.

7.8.4 Comparison of policies

Unlike the other two shocks studied, a reduced flow of foreign finance has more generalized negative impacts on the country's prospects of achieving its main macroeconomic goals. These impacts are given in terms of output contraction, exchange reserves losses, higher inflation, lower investment and a more inequitable income distribution; these became more apparent as the economy moves to a foreign-exchange-constrained position. In terms of the RF-CGE model, this situation is defined as a position where the ex-post levels of output and investment are determined by the maximum capacity of the economy to import intermediate inputs and capital goods. Under these circumstances, although the external shock has a negative effect on aggregate demand, the supply shock produced by the foreign exchange gap is even stronger. As a result, the mark-up sectors begin to adjust through higher mark-up rates rather than through output increases. Lower capital inflows also have direct negative impacts on the balance of payments position. Reserves fall over the whole period of the simulation.

The orthodox policy is more effective in controlling price increases and reserve losses in that it concentrates on attacking the external imbalances by increasing domestic interest rates and therefore discouraging capital flight, by increasing exports through a nominal exchange rate devaluation, and by reducing government consumption in order to alleviate the pressure on the foreign exchange market. As a result of all these measures, official reserve losses are partly reversed. These measures also help the economy to alleviate its foreign-exchange-constrained position; as a result, output contraction and price increases are not as severe as in the no-policy case. Income distribution does not improve under the orthodox policy.

The heterodox policy exhibits better results in terms of mitigating output contraction and improving income distribution by maintaining aggregate demand. Nominal devaluation, however, again proves to be less effective in promoting exports when applied under the heterodox as opposed to the orthodox policy.

7.9 Shock Resulting from a Coca Crop Reduction Program

The need to reduce the level of coca crop production in excess of that required for traditional consumption (and, hence, used in the production of narcotics) has been a very important issue, one which has dominated Bolivia's relations with the international community. The international pressure on successive Bolivian governments to eradicate surplus coca production led them to implement various coca substitution or reduction programmes.

The simulation exercise discussed in this section is very illuminating in terms of the effects that a coca crop reduction programme would have on the external and internal balances of the economy. The specific simulation exercise run through the model is a 5 per cent annual rate of coca output reduction over a time horizon of ten years. The results obtained through the simulation are then compared to the base-run simulation.

In the first year of the coca crop reduction programme, the rate of growth of GDP falls by more than 0.3 per cent (see Figure 7.4a). Subsequently, GDP growth exhibits higher growth rates, albeit always at lower levels compared to the base-run scenario. These reductions may be explained by three factors. First, lower levels of consumption due to reduced income levels. Second, lower levels of investment, due to households' reduced savings. And third, diminished export levels (which are mainly due to the drop in coca exports). The level of imports also falls as a consequence of lower levels of activity, consumption and investment.

The effects of this shock on sectoral output growth are different for each sector. On the one hand, output growth rates in the agriculture, mining, hydrocarbons, and modern services sectors do not experience a significant change compared to the base-run scenario. On the other hand, the output growth rates decline in the manufacturing, construction and informal services sectors, because these sectors are demand-driven, and thus output adjusts to the lower levels of demand.

The fiscal balances present higher deficits than those observed in the base run, since lower levels of activity reduce tax revenues. As a result, domestic finance is slightly less contractionary than in the base run. The effects on the external sector are more sizeable.

The current account deficit of the balance of payments exhibits slightly higher deficits, albeit at a lower levels of exports and imports.

Inflation falls in the first year of the eradication programme is implemented, due to the contractive effect on aggregate demand (see Figure 7.4e). Lower demand reduces the prices of agricultural products, which have a large weight in the consumer price index (CPI). As a result of the reduced inflation, real wages increase much faster under the eradication programme compared to the base-run scenario. Unemployment also increases due to job losses not only in the coca sector resulting from implementation of the eradication programme, but also in the rest of the

Figure 7.4 *Comparison of key macroeconomic variables behaviour following a coca-crops eradication programme (deviations from the base-run scenario)*

(a) GDP growth rate

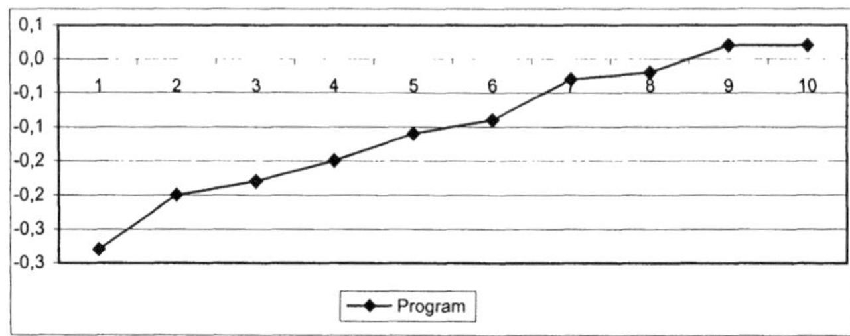

(b) Fiscal deficit (% of GDP)

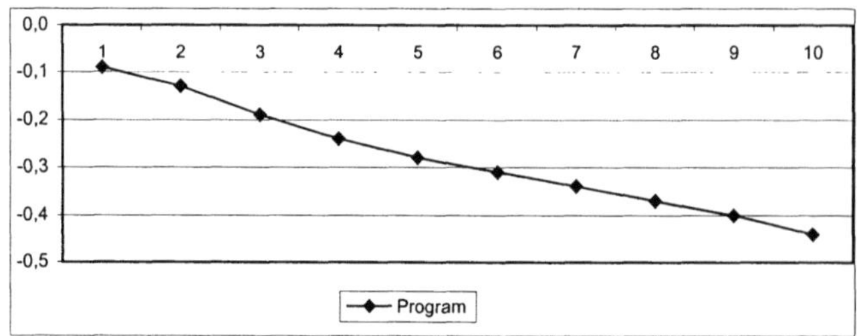

(c) Current account deficit (% of GDP)

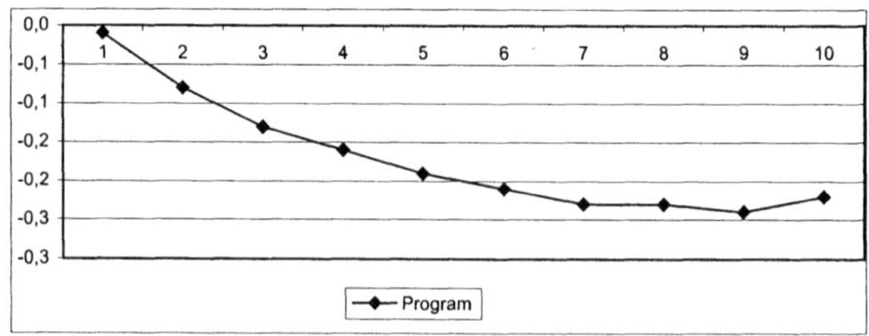

Figure 7.4 *Comparison of key macroeconomic variables behaviour following a coca-crops eradication programme (deviations from the base-run scenario), continued*

(d) Total investment (% of GDP)

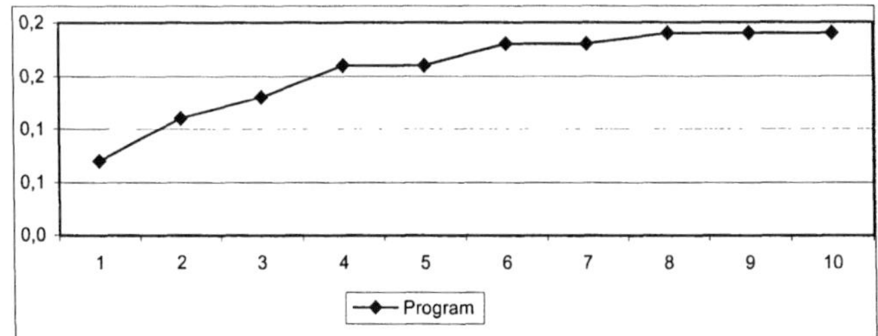

(e) Inflation rate (%)

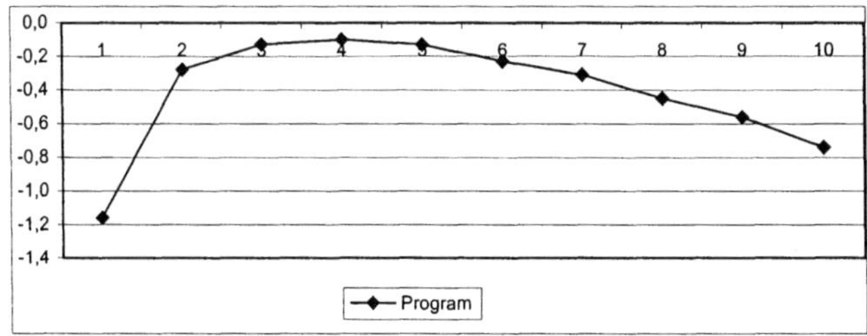

(f) Real wage rate

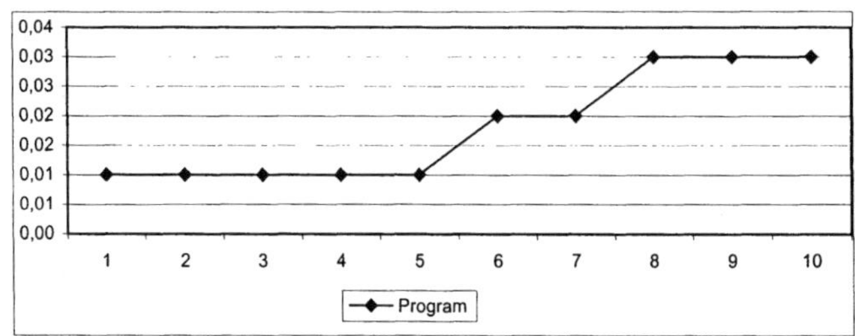

Figure 7.4 Comparison of key macroeconomic variables behaviour following a coca-crops eradication programme (deviations from the base-run scenario), continued

(g) Unemployment rate

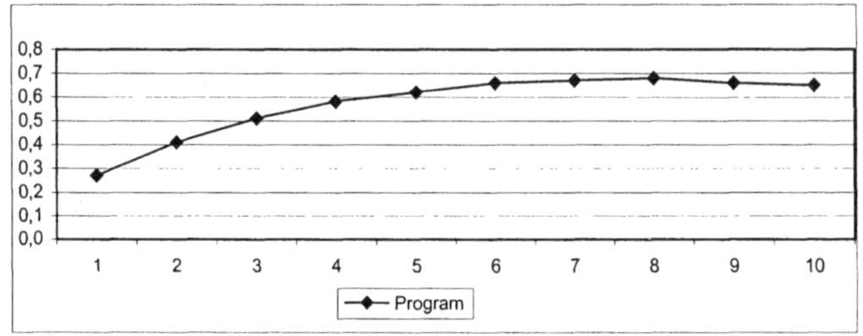

productive sectors because of the recessionary effects of the programme implementation (see Figure 7.4g).

7.10 Shock Resulting from an Increase in Foreign Direct Investment

The reform programme implemented from 1993 onwards comprises the capitalization of the main public enterprises. This process will be accomplished through the inflow of foreign direct investment into the six largest public enterprises. As discussed in this book, the strategic investors that capitalized the public companies have committed about US$ 1.7 billion to be invested in these firms over the next seven years. This process is expected to have a highly beneficial effect on the economy by increasing investment, output growth, employment, savings and exports.

The simulation exercise discussed in this section tests the effects that an increased inflow of foreign direct investment to the former public enterprises would have on the main macroeconomic variables. The results obtained are compared to the base-run simulations.

The effects of the increased inflow of foreign investment are tested under two scenarios. First, with inflows allowed to work their way through the system, and no complementary policy being implemented. And second, when the investment shock is accompanied by complementary policies, aimed at increasing productivity of salaried labour and self-employed workers.

The results of these two simulation exercises are discussed in the following two subsections.

7.10.1 Increased investment flows without complementary policies

The increased investment flows received by the former public companies, when no complementary policies are implemented, increases the rate of growth of GDP between 0.5 and 1 per cent point over the whole period of the simulation (see Figure 7.5a). These increased growth rates are initially fuelled by investment, whose growth rate is more than three times higher than the growth rate observed in the base-run scenario. Exports also exhibit higher growth rates due to the larger productive capacity created by the investment inflows. The increased growth rates of investment and of exports crowd-out private consumption, whose growth rate shrinks by almost 1.5 per cent compared to the base-run scenario. Imports also show higher growth rates, mainly in response to the greater dynamic shown by investment.

As a result of the increased investment inflows, sectoral behaviours exhibit different patterns. For those sectors in which incorporated firms account for a large share of sectoral output (such as mining and hydrocarbons), output growth rates show significant increases in the medium term. Output in the mark-up sectors (i.e. manufacturing and construction) also grows very rapidly in response to higher investment demand. For those sectors with a large share of informal activities in output generation (namely, agriculture and informal services), output growth rates increase, all be it in a more modest fashion. These diverse output responses occur because the flows of direct foreign investment are totally geared to increasing the productive capacity of corporate enterprises (that is, of the formerly publicly owned enterprises). Thus, output growth booms occur in all those sectors with relatively large participation of incorporated firms, while output does not react very strongly in those sectors with a large participation of informal unincorporated firms.

With the increase in the level of direct foreign investment, the investment rate increases by between 1.5 and 2 per cent of GDP over the whole period of the simulation (see Figure 7.5d). Private investment in-

Figure 7.5 Comparison of key macroeconomic variables behaviour under two policy alternatives, following an increase in foreign direct investment flows (deviations from the base-run scenario)

(a) GDP growth rate (deviations from base-run)

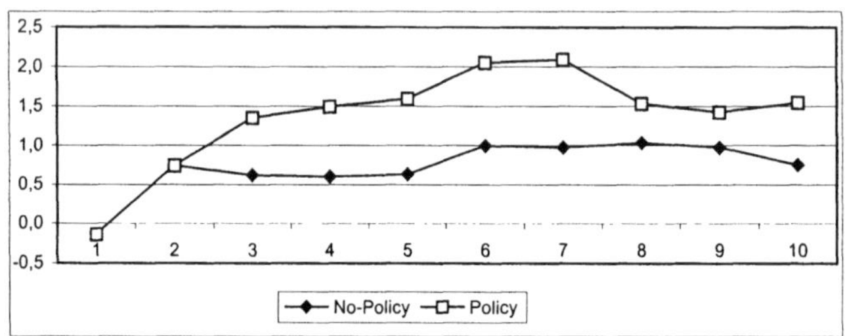

(b) Fiscal deficit (% of GDP)

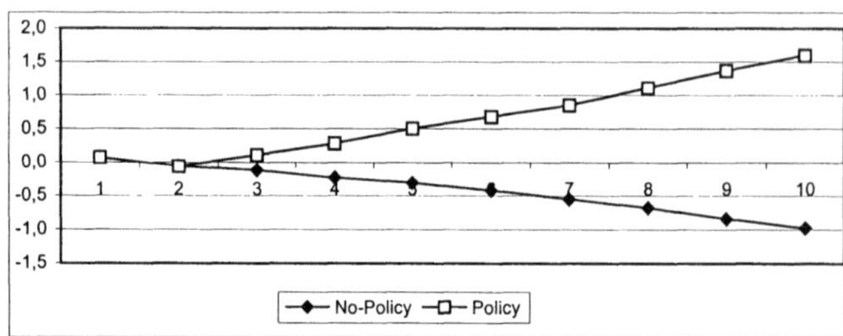

(c) Current account deficit (% of GDP)

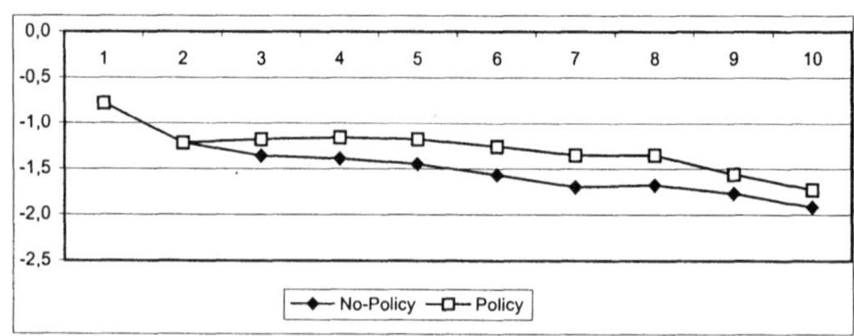

Figure 7.5 Comparison of key macroeconomic variables behaviour under two policy alternatives, following an increase in foreign direct investment flows (deviations from the base-run scenario), continued

(d) Total investment (% of GDP)

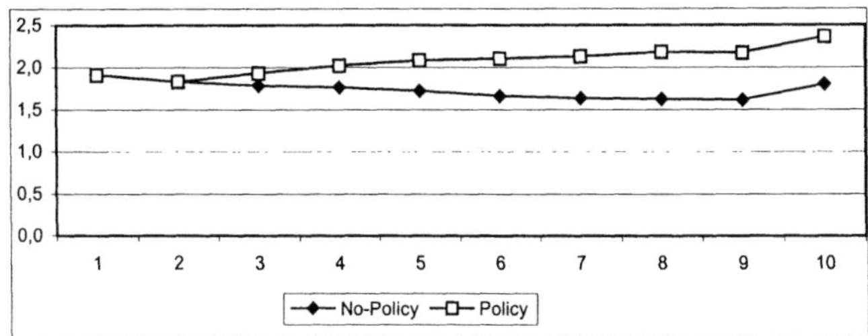

(e) Inflation rate (%)

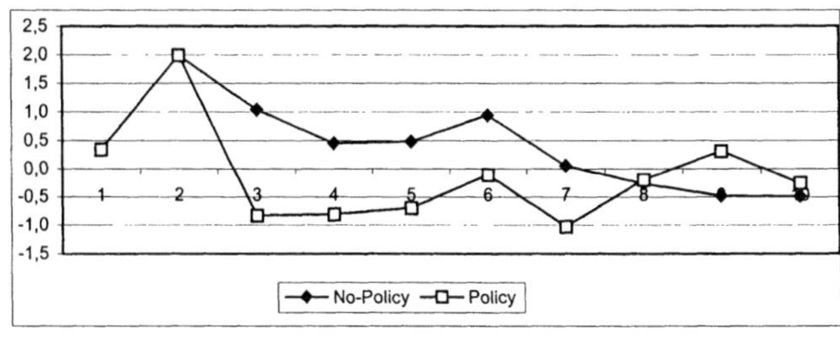

(f) Real wage rate

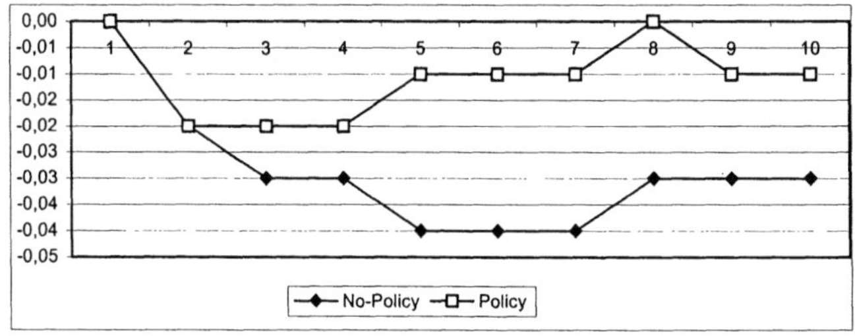

Figure 7.5 *Comparison of key macroeconomic variables behaviour under two policy alternatives, following an increase in foreign direct investment flows (deviations from the base-run scenario), continued*

(g) Unemployment rate

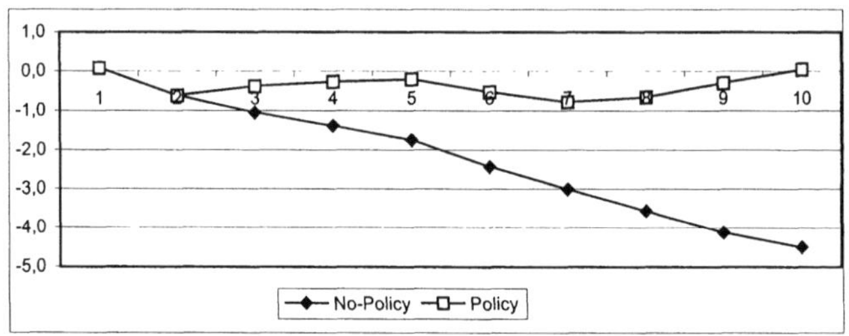

creases from 6.7 per cent of GDP in the base year to more than 12 per cent of GDP in the tenth year. Government investment decreases as a share of GDP, from 8.8 per cent to 4.8 per cent. This is explained by the fact that all the investment carried out by public firms in the base year is transferred to the private sector through the capitalization process.

Private savings increase from 2.6 of GDP in the base run to 6.5 in the tenth year. Government savings, on the other hand, exhibit an initial reduction of 2 per cent of GDP during the first two years of the simulation and, subsequently, stabilize at around 4 per cent of GDP up to year ten. External savings increase due to larger capital inflows, reaching 8 per cent of GDP in the third year. Subsequently, savings slowly decrease settling at a level of 6 per cent of GDP.

The inflation rate increases considerably over the whole period of the simulation, due to higher levels of activity and employment. Because of the higher inflation rates recorded, the real wage rate decreases in relation to the levels observed in the base-run scenario (see Table 7.5f).

7.10.2 Increased investment inflows with complementary measures

The Bolivian economy suffers from widespread low labour productivity across activity branches. In practically all sectors of the economy, unincorporated firms, with low levels of productivity, account for an important share of output, employment and investment. As was shown in the previous section, under these conditions, a significant increase in foreign investment inflows will increase output growth only marginally and enlarge income distribution inequalities.

The impacts of increased foreign investment inflows are quite different when they are accompanied by policies aimed at increasing informal workers' productivity.

In the first place, the overall growth rate of GDP is substantially increased during the whole period of the simulation, by an average of almost 2 percentage points of GDP, when compared to the base-run scenario. Growth also becomes more balanced across productive activities. In all those sectors where unincorporated firms account for a large share of total output, employment and investment exhibit higher growth rates, which makes growth rate differentials across sectors much smaller than in the no-complementary-policy scenario.

The growth rates of consumption, investment and exports are not only higher than in the no-complementary-policy scenario, but also exhibit a more consistent and self-sustainable pattern over the whole period of the simulation.

As was argued previously, the export sectors (mining and hydrocarbons) present about the same growth rates as those observed in the no-complementary-policy alternative. However, the remaining sectors (agriculture, manufacturing, construction, and services) exhibit higher growth rates due to the greater dynamic presented under the complementary-policy scenario.

The external balance improves slightly under the complementary-policy scenario. Although there are higher exports due to increased productivity, imports are also greater because of the higher levels of consumption and investment.

The fiscal balance is substantially improved as the fiscal deficit falls much faster in spite of higher levels of public investment. This is explained by the increased tax revenues, which result from higher activity levels. Lower fiscal deficits also imply a reduced requirement for domestic credit to finance the public sector.

Under the complementary-policy option, inflation is lower than under the no-complementary-policy alternative. This is explained by the increased supply of goods and services resulting from the productivity gains of labour. Lower inflation also implies a higher real wage rate.

Domestic savings are higher with the complementary policies. However, the composition of savings is quite different, with a greater share for public savings and a lower share for private savings. Additionally, investment increases because of the higher levels of public and private investment demand.

7.10.3 Comparison of scenarios

It is clear from the above discussion that an increased inflow of foreign direct investment, received by the private incorporated sector, is highly beneficial for the economy as a whole, since it increases output growth, domestic savings, investment, exports, employment, and the fiscal and the external balances. However, the results are less satisfactory in relation to a number of other aspects.

First, there are substantial growth differentials across sectors, since those sectors where incorporated firms have a large share of output present higher growth rates, while those sectors where unincorporated firms have the largest share in output exhibit lagging growth rates. This uneven pattern, followed by output growth across sectors, is the result of the large differentials in the shares of unincorporated firms in total output, employment and investment across sectors.

Second, the lagged growth of unincorporated firms' output and the large share of unincorporated firms in sectoral output also imply lower growth rates for the economy as a whole.

The beneficial effects of the increased capital inflows are greatly enhanced by the complementary policies aimed at increasing labour productivity, especially of unincorporated firms. As a result of these policies, those activities dominated by informal or unincorporated firms exhibit higher growth rates, similar to those presented by activities dominated by formal incorporated firms. Thus, economic growth across sectors becomes more balanced than in the no-complementary-policy option, and growth for the economy as a whole increases to a significant extent.

In summary, the role of informal unincorporated firms in economic growth cannot be neglected if a more balanced, equitable, self-sustainable economic growth is desired. The capitalization of the main public enterprises in Bolivia has secured large inflows of foreign direct investment to the country for the coming years. These resources will be received by formal incorporated firms in the hydrocarbons, telecommunication, transport, energy, and mining sectors. These inflows will undoubtedly increase investment and growth. However, these growth prospects will be greatly diminished if the unincorporated firms are left aside and no specific policies are undertaken to improve productivity in these sectors, as was clearly demonstrated in this section's simulation exercises.

Policies aimed at increasing labour productivity, such as the education reform and the Strategy for the Productive Transformation of the agricultural sector, were presented as official strategies of the Bolivian government to increase labour productivity, improve employment opportunities for the poor, increase the living standards of the population, and eventually defeat poverty. These strategies, and other policies aimed at increasing labour productivity in the unincorporated sector, are vital for the country's economic growth and development perspective.

7.11 Conclusions

This chapter has largely confirmed the importance of undertaking a more detailed approach to the analysis of macroeconomic adjustment in developing countries. The effects of the shocks and of the policy options tested tended to differ both quantitatively and qualitatively as their effects are transmitted into the economy along different channels. This section summarizes and compares the effects of the various shocks and policies applied, with reference to the outcomes and mechanisms that brought them about.

7.11.1 External shocks

Based on the simulations carried out and discussed in this chapter, it is evident that external shocks tend to have extremely negative effects on the country's economic performance. All shocks gave rise to recessionary tendencies in the system; prices went down in all cases, and output, employment, growth, external balance and income distribution were negatively affected. As highlighted previously, the shocks worked their way through the system along different channels.

(a) The terms of trade shock primarily had a negative effect on output as unfavourable relative prices discouraged activity in the export sectors. Lower exports had a recessionary effect on the activities of non-exporting sectors through the multiplier effect.

Lower official export prices also reduced revenues from the exporting activities. Thus, the incomes and savings of the agents controlling those activities (namely private companies and state enterprises) deteriorated; as a result, corporate savings fell and the fiscal deficit widened. The outcome was a continuous expansion in domestic credit, which brought about an equally steady reduction in the level of foreign exchange reserves.

Because lower export revenues mostly reduce the incomes of wealthy groups with relatively low propensities to consume, the deterioration of output also tends to be relatively low since the multiplier effect of the initial shock tends to be smaller.

(b) A higher international interest rate tended primarily to discourage investment demand. The most negative impact was on investment by companies and upper-income households, as these two sectors reorganized their portfolio structures in favour of external financial assets. In turn, the lower levels of investment also had recessionary impacts on other sectors through the multiplier effect.

Higher external interest rates also had significant effects on the fiscal balance. The fiscal deficit widened because of higher interest payments on the public external debt. Higher interest rates, however, produced relatively smaller reductions in reserves, as a deeper recession was associated with lower levels of imports.

Income distribution also worsened as the recession caused wage earnings and peasant incomes to fall.

(c) Reduced capital inflows had the most negative effects of all shocks analysed. The outcomes were lower levels of output and investment, higher inflation, larger foreign exchange losses and more unequal income distribution.

A reduced level of capital inflows primarily reduced investment demand by government and by state enterprises by operating through their investment demand functions. Government consumption was also reduced through the same mechanism. Moreover, lower capital inflows substantially reduced the formal sector's import capacity. As a result, output and investment went down due to the binding foreign exchange gap.

These two combined effects had a strong stagflationary effect on the economy. Although consumption and investment demand fell, aggregate supply fell even further again due to the binding foreign gap. As a result, prices went up.

The shock also brought about lower tax revenues for government. However, due to lower levels of public sector consumption and investment, however, the fiscal deficit reduced slightly.

Although lower levels of activity were associated with lower imports, this shock had a negative net effect on reserves.

7.11.2 Policy options

The simulations showed that there is little room for policy manoeuvres when the economy is exposed to an external shock. The negative effects of the shocks proved to be very difficult to reverse under the three alternative policy options tested. For instance, output contractions resulting from the shocks could not be reversed under any of the stabilization policies applied. The difficulties faced by the economy in increasing investment and long-term growth were also made explicit through the simulations. Both orthodox and heterodox policies were shown to have little power to increase investment to levels consistent with sustainable long-term growth. Investment by companies and upper-income households proved to be highly sensitive and to shrink very quickly in response to changes in the profitability of alternative assets, namely a higher international interest rate. This susceptibility obviously introduces great instability into the system. Besides, investment by lower-urban and rural households, which accounts for the bulk of the population, was very much constrained by the low availability of savings and finance. These two groups proved to be too poor to generate enough savings and investment to attain long-term growth.

In spite of the reduced room for economic policy design imposed by the shocks and by the structural constraints that characterize the Bolivian economy, the simulations still showed that orthodox and heterodox policies produced different results in terms of the various macroeconomic objectives. The heterodox stabilization programme consistently produced better results in terms of alleviating output losses and improving income distribution. However, this policy alternative was also associated with higher rates of inflation and less positive behaviour in the external sector. Conversely, the orthodox programme consistently yielded better results in terms of gains in official foreign exchange reserves and lower price increases. Output and income distribution always tended to deteriorate.

This obviously goes to show the different priorities that the two policies assign to the various macroeconomic goals.

(a) In essence, orthodox policies give priority to the external sector and try to bring about balance of payments equilibrium by controlling aggregate demand and by promoting export growth.

The orthodox policies simulated in this book attempted to attain aggregate demand reductions by controlling government consumption and by lowering wages. Lower demand was associated with reduced levels of activity in the mark-up sectors and lower imports. The outcome was an improvement in the official exchange reserves position.

Other complementary measures (such as increased prices for public sector goods) were aimed at increasing fiscal revenues. This measure, coupled with lower government consumption demand, went to reduce the fiscal deficit. As a result, domestic credit creation and exchange reserves losses were reduced.

Devaluation had a very positive effect on the quantities exported by formal sector activities (namely modern agriculture, manufacturing and modern services).

A higher domestic interest rate also tended to promote deposits in the domestic financial system, and therefore to discourage capital flight by upper-income households.

The negative effects of the orthodox policy were mostly in terms of output losses and income distribution deterioration. In fact, the output contraction due to the orthodox policy added to the recessionary effects of the shocks and mostly affected the mark-up sectors. Income distribution under the orthodox policy deteriorated as wage controls and demand restraint reduced wage earnings and employment. Peasants' incomes also declined as the lower level of demand led to a reduction in traditional agricultural prices.

(b) Heterodox programmes give priority to output growth, employment and income distribution; policy measures are therefore focused on avoiding aggregate demand restraint that could cause unnecessary idle capacity in the mark-up sectors.

The heterodox policy simulated through the RF-CGE model relied largely on increased income taxes on upper-income groups. This measure allows the government to maintain demand without increasing its deficit; thus inflation and foreign exchange losses were not as severe as they would otherwise have been.

High tax revenues permitted the government to increase investment in infrastructure, which had a positive long-term crowding-in effect on company investment. Wage reductions were also avoided, with positive effects on aggregate demand, output and income distribution.

Devaluation was also included as part of the heterodox programme, because there is a growing consensus in Bolivia about the necessity to maintain a competitive exchange rate in order to promote export growth. But devaluation proved to be more effective when applied under the orthodox policy. This was due to the deflationary effects induced by the orthodox measures, which managed to produce a larger foreign exchange devaluation in real terms.

7.11.3 Coca reduction programme

The application of a coca crop reduction programme seems not to have had a significant impact on the Bolivian economy. The share of coca value added in the Bolivian GDP has greatly diminished in the last six years. In 1996, coca value added accounts for only 2 to 3 per cent of GDP. The impacts on the fiscal sector, balance of payments, and financial sector are also limited. However, the impacts on employment are relatively more important.

7.11.4 Increased inflows of direct foreign investment

The increased inflows resulting from the investment commitments made by strategic investors when the public enterprises were capitalized succeeded in increasing the overall growth rate of the economy. Growth, however, proved to be unbalanced, as investment flows promote growth in the formal sector of the economy, controlled by large incorporated national and foreign companies, including the capitalized public firms. Thus, those sectors where incorporated firms have a large share in production and investment, such as hydrocarbons and modern services will show the fastest growth rates, while in those sectors dominated by small-scale firms, growth will fall behind. This uneven growth pattern of the incorporated and unincorporated activities will also diminish the performance of the economy as a whole.

Finally, the model was used to test the impact of increased investment inflows, when they were accompanied by specific policies aimed at increasing productivity of unincorporated firms. The results obtained show that this complementary policy will eliminate growth differentials between sectors by substantially raising growth in the informal sector. This will increase the overall output growth rate of the economy, given the large share that unincorporated firms have in output and employment in Bolivia.

Note

1. The distributional impacts of shocks and policies are normally measured in terms of the Gini coefficient, which measures the changes in the income shares of socioeconomic groups. In this CGE model, the Gini coefficient captures distributional shifts across groups which are associated with different factor sources of income, as identified within the 1989 SAM (i.e. peasants, informal workers, unskilled and skilled wage-earners, small-scale producers and capitalists).

8 Summary and Conclusions

This closing chapter summarizes the most important conclusions arrived at in this book.

As was advanced in the introduction, this book put forward an appropriate approach to the study of external shocks, stabilization policies and structural reforms in a developing country like Bolivia.

The book began by arguing that existing and leading theories of capital inflows, adjustment and stabilization cannot satisfactorily explain adjustment in a developing country such as Bolivia. Three serious shortcomings in the approaches to explaining adjustment in LDCs were identified: (i) they are a-temporal in their analyses, since adjustment rules are regarded as unchangeable over the period studied; (ii) they tend to be partial in their approach in that they tend not to include all sectors of the economy in their analytical frames; and (iii) their analytical frameworks do not capture the heterogeneous nature of a developing economy because their analyses are presented at a very aggregated level.

The discussion in this book largely demonstrated the above-mentioned shortcomings in a number of different ways.

First, it demonstrated that both markets' adjustments to external shocks are anything but homogeneous in Bolivia. Each productive sector exhibited particular adjustment mechanisms (such as prices, quantities and imports) that were determined by specific institutional settings. For instance, adjustment in those sectors that produce goods and services to be sold in domestic markets (such as agriculture, manufacturing, construction or services) follow completely different patterns compared to market adjustment in export sectors such as hydrocarbons and mining. The following market adjustment patterns have been identified over the last two and a half decades:

(a) The agricultural sector supply in Bolivia, has been quite dependent on weather conditions and has tended to be inelastic in the short term; thus, adjustment in this sector has mostly taken place through price changes.
(b) In the mining sector, producers were international price takers, and export supply depended mostly on past investment.
(c) The hydrocarbons sector showed two different adjustment rules. Export price and quantities were determined through sell contracts of natural gas, which were periodically revised depending on demand condition changes of Bolivia's main customer, Argentina. Domestic sales of hydrocarbons (refined oil products) depended on supply and demand growth; domestic prices were administratively determined, very often based on fiscal objectives.
(d) Manufacturing presented a more elastic supply in the short term. However, supply depended on imported inputs; thus, a foreign exchange constraint situation sometimes limited supply responses to changes in demand. Prices in this sector were determined following the mark-up rule.
(e) Construction has been more responsive to investment demand, mainly by households and by the government. Supply responses have also been elastic in the short term with supply less dependent on imported inputs.
(f) Services output mostly depended on demand conditions.

Second, from the discussion carried-out in the different chapters of the book, it is clear that the different socioeconomic agents of the economy reacted to shocks and policy interventions in quite different ways. These uneven responses to shocks and policies, and the interactions among agents through the different markets of the economy in which they operate, bring about a particular adjustment pattern at the macroeconomic level. The following general patterns were observed:

(a) Poor households' production activities (that is, rural peasants and urban informal) mostly responded to subsistence objectives. They operated in competitive markets, where price adjustments dominated. Households' access to bank credit was constrained by banks' credit rationing behaviour, or lack of collateral. Thus, households' investment was constrained by their own savings.

(b) Companies' production activities were mostly guided by objectives of profit or market share maximization. Very often they enjoyed an oligopolistic position in the markets in which they operated and thus were able to determine prices following the mark-up rule. Companies' access to bank credit was facilitated by personal contacts or because companies or banks belonged to the same economic group.

(c) Development objectives determined government and public enterprises' actions. The public sector investment projects to promote development were financed at different periods of time through foreign credits from international financial creditors. When foreign finance was lacking, the public sector resorted to domestic finance, either from the Central Bank or from the private sector. Each of these alternative sources of finance embodied different costs for the economy at the macro level.

(d) The financial institutions lent mostly to companies and to the government. The domestic banking system exhibited an oligopolistic structure, where a few large banks dominate in terms of the taking of deposits and provision of loans. The lack of competition kept interest rates at very high levels after financial liberalization.

Third, discussion in this book also demonstrated that the adjustment rules for the different social groups and institutions did not remain constant but rather changed over time, depending on the changes in the institutional settings and international conditions that govern adjustment:

(a) During the 1970s, a positive shock of export and capital inflows boosted economic activity and employment fuelled by government investment. The public sector acquired a large external debt while the private sector accumulated a large amount of financial assets abroad.

(b) During the first half of the 1980s, capital inflows ceased and government financed its increased deficits through Central Bank credit. The outcome was hyperinflation and a profound economic crisis in the formal sector of the economy. Additionally, the private sector started to receive large amounts of external resources through the drug trade, which, during the 1980s, became the booming sector of the economy.

(c) After the 1985 stabilization programme, government expenditures adjusted to fundable levels and inflation was controlled. The policies included the liberalization of domestic prices, foreign trade and the financial system. The fiscal deficit was reduced but not completely eliminated. Excess liquidity resulting from the deficit was sterilized through open market operations, which prevented further reductions in the interest rate. The private sector reacted to the high interest rates by repatriating deposits; as a result, domestic bank deposits and international reserves increased sharply.

(d) The structural reforms introduced after 1993 are expected to change substantially the adjustment rules of the different social groups and institutions. The reforms included the capitalization (privatization) of public enterprises, Central Bank autonomy, pension reform, decentralization of public expenditures, and education reform. The capitalization process is expected to bring about a large increase in foreign investment inflows, while greater Central Bank autonomy will reduce public sector access to domestic credit.

We can confidently argue that the approach presented in this book has succeeded in overcoming the limitations of the leading theoretical approaches in several ways:

The analytical framework developed here for the study of macroeconomic and sectoral adjustment included considerable disaggregation of the productive sector (including the informal sector), of socioeconomic groups and institutions, and of the financial sector. This framework was developed through the following steps:

(a) The first step was to identify the stylized facts of the individual accumulation balance behaviour for all the relevant sectors (productive activities, economic agents and institutions, financial institutions and the external sector). That was carried out through a detailed discussion of the most relevant economic events that occurred in Bolivia over the last two decades at the sectoral level.

First, the most important adjusting mechanisms in the supply-demand balance for each productive activity were identified in light of the sectoral behaviours observed over the last two decades (such as prices, output, competitive imports and exports). These mechanisms were later formalized in the construction of individual microeconomic models for each productive sector.

Second, key institutional factors that determine adjustment in the accumulation balance for each socioeconomic group and institution were identified based on the analysis of the events observed. Relevant closures were recognized in the accumulation balance for each agent (such as saving-investment, access to credit and portfolio decisions). These mechanisms were later incorporated into individual behavioural microeconomic models for each agent.

Third, the ways in which the financial institutions adjusted to the external shocks over the last two decades were analysed in detail. The stylized facts identified were later utilized to define adjustment rules, closures and behavioural equations for the variables included within the balance for each financial institution. These stylized facts were later included in the microeconomic models of the financial institutions.

Fourth, the same approach was followed to model the balance adjustment for the external sector. The modelling of the external sector was important because the variables identified as closures in this balance were also the closing variables of the whole system at the macroeconomic level (such as the parallel foreign exchange rate, foreign reserves and import capacity). Therefore, the degrees of freedom in the selection of this balance's closures were limited in that they had to be consistent with the closures already specified and defined within the balances for all other sectors.

(b) A more disaggregated framework was constructed. Initially, it was analytically developed in algebraic terms, using a reduced SAM-based model with some disaggregations of the productive sector and of socioeconomic groups. The reduced model was used to trace the shocks and adjustments that occurred in Bolivia during three separate periods: 1970s, 1980–85 and 1985–89. The alternative adjustment mechanisms for each period were clearly specified within the consistent and integrated framework provided by the reduced-SAM model.

The reduced-SAM model helped to clarify the differences in the adjustment behaviour of the agents; the changing nature of the rules that conditioned sectoral adjustment over time; and confirmed the value of adopting a disaggregated approach to the study of macroeconomic adjustment in an LDC.

(c) All the sectoral microeconomic models developed were then integrated within the RF-CGE model. The CGE framework helped to consolidate the individual sectoral-models within a single and consistent macroeconomic system.

(d) The RF-CGE model was utilized to test the macroeconomic effects of different external shocks and policy packages. The shocks tested were: (i) a reduction in the country's terms of trade; (ii) an increase in the real international interest rate; and (iii) a reduction in the level of capital inflows. Orthodox and heterodox policy alternatives were introduced in response to the shocks. The relative effectiveness of these policies was judged in terms of the five macroeconomic objectives: growth, income distribution, inflation, employment and the balance of payments.

The results of the simulations showed that neither of the policy alternatives applied succeeded in reversing the negative effects of the shocks. However, the orthodox policies produced better results in terms of achieving external equilibrium and price stability, while the heterodox policies performed better in terms of improving economic activity and income distribution.

(e) The model was also used to test the impact of a large increase in foreign investment inflows to the country. These increased inflows result from the investment commitments made by the strategic investors when the public enterprises were capitalized. The results obtained are quite illuminating. Larger investment inflows will succeed in increasing the overall growth rate of the economy. Growth, however, will be unbalanced, as investment flows will promote growth in the formal sector of the economy, controlled by large incorporated national and foreign companies, including the capitalized public firms. Thus, those sectors where incorporated firms have a large share in production and investment (such as hydrocarbons and modern services) will show the fastest growth rates, while in those sectors dominated by small-scale firms, growth will fall behind. This uneven growth pattern of the incorporated and unincorporated activities will also diminish the performance of the economy as a whole.

Additionally, the model was used to test the impact of the increased investment inflows, when they were accompanied by specific policies aimed at increasing productivity of unincorporated firms. The results obtained show that this complementary policy will eliminate growth differentials between sectors by substantially raising growth in the informal sector. This will increase the overall output growth rate of the economy, given the large share that unincorporated firms have in output and employment in Bolivia.

Several aspects can be highlighted to demonstrate the usefulness of the model constructed in this research.

(a) The 1995 SAM-based RF-CGE model proved to be an ideal tool for the specific purposes of this research. It represented a perfect device for modelling sectoral microeconomic behaviours within a consistent and integrated macroeconomic framework. The accounting structure of the 1995 SAM provided separate, detailed accumulation balances for each economic agent. The balances greatly facilitated the construction of separate sectoral behavioural models for all agents, always maintaining consistency at the macroeconomic level.

By making the accumulation behaviours of the various socioeconomic groups and institutions the focus of the analysis, it was much easier to identify the linkages existing among the processes of production, factor and institutional income distributions, saving-investment decisions and the financial and external sectors. Thus, income distribution became a paramount factor in the process of macroeconomic adjustment.

First, each agent's capacity to generate income was linked to a particular productive activity (peasants to traditional agriculture, companies to export activities, and so on). As a result, the differentiated abilities of these groups to control commodity market adjustments were modelled more straightforwardly in the supply demand balance for each activity.

Second, the linkages between the factor and institutional income distribution processes made the current incomes of each of the groups institutionally dependent on their relative endowments of factors of production. Thus, the structural institutional factors (namely the distribution of wealth among groups) that determine income distribution were fully reflected in the model.

Third, by bringing into the system an integrated financial sector, the modelling of accumulation decisions by individual groups was greatly enhanced. The individual saving-investment decisions of each group were modelled in terms of portfolio decisions. Each agent could choose among different assets (physical capital, domestic financial and external financial assets), but subject to different sets of constraints (for example, credit rationing for peasants and lower-income households).

(b) The inclusion of a proper financial sector in the model also represented an attempt to fill a gap left in other modelling experiences. As Rosensweig and Taylor (1990, p.330) point out, 'Aside from … several models for developing countries which do flow-of-funds calculations posterior to the real solution, there seem to be few examples in the literature of computable models that integrate markets for goods and assets'.

The inclusion of a complete financial sector within the RF-CGE model, in the form undertaken here, helped to clarify various macroeconomic phenomena that had not been properly understood.

First, by including full accounting matrices for asset stocks at the beginning and end of each period, it was possible to trace the asset-liability positions of individual agents during the adjustment process. The ways in which external shocks affect the wealth positions of groups were also clearly identified and the effects of each agent's portfolio decisions on the direction of the adjustment made explicit. For instance, the fact that capital flight was included as a portfolio choice open to upper-income households tended to produce a constant drain on the availability of savings and foreign exchange to finance investment in physical capital; as a result, some sectors had to adjust their investments due to lack of finance (poor households, for example) or due to lack of foreign exchange (companies and the government, for example).

Second, the inclusion of asset stock revaluations allowed portfolio changes to be split into those due to actual flows and those due to revaluations of existing assets. This helped to capture the wealth transfers among groups due to differentials in each of the agents' portfolio revaluations.

(c) The RF-CGE model also has clear advantages over other analytical frameworks constructed for studying macroeconomic adjustment in Bolivia. Although UDAPE has widely utilized CGE models to analyse different issues (see UDAPE 1990a, b), these models did not include the financial part of the economy; thus they did not incorporate differentiated accumulation behaviours for the various social groups and institutions. Savings decisions were differentiated only in terms of average savings propensities, while investment decisions were not differentiated at all.

In the analysis of macroeconomic adjustment in Bolivia, the RF-CGE model helped to bring together issues such as income distribution and poverty, market controls, the informal sector, financial market segmentation, the 'dollarization' of the financial system, the parallel foreign exchange market and capital flight. Although these issues have been addressed by many observers, they have never been analysed within an integrated and consistent micro-macro framework.

The sectoral disaggregation included in the RF-CGE model, both in its financial and non-financial sectors, allows all of these phenomena to be captured by incorporating a wide variety of sectoral adjusting mechanisms that come into operation after a shock or policy is introduced into the system. These mechanisms come into operation at different stages in the adjustment process.

First, income distribution played a key role in bringing adjustment to the system. The model simulations put into evidence the large disparities in sectoral output and price behaviours during the adjustment, as the effects of the shocks and policy interventions tended to work their way through the economy along different channels. The differentiated sectoral closures introduced into the model were very easily followed, and proved to be essential in explaining macroeconomic adjustment. For example, changes in mining, hydrocarbons and modern agricultural output were closely associated with changes in exports; on the other hand, construction sector output was more closely correlated with investment, while the output of the manufacturing and modern services sectors responded mostly to changes in domestic consumption.

Because the incomes of different socioeconomic groups were explicitly associated with particular productive activities, the roles played by different sectoral price and output behaviours in determining income distribution and adjustment were also clearly identified throughout the model simulations.

Second, the informal sector was explicitly identified within the 1995 SAM framework, and its specific behavioural rules were incorporated into the RF-CGE model. The linkages between the formal and informal sectors were clearly identified, in terms of both financial and non-financial flows.

Third, the segmented nature of the Bolivian financial system was captured by imposing credit rationing on some sectors (specifically on poor households) and by allowing other sectors to have a preferential access to financial credit (for example, companies and upper-income households).

Fourth, the impact of the ever-increasing degree of 'dollarization' of the Bolivian financial system was well captured by the explicit modelling of asset stock revaluations. Thus, agents with more power to protect their assets against inflation would benefit the most from changes in the price of the key asset of the Bolivian economy: the US dollar.

(d) The RF-CGE model also demonstrated the importance of having an analytical framework that allows the comparison of orthodox and heterodox policies in a single model frame against multiple criteria. The relevance of such a framework is evident for future policy studies, as the effectiveness of individual policy tools can be assessed and thus an optimal policy mix can be derived.

(e) Finally, there are some implications for future research. This book has covered almost every area of the Bolivian economy; thus the analytical and empirical rigour of the individual sectoral models was sometimes not as high as desired. Therefore, the sectoral models included within the RF-CGE model can be greatly improved at the microeconomic level. Further, research on the accumulation behaviour of the various economic agents could greatly contribute to a better understanding of the institutional factors that govern the adjustments for individual agents.

The results obtained through the simulations were demonstrated to be quite consistent with what was observed in reality. This obviously highlights the potential of the model in the evaluation of more concrete policy packages and long-term economic strategies; the possibilities for manipulating policy variables and external shocks within the model are countless. Although the RF-CGE model was utilized here to analyse external shocks, macroeconomic adjustment, stabilization policies, and structural reforms, the framework created can also be utilized in the analysis of a wide range of phenomena that link micro-macro behaviours.

Appendix A
A Social Accounting Matrix for Bolivia

A.1 Introduction

The reduced-SAM model presented in Chapter 6 has been demonstrated to provide a better analytical framework than aggregated theoretical models for understanding macroeconomic adjustment in developing countries. That framework is still too aggregated, however, in that it hides some institutional characteristics that could further enhance macroeconomic analysis. In this appendix an additional step is made to construct a more disaggregated analytical framework. It summarizes the main characteristics of a detailed social accounting matrix for the Bolivian economy (1995 SAM) with a considerable disaggregation of the productive sector, including the informal sector, and socioeconomic groups. Eventually the 1995 SAM will provide a database for the construction of the Real Financial (RF) computatable general equilibrium (CGE) model for Bolivia, focusing on the financial behaviour of these sectors and groups. This model was used in simulation exercises that show in detail how the various sectors and groups in the Bolivian economy react to external shocks and domestic policy.

The SAM describes in a consistent and coherent manner the channels through which the process of production is interrelated with the processes of income distribution, consumption, saving, accumulation and foreign trade. Moreover, the mechanisms through which financial resources are transferred from surplus to deficit sectors can also be monitored if a detailed flow of funds subsystem is compiled and incorporated into the SAM analysis.

The SAM constructed as part of this research describes, the real and monetary balances of the economy, which present a very detailed ex-post macroeconomic equilibrium.

Aspects such as the overall design of the system, data sources utilized, base year chosen, and the final results obtained are discussed and presented in this appendix.

A.2 General Relationships between the Reduced-SAM and the 1995 SAM

The RF-CGE model is not only a highly disaggregated version of the reduced-SAM model, but also comprises other features that were not included within the reduced version in a deliberate attempt to simplify the exposition in Chapter 6. This section explains the most important adjustments introduced in the reduced-SAM of Chapter 6 in order to obtain the 1995 SAM presented in this chapter, the latest being the basic framework of the RF-CGE model.

(a) Within the reduced-SAM model, the accumulation balance closures were discussed in terms of flows. In the 1995 SAM, and later within the RF-CGE model, financial balances are expressed in terms of stocks. There are at least two justifications for the utilization of the stock approach:

First, there is the argument that in economic theory the demand for financial stocks is conceptualized in terms of stocks rather than flows. This argument is based on Tobin's analytical framework of macroeconomics and monetary theory (Tobin 1982) and is grounded in the integration of savings and portfolio decisions. Tobin specifies accumulation functions for particular assets which add up to total liability and wealth accumulation for the period. The markets which determine asset and liability prices, and the interest rates, coordinate these demand flows with the supply flows arising from real investment, the government deficit, and the external current account. The markets handle simultaneously flows arising from savings and accumulation, and those arising from the reshuffling of portfolios, both by private agents on the demand side and by the monetary authorities on the supply side. By the end of the period, simultaneously with the determination of the asset and liability prices for the period, these market participants have the stock of assets, liabilities and of the total wealth they desire at prevailing prices at that time.

An essential part of Tobin's analytical framework is therefore the relation between the dynamics of flows and stocks. According to this concept, there is a close relationship between investment and capital, savings and wealth, specific forms of savings and asset stocks. Consequently, according to Tobin, '… It is not generally defensible to ignore these relations on the excuse that the analysis refers to so short a time that stocks cannot change significantly'.

The second argument for using 'stocks' in the analysis of financial balance closures is related to the fact that within the stock approach it is possible to include not only the flows that close the sectoral balances but also the effect that the revaluation of existing stocks has on the different institutions' asset, liability and wealth positions. This is particularly important in understanding adjustment in a highly inflationary or in a highly indexed economy, which was the case in Bolivia during the 1970s, 1980–85 and 1985–96.

(b) The 1995 SAM presents a more disaggregated framework than the reduced-SAM. The main disaggregations undertaken are as follows.

First, production accounts, which are disaggregated into formal and informal activities within the reduced-SAM model, are further disaggregated into eleven sectors. In general, the 1995 SAM sectors that can be classified as 'formal' are modern agriculture, mining, oil and gas, manufacturing, electricity, construction, modern services and public services. On the other hand, traditional agriculture, coca and informal services can be regarded as informal activities.

The way in which the National Accounts' categories have been matched to each of the SAM categories is as follows:

Agricultural sector. In Bolivian National Accounts statistics, agriculture, livestock, forestry, fishing and hunting activities are grouped according to the International Standard Industrial Classification of All Economic Activities (ISIC; United Nations 1968).

Coca. The coca sector comprises both the traditional harvest of coca leaves (including that for customary local consumption) and the illicit production and export of coca by-products as part of the illegal international drug trade.[1]

Mining and basic metals. Following standard SNA conventions, the Bolivian National Accounts Office explicitly keeps separate records for the value added, intermediate consumption and gross output for both mining activities and the manufacturing of basic metals. Basic metal activities are eventually grouped within the manufacturing sector (major division 3 ISIC).

Oil and gas. National accounts separate the value added generated in the production of natural gas and crude petroleum from that generated in the refining of hydrocarbons (the latter is now included in the manufacturing sector: major division 3 ISIC). Given the characteristics of this sector, updated data on the value and quantity produced are highly reliable and easily available.

Manufacturing. The SAM 'manufacturing' category includes the following SNA activities: fresh and processed meat; dairy products; grain mills and bakeries; other food manufactures; beverages; tobacco; textiles, clothing, and leather products; wood and wood products; paper and paper products; chemical products; non-metallic minerals; machinery and equipment; and other manufactures.[2]

Construction. This sector corresponds to the SNA category 'construction and public works' (major division 5 ISIC).

Services. Although services accounted for 46 per cent of GDP in 1989, data for this sector are amongst the weakest. Although there are indicators on activity changes for some services (transport, communications, financial), they only cover those activities that operate in the formal sector of the economy.

The SNA includes separate records for the following services: commerce; transport and storage; communications; finance, insurance and business services; ownership of dwellings; and community, social and personal services.

From the SAM perspective, this wide variety of services have been grouped in two categories: (a) modern services, which include all activities that have a capitalist form of organization and are profit-oriented; and (b) informal services, which include all activities that provide a subsistence alternative to a large number of unskilled unemployed workers in urban areas (Kritz 1986; Casanovas 1989).

The SNA categories directly considered as 'modern' are: transport and storage; communications; financial services; services to firms; ownership of dwellings; community, social and personal services. Domestic services, part of commerce, and part of transport are directly grouped as 'informal'.

Second, the 1995 SAM includes the following socioeconomic groups:

(i) Households comprise all household categories analysed in chapter 5, including rich and poor households in the urban areas, and peasant households in the rural areas.

(ii) Companies comprise large- and medium-scale privately owned firms (more than five workers) that use relatively modern technology and forms of organization.

(iii) The government comprises the central government, local and regional governments, regional development corporations, universities and the social security system.

(iv) Public enterprises or state-owned corporations operate in several sectors of the economy such as mining (COMIBOL, ENAF), hydrocarbons (YPFB), transport (LAB, ENFE) and communications (ENTEL).

(v) Rest of the world comprises all other countries that maintain economic relations with Bolivia.

(vi) Financial institutions. Separate accounts have been opened for each of the financial institutions incorporated in the SAM analysis: the Central Bank of Bolivia and commercial banks. This latest category includes private commercial banks, both national and foreign.

A.3 Data Sources

Although the quality of statistics in Bolivia has improved substantially over the last decade, nevertheless, in their present state the construction of a social accounting matrix remains a very difficult task. Whereas some important efforts have been made to improve statistics in some sectors (namely fiscal, monetary, balance of payments and external debt statistics), there has been a deterioration in the flow of information from other sectors. Neither has the quality of statistics on national income and components of national expenditure improved. Moreover, the methodology used to compile the available estimates has remained the same, despite changes in the inter-sectoral dependences, cost structures, and final demand patterns. In the estimation of the gross domestic product, less than half of the value added is estimated directly, while the rest either is assumed to grow at a trend rate or is estimated endogenously in a Leontieff-type model (INE 1990). Value added in construction is calculated as a multiple of the value of certain material inputs, while investment is derived largely as the value of output of construction plus a proportion of the c.i.f. value of imported machinery and equipment. Even estimates of output of major crops are suspect, because reliable estimates of areas planted are not available for potatoes, maize and wheat crops (let alone coca crops). In several instances, domestic consumption in real terms is derived from estimates of constant per capita consumption obtained several years earlier, despite significant increases in the prices of consumer commodities over the years. Estimates of the changes of inventories are simply not available for most commodities. Despite the overwhelming concern with unemployment, statistics on employment are dubious. Therefore, the general unreliability of the Bolivian statistics was a problem to be aware of during the construction of the SAM.

However, the degree of unreliability of the data sources utilized was not consistent, as will be explained in more detail later. Some sources were considered as relatively more reliable. Public sector operations, for instance, are recorded rather accurately. These figures were thus incorporated in the SAM with some degree of confidence.

Since the data used in the construction of the 1995 SAM were obtained from different sources,[3] there were very often data problems such as lack of comparability between concepts, definitions, sampling methods, and valuations, making reconciliation difficult. Stone (1977) highlights that

> ... in order to deal with the problem of reconciliation, a view has to be taken of the reliability of the different data sources. Accepting that the more reliable sources are accurate, an attempt has to be made to meet the arithmetic and accounting constraints of the SAM by adjusting the estimates contained in what are deemed to be the less reliable sources. Since it may prove impossible to do this in a plausible way, it is necessary to reconsider the supposedly reliable sources. In practice, a certain amount of iterations between earlier and later stages cannot be avoided. However, the aim remains the same throughout, namely to adjust what are believed to be weaker estimates and preserve as far as possible those believed to be the stronger.

This method requires a great deal of information and judgement.[4] Besides, it mostly features cases where there is excess data and alternative sources provide conflicting estimates of the same items. In the construction of the Bolivian SAM the problems arose mainly from the lack of data. Nevertheless, the sources used were:

(a) National Accounts (INE 1996, 1997)
(b) Continuing Survey of Households (INE 1995)
(c) Wage Statistics (INE 1997)
(d) Non-Financial Public Sector Operations (UDAPE 1997a)
(e) Statistical Bulletin (BCB a; various issues)
(f) External Sector Bulletin (BCB b; various issues)
(g) Statistics on Taxation by Economic Sector and Income Category in 1995 (UDAPE 1997a)
(h) Central Bank Balances (BCB c; various issues)

A.4 Overall Design of the System and Numeric Results

The overall design of the 1995 SAM is presented in Table A1.

The first column of the matrix shows the components of domestic supply: intermediate consumption and factor value added (including indirect taxes received by government). The numeric results of this part of the matrix are presented in Table A2.

The second column of the schematic SAM shows how factor income is redistributed among the various institutional economic agents (households, companies, public enterprises, and the rest of the world), according to their respective factor endowments. The third column of the schematic SAM shows the uses that the institutional economic agents give to their factor income. Part of it is consumed, part is redistributed among the institutional agents themselves, and the remainder is saved. The numerical results of both the factor income distribution and the uses given to those incomes are presented in Table A3.

The last column of the schematic SAM presents the financial and physical accumulation of the institutional agents. The 1995 SAM has been constructed based on the concept of sources and uses of funds, according to which each economic agent, at any moment, balances total sources of funds (liabilities plus net wealth) and total uses of funds (assets).

Total uses of funds = Total sources of funds

Total assets = Total liabilities + net wealth

An increase in the stock value of any asset held by a particular economic agent has to be compensated (financed) by a reduction in the stock value of one or more of its remaining assets, an increase in the stock value of one or more of its liabilities, or an increase in its net wealth.

A number of factors can bring about changes in the stock value of assets, liabilities and the net wealth of an economic agent:

(i) The stock value of assets and liabilities may change due to either the acquisition of a new financial asset/liability by the agent (flow of funds), as when the Central Bank increases its reserves through foreign exchange operations; or to a change in the price of an asset/liability held by the agent (asset revaluation), as when the Central Bank increases the value of its foreign exchange reserves expressed in local currency, due to changes in the foreign exchange rate. The total change in the stock value of a particular asset or liability can therefore be expressed as:

$$\Delta ASV = P_t.A_t - P_{t-1}.A_{t-1} \qquad (A.1)$$

This expression can be rearranged as:

$$\Delta ASV = P_t.(A_t - A_{t-1}) + (P_t - P_{t-1}).A_{t-1} \quad (A.2)$$

where:

ΔASV = Total change in the stock value of an asset
A_{t-1} = Initial asset stock
A_t = Final asset stock
P_{t-1} = Initial asset price
P_t = Final asset price

The right-hand side of equation (A.2), $P_t.(A_t - A_{t-1})$, represents net asset acquisition, while $(P_t - P_{t-1}).A_{t-1}$ represents the net asset revaluation due to changes in the price of the asset.[5]

(ii) Changes in net wealth arise from savings generated during a particular period plus net wealth gains (losses) due to changes in the prices of assets/liabilities. Net wealth gains are the difference between total asset and total liability revaluations.

(iii) Finally, increases in the fixed capital stock are the result of gross investment, and reductions are the result of depreciation of existing capital stock during the period.

The schematic matrix captures the above mechanisms. Row 1 shows the initial asset portfolios held by various economic agents (companies, households, government and state enterprises (public sector), the rest of the world and financial institutions). The last row presents the agents' final asset portfolios. The differences between the first and last rows are entirely explained by the rows in between: the agents' gross investments (row 2), their net asset acquisitions (row 5) and asset stock revaluations due to price changes at the beginning of the period (row 6). The numerical results of this part of the matrix are presented in Table A4.

Table A.1 *Schematic SAM*

				Institutions	
		Activities	Factors of Production	Current Account Transactions	Capital Account Transactions
INST	Stocks of Assets-Liabilities				Beginning of the period
	Activities	Input-output		Consumption-exports	Investment
	Factors of Production	Income distribution to factors			
INSTITUTIONS	Current Account Transactions		Income distribution to institutions	Secondary distribution of income	
	Capital Account Transactions			Savings	Flow of funds
	Revaluation of Assets				Revaluation
	Stocks of Assets-Liabilities				End of the period

Table A.2 *Social Accounting Matrix for Bolivia – 1995, Input-Output, Income Distribution, Taxes, and Imports (in millions of bolivianos)*

		AG *11*	CC *12*	MN *13*	HD *14*	MF *15*	CN *16*	MS *17*	IS *18*	TOTAL	Imp. Goods *19*	TOTAL	
Agriculture	*11*	567		21		2 448	42	131	39	3 250		5 740	*11*
Coca	*12*											304	*12*
Mining	*13*			394	7	231	130	1		766		2 696	*13*
Hydrocarbons	*14*	30		62	839	211	14	1 218	4	2 382		3 468	*14*
Manufacturing	*15*	191	4	73	20	1 532	571	1 681	328	4 403		13 070	*15*
Construction	*16*			1	2	3		36	86	130		2 625	*16*
Modern Services	*17*	548	3	309	442	1 895	279	4 861	345	8 685		22 143	*17*
Informal Services	*18*	11		1	9	79	4	419	27	553		3 932	*18*
Total		1 350	8	864	1 321	6 402	1 042	8 349	832	20 172		53 981	
Imports	*19*	225	12	233	89	1 746	433	997	175	3 913		9 683	*19*
TOTAL		1 575	21	1 098	1 411	8 149	1 475	9 346	1 007	24 085		63 664	
Wages	*20*	568	149	288	257	1 731	483	7 291	808	11 577		11 616	*20*
Profits	*21*	3 578	133	1 229	1 099	2 759	460	4 962	1 962	16 186			
Non-corporate	*22*	3 454	133	821		2 008	308	4 201	1 962	12 890		12 890	*21*
Corporate	*23*	123		408	1 099	750	152	761		3 296		3 296	22
TOTAL		4 146	282	1 518	1 357	4 490	943	12 254	2 771	27 764		27 803	
Households	*23*											28 448	*23*
Companies	*24*											4 262	*24*
Public Firms	*25*											2 704	*25*
Government	*26*	18		79	699	430	206	542	153	2 130	1 411	6 696	*26*
Rest of the World	*27*										8 271	9 450	*27*

Table A.3 *Social Accounting Matrix for Bolivia – 1995, Income, Consumption, Exports, and Savings (in millions of bolivianos)*

		Wages 20	Non-corporate 21	Corporate 22	TOTAL	HH 23	Companies 24	Public Ent. 25	Government 26	RoW 27	TOTAL	
Agriculture	*11*					1 749				640	5 740	*11*
Coca	*12*					36				266	304	*12*
Mining	*13*									1 852	2 696	*13*
Hydrocarbons	*14*					403				714	3 468	*14*
Manufacturing	*15*					7 031				1 581	13 070	*15*
Construction	*16*										2 625	*16*
Modern Services	*17*					7 941			4 097	1 293	22 143	*17*
Informal Services	*18*					3 374				4	3 932	*18*
Total						20 536			4 097	6 352	53 981	
Imports	*19*					3 935					9 683	*19*
TOTAL						24 472				6 352	63 664	
Wages	20									38	11 616	20
Profits												
Non-corporate	21										12 890	21
Corporate	22										3 296	22
TOTAL										38	27 803	
Households	23	11 569	12 890		24 459		2 869		638	481	28 448	23
Companies	24			1 697	1 697	1 951		93	275	244	4 262	24
Public Firms	25			1 598	1 598	361	460		283		2 704	25
Government	26					981	632	1 539			6 696	26
Rest of the World	27	47			47	45	144	294	647		9 450	27
Stock Changes	28										-139	28
Households	29					635					1 028	29
Companies	30						155				1 674	30
Public Firms	31							776			590	31
Government	32								754		1 894	32
Central Bank	33										259	33
Private Banks	34										1 376	34
Rest of the World	36									2 333	3 477	36
TOTAL						635	155	776	754	2 333	10 301	

Table A.4 *Social Accounting Matrix for Bolivia – 1995, Initial Stocks, Investment, Flow of Funds, and Stock Changes (in millions of bolivianos)*

		S.Ch.	HH	Comp.	Pub. Ent.	Gov.	Cent.Bank	Prv.Banks	RoW	Liabilities	Net Wealth	TOTAL	
		28	29	30	31	32	33	34	36		37		
Households	1							4 830		4 830	25 699	30 529	1
Companies	2		5 464					9 315	2 668	17 447	9 035	26 482	2
State Firms	3			2 176			407		3 322	5 906	8 990	14 897	3
Government	4			1 522			4 504		15 029	21 057	-8 328	12 728	4
Central Bank	5		1 436	904	473	3 167		1 410	3 612	11 004	193	11 197	5
Private Banks	6		7 253	3 054		229	2 512		356	13 405	2 370	15 776	6
Rest of the World	8		2 240	774			3 772	220		7 007	17 980	24 988	8
Physical Capital	9		14 135	18 049	14 423	9 331						55 939	9
TOTAL			30 529	26 482	14 897	12 728	11 197	15 776	24 988	80 658	55 939	192 538	
Agriculture	11	27	10	23		38						73	11
Coca	12												12
Mining	13	77											13
Hydrocarbons	14	-31											14
Manufacturing	15	-24	5	58	3	11						79	15
Construction	16		413	325	266	1 490						2 495	16
Modern Services	17	-106	40	111	39	39						231	17
Informal Services	18												18
Total		-57	470	518	310	1 580						2 879	
Imports	19	-81	279	879	384	371						1 915	19
TOTAL		-139	750	1 398	694	1 951						4 795	
Stock Changes	28		-42	-96								-139	28
Households	29							392		392	635	1 028	29
Companies	30		-413					383	1 548	1 518	155	1 674	30
Public Firms	31			-20			-302		137	-186	776	590	31
Government	32			486			–370		1 024	1 139	754	1 894	32
Central Bank	33		298	-810	-71	492		290	218	417	-158	259	33
Private Banks	34		272	170		-50	276		549	1 218	158	1 376	34
Rest of the World	36		162	547			656	310		1 677	1 800	3 477	36
TOTAL			1 028	1 674	590	1 894	259	1 376	3 477	6 177	4 123	10 301	

Notes

1. Three stages can be identified in the processing of coca leaf into cocaine products: Paste, base and hydrochloride (US Embassy 1990; UDAPE 1990b).

2. In the 1989 SAM, the production of basic metals and refinery were grouped together with mining, and oil and gas activities, respectively. In the SNA, however, they belong to the manufacturing sector (major division 3 ISIC).

3. From a statistical point of view, in principle all available socioeconomic statistics can (and in fact should) be used in the construction of a SAM, as long as they meet two requirements (Keuning and de Ruijter 1991): the information should cover a year close to the SAM base year; and it must be possible to classify the raw data in accordance with the taxonomies applied in the SAM.

4. Since this method represents an attempt to use subjective judgements about the reliability of initial estimates, Stone (1977, p.xxi) has proposed a formal mathematical treatment for handling inconsistent data.

5. Not all assets have the same capacity to maintain their value against inflation. Currency, for instance, is not indexed to price changes, so that when prices are increasing it presents a loss to those holding currency and a gain to the Central Bank, the issuerof currency. Foreign exchange, on the other hand, can maintain its value in as much as foreign exchange is devalued. The different capacities of assets to maintain their value against inflation bring about transfers of wealth among the different economic agents holding them.In Bolivia, economic agents take the exchange rate as a key indicator of changes in asset values. All types of assets are increasingly being indexed to the foreign exchange rate. Bank deposits are expressed in foreign currency, and the value of physical capital in company balance sheets are corrected from year to year using the rate of foreign exchange rate devaluation. Therefore, in the financial SAM, the wealth shifts among economic agents can be traced if assets are grouped according to their degree of indexation to the price of the dollar.

Appendix B
The Real Financial CGE Model for Bolivia

B.1 General Characteristics of CGE Models

General equilibrium models have a long history dating back to Walras, who, around 1875, formulated the economic system as a set of excess demand equations in as many unknown prices, for which a solution could be found via a successive price revision procedure.

In the literature on developing countries, CGE models represent an incremental step in a long tradition of work with multi-sectoral programming models (Devarajan et al. 1986). A CGE model incorporates the fundamental general equilibrium links among production structure, incomes of various groups and the pattern of demand. A CGE model works by simulating the interactions of these various economic agents across markets. Specific behavioural rules for individual agents are assumed and incorporated into the equations that describe them. The CGE framework requires a complete specification of both the supply and demand sides of all markets, including all the nominal magnitudes in the circular flow. The models are therefore structural in spirit, capturing the market mechanisms explicitly (Robinson 1987).

The SAM provides the underlying data framework for CGE models, with an income-expenditure account and an accumulation balance for each social agent included in the model. As discussed previously, however, the SAM gives a consistent picture of an ex-post equilibrium of variables whose nominal values appear in the cells. Since the SAM is only an accounting framework it does not describe the underlying technical or behavioural relationships between the cells, nor does it distinguish price from volume components of each cell. When complemented with information on volumes or prices, the SAM is a useful basis for modelling. Some functional relationships can be calculated directly from the SAM; for instance, the input-output coefficient can be calculated by dividing the value of an intermediate delivery by the column sum (total value of production) of a sector, and the expenditure shares can be calculated by dividing the total of consumption of a category by the total consumption (partial column sum) of a household group.

The use of the SAM for parameter calculation is restricted to linear relationships without constants. If fixed proportions between the value entries of the SAM cannot be assumed, data for other years are needed and the formation of prices corresponding to the cells is described.

A CGE model normally comprises the following components (Ginsburgh and Waelbroeck 1981):

The *socioeconomic actors* whose behaviour is to be analysed, such as households, companies, government, and rest of the world. A simple Walrasian model would include only producers and households.

Particular *behavioural rules* for each economic agent that reflect their assumed saving-investment behaviour. For example, investments by peasants and urban informal workers are savings-constrained, while those of capitalists and the government determine savings availability.

Agents make decisions based on the *signals* they observe. For example, in a Walrasian model, prices are the only signals agents need to know.

The *institutional structure* of the economy delineates the 'rules of the game' according to which the various agents interact.

The *equilibrium conditions* of the model are the *system constraints* that must be satisfied, but are not taken into account by any agent in making his decisions. Formally, an equilibrium can be defined as a set of signals such that the resulting decisions of all agents jointly satisfy the system constraints. The signals represent the equilibrating variables of the model. For example, a market equilibrium in a competitive model is defined as a set of prices and associated quantities such that all excess demands are zero. In a market economy, prices are the equilibrating variables that vary to achieve market clearing.

The definition of equilibrium conditions is a fundamental requirement of a model. The specification of equilibrating variables and of system constraints that characterize an equilibrium can be seen as a simplifying device that provides a way to describe the results of the workings of an actual economy (Robinson 1987, p.33). This implies that some variables must adjust in order to bring equilibrium to the model (model closure).

The definition of the system's closure is a fundamental property of a model. Distinct theoretical approaches tend to emphasize different variables as the most relevant in the economic adjustment process.

The description of actors' behavioural rules, institutional structure, signals, and system constraints apply to computable (CGE) as well as to applied general equilibrium models (AGE). CGE models are generally applied to analyse the effects of changes in parameters or exogenously determined variables. In contrast, in AGE modelling, as in programming models, one must also specify the form of the objective function.

B.2 The CGE Model for Bolivia

This section gives a detailed description of the main parts of the model, determining all variables which are endogenous, exogenous and parameters in the current period. The basic structure of the model is based on the accounting identities supplied by the SAM structure outlined in appendix A:

(i) supply-demand balances for all economic activities,
(ii) income generation and distribution system,
(iii) accumulation balances for all economic agents,
(iv) financial balances,
(v) external balance.

B.2.1 Basic characteristics of the model

The main characteristics of the CGE model for Bolivia are:

(a) In the productive sector there are five activities that have production functions: agriculture, coca, mining, hydrocarbons and modern services. Domestic prices in the agricultural sectors are flexible.

(b) The other three sectors (manufacturing, construction and informal services) are fix-price sectors (mark-up); excess demand in these markets is cleared through changes in output. Output adjustment however, only takes place until a maximum level of output has been reached. This maximum is determined by import capacity (foreign-exchange gap) or by the maximum supply of labour.

(c) The accumulation balance adjustment for households follows the 'prior-saving' approach. The level of investment and the accumulation of other financial assets adjust to the availability of funds that is determined exogenously to households. Households, however, can choose their portfolio structure following profitability criteria.

(d) Companies can decide on their level and structure of assets in the first place and finance may be secured later ('investment-leading-savings' approach). Companies can determine their asset portfolio as well as their structure of finance based on profitability differentials and on the cost of alternative sources of finance. The level of investment realized by companies can be constrained by the amount of foreign exchange available to import capital goods ('exchange gap') or by the total amount of finance made available to them ('budget constraint').

(e) Public enterprises and government can decide on their level of investment in physical and financial assets. Credit from the Central Bank will eventually act as the closure to their accumulation balances. Again, investment might be constrained by either the amount of foreign exchange available to import capital goods or by the total amount of finance they can obtain.

(f) Whereas companies, which enjoy preferential lending status, determine their own loans from private commercial banks, loans to households and public financial institutions are determined by the banks themselves based on profitability criteria. Finance is secured through deposits and through credit from the Central Bank, which eventually acts as the balance closure.

(g) As explained above, the Central Bank fulfils its customary functions of lender of last resort to the financial system. The ultimate sources of finance for an expansion of credit by the Central Bank are its own exchange reserves. In a foreign exchange constrain situation, however, import capacity and the emergence of a parallel foreign exchange act as overall closure for the model.

B.2.2 Basic notation

(i) Productive sectors:
- generic notation (i or j)
- individual notation: agriculture (AG), coca (CO), hydrocarbons (HD), mining (MN), manufacturing (MF), construction (CT) modern services (SM) and informal services (SI).

(ii) Factors of production:
- generic notation (f)
- individual notation: labour (LB), unincorporated profits (UP), corporate profits (CP).

(iii) Institutions:
- generic notation (k)
- individual notation: households (HH), unincorporated enterprises (UE), corporate enterprises (CE), public enterprises (SE) and government (GV).

(iv) Households:
- generic notation (h)

(v) Financial institutions:
- generic notation (k)
- individual notation: Central Bank (CB) and private financial institutions (PB).

vi) Rest of the World (RW).

B.3 Model's Equations

The model comprises 323 equations that solve 323 endogenous variables. The equations are:

B.3.1 Supply demand balances

$X_i \equiv XD_i + E_i$	Domestic output (X_i) is equal to domestic absorption (XD_i) plus exports (E_i). (for all productive sectors (a.p.s.) (8 equations)).
$XD_i \equiv \Sigma a_{i,j}.X_j + C_i + G_i + \Sigma\lambda_{i,k}.IR_k + \Delta SK_i$	Domestic absorption specification (for a.p.s. (8)).

$E_i = E_{i0}.(PE_i/P_i)\ \varepsilon i\ .\ X_i$	Exports are responsive to changes in relative prices. E_{i0} is the level of exports in the base year, ε_{i0} is the export to output ratio in the base year and ξ_i is the export elasticities) (for a.p.s. but CO, MN and HD (5)).

B.3.2 Price equations for all sectors

$P_j = (PD_j.XD_j + PE_j.E_j)/X_j$	Composite prices (for a.p.s. (8)).
$PE_j = e.PW_j$	Export prices (for a.p.s. (8)).
$PD_{MP} = e.PW_{MP}$	Domestic price of imports (1).
$PD_{MN} = PE_{MN}$	Domestic prices in the coca, hydrocarbons and mining sectors take after international prices (3).

B.3.3 Corporate and unincorporated capital

$KC = K_{CE} + K_{SE} + K_{GV}$	Corporate capital defined as that belonging to companies, state enterprises and government (1).
$KU = K_{HH} + K_{GV}$	Unincorporated capital is defined as that belonging to households. Government capital (e.g. infrastructure) has a crowding-in effect on households' production (1).

B.3.4 Output and price adjustment

There are two types of productive sectors in the model (sectors with production functions and mark-up sectors), each with their own adjustment rules.

In each of these categories of productive activities, different factors of production take part in the productive process: intermediate domestically-produced inputs, imported inputs (M), labour (L), corporate capital (KC) and unincorporated capital (KU). Each of these factors has its own 'price': input prices (PD_j), imported-input price ($e.PW_{MP}$), wage rate (w), profitability rate of corporate capital (rc_j) and profitability rate of corporate capital (ru_j).

The equation system defined for each of the sectors must solve output (X) and prices (P) for each commodity produced; and the prices for and quantities of each of the factors demanded. Some of the variables are determined outside the system, somewhere else in the model; in all cases, KC and KU are solved within the sectoral accumulation balances for the agents; the exchange rate (e) is a policy variable, the world prices for imported inputs (PW_{MP}) are exogenous variables and the wage rate is determined in the labour market (see section xx). The variables that are determined within the system of equations are: sectoral output and prices (X_j and P_j), the quantities of labour (L_j) and intermediate inputs (M_j) used, and the sectoral profitability of corporate (rc_j) and unincorporated (ru_j) capital.

B.3.4.1 Sectors with production functions

In the sectors with production functions, there are substitution possibilities among production factors. This is captured through a constant elasticity of substitution (CES) function. The CES comprises a consistent system of equations including the CES cost function and the individual demand functions for inputs which are derived by applying Shepard's lemma (cf. Varian 1984, 54–57), which states that factor input ratios are equal to the partial derivatives of the cost function.

In terms of the CGE-model discussed here, the CES cost function together with the demand functions discussed in section B.7.1, determine P_j and X_j; while the individual input demand functions determine ru_j, rc_j, L_j and M_j.

$$P_j = \{(1+txi_j).[\Sigma(PD_i/P_j^{\rho j}).a_{i,j} + ß_{CP,j}.(rc_j.P_j)^{1-\rho j} + ß_{UP,j}.(ru_j.P_j)^{1-\rho j} + ß_{LB,j}.(w)^{1-\rho j} + a_{MP,j}.(PD_{MP})^{1-\rho j}]\}^{1/(1-\rho j)}$$

CES cost functions for sectors with production functions (5).

$$KU= ß_{UP,j}.(ru_j)^{-\rho j}.X_j$$

Demand for unincorporated capital (where: $ß_{UP,j}$ is the share of unincorporated profits in sector j's total output, ru_j is the profitability of unincorporated capital in activity j, and ρ_j is the CES coefficient in sector j's production function) (5).

$KC = ß_{CP,j}.(rc_j)^{-\rho j}.X_j$	Demand for corporate capital in sector j (5).
$L_j = ß_{LB,j}.(w/PD_j)^{-\rho j}.X_j$	Demand for labour in sector j (5).
$M_j = a_{MP,j}.(PD_{MP}/PD_j)^{-\rho j}.X_j$	Demand for imported intermediate inputs in sector j (where $a_{MP,j}$ is the input-output coefficient for imported inputs in sector j) (5).
$\Gamma_j = (rc_j.KC + ru_j.KU)/(KC + KU)$	Profitability of total physical capital in sector j as a weighted average of ru_j and rc_j (5).
$(\tau_j/((1+\tau_j) = [\Gamma_j.(1+txi_j)].[(KU+KP)/X_j]$	Mark-up rate determination for sector j (5).

B.3.4.2 'Mark-up' sectors

Adjustment in the mark-up sectors, in principle, takes place through changes in the level of output (X_j); thus, prices are determined through the mark-up rule.

Output adjustment however cannot take place indefinitely. There is a maximum output level set by either the availability of foreign exchange to import intermediate inputs or by the total supply of labour. Once output has reached that maximum (X_j^{max}), further increases in demand will be matched by higher mark-ups.

In terms of the CGE-model discussed here, the conditioned output-price adjustment is captured by the first four equations listed below (the mark-up is also determined here). The other equations help to determine demand for labour and imports, plus total and sectoral physical capital profitability.

$P_j = (1+txi_j).(1+\tau_j).[\Sigma PD_i.a_{i,j} + w.b_j]$	Price functions for mark-up sectors (3).
$(Xj^{max} - X_j).(\tau_j - \tau_{0j}) = 0$	Output – mark-up determination (3).
$X_j \leq X_j^{max}$ and $\tau_j \geq \tau_{0j}$	Additional constraints to the previous equation.

$Xi^{max} = X0_i.(CM/CM0)$ — Maximum level of output for the mark-up sectors are set by the minimum bind between the 'exchange-gap' and the maximum labour supply; (where : CM0 and CM are respectively the capacity to import intermediate goods in the base year and during the current period; and CL0 and CL are the maximum labour supply available in the base year and in the current period) (3).

$L_j = \beta_{LB,j}.X_j$ — Demand for labour in sector j (3).

$M_j = a_{MP,j}.X_j$ — Demand for imported intermediate inputs (3).

$G_j = (\tau_j/((1+\tau_j).(1+txi_j))).(X_j/(KU+KP))$ — Profitability of total physical capital for sector j (3).

$ru_j = [(\kappa_{u,j}.KU)/(\kappa_{u,j}.KU + \kappa_{c,j}.KC)].[(KU+KC)/KU].\Gamma_j$ — Determination of sectoral profitability of unincorporated capital (where $_{u,j}$ is the unincorporated-profits/unincorporated-capital coefficient in sector j) (3).

$rc_j = [(\kappa_{c,j}.KC)/(\kappa_{u,j}.KU + \kappa_{c,j}.KC)].[(KU+KC)/KC].\Gamma_j$ — Determination of sectoral profitability of corporate capital (3).

B.3.5 Income distribution

B.3.5.1 Factorial income distribution

$Y_{LB} = \Sigma w.L_j + e.RFA$ — Labour income (wage earnings plus remittances from abroad)(1).

$Y_{UP} = \Sigma(ru_j.P_j.KU)$ — Unincorporated capital income (1).

$Y_{CP} = \Sigma(rc_j.P_j.KC)$ — Corporate capital income (1).

B.3.5.2 Income distribution to institutions

$GY_{kf} = [\gamma_{kf}.K_{kf}/(\Sigma\gamma_{kf}.K_{kf})].Y_{CP}$ — Distribution of corporate profits to institution kf (kf = CE and SE), according to their physical capital endowment (where γ_{kf} is the profit/capital ratio for agent kf) (2).

B.3.6 Rates of return per type of asset

Five type of assets and liabilities are distinguished in the model, each of them with a differentiated rate of return (the exception being 'currency'): (1) physical capital (K); (2) government's assets and liabilities (including government bonds, deposits in and loans from the Central Bank); (3) domestic currency (CU); (4) private assets and liabilities (including deposits in and loans from the private domestic financial system); and (5) external assets and liabilities (including deposits abroad, foreign reserves and external debt).

For the purpose of calibration, the different assets' and liabilities' returns are expressed as indexes, the base year being equal to one.

B.3.6.1 Basic rates of return indexes

$rpc_c = [1 + ((\Sigma rc_j.P_j)/\Sigma P_j)] / [1 + ((\Sigma rc_{0j}.P_{0j})/\Sigma P_{0j})]$ — Profitability of corporate physical capital (1).

$rpc_u = [1 + ((\Sigma ru_j.P_j)/\Sigma P_j)] / [1 + ((\Sigma ru_{0j}.P_{0j})/\Sigma P_{0j})]$ — Profitability of unincorporated physical capital (1).

$rg = (1+i^a)/(1+i^a_0)$ — Profitability on public domestic assets (government's bondsand loans from Central Bank) (i^a = administered interest rate) (1).

$rp = (1+i)/(1+i_0)$ — Profitability on private domestic assets (deposits in private banks and private banks loans) (i = rate of interest determined in the market) (1).

$re = (1+i^*)/(1+i_0^*)$ — Return on foreign assets/liabilities (i.e. banks' reserves, foreign debt) (1).

B.3.6.2 Allocation of each of the basic rates of return to the different financial transactions and to physical capital

$rf_{RW,k} = (e/e_{t-1}).re$	The official exchange rate (e) applies for all RW's claims on all domestic institutions (e.g. external debt) (7).
$rf_{kz,RW} = (e/e_{t-1}).re$	For domestic agents' official holdings of foreign exchange (e.g. banks' reserves) (kz = all institutions excluding households) (5).
$rf_{HH,RW} = (e^P/e^P_{t-1}).re$	The parallel exchange rate (e^P) applies for domestic agents' (i.e. households') holdings of foreign exchange (e.g. capital flight) (1).
$rf_{ks,kn} = rg$	rg applies for assets held by state institutions (e.g. Central Bank credit) (ks = SE, GV and CB, and kn = all domestic institutions) (18).
$rf_{kp,kx} = rp$	rp applies for assets held by private institutions (e.g. bank deposits) (kp = HH, CE and PB; and kx = HH, SE, and PB) (9).
$rf_{kp,GV} = rg$	rg applies to bonds issued by the government (3).
$rf_{kp,CB} = 1$	currency's rate of return is set to be 1 (3).
$rf_{HH,CE} = rpc_c$	Households' demand for shares depend on companies' profitability (1).
$rf_{kc,CE} = rp$	rp applies for the corporate sector's claims on companies (e.g. bank credit) (kc = CE and PB) (2).
$rk_{HH} = rpc_u$	Return on unincorporated capital applies for households (1).
$rk_{kk} = rpc_c$	Return on corporate capital applies for companies, state enterprises and government (3).

B.3.6.3 Weighted average rates of return for each agent's asset portfolio

$ra_{kw} = [\Sigma\alpha_{kw,k}.(rf_{kw,k})^{\sigma k}]^{(1/\sigma k)}$ Weighted profitability of RW and financial institutions' portfolio (kw = RW, CB and PB) (3).

$ra_{kd} = [\Sigma\alpha_{kd,k}.(rf_{kd,k})^{\sigma k} + \alpha_{k,K}.(rk_{kd})^{\sigma k}]^{(1/\sigma k)}$ Weighted profitability of non-financial institutions' portfolio (kd = HH, CE, SE and GV) (4).

B.3.7 Common accumulation balances for all sectors

All economic agents maintain a balance between, their total asset stock holdings on one hand, and their total liabilities plus their net wealth on the other.

$ASS_k \equiv LBT_k + WTH_k$ Stock balances (6).

The differences in sectoral accumulation behaviours are captured by differentiating the way each of the agents' balances closes. For those sectors where the 'investment-leading-saving' approach holds (companies, state enterprises and government) ASS_k is fully determined by the agent (i.e. within its accumulation balance); this implies that one of the variables in the right hand side of the equation (i.e. LBT_k) will be the closure of the balance. Conversely, for households' balance adjustment, where the 'prior saving' principle holds, LBT_{HH} is determined outside households' control (i.e. in other agents' balances); thus, one of the variables within ASS_{HH} must be the closing variable of the balance (i.e. HH's investment).

B.3.7.1 For non-financial institutions (k = HH, CE, SE and GV)

(a) Assets

$ASS_k \equiv \Sigma AA_{k,l} + KN_k$ Asset structure (4).

$KN_k \equiv KN_{k(t-1)} + IN_k + STK_k$ Nominal capital definition (4).

$IN_k \equiv \Sigma(\lambda_{i,k}.PD_k).IR_k$ Nominal investment definition (4).

$K_k \equiv (1-dr).K_{k(t-1)} + IR_k$ — Physical capital stock hold by each agent at the end of the period. (i.e. dr = depreciation rate) (4).

(b) Liabilities

$LBT_k \equiv \Sigma AA_{l,k}$ — Liability structure (4).

(c) Net wealth

$WTH_k \equiv WTH_{k(t-1)} + SV_k + REV_k$ — Net wealth definition (4).

$REV_{HH} = ((e^{P} - e^{P}_{t-1})/e^{P}_{t-1}).AA_{HH,RW}$ — Revaluation of HH's foreign assets (1).

$REV_k = ((e-e_{t-1})/e_{t-1}).(-AA_{RW,k(t-1)})$ — Revaluation of CE, SE and GV's net wealth comprise only that due to CE's external debt (3).

B.3.7.2 Balances for financial institutions (k = CB and PB)

(a) Assets

$ASS_k \equiv \Sigma AA_{k,l}$ — Asset structure (2).

(b) Liabilities

$LBT_k \equiv \Sigma AA_{l,k}$ — Liability structure (2).

(c) Net wealth

$WTH_k \equiv WTH_{k(t-1)} + REV_k$ — Net wealth definition (2).

$REV_k = ((e-e_{t-1})/e_{t-1}).(AA_{k,RW} - AA_{RW,k})$ — Net revaluation of financial institution k's foreign asset-liability stocks (2).

Rest of the world

(a) Assets

$ASS_{RW} \equiv \Sigma AA_{RW,l}$	Asset structure (1).

(b) Liabilities

$LBT_{RW} \equiv \Sigma AA_{l,RW}$	Liability structure (1).

(c) Net wealth

$WTH_{RW} \equiv WTH_{RW(t-1)} + SAV_{RW} + REV_{RW}$	Net wealth definition (1).
$REV_{RW} = -\Sigma REV_k$	Net revaluation for the rest of the world's assets-liabilities (1).

B.3.8 Households' balances (HH)

B.3.8.1 Households' income and savings

$GY_{HH} = Y_{LB} + Y_{UP} + DIV_{HH} + \Sigma CT_{k,HH}$	Households' gross income, including labour income, unincorporated profits, distributed profits (DIV) and current transfers to households ($CT_{k,H}$ from state enterprises, government and from the rest of the world) (1).
$YD_{HH} = (1-txd_{HH}).GY_{HH} - \Sigma CT_{HH,CE}$	Disposable income per household category after direct taxation and current transfers to companies ($CT_{HH,CE}$; i.e. interest payments) and to the rest of the world ($CT_{HH,RW}$; i.e. remittances out of coca proceeds) (1).
$CT_{HH,CE} = rf_{CE,HH}.\ \xi_{HH,CE}.AA_{PB,HH(t-1)}$	Comprises interest payments by households to companies (i.e. private banks) (1).
$CT_{HH,RW} = \Psi_{HH\ RW}.ru_{CO}.P_{CO}.KU$	Comprises remittances out of coca proceeds (1).

$SV_{HH} = \Lambda_1.YD_{HH} - \Lambda_2.(WTH_{HH(t-1)} + REV_{HH})$

Savings by households are determined as an incomplete attempt by households to adjust their net wealth to a proportion Λ_1 of their disposable income ($\Lambda_1 > 0$; and $\Lambda_2 < 0$) (1).

$NC_{HH} = YD_{HH} - SV_{HH}$

Households' nominal consumption as function of disposable income (1).

$C_i = \Theta_i + \mu_i.((NC_{HH} - \Sigma PD_i.\Theta_{i,})/PD_i)$

LES type consumption demand (including consumption of imported goods) where: Θ_i = floor level of consumption of commodity i; and μ_i = marginal budget shares (9).

B.3.8.2 Portfolio determination

$AA_{HH,k} = \alpha_{HH,k}.(rf_{HH,k}/ra_{HH})^{\sigma}.ASS_{HH}$

Households can only determine their asset-portfolio composition. HH's demand for financial assets are determined through this set of equations. Households' demand for physical capital is implicitly determined and does not need to be explicitly specified (7).

B.3.9 Companies' balances (CE)

CE's accumulation balance behaviour critically depends on companies' accumulation of physical capital. This accumulation is, in turn, conditioned by different types of constraints that come into operation under different circumstances. There are three alternative ways in which CE's investment (and therefore CE's accumulation of physical capital) might be determined: a) by CE's investment-demand function (IRF_{CE}) which, in turn, is dependent on the level of economic activity (accelerator term); b) by the availability of foreign exchange to import capital goods (IRE_{CE}) (foreign-exchange constraint); and c) by the availability of funds to finance investment (IRB_{CE}) (budget constraint). The ex-post level of CE's investment will be the minimum among these three alternative investment levels.

Section B.3.9.2 shows the way IRF_{CE} and IRE_{CE} are calculated. IRB_{CE} determination is explained in section B.3.16.

B.3.9.1 Companies' income and savings

$YBT_{CE} = GY_{CE} + \Sigma CT_{h,CE} + CT_{SE,CE} + CT_{RW,CE} - DIV_{HH} - CT_{CE,SE} - CT_{CE,RW}$

Companies' incomes before taxation (1).

$DIV_{HH} = \zeta . GY_{CE}$

Distributed profits to households as function of companies gross profits (1).

$CT_{CE,SE} = rf_{SE,CE} . \xi_{CE,SE} . \Sigma\Sigma AA_{kg,kc(t-1)}$

Current transfers from companies (i.e. firms and private banks (kc)) to state enterprises (i.e. state firms and Central Bank (kg)) mostly due to interest payments (1).

$CT_{CE,RW} = rf_{RW,CE} . \xi_{CE,RW} . \Sigma AA_{RW,kc(t-1)}$

Interest payments due to the corporate private sector's external debt (1).

$SV_{CE} = YBT_{CE} - txd_{CE} . GY_{CE}$

Companies' savings (1).

B.3.9.2 Investment demand

$IR_{CE} = \min(IRF_{CE}, IRE_{CE})$

CE's real investment is given by the minimum among: CE's investment demand function (IRF), CE's foreign-exchange-constrained investment level (IRE), and CE's budget-constrained investment level (IRB) (1).

$IRF_{CE} = IR_{CE} + \chi_1 . IR_{CE(t-1)} + \chi_2 . (GDP - GDP_{t-1}) + \chi_3 . DFI$

CE's investment demand function is dependent on CE's investment in the previous period, on an accelerator term reflected by changes in GDP and on the level of direct foreign investment (DFI) (1).

$IRE_{CE} = IR0_{CE} . (CM/CM0)$

CE's foreign-exchange-constrained investment depends on the current import capacity (CM) (1).

B.3.9.3 CE's financial portfolio determination

$AA_{CE,k} = (\alpha_{CE,k}/\alpha_{CE,K}).(rf_{CE,k}/rk_{CE})^{\sigma}.KN_{CE}$	CE's financial portfolio structure is determined as function of CE's capital stock (KN_{CE}). In this way, changes in KN_{CE} (given by CE's investment) will bring about changes in CE's level of working capital (7).

B.3.10 Public enterprises' balances (SE)

As in the case of companies, public enterprises' accumulation behaviour is crucially determined by SE's investment and accumulation of physical capital.

Ex-post SE's investment for their part also being calculated as the minimum among IRF_{SE}, IRE_{SE} and IRB_{SE}.

B.3.10.1 Public enterprises' income and savings

$YBT_{SE} = GY_{SE} + CT_{CE,SE} - \Sigma CT_{SE,kl}$	SE's income before taxation (kl = HH, CE and RW) (1).
$CT_{SE,HH} = \Psi_{SE\ HH} . GY_{SE}$	SE's transfers to households as function of SE's gross profits (1).
$CT_{SE,CE} = rf_{PB,SE}.\xi_{SE,CE}.\Sigma\Sigma AA_{kc,kg}$	Current transfers from state enterprises (i.e. state firms, Central Bank and development banks (kg)) to companies (i.e. firms and private banks (kc)) mostly comprise interest payments (1).
$CT_{SE,RW} = rf_{RW,SE}.\xi_{SE,RW}.\Sigma AA_{RW,kg}$	Interest payments due to the corporate public sector's external debt (1).
$SV_{SE} = YBT_{SE} - txd_{SE}.GY_{SE}$	Public firms' savings (1).

B.3.10.2 Investment demand

$IR_{SE} = \min(IRF_{SE}, IRE_{SE})$	SE's real investment is given as the minimum among SE's IRF, IRE, and IRB (1).

$IRF_{SE} = IR0_{SE}$	SE's investment demand function only imposes a ceiling on SE's investment. This ceiling is given by SE's investment in the base year (1).
$IRE_{SE} = IR0_{SE}.(CM/CM0)$	SE's foreign-exchange-constrained investment (1).

B.3.10.3 SE's financial portfolio determination

$AA_{SE,k} = (\alpha_{SE,k}/\alpha_{SE,K}).(rf_{SE,k}/rk_{SE})^{\sigma}.KN_{SE}$	SE's financial portfolio structure is determined in relation to their capital stock (KN_{SE}) (7).

B.3.11 Government's balances

As in the previous two cases, government accumulation balance behaviour is closely determined by its investment demand. Again, ex-post GV's investment is solved as the minimum between IRF_{GV}, IRE_{GV} and IRB_{GV}.

B.3.11.1 Government income and savings

$SV_{GV} = GRV - GEX$	Government savings equal to the difference between its revenues and expenditures (1).
$GRV = \Sigma(txi_j/(1+txi_j)).P_j.X_j + txd_{HH}.GY_{HH} + txd_{CE}.GY_{CE} + txd_{SE}.GY_{SE} + e.CT_{RW,GV}$	Government revenues (1).
$GEX = PD_{SM}.G + CT_{GV,HH} + CT_{GV,RW}$	Government expenditures (1).
$CT_{GV,HH} = \Psi_{GV\,HH}.PD_{SM}.G$	Current governmental transfers to households (1).
$CT_{GV,RW} = rf_{RW,GV}.\xi_{GV,RW}.AA_{RW,GV}$	Interest payments due to the government's external debt (1).

B.3.11.2 Investment demand

$IR_{GV} = \min(IRF_{GV}, IRE_{GV})$	GV's real investment is given as the minimum among GV's IRF, IRE, and IRB (1).

$IRF_{GV} = IR_{GV} + \varphi.\Delta F_{GV}$

GV's investment demand function comprises an autonomous investment term plus another part that is a function of the current capital inflows to the government (1).

$IRE_{GV} = IR0_{GV}.(CM/CM0)$

GV's foreign-exchange-constrained investment (1).

B.3.11.3 GV's financial portfolio determination

$AA_{GV,k} = (\alpha_{GV,k}/\alpha_{GV,K}).(rf_{GV,k}/rk_{GV})^{\sigma}.KN_{GV}$

GV's financial asset portfolio structure is determined based on the level of physical capital stock (KN_{GV}) (7).

B.3.13 Private financial institutions (PB)

$AA_{PB,ka} = \alpha_{PB,ka}.(rf_{PB,ka}/ra_{PB})^{\sigma}.ASS_{PB}$

As explained before, PBs determine all their assets but credit to companies, government, and state enterprises ($AA_{PB,CE}$) which is implicitly determined in these agents' accumulation balances. CE's balance closure however takes place through a variable in LBT_{PB} (i.e. credit from the Central Bank) (ka = HH, PB,CB and RW) (4).

B.3.14 Central Bank (CB)

$AA_{CB,kq} = \alpha_{PB,kq}.(rf_{PB,kq}/ra_{PB})^{\sigma}.ASS_{PB}$

As discussed previously, CB can only partially determine their portfolio as credit private banks have been implicitly determined within PS's balances. CB's balance adjustment eventually takes place though its foreign-exchange reserves, as will be explained in more detail in section B.3.14.3 (kq = HH, CE, GV,SE and CB) (5).

B.3.15 External balance

B.3.15.1 Current balance

$SV_{RW} = RWRV - RWEX$	External savings (current account balance) (1).
$RWRV = PD_{MP}.(\Sigma M_j + C_{MP,HH} + \Sigma\Theta_{MP,k}.IR_k + \Delta SK_{MP}) + \Sigma CT_{k,RW}$	Payments to the rest of the world (1).
$RWEX = e.\Sigma PW_i.E_i + e.RFA + e.\Sigma CT_{RW,k}$	Payments from the rest of the world (1).

B.3.15.2 Capital account

$AA_{RW,k} = (e/e_{t-1}).AA_{RW,k(t-1)} + e.\Delta F_k$	RW's assets comprise domestic agents' external debt. Capital inflows within the period (ΔF) are determined exogenously (7).

B.3.15.3 Import capacity

$MC = \Sigma PW_i.E_i + RFA + \Sigma CT_{RW,k}$ ab$-PW_{MP}.[C_{MP,HH} + \Sigma M_j + \Sigma\Theta_{MP,k}.IR_k + \Delta SK_{MP}] - \Sigma(CT_{k,RW}/e) + \Sigma[(AA_{k.RW(t-1)}/e_{t-1}) - AA_{k,RW}/e] - [AA_{CB\,RW(t-1)}/e_{t-1}) - MIRES] + \Sigma\Delta F_k$	Capacity to import non-competitive goods; i.e. intermediate for the mark-up-sectors and capitalgoods for the investment of CE, GV and SE (MIRES = minimum desired Central Bank's foreign reserves) (1).

B.3.16 Stock changes

$DSK_i = \Phi_i.X_i$	Changes of stocks by activities depend on each sector's level of production (i = all commodities but imports) (8).
$SK_{MP} = \Phi_{MP}.(\Sigma M_j + \Sigma C_{MP,h} + \Sigma\Theta_{MP,k}.IR_k)$	Changes of stocks for imported commodities depend on total imports (1).

$STK_k = \gamma_k.\Sigma PD_i.SK_i$	Stock changes are allocated among agents according to a fixed proportion γ_k (4).

B.3.17 Labour market

$w = cw_0 + cw_1.CPI - cw_2.U + cw_3.w_{t-1}$	Nominal wage rate is a function of the consumer price index (CPI), unemployment rate (U) and the wage rate in the previous period (w_{t-1}) (1).
$TLD = \Sigma\lambda_i.L_i$	Total labour demand (1).
$TLS = TLS_0.(1+n)^t$	Total labour supply (1).
$U = (TLS - TLD)/TLS$	Unemployment rate (1).
$CL = TLS - \Sigma\lambda_{iq}.L_{iq}$	Maximum labour supply to the mark-up sectors (iq = sectors with production functions) (1).

B.4 List of Variables, Parameters and Coefficients

B.4.1 Endogenous variables

There are 447 endogenous variables:

Var.	Number of cases	
X_i	8	total production by activities
XD_i	8	domestic absorption
E_i	8	exports by activities
P_i	8	composite price per activity
PE_i	8	export price per activity
PD_i	9	domestic price per activities and for imported commodities
KC	1	corporate capital stock
KU	1	unincorporated capital stock
K_k	4	capital stock held by agents
ru_i	8	profitability of unincorporated capital per activity
rc_i	8	profitability of corporate capital per activity
L_i	8	employment by activities
M_i	8	demand for imported inputs by activities
Γ_i	8	profitability of total capital per activity
τ_i	8	mark-up rate per activity
X_i^{max}	3	maximum output in the mark-up sectors
Y_f	3	total income by productive factor categories
GY_k	2	allocation of corporate profits to institutions
rpc_f	2	profitability per category of physical capital
rg	1	profitability of public bonds
rp	1	profitability of private domestic assets
re	1	profitability of external assets
$rf_{k,l}$	49	rofitability of financial assets
rk_k	4	profitability of capital by agents
ra_k	7	average portfolio profitability by agents
ASS_k	7	total assets by agents
LBT_k	7	total liabilities by agents
WTH_k	7	total wealth by agents
KN_k	4	nominal value of physical capital by agents
$AA_{k,l}$	49	financial assets issued by agent l and held by agent k
IN_k	4	nominal investment by agent k
IR_k	4	real investment by agent k
SV_k	5	savings by agent
REV_k	7	net revaluation of assets per agent

GY_{HH}	1	households' gross income
YD_{HH}	1	disposable income by households
NC_{HH}	1	nominal consumption by households
C_i	9	real consumption of commodity i by households
YBT_k	2	income before taxes by companies (i.e. CE and SE)
DIV_{HH}	1	distributed corporate profits to households
$CT_{k,l}$	9	current transfers from agent k to agent l
IRF_k	3	investment demand by economic agents
IRE_k	3	foreign-exchange constraint investment by agent
GRV	1	government revenues
GEX	1	government expenditures
RWRV	1	rest of the world revenues
RWEX	1	rest of the world expenditures
MC	1	maximum capacity to import
ΔSK_i	9	changes of stock by commodities
STK_k	4	changes of stocks by agents
w	1	nominal wage rate
TLD	1	total demand for labour
TLS	1	total supply of labour
U	1	unemployment rate
e^P	1	parallel exchange rate

B.4.2 Exogenous variables

G	1	government final consumption
e	1	official exchange rate
PW_i	8	world price for commodities
RFA	1	remittances from the RW
ia	1	interest rate on government bonds
i	1	market interest rate
i*	1	world interest rate
ΔF_k	6	capital inflows received by agent k during the period
$CT_{RW,k}$	3	current transfers from the rest of the world
MIRES	1	minimum (or target) level of exchange reserves
$K_{k(t-1)}$	4	capital stock at the beginning of the period
$WTH_{k(t-1)}$	7	net wealth by agent at the beginning of the period
$AA_{k,RW(t-1)}$	4	holdings of foreign exchange by agent
$AA_{RW,k(t-1)}$	6	external debt by institution
$e_{(t-1)}$	1	official exchange rate in the previous year
$e^P_{(t-1)}$	1	parallel exchange rate in the previous period
$IR_{CE(t-1)}$	1	companies' investment in the previous period
w_{t-1}	1	wage rate in the previous period
DFI	1	direct foreign investment flow within the period

B.4.3 Parameters

E_{i0}	6	exports by activity in the base year
ε_i	6	export elasticity by activity
$\lambda_{i,k}$	28	coefficients linking investment by agents and by commodities
ρ_i	5	constant elasticity substitution coefficient among factors for activities with production functions
$a_{i,j}$	72	input-output coefficients
b_i	8	labour-output coefficient for all sectors
txi_i	8	indirect tax rate per activity
τ_{i0}	3	mark-up rate in the base year for the mark-up sectors
$\kappa_{u,j}$ and $\kappa_{c,j}$	6	profit-capital coefficient for unincorporated and corporate capital
γ_k	4	profit-capital coefficient for economic agents
$\alpha_{k,l}$	4	portfolio shares for economic agents
σ_k	7	elasticities of substitution for agents portfolios
txd_k	4	direct tax rate per agent
Λ_1 and Λ_2	2	households' propensities to save out of income and out of net wealth
Θ_i	9	households' floor consumption levels by commodity
μ_i	9	households' marginal budget shares by commodity
$\xi_{k,l}$	6	implicit interest rate by agents
ζ_{HH}	1	distributed profit coefficients by companies to households
Ψ_{HH}	1	current transfers to households as share of government final demand
χ_1, χ_2, χ_3	3	investment demand coefficients for companies
φ	1	investment demand coefficient for government

References

Afcha, G. 1989. *Desintermediación y Liberalización Financiera en Bolivia: 1980–1988*, La Paz, Unidad de Análisis de Políticas Económicas (UDAPE).

Agénor, P.R. and P. Montiel. 1996. *Development Macroeconomics*, Princeton, NJ, Princeton University Press.

Alarcón, J., J. Van Heemst, S. Keuning, W. De Ruijter and R. Vos. 1991. *The Social Accounting Framework for Development*, Aldershot, Gower/Avebury.

Antelo, E. 1994. 'Reglas, Discreción y Reputación: Una explicación para las elevadas tasas de interés en Bolivia', *Análisis Económico*, no.9, La Paz, UDAPE, pp.7–21.

Apt, J. and E. Schargrodsky. 1995. 'Market Structure of the Bolivian Banking System' (unpublished paper), Cambridge:Harvard University.

Bacha, E.L. 1984. 'Growth With Limited Supplies of Foreign Exchange: A Reappraisal of the Two-Gap Model' in [M. Syrquin, L. Taylor and L. Westphal (eds), *Economic Structure and Performance: Essays in Honor of Hollis B. Chenery*, New York, Academic Press, pp. 263–80.

Bacha, E.L. 1990. 'A Three-gap Model of Foreign Transfers and the GDP Growth Rate in Developing Countries', *Journal of Development Economics* vol. 32, pp. 279–96.

Balassa, B. 1987. 'Structural Adjustment Policies in Developing Economies', *World* Bank Staff Working Papers, no. 464, March.

Baran, P. 1968. *The Political Economy of Growth*, New York, Modern Research Paperbacks.

Barnum, H.N. and L. Squire. 1979. *A Model of an Agricultural Household, Theory and Evidence,* Occasional Paper no. 27, Washington, DC, World Bank.

Bascopé, S. 1982. *La Veta Blanca*, La Paz, Ediciones Aqui.

Banco Central de Bolivia (BCB). 1983. *Indice del Costo de la Construcción de Viviendas en la Ciudad de La Paz*, no. 1, La Paz, Banco Central de Bolivia.

BCB (various issues-a) *Boletín Estadístico*, La Paz, Banco Central de Bolivia

BCB (various issues-b) *Boletín Sector Externo*, La Paz, Banco Central de Bolivia.

BCB (various issues-c) *Memoria Anual*, La Paz, Banco Central de Bolivia.

Behrman, J. 1991. 'Human Capital and International Perspective on Bolivian Performance and Policy Options', paper prepared for the conference 'Structural Adjustment and Economic Growth', La Paz, UDAPE-HIID-USAID/B.

Bird, G. 1984. 'Balance of Payments Policy' in T. Killick (ed.) *The IMF and Stabilisation: Developing Country Experiences*, London, Heinemann Educational Books.

Blanes Jimenez, J. 1989. 'Cocaine, Informality, and the Urban Economy in La Paz, Bolivia' in A Portes, M. Castells and L. Benton (eds.) *The Informal Economy: Studies in Advanced and Less Developed Countries*, Baltimore, MD: Johns Hopkins University Press.

Boada, R. 1991. 'Comentarios' in C. Toranzo (ed.) *Panel: Ajuste Estructural y Crecimiento*, La Paz, UDAPE-HIID-USAID/B-Foro Económico-ILDIS, pp. 53–54.

Brugger, E. (ed.) 1990. *The Business Environment of Small Industrial Enterprises in Bolivia*, La Paz, FUNDES.

Calvo, G. 1991. 'Exposición' in C. Toranzo (ed.) *Panel: Ajuste Estructural y Crecimiento*, La Paz, UDAPE-HIID-USAID/B-Foro Económico-ILDIS, pp. 17–19.

Candia, F. 1991. 'Comentarios' in C. Toranzo (ed.) *Panel: Ajuste Estructural y Crecimiento*, La Paz, UDAPE-HIID-USAID/B-Foro Económico-ILDIS, pp. 51–52.

Carbonetto, D. 1985. 'La Heterogeneidad Productiva en el Sector Informal', in *El Sector Informal en los Paises Andinos*, Quito, ILDIS, pp. 45–68.

Cariaga, J.L. 1982. 'The Economic Structure of Bolivia after 1964' in J.R. Ladman (ed.) *Modern-Day Bolivia: Legacy of the Revolution and*

Prospects for the Future, Tempe, AZ, Center for Latin American Studies, Arizona State University, pp. 147–63.

Carter, W. 1981. 'Medicinal Uses of Coca in Bolivia' in: J. Bastian and J. Donahue (eds) *Health in the Andes*, Washington, DC, American Anthropological Association.

Casanovas, R. and S. Escobar .1988. *Los Trabajadores por Cuenta Propia en La Paz, Funcionamiento de las Unidades Economicas, Situacion Laboral e Ingresos*, La Paz, CEDLA.

Casanovas, R. 1989. 'Informalidad e Ilegalidad: Una Falsa Identidad' in A. Perez, R. Casanovas, S. Escóbar and H. Larrazábal (eds) *Informalidad e Ilegalidad: Una Falsa Identidad*, La Paz, CEDLA.

Castells, M. and A. Portes 1989. 'World Underneath: The Origins, Dynamic, and Effects of the Informal Economy' in A. Portes, M. Castells and L. Benton (eds.) *The Informal Economy: Studies in Advanced and Less Developed Countries*, Baltimore, MD, Johns Hopkins University Press, pp. 11–37.

Centro de Estudios pare el Desarrollo Laboral y Agrario (CEDLA). 1989. *Encuesta de Establecimientos Semi-empresariales y Familiares*, La Paz.

Chenery, H.B. 1969. 'The Two Gap Approach to Aid and Development: A Reply to Bruton', *American Economic Review* vol. 59 (June), p. 446.

Chenery, H.B. and A. Strout. 1966. 'Foreign Assistance and Economic Development', *American Economic Review* vol. 56(4), pp. 679–733.

Cobas, E. 1987. *Informe de la Primera Etapa de la Cooperación Técnica para el Establecimiento de una Estrategia de Desarrollo Industrial. Resumen*, La Paz, Gobierno de Bolivia-BID.

Cornia, G.A., R. Jolly and F. Stewart (eds) 1987. *Adjustment with a Human Face, Protecting the Vulnerable and Promoting Growth*, Oxford, Clarendon Press.

Davis, E. and J. Pointon. 1984. *Finance and the Firm*, Oxford, Oxford University Press.

De La Piedra, E. 1986. 'El Sector Informal Urbano: La Inconsistencia del Paradigma Convencional y un Nuevo Enfoque', *Revista Apuntes*, primer semestre, La Paz.

Dervis, K., J. De Melo and S. Robinson. 1982. *General Equilibrium Models for Development Policy*, Washington, DC, World Bank.

Devarajan, S., J. Lewis and S. Robinson 1986. *Bibliography of Computable General Equilibrium (CGE) Models Applied to Developing Countries*, Working Paper no. 400, Department of Agricultural and Resource Economics, Berkeley, University of California.

Devlin, R. 1978. 'External Finance and Commercial Banks, Their Role in Latin America's Capacity to Import between 1951 and 1975', *CEPAL Review*, first half of 1978, Santiago, CEPAL.

Devlin, R. 1986. 'Private Banks, Debt, and the Bargaining Power of the Periphery: Theory and Practice', in Economic Commission for Latin America and the Caribbean, *Debt, Adjustment, and Renegotiation in Latin America: Orthodox and Alternative Approaches*, Boulder, CO, Lynne Rienner, pp. 3–28.

Devlin, R. and M. Mortimore. 1983. *Los Bancos Trasnacionales, El Estado y el Endeudamiento Externo en Bolivia*, Estudios e Informes de la Cepal, Santiago, CEPAL.

Dornbusch, R. 1980. *Open Economy Macroeconomics*, New York, Basic Books.

Drake, P.J. 1980. *Money, Finance and Development*, Oxford, Martin Robertson.

Dunkerley, J. 1984. *Rebellion in the Veins: Political Struggle in Bolivia 1952–1982*, Thetford, Norfolk, Thetford Press.

Dunkerley, J. (1992) 'Political Transition and Economic Stabilization: Bolivia 1982–89' in J. Dunkerley (ed.) *'Political Suicide in Latin America' and Other Essays*, London, Verso.

Ellis, F. 1988. *Peasant Economics, Farm Households and Agrarian Development*, Cambridge, Cambridge University Press.

Escóbar, S. 1990. *Crisis, Política Económica y Dinámica de los Sectores Semi-Empresariales y Familiares: La Paz, Cochabamba, Santa Cruz (1985–1989)* Serie: Estudios e Investigación, Temas Urbanos, La Paz, CEDLA.

Eshag, E. 1983. *Fiscal and Monetary Policies and Problems in Developing Countries*, Cambridge, Cambridge University Press.

Espejo, J., R. Gomez and C. Machicado 1988. *Elementos para una Estrategia Industrial en Bolivia*, La Paz, Ministerio de Industria, Comercio y Turismo-Deutsche Gesellschaft für technische Zusammenarbeit (GTZ).

Fisher, S. 1991. 'Exposición' in C. Toranzo (ed.) *Panel: Ajuste Estructural y Crecimiento*, La Paz: UDAPE-HIID-USAID/B-Foro Económico-ILDIS, pp. 13–15.

FitzGerald, E.V.K. 1976. 'The Urban Service Sector, the Supply of Wage-goods and the Shadow Wage Rate', *Oxford Economic Papers*, Vol. 28(2), pp. 228–239.FitzGerald, E.V.K. 1986. *Kalecki on Planned Growth in the Mixed Economy*, Working Paper no. 18, Subseries on

Money, Finance and Development, The Hague, Institute of Social Studies.

FitzGerald, E.V.K. and R. Vos. 1989. *Financing Economic Development: A Structuralist Approach to Monetary Policy*, Aldershot, Gower Press.

FitzGerald, E.V.K. and K. Sarmad. 1990. *Public and Private Sector Capital Account Behaviour in Less Developed Countries, 1970–1988*, Working Paper no. 36, Subseries on Money, Finance and Development, The Hague, Institute of Social Studies.

FitzGerald, E.V.K. 1991. 'Some Notes on the Finance of Firms and Households in LDCs', Finance and Development Research Group, The Hague, Institute of Social Studies.

Flores, G. and J. Blanes. 1984. *¿Dónde va el Chapare?*, Cochabamba, Centro de Estudios de la Realidad Económica y Social (CERES).

Foxley, A. 1981. 'Stabilization Policies and their Effect on Employment and Income Distribution: A Latin American Perspective' in W.R. Cline and S. Weintraub (eds) *Economic Stabilization in Developing Countries*, Washington, DC, Brookings Institution.

Frenkel, J. and H. Johnson (eds). 1976. *The Monetary Approach to the Balance of Payments*, London, George Allen and Unwin.

Frenkel, J. and A. Razin. 1987. 'The Mundell-Fleming Model a Quarter of a Century Later: A Unified Exposition', *IMF Staff Papers* vol. 34(4), pp. 567–620.

FundaPro. 1997. 'El Problema de las Garantías en el Crédito para la Pequeña y la Microempresa en Bolivia', Foro de Microfinanzas, Los Andes-Fundes-Sartawi, Serie Crédito no. 1, La Paz, Fundación para la Producción

García-Rodriguez, L.E. 1982. 'Structural Change and Development Policy in Bolivia' in J.R. Ladman (ed.) *Modern-Day Bolivia: Legacy of the Revolution and Prospects for the Future*, Tempe, AZ, Center for Latin American Studies, Arizona State University, pp. 165–92.

Ginsburgh, V. and J. Waelbroeck. 1981. *Activity Analysis and General Equilibrium Modelling*, Amsterdam, North-Holland.

Graham, C. 1997. 'Building Support for Market Reforms in Bolivia: The Capitalization and Popular Participation Programs' in Peirce M.H. (ed.) *Capitalization: The Bolivian Model of Social and Economic Reform*, the Woodrow Wilson Center, Washington, DC, pp. 23–69.

Healy, K. 1986. 'The Boom within the Crisis: Some Recent Effects of Foreign Cocaine Markets on Bolivian Rural Society and Economy' in D. Pacini and C. Franquemont (eds) *Coca and Cocaine: Effects on People and Policy in Latin America*, Cultural Survival Report no. 2, Peterborough, NH, Cultural Survival Inc. and LASP, pp. 101–43.

Hinojosa, J. and J. Espinoza. 1983. *Estrategia de Desarrollo Basado en el Endeudamiento Externo: Algunas Consideraciones Sobre el Caso de la Deuda Directa de la Banca Comercial Privada, 1970–1982*, XX Reunión de Técnicos de Bancos Centrales del Continente Americano, La Paz, Banco Central de Bolivia.

IMF. 1977. *The Monetary Approach to the Balance of Payments*, Washington, DC, International Monetary Fund.

IMF. 1987a. *Theoretical Aspects of the Design of Fund-Supported Adjustment Programmes*, Occasional Paper 55, Washington, DC,International Monetary Fund.

IMF. 1987b. 'Bolivia Breaks Hyperinflation: Creating Conditions for Sustained Growth', *National Economies: IMF Surveys*, Washington, DC, International Monetary Fund (January) , pp. 18–21.

IMF. 1996. 'Bolivia: Staff Report for the 1995 Article IV Consultation and Request for Second Annual Arrangement Under the Enhanced Structural Adjustment facility', Prepared by the Western Hemisphere Department, March, (unpublished paper), Washington DC, International Monetary Fund.

INE. 1978. *Resultados del Censo Nacional de Población y Vivienda-1976*, La Paz, Instituto Nacional de Estadística.

INE. 1980. *Encuesta Sector Informal Urbano y Rural* , La Paz, Instituto Nacional de Estadística.

INE. 1983. *Directorio Nacional de Establecimientos Económicos*, La Paz, Instituto Nacional de Estadística.

INE. 1988. *Principales Resultados de la Encuesta Permanente de Hogares 1980–87*, La Paz, Instituto Nacional de Estadística.

INE. 1989a. *Encuesta Integrada de Hogares*, La Paz, Instituto Nacional de Estadística.

INE. 1989b. *Cuentas Nacionales Definitivas: 1978–1986*, La Paz, Instituto Nacional de Estadística.

INE. 1990. *Boletín de Cuentas Nacionales* Nos. 3, 4, La Paz, Instituto Nacional de Estadística.

INE. 1995. *Encuesta Integrada de Hogares*, La Paz, Instituto Nacional de Estadística.

INE. 1996. *Cuentas Nacionales 1988–1992*, La Paz, Instituto Nacional de Estadística.

INE. 1997. *Anauario Estadístico 1997*, La Paz: Instituto Nacional de Estadística.

Irvin, G. 1979. *Planning Investment in Bolivia: The Changing Role of the Public Sector*, The Hague, Institute of Social Studies.

Jansen, K. 1987. *International Capital Flows and Economic Adjustment in Developing Countries*, Working Paper no. 21, Subseries on Money, Finance and Development, The Hague, Institute of Social Studies.

Jemio, L.C., and E. Antelo, 1996. 'Una Visión Sobre las Perspectivasde Crecimiento de la Economía Boliviana a Partir del Modelo de las 3 Brechas', *Análisis Económico*, no. 16, La Paz, UDAPE, pp. 37–63.

Kalecki M. 1976. *Essays on Developing Economies*, Brighton, Harvester Press.

Keuning, S. and W. de Ruijter. 1991. 'The Social Accounting Framework: Outline of Construction Stages and Organization of Work' in J. Alarcón et al., *The Social Accounting Framework for Development*, Aldershot, Gower/Avebury, Institute of Social Studies, pp. 191–219.

Khan, M.S. and M.D. Knight. 1981. 'Stabilization Programs in Developing Countries: A Formal Framework', *International Monetary Fund Staff Papers* vol. 28(1) (March), pp. 1–53 .

Killick, T. (ed.) 1984a. *The IMF and Stabilisation: Developing Country Experiences*, London, Heinemann Educational Books.

Killick T. (ed.) 1984b *The Quest for Economic Stabilisation: The IMF and the Third World*, London, Heinemann Educational Books.

Kritz E. 1986. *Analisis del Sector Informal Urbano en America Latina*, La Paz, CEDLA-FLACSO .

Krugman, P. 1988. 'External Shocks and Domestic Policy Response' in R. Dornbusch and L. Helmer (eds) *The Open Economy: Tools for Policy Makers in Developing Countries*, Oxford, Oxford University Press (Economic Development Institute), pp. 54–79.

Krugman P. and L. Taylor. 1978. 'Contractionary Effects of Devaluation', *Journal of International Economics* vol. 8., p. 445.

Ladman, J.R. 1982. 'The Political Economy of the "Economic Miracle" of the Banzer Regime' in J.R. Ladman (ed.) *Modern-Day Bolivia: Legacy of the Revolution and Prospects for the Future*, Tempe, AZ, Center for Latin American Studies, Arizona State University, pp. 321–43.

Leff, N.H. 1976. 'Capital Markets in Less developed Countries: The Group Principle' in R.I. McKinnon (ed.) *Money and Finance in Economic Growth and Development*, New York, Marcel Dekker.

Lehwing, T. 1989. *Programa Monetario: Un Enfoque Práctico al Caso Boliviano*, La Paz, Banco Central de Bolivia.

Lopes, J. 1983. 'Financiamiento Externo Público en el largo plazo, 1950–1981', *Revista Puntos de Vista* no. 2, La Paz, Banco Central De Bolivia, pp. 7–37.

Machicado, F. (1991) 'Comentarios' in C. Toranzo (ed.) *Panel: Ajuste Estructural y Crecimiento*, La Paz: UDAPE-HIID-USAID/B-Foro Económico-ILDIS, pp. 36–7.

Mann, A.J. and M. Pastor. 1989. 'Orthodox and heterodox Stabilization Policies in Bolivia and Perú, 1985–88', *Journal of Inter-American Studies and World Affairs* vol. 31(4), pp. 163–92.

Mercado, R. 1988. *El Sistema Bancario y el Proceso de Reactivación Económica en Bolivia: Aspectos Financieros*, Taller de Investigaciones Socio-Económicas, La Paz, ILDIS.

Mierau-Klein, B. and J. Page. 1991. *Bolivia's Supply Response to Adjustment, 1985–1990*, paper prepared for the conference 'Structural Adjustment and Economic Growth', La Paz, UDAPE-HIID-USAID/B.

Miller, C.J. and J.R. Ladman. 1982. 'Factors Impeding Credit Use in Small-Farm Households in Bolivia', *Journal of Development Studies*, vol. 19(4), pp. 522–38.

Ministerio de Asuntos Campesinos y Agropecuarios (MACA). 1989. *Plan Integral de Desarrollo y Sustitución (PIDYS), La Paz,* Subsecretaria de Desarrollo Alternativo y Sustitución de Cultivos de Coca (SUBDESAL).

Ministerio de Planeamiento y Coordinación. 1989. *Estrategia de Desarrollo Económico y Social 1989–2000*, La Paz.

Ministry of Finance. 1996. 'Strategy for the Productive Transformation of Agriculture', Presentation by the Bolivian Government to the 9th Consultative Group Meeting, Paris, March 14–15, 1996. Ministry of Finance. 1997. 'Bolivia's Structural Reforms: Achievements and Prospects for the Future', Presentation by the Bolivian Government to the 10th Consultative Group Meeting, Paris, April, 1997. Moller, A. 1980. *Los Trabajadores por Cuenta Propia en Santiago*, Santiago de Chile, PREALC.

Morales, J.A. 1982. 'The Bolivian External Sector after 1964' in J.R. Ladman (ed.) *Modern-Day Bolivia: Legacy of the Revolution and Prospects for the Future*, Tempe, AZ, Center for Latin American Studies, Arizona State University, pp. 193–231.

Morales, J.A. 1987a. 'Estabilizacion y Nueva Politica Economica en Bolivia', *El Trimestre Economico*, vol. 54, pp. 179–211.

Morales, J.A. 1987b. *Precios, Salarios, Politica Economica Durante la Alta Inflacion Boliviana, de 1982 a 1985*, Estudio, Diagnostico, Debate, La Paz, ILDIS.

Morales, J.A. 1990. 'Impacto de los Ajustes Estructurales en la Agricultura Campesina Boliviana' in C. Toranzo (ed.) *Política de Ingresos, Política de Gasto y Administración de la Inversíon Pública, Taller de Investigaciones Socio-Económicas*, La Paz, ILDIS.

Morales, J.A. and J. Sachs. 1989. 'Bolivia's Economic Crisis' in J. Sachs (ed.) *Developing Country Debt and Economic Performance*, Chicago, University of Chicago Press for NBER.

Morales, R. 1984. *Desarrollo y Pobreza en Bolivia: Análisis de la Situación del Niño y la Mujer*, La Paz, UNICEF.

Morales, R. 1985. *Las Crisis Económica en Bolivia y su Impacto en las Condiciones de Vida de los Niños*, La Paz, UNICEF.

Morales, R. 1987a *Tasa de Interés y Tipo de Cambio: 1981–1987*, Estudio, Diagnostico, Debate, La Paz: ILDIS.

Morales R. (1987b) *Bolivia: Efectos Sociales de la Crisis y de las Politicas de Ajuste*, Estudio, Diagnostico, Debate, La Paz: ILDIS.

Morgan Guarantee. 1986. 'LDC Capital Flight', *World Financial Markets*, March, pp. 13–15.

Naylor, R.T. 1987. *Hot Money and the Politics of Debt*, London, Unwin Hyman.

O'Connell, J. 1987. 'Kaldor's Distribution Theory', *Journal of Post-Keynesian Economics*, vol. 9(4).

Pastor, M. Jr. 1987. 'The Effects of IMF Programs in the Third World: Debate and Evidence from Latin America', *World Development*, vol. 15(2), p. 249+.

Pastor, M. Jr. 1991. 'Bolivia: Hyperinflation, Stabilization, and Beyond', The Journal of Development Studies vol. 27(2) (January), pp. 211–237.

Plowman, T. 1986. 'Coca Chewing and the Botanical Origins of Coca (Exythroxylum spp.) in South America' in D. Pacini and C. Franquemont (eds) *Coca and Cocaine: Effects on People and Policy in Latin America*, Cultural Survival Report no. 2, Peterborough, NH: Cultural Survival Inc. and LASP.

PREALC. 1978. *Sector Informal, Funcionamiento y Políticas*, Santiago, ILO.

PREALC. 1979. *Distribución del Ingreso, Migración y Colonización: Una Alternativa para el Campesino Boliviano*, Document de Trabajo 176, La Paz, ILO.

Pyatt, G. and J. Round. 1979. 'Accounting and Fixed-Price Multipliers in a Social Accounting Matrix Framework', *Economic Journal*, vol. 89 (December), pp. 850–73.

Pyatt, G. and J. Round. 1984. *Improving the Macroeconomic Data Base: A SAM for Malaysia 1970*, World Bank Staff Working Paper no. 646, Washington, DC, World Bank.

Ramirez, J.R. and J. De la Viña. 1992. *Tasas de Interés en la Post-estabilización*, La Paz, ILDIS.

Ramos, P. 1980. *Siete Años de Economía Boliviana*, La Paz, Universidad Mayor de San Andrés.

Ramos, P. 1989. 'Las Políticas Económicas Aplicadas en Bolivia: 1952–1987' in C. Toranzo (ed.) *Bolivia Hacia el Año 2000: Desafíos y Opciones*, La Paz, ILDIS-Nueva Sociedad-Los Amigos del Libro-UNITAR/PROFAL.

Requena, J.C. 1990. 'Notas Sobre la Política de Gasto' in C Toranzo (ed.) *Política de Ingresos, Política de Gasto y Administración de la Inversíon Pública, Taller de Investigaciones Socio-Económicas*, La Paz, ILDIS.

Riordan J.T. 1977. 'An Assessment of the Target Region for USAID/Bolivia's agricultural sector Loan II', Washington, DC, US Agency for International Development, LA/DR/RD. (unpublished paper). Rivas, H. 1989. *Modelo Económico y Deuda Externa: Bolivia 1972–1987*, Documento de Análisis no. 6, La Paz, CIPCA-UNITAS.

Robinson, S. 1987. *Multisectoral Models of Developing Countries: A Survey, Deparment of Agricultural and Resource Economics*, Berkeley, University of California Press.

Romero, S. 1982. 'The Role of the State in the Rural-Urban Configuration' in J.R. Ladman (ed.) *Modern-Day Bolivia: Legacy of the Revolution and Prospects for the Future*, Tempe, AZ, Center for Latin American Studies, Arizona State University, pp. 301–17.

Rosensweig, J. and L. Taylor. 1990. 'Devaluation, Capital Flows and Crowding-out: A CGE Model with Portfolio Choice for Thailand'in L. Taylor (ed.) *Socially Relevant Policy Analysis for the Developing World: Structuralist Computable General Equilibrium Models*, Cambridge, MA, MIT Press, pp. 302–32.

Round, J. and G. Pyatt. 1985. *Social Accounting Matrice, A Basis for Planning*, A World Bank Symposium, Washington, DC, World Bank.

Sachs, J. 1987. 'The Bolivian Hyperinflation and Stabilization', *American Economic Review* vol. 77(2), pp. 279–83.

Sage, C. 1989. 'Drugs and Economic Development in Latin America: A Study in the Political Economy of Cocaine in Bolivia' in P.M. Ward (ed.) *Corruption, Development and Inequality: Soft Touch or Hard Graft?*, London, Routledge, pp. 38–57.

Schuh, G.F. 1991. 'The Potential Role of Agricultural Technology in Bolivia's Economic Growth', paper prepared for the conference 'Structural Adjustment and Economic Growth', La Paz, UDAPE-HIID-USAID/B.

Sethuraman, S.V. 1976. *The Urban Informal Sector: Concept, Measurement and Policy*, Working Paper, World Employment Programme Research, Urbanization and Employment Research Programme, Geneva, ILO.

Sethuraman, S.V. 1981. *The Urban Informal Sector in Developing Countries: Employment, Poverty and Environment*, Geneva, ILO.

Srivastava, P. 1991. 'Interest Rate, Peso Problem and Dollarization in Bolivia', paper prepared for UDAPE, La Paz, HIID-Harvard University. Stone, R. 1977. 'Foreword' to G. Pyatt and A. Roe. *Social Accounting for Development Planning With Special Reference to Sri-Lanka*, New York, Cambridge University Press, pp. xvi–xxxi.

Tanzi, V. 1982. 'Fiscal Disequilibrium in Developing Countries', *World Development*, vol. 10(12), pp. 1068–82.

Taylor, L. 1983. *Structuralist Macroecroeconomics, Applicable Models for the Third World*, New York, Basic Books.

Taylor, L. 1987. 'Macro Policy in the Tropics: How Sensible People Stand', *World Development*, 15(12), pp. 1407–35.

Taylor, L. (ed.) 1990. *Socially Relevant Policy Analysis, Structuralist Computable General Equilibrium Models for the Developing World*, Cambridge, Massachusetts and London, England, The MIT Press.

Tobin, J. 1982. 'Money and finance in the Macroeconomic Process', *Journal of Money, Credit and Banking*, vol. 14(2), pp. 171–204.

Toranzo, C. 1991. '*Comentarios*' in C. Toranzo (ed.) *Panel: Ajuste Estructural y Crecimiento*, La Paz, UDAPE-HIID-USAID/B-Foro Económico-ILDIS, pp. 39–42.

Toranzo, C. and M. Arrieta. 1989. *Nueva Derecha y Desproletarización en Bolivia*, La Paz, UNITAS-ILDIS.

Torrico, J.I. 1982. 'The Public Sector in Bolivian Agricultural Development' in J.R. Ladman (ed.) *Modern-Day Bolivia: Legacy of the Revolution and Prospects for the Future*, Tempe, AZ, Center for Latin American Studies, Arizona State University, pp. 255–74.

Triennial Anti-Narcotics Plan. 1987. Presented by the government of Bolivia to the meeting of the United Nations Fund for Drug Abuse Control, Vienna.

Trigo, J. 1991. 'Comentarios' in C. Toranzo (ed.) *Panel: Ajuste Estructural y Crecimiento*, La Paz, UDAPE-HIID-USAID/B-Foro Económico-ILDIS, pp. 49–50.

UDAPE. 1990a. 'La Política Anti-Inflacionaria de Choque y el Mercado de Trabajo' in PREALC, *Estabilización y Respuesta Social*, Santiago, PREALC, pp 137–96.

UDAPE. 1990b. *La Economía de la Coca y el Desarrollo Económico en Bolivia: Un Enfoque Alternativo*, Documento Técnico, La Paz, UDAPE.

UDAPE. 1990c. 'Análisis de Impacto de las Políticas Macroeconómicas y Factores Externos en el Sector Agrícola' in C. Toranzo (ed.) *Política de Ingresos, Política de Gasto y Administración de la Inversíon Pública, Taller de Investigaciones Socio-Económicas*, La Paz, ILDIS.

UDAPE. 1990d. *Matriz de Contabilidad Social Para la Evaluación de la Inversión Pública*, La Paz, UDAPE.

UDAPE. 1991. 'Ajuste Estructural y Crecimiento Económico: Evaluación y Perspectivs del Caso Boliviano', paper prepared for the international seminar 'Ajuste Estructural y Crecimiento Económico', La Paz, UDAPE-HIID-USAID/B.

UDAPE. (1997a) Determinantes del Spread en las Tasas de Interés Bancarias en Bolivia, La Paz: UDAPE.

UDAPE. (1997b) *Dossier de Información de Estadísticas Económicas de Bolivia*, no. 7, La Paz, UDAPE.

Ugarteche, O. 1986. *El Estado Deudor, Economía Politica de la Deuda: Peru y Bolivia 1986–1984*, Lima, Instituto de Estudios Peruanos.

United Nations. 1968. *International Standard Industrial Classification of All Economic Activity (ISIC)* Series M, no. 4, rev. 2, New York, United Nations.

Uribe-Echeverría, F. 1991. *Beyond the Informal Sector, Labour Absorption in Latin American Urban Economies: The Case of Colombia*, Working Paper Series, no. 111, The Hague, Institute of Social Studies.

Urioste, M. 1989a 'Los Campesinos y el Desarrollo Rural'in C. Toranzo (ed.) *Bolivia Hacia el Año 2000: Desafíos y Opciones*, La Paz,

ILDIS-Nueva Sociedad-Los Amigos del Libro-UNITAR/PROFAL, pp. 313–46.

Urioste, M. 1989b. *La Economía del Campesino Altiplánico en 1976*, La Paz, CEDLA.

US Embassy. 1990. *Analysis of Coca Industry Generated from Chapare Leaf Production*, La Paz, US Embassy (unpublished paper). .

Varian, Hal R. 1984. *Microeconomic Analysis*. 2nd ed. New York, Norton.

Veliz, C. 1980. *The Centralist Tradition of Latin America*, Princeton, NJ, Princeton University Press.

Vos, R. 1990. *Private Foreign Asset Accumulation: Magnitude and Determinants. The Case of The Philippines*, Working Paper no. 33, Subseries on Money, Finance and Development, The Hague, Institute of Social Studies.

Vos, R., H. Lee and J.A. Mejía. 1998. 'Structural Adjustment and Poverty' in van Dijck (ed.) *The Bolivian Experiment: Structural Adjustment and Poverty Alleviation*, Latin American Estudies, Amsterdam: CEDLA, pp. 83–139.

Whitaker, M.D. and E.B. Wennergren. 1982. 'Bolivia's Agriculture Since 1960: Assessment and Prognosis' in J.R. Ladman (ed.) *Modern-Day Bolivia: Legacy of the Revolution and Prospects for the Future*, Tempe, AZ, Center for Latin American Studies, Arizona State University, pp. 233–254.

Wolf, E.R. 1966. *Peasants*, Englewood Cliffs, NJ, Prentice-Hall.

World Bank. 1985a. *Structural Adjustment Lending: An Evaluation of Program Design*, Staff Working Paper no. 735, Washington, DC, World Bank.

World Bank. 1985b. *Country Report: Bolivia*, Washington, DC, World Bank.

World Bank. 1988. *World Development Report*, Oxford, Oxford University Press.

World Bank. 1989. *Bolivia: Country Economic Memorandum*, Report no. 7645-BO, Washington, DC, World Bank.

World Bank. (1990) *Bolivia: Poverty Report*, Report no. 8643-BO, Washington, DC, World Bank.

World Bank. Various issues. *World Debt Tables*, Washington, DC: World Bank.

World Bank. 1991. *Bolivia: From Stabilization to Sustained Growth*, Report no. 9763-BO, Washington, DC, World Bank.

World Bank. 1992. *Updating Country Economic Memorandum*, Report no. 11123-BO, Washington, DC, World Bank.

World Bank. 1994. How Legal Restrictions on Collateral Limit Access to Credit in Bolivia, Report no. 13873-BO, Washington, DC, World Bank.

World Bank. 1996. *Bolivia: Poverty, Equity, and Income*, Selected Policies for Expanding Earning Opportunities for the Poor, Report no. 15272-BO, Washington, DC, World Bank.

Index